Principles
of Database Design

Volume I:
Logical Organizations

S. Bing Yao, ed.
University of Maryland

Prentice-Hall, Inc.
Englewood Cliffs, N.J. 07632

Library of Congress Cataloging in Publication Data
Main entry under title:

 Principles of database design.

 (Prentice-Hall series in advances in computing
science and technology)
  Bibliography: p.
  Includes index.
  Contents: v. 1. Logical organizations.
  1. System design.   2. Database management.
I. Yao, S. Bing.   II. Series.
QA76.9.D3P73   1985   001.64   84-50573
ISBN   0-13-708876-0

Editorial/production supervision and
  interior design: *Nancy Milnamow and Tracey L. Orbine*
Cover design: *Chris Wolf*
Manufacturing buyer: *Gordon Osbourne*

© *1985 by Prentice-Hall, Inc., Englewood Cliffs, New Jersey 07632*

Printed in the United States of America

10 9 8 7 6 5 4 3 2 1

ISBN 0-13-708876-0   01

Prentice-Hall International, Inc., *London*
Prentice-Hall of Australia Pty. Limited, *Sydney*
Editora Prentice-Hall do Brasil, Ltda., *Rio de Janeiro*
Prentice-Hall Canada Inc., *Toronto*
Prentice-Hall Hispanoamericana, S.A., *Mexico*
Prentice-Hall of India Private Limited, *New Delhi*
Prentice-Hall of Japan, Inc., *Tokyo*
Prentice-Hall of Southeast Asia Pte. Ltd., *Singapore*
Whitehall Books Limited, *Wellington, New Zealand*

Contents

10 Schema Implementation and Restructuring
(Shamkant B. Navathe)   **361**

Preface

One of the most important steps in developing a database application is the design of an effective database structure. The complexity and size of the problem usually make it a difficult task. In the past several years there has been much effort devoted to the development of systematic techniques for database design. The purpose of this series is to bring together a collection of state-of-the-art methods that address all phases of the database design process.

The goal of database design is to organize databases for effective processing. This involves a wide spectrum of activities from problem definition to system implementation. These activities can be divided into two classes: 1) Logical database design is concerned with requirement specification, data and process modeling, normalization, model integration, and structural analysis; and 2) Physical database design is concerned with file and index optimization, storage allocation, performance evaluation, and reorganization and security. This first volume will focus on the design of logical structures that provide the foundation for an effective database design.

The solution of a problem usually depends on how well it is stated. Successful database design must begin with an accurate requirement specification. Specifying the requirements for a database application often forces people to cope with a large amount of potentially inconsistent and incomplete information. This is an area in which computer based tools can be highly useful. In **Chapter 1**, practical methods for requirement analysis and specification are introduced. The chapter begins with a thorough analysis of the contents of a requirement document, which includes both data and process requirements. Example approaches of requirement specification are also discussed. Manual techniques surveyed include language-oriented and graphics-oriented methods. Computer-aided techniques are illustrated with detailed examples using the PSA/PSL system.

The design of logical database structures must eventually be implemented in a database system using a particular data model. To provide the reader with the necessary background, **Chapter 2** reviews conventional data models in the context of the ANSI/X3/SPARC database architecture. The three principal data models—network, hierarchical and relational—are introduced and compared using a simple example database.

It is often desirable to represent the result of requirement specification in a system-independent model that is more expressive than conventional data models. **Chapter 3** introduces semantic data models for the representation of data requirements. The limitations of conventional, record-based data models are reviewed. This is followed by a survey of major concepts in contemporary semantic data models. An integrated model that combines many of the reviewed features is also introduced.

Chapter 4 introduces the modeling of process requirements using three types of specification languages. They are based on the representation of data item usage, query description and transaction descriptions, respectively. Together with the semantic models, this forms a complete specification of the design requirement.

Manual database design methods can be useful during the initial design stages to obtain an approximate design solution. These methods often depend on the designer's skill and experience. Graphical notations could be valuable tools for the representation and communication of the design result. One of the popular notations, Entity-Relationship Diagrams, is presented in **Chapter 5**. Examples are given to show the design of system independent logical structures and their mapping to conventional data models. The importance of this method derives from its simplicity and clarity, which make it easily understandable and usable by most data processing practitioners.

The next part of this volume presents specific methods for designing logical database structures for particular data models. **Chapter 6** surveys relational, normalization, and decomposition techniques with explicit algorithms for their implementation. The significance of these techniques lies in their thorough treatment of the fundamental properties of data. Some methods for relational database design are also adaptable to other data models.

Chapter 7 introduces the application of the normalization technique to the design of hierarchical data structures. Practical considerations for constructing a design tool for such structures are discussed in detail.

Chapter 8 reviews the design of network structures using heuristic and mathematical optimization techniques.

When designing logical structures that span more than one application area, the local models designed for each area must be integrated to form a global model. It is recognized that the integration of models must be guided by both semantic information about data entities and process requirements. **Chapter 9** introduces a computer-aided logical structure design and integration technique that allows the designer to interactively construct an integrated model.

Chapter 10 analyzes logical restructuring methods for the design and redesign of the logical database structures. Operators for restructuring logical structures are reviewed and illustrated with examples.

This book can be used as a textbook for graduate or upper-level undergraduate courses in database design. It can also be a valuable reference for database practitioners.

Finally, I would like to take this opportunity to thank all of the contributing authors for the effort put forth in making this volume possible.

S. Bing Yao

1

Requirement Specification Techniques

B. K. Kahn
Boston University

1.1 REQUIREMENTS FOR A SUCCESSFUL DATABASE DESIGN

Designing database, one of the major activities of the system development process, is a difficult, complex, and time-consuming task. Inadequate designs have presented many problems. The failure to specify clearly the organizational goals and requirements has resulted in databases of limited scope and usefulness, which are unable to adapt to change [19]. In many cases, these problem-ridden databases have prevented database management systems (DBMSs) from becoming an effective data processing tool [40, 29].

A successful database design must satisfy three criteria. First, the input to the design process must be complete, consistent, and usable. Second, the design methodology must be sound and must effectively use the input provided. Third, technical and user personnel must interact and communicate effectively. In addition, the design methodology and input preparation procedures must be followed and utilized by the personnel.

All three—input, methodology, and personnel—must exist and interact well. Good personnel may compensate for a poor methodology or vice versa. However, neither good methodology nor excellent personnel can compensate for inadequate input. The adage "garbage in, garbage out" applies to database design. If the input is wrong or incomplete, then the database based on this input will be unusable. In time, this will result in repetition of the design process with "good" input. This duplication wastes organizational resources, especially money and personnel.

The input to the database design process is the organization's statement of requirements. Poor definition of these requirements is a major cause of exceeding proposed budgets. The requirements are a statement of *what* the ensuing (information) system should do, the activities to be supported, the information required, and the other perceived organizational needs. They may be expressed in one or more documents and may come from a variety of organizational sources. The content and format of a requirements document are described in Section 1.2.

The system development process is divided into a number of phases. The requirements document is developed during the requirements phase.

The requirements phase consists of three activities:

1. Collection of the requirements.
2. Documentation of the requirements.
3. Analysis of the requirements.

The type of information collected and documented depends on the system's characteristics. These characteristics are determined during the first activity of the requirements phase, called *gross systems analysis*, during which the following information is identified:

1. Level(s) of management served (i.e., first-level, middle-level, or upper-level management).
2. Type(s) (i.e., operational control, management control, tactical planning, and strategic planning).
3. The amount and spectrum of system structure (i.e., the percent of activities that are structured, semistructured, and unstructured).
4. User population.

The first three types of information can be obtained by interviewing a few key individuals. There is a direct relationship between system type(s) and level(s) of management served (summarized in Figure 1.1). The system type gives an indication of the level of management served and vice versa. Low-level managers usually interact with operational control systems. Middle-level managers usually interact with management control and tactical planning systems. High-level managers are most concerned with strategic planning systems. However, any level of management can be concerned with or may interact with any type of system.

The amount of system structure gives an indication of the dominant type of activities. This information can be used to classify the system according to the Gorry and Scott-Morton framework [1971]. Example types of information systems classified according to this framework are shown in Figure 1.2. The system classification affects the contents of the requirements document.

The user population can be identified through interviewing management and studying organizational charts. The user population consists of all individuals who use or are impacted by a report to be produced by the system, who are concerned with transactions processed, who have questions that can be potentially answered by

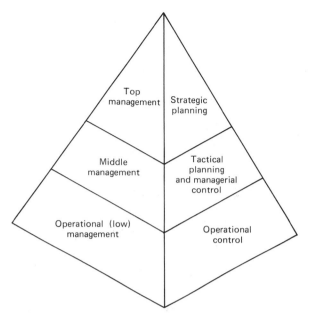

Figure 1.1 Summary of system characteristics and level of management.

	Operational Control	Managerial Control	Strategic Planning
Structured	Accounts receivable Order entry	Budgeting Short term forecasting	Tanker fleet mix Warehouse location
Semistructured	Inventory control Production scheduling	Variance analysis	New product introduction
Unstructured	Cash management	Personnel management	R & D planning

Figure 1.2 Gorry and Scott-Morton framework. Reprinted from "A Framework for Management Information Systems" by G. Anthony Gorry and Michael S. Scott Morton, *Sloan Management Review* Vol. 13, No. 1, pp. 55–70, by permission of Sloan Management Review. Copyright 1971 by the Sloan Management Review Association. All rights reserved.

the system, who operationally use the system, or who are in anyway impacted or interact with the system being developed. The potential user population is usually quite large and it is impossible to interview and collect requirements from each member. Therefore, a representative sample from the potential user population must be identified. The identification of a representative sample of users will be covered in Section 1.3.

1.2 REQUIREMENTS DOCUMENTS

Requirements are a statement of an organization's needs that should be satisfied by the ensuing information system, including its database. The requirements are gathered in the requirements phase. This phase is concerned primarily with documenting the organizational needs and secondarily with enumerating the means to satisfy these needs. In this phase, the analyst should be concerned only with determining the goals of the ensuing (computerized) system, and in a later phase of the system development process the programmer and data processing staff should select the best (computerized) means. Unfortunately, all too often the analyst worries about the best computer means (e.g., best file structure) and the programmer worries about the goal (e.g., is this report really needed?); both then may do their jobs ineffectively. Care must be taken to avoid this role reversal or at least minimize it.

Requirements must be determined when a major system development effort is undertaken—for example, in the extensive redesign of an existing system, the integration of systems, and the development of a new system. These requirements should be documented formally, but this is not always done.

Formal requirements are an integral part of any successful system development effort and provide direction to this effort. Without formal requirements, there is no record of the needs to be satisfied by the developing information system. In addition, when the system is operational, there is no way to verify that the system satisfies organizational needs or aids in solving overall organizational objectives. The lack of formal requirements is the major cause of the proliferation of unusable and underutilized information systems, high maintenance costs, and high development costs. The repercussions from absence of formal requirements become even more severe as system complexity increases. With a complex system that serves many users and requires a large system development staff, the formal requirements documented in one or more documents become a crucial factor.

1.2.1 Composition of Requirements Document

If requirements are to support adequately the system development process, the requirement document(s) must be:

> Complete.
> Consistent.
> Up to date.

Understandable to users, analysts, and designers.

Analyzable.

Well structured.

A method of ensuring these characteristics is to divide each requirements document into manageable parts and to provide a perspective to model each part.

The two major types of information in a requirements document are information requirements and processing requirements. They should be modeled in a well-structured and usable manner that lends itself to representing various levels of detail.

> *Information requirements* define all the information to be used in the ensuing system. They depict the intrinsic and conceptual relationships of all data and describe the properties of entities, groups, attributes, and relationships.

> *Processing requirements* are the definition of the (data-manipulation) processes of the ensuing system. They describe process precedence, including how often and when each process is performed and the relationships between processes and data (i.e., how data is utilized in the system).

The specifications of both information and processing requirements define integrity constraints. *Integrity constraints* are rules that define the criteria for data correctness and consistency in order to protect the ensuing database from nonmalicious errors. Examples of integrity constraints that should be included in a requirements document are given in Sections 1.2.2 and 1.2.3.

In addition to information requirements and processing requirements, other descriptive information is necessary for the requirements document(s). *General descriptive information* describes the characteristics of data presented in the definition of either or both information and processing requirements. This information is very similar to that contained in a data dictionary and should be accessible through the commercial packages currently available, such as Datamanager and IBM's Data Dictionary [9, 35, 49, 55]. A *data dictionary* is an integral part of any database design methodology. Each data item specified in the processing requirements and each attribute defined in the information requirements should be included in the data dictionary. Dictionary entries should consist of at least the following properties: definition, synonyms, type, length, value set size, and legal values. The role of a data dictionary in the requirement process is described in Section 1.8.

1.2.2 Information Requirements

There are many different ways to model information requirements. The *information-structure perspective* (*ISP*) [30, 32] is a simple model for this purpose. Several other approaches can be found in Chapters 3 and 9. The ISP depicts the intrinsic and conceptual relationships of all data in the information system as viewed by the entire user community (i.e., global information structure) or by an individual user (i.e., local information structure). Information requirements are usually obtained by interviewing people at various levels of the organization, especially users of the system. Information requirements may be bound to a particular application, but the model should represent the natural clusterings of information. Additionally, this model should express the basic semantic properties and integrity constraints. Also expressed in information requirements are details about the entities in the information system and the relationships between these entities. The representation of natural relationships and details in the database provides the basis for handling unstructured and unanticipated queries or requests for information.

The ISP is based on three primitives: entity, attribute, and relationship. According to the ANSI SPARC Report [2], an *entity* is a person, place, thing, concept, or event, real or abstract, of interest to the organization (system). An *attribute* is an elementary piece of information describing an entity that can be assigned a value. A *relationship* is a connection between entities.

The entity is the foundation of the ISP. Entity types represent a general classification or description of the components of the user's entity scheme. An *entity type* has a unique name, which should connote the semantics of the object that the entity represents in the real world. Entities are characterized by attributes, the smallest named piece of information in this model. An entity can be viewed as an "*n*-ary" collection of attributes. An *entity occurrence* can be viewed as a collection of attribute values. Each entity should have at least one identifier. An *identifier* is an attribute or collection of attributes whose value is in one-to-one correspondence with the entity occurrences. If a given entity type has more than one identifier, one will be designated as the *primary identifier*. For example, the entity EMPLOYEE includes the identifier EMPLOYEE-ID and the attributes ADDRESS, TELEPHONE-NO, PAY-RATE, POSITION, and so on. In some applications, one may be interested only in the existence of an entity and not in the entity itself or its characteristics. For example, a system may be concerned with the number of occurrences of the entity EMPLOYEE but not at all interested in any more detail about EMPLOYEE.

In this model there are two criteria for the existence of an *attribute*. First, an *attribute* must have a unique name which is used to identify it. Second, an attribute must have an associated set of valid values, referred to as its *domain*. For example, the identifier attributed to EMPLOYEE is named EMPLOYEE-ID and has a domain defined as all six-digit positive integers.

Entities may be described also by groups. A *group* is a named association or combination of one or more attributes and/or groups. Attributes are collected into groups for two reasons. First, groups provide a way of treating associated attributes as a single unit. In a group of this type, their component attributes are not usually referred to individually. For example, the group DATE, consisting of the attributes DAY, MONTH, and YEAR, is usually considered as a single unit. This type of group will be referred to as a *non-decomposable group*. Second, groups provide a representation and indexable sequence for multivalued attributes or groups. This type of group is exemplified by the group MONTHLY-AMOUNT-SOLD, which represents the amount of goods sold each month over the last year, where the

MONTHLY-AMOUNT-SOLD repeats twelve times. This second type of group is called a *decomposable group* and is often referred to in the literature as a *repeating group*.

The third primitive of the ISP is a relationship. A *relationship* presented in a requirements document is defined as a binary mapping between entities. Generally, a relationship is defined as an *n*-ary mapping between entities and relationships. A relationship may have associated with it attributes called *intersection data*.

There are two criteria for the existence of a relationship. First, a relationship must have a unique name, and this name should reflect the entities connected. Second, the relationship definition must state the set of entity occurrences of each type that are being logically connected. This is the definition of the range and domain components of the relationship. The range and domain may be the same. For example, a relationship that connects the entities EMPLOYEE and DEPART-MENT could be named EMPLOYEE's-DEPARTMENT. (*Note*: There may exist many relationships between EMPLOYEE and DEPARTMENT.) This relationship connects two sets of entities, where each set is one entity type. If EMPLOYEE were subdivided into two entities, SALARIED-EMPLOYEES and HOURLY-EMPLOYEES, then the relationship would connect SALARIED-EMPLOYEES and HOURLY-EMPLOYEES to DEPARTMENT. Even though the domain of this relationship is two entity types, the relationship is still binary.

Conditionality is another characteristic of relationships. Not all occurrences of the entity types involved in the relationship may participate in the relationship. For example, in a relationship called MANAGES that connects the entities EMPLOYEE and DEPARTMENT, not all occurrences of EMPLOYEE manage a DEPART-MENT and therefore these occurrences do not participate in the MANAGES relationship. Thus, an occurrence of EMPLOYEE conditionally participates in this relationship.

The *connectivity* of a relationship denotes the expected number of occurrences of one entity type to a given occurrence of the other entity type. There are two distinct connectivities for a given binary relationship, one for each direction. There are three classes of connectivity: one-to-one relationship (1:1), one-to-many relationship ($1:N$), and many-to-many relationship ($M:N$). A *one-to-one relationship* is one whose connectivity is 1-to-1 in both directions. For example, consider the relationship MANAGED-BY between EMPLOYEE and DEPARTMENT. An employee can be a manager of at most one department, and a department has only one employee acting as manager. A *one-to-many relationship* has a connectivity of 1-to-1 in one direction and one-to-many in the other. For example, consider the relationship EMPLOYED-BY between DEPARTMENT and EMPLOYEE. A DEPART-MENT employs many EMPLOYEES and an EMPLOYEE is employed by only one DEPARTMENT. Therefore, EMPLOYED-BY is a one-to-many relationship. A *many-to-many relationship* is one which is one-to-many ($1:N$) in both directions (the value of N is usually different in each direction). For example, consider the relationship TAUGHT-BY between STUDENT and PROFESSOR. A STUDENT is taught by many PROFESSORS, and a PROFESSOR teaches many STUDENTS.

It is useful to determine the maximum, minimum, and average connectivity in each direction. For example, consider the relationship TAUGHT-BY between the entities STUDENT and PROFESSOR. The (average) connectivity for direction STUDENT to PROFESSOR is 1-to-4 (1:4) if, on the average, a student has four professors, and the connectivity range (i.e., minimum to maximum) could be 0-to-6, implying that a student can be in as few courses as none and in a maximum of six courses. Additionally, the connectivity is 1-to-30 (1:30) for PROFESSOR to STUDENT if a professor teaches, on the average, a course of thirty students, and the

Information Structure

    List of attribute descriptions (*) (at least one attribute)
    List of group descriptions
    List of entity descriptions (*) (at least one entity)
    List of relationship descriptions

Attribute

    Attribute name (*)
    Value set (*)
    Cardinality

Group

    Group name (*)
    Group type (*) (decomposable or nondecomposable)
    Group contents (*)
        Identifier (*DG)
        List of nonidentifier attributes/groups
    Cardinality

Entity

    Entity name (*)
    Identifier (*, M) (attribute or group name)
    List of nonidentifier attribute/group names
    List of attributes/groups
    Characteristics of attributes/groups
        Picture, value set
        Repetition factor

Relationship

    Relationship name (*)
    Domain entity set (*) (list of entity names or NULL)
    Range entity set (*) (list of entity names or NULL)
    Intersection data (list of attribute/group names)
    Cardinality
    Connectivity in both directions (*)
    Probability of existence in both directions

Key

        * = Required
        M = More than one allowed
     *DG = Required for a decomposable group

Figure 1.3 Summary of the contents of the information-structure perspective.

connectivity range could be 5-to-200, denoting that class size ranges from five to two hundred students.

Another characteristic of the ISP is the identification of integrity constraints. As defined formally by Benci et al. [5], *integrity constraints* are predicates defined on the elements of the information structure in order to provide the user with error-free data. Integrity constraints can limit both the set of possible values that entities, attributes, and relationship types can include and the valid set of possible operations on the database. The integrity constraints of the ISP include: existence conditions for entity types and their occurrences, attribute repetition factors, interdependencies between attributes, definition of instances of entities composing the domain and range of relationships, and organizational policies. The components composing the information-structure perspective are summarized in Figure 1.3. An example ISP definition is shown in Figure 1.4.

A requirements document includes multiple levels of descriptive detail. The first level corresponds to a nonquantitative definition of entities, attributes, and relationships and it forms the functional statement of requirements. However, another, more detailed level of description is necessary to support the subsequent phases of design. The required information is quantitative and includes:

1. The cardinality (expected number of entity occurrences) for entities.
2. The repetition factor, length, cardinality (value set size), and probability of existence for attributes.
3. The connectivity, cardinality, and probability of existence for relationships.

Information	*Example*
1. Entity description	
* Name	Employee
• Cardinality (number of occurrences)	100 (expected number of employees)
2. Attribute description	
* Name	Social security number
• Repetition factor	1
• Length	9
• Number of unique values	Cardinality of employee
• Probability of existence	1.0
3. Relationship description	
* Name	Employed-by
* Entities defined over	Employee, department
• Connectivity (mapping)	1 : 1 (departments per employee)
	1 : Many (employees per department)
• Cardinality (number of occurrences)	100 (expected number of employees)
• Probability of existence	.95 (employee), 1 (department)

Key: * = Descriptive information
      • = Volume information

Figure 1.4   Example of the information-structure perspective.

1.2.3 Processing Requirements

There are many ways to model processing requirements. Some of the modeling approaches are presented in Chapter 4. One example model [32] will be used to illustrate the idea. The *usage perspective* (UP) is a model of the system's processing requirements. It describes the structure, precedence, and frequency of a process and the relationship between processes and data (i.e., how data is utilized in the system). "Data" in the UP usually refers to attributes or nondecomposable groups, both of which are elementary pieces of information. The system's processing requirements can be determined by analyzing the system's input, output, and updating requirements and by evaluating current and possible future applications.

The system to be supported by the database being designed consists of a collection of functions. Each function is an independent unit and can be broken down into a series of applications, and each application can be decomposed into a series of "execution units." In the requirements document the distinction between applications and execution units should be ignored. These lower level functions will be called processes. Thus, a *function* can be decomposed into a collection of *processes* whose processing requirements could be represented by a series of *data-manipulation operations*.

Besides describing these primitives, the requirements document must also include integrity constraints which describe processing conditions and the dependencies between processes. These constraints include the statement of process inception or triggering conditions, interprocess interactions, such as the ability to have parallel processing, and allowable data manipulation operations or evolution rules. The form and content of processing requirements can be stated as follows:

> *Processing requirements*:
> Process structure.
> List of process descriptions.
> *Process description*:
> Process name.
> Process frequency.
> List of process data interactions:
> 1. Data list with data associations (a data list is a list of attribute or group names and a data association is a collection of binary pairs of data) or
> 2. Data-manipulation language (DML) operation with operation frequency, where a DML operation has the form of operator (i.e., add, delete, find, etc.) followed by data list.

The amount of processing-requirements description included in the requirements documents depends upon the type of system and the analysis approach. As the level of management served by the system increases, the amount of detailed information used and the amount of structured processing requirements decreases (as shown in Figures 1.1 and 1.2). Three different levels of detail compose the contents of processing requirements. The first level is the most basic and supplies the least amount of information. For high-level systems, such as strategic planning systems, only classes of process that correspond to high-level organizational functions and the entities required for these functions are specified.

The first level of processing-requirements description is the statement of functions, process structure, and process data interactions. A *process structure* defines the hierarchies of processes that comprise the processing requirements. The next level of description adds process frequency and the volume of data processed. The last and most detailed level describes those processes that comprise most (80 to 90 percent) of the system workload in terms of the operations that should be used [42]. A format for specifying processing requirements and an example are included in Figure 1.5.

The next level of detail is the refinement of the specification at the first level. In the specification of the process structure, the functions are decomposed into lower-

Level	*Information*	*Example*	
1. Functional		Payroll	
	(a) Process Structure	Wagecalc	Taxcalc
	(b) Name	Wage-calculation	
	(c) Data required	Employed, Time card, Payrate	
	(d) Priority	High	
2. Volume			
	(a) Frequency of occurrence	Weekly	
	(b) Probability of occurrence	1.0	
	(c) Volume of data	100 employees	
3. Operators			

How Data Used Expressed in DML Primitives:

Operator	Search criteria	All or unique	Output	Associations	Statistics
Find	Data		Data	Data	Frequency
Add				and/or	Priority
Delete				relations	Probability
Modify					

Operator	Find
Search criteria	Employee
Number of instances retrieved	All
Associations used	Status-active
Probability of occurrence	1.0
Probability of retrieved being used	.95

Figure 1.5 Usage perspective components.

level processes. As this decomposition proceeds, the pieces of information required can be pinpointed. For each process, its relative frequency, weight (priority), and data required with data volume should be specified. This information should be available for all management control or tactical planning systems and is readily available for operational control systems.

The last level of description is the most detailed and most time-consuming to collect and document. Additionally, it is not appropriate for all types of systems or for all processes. Those processes that are most important and constitute most of the systems workload should be analyzed first. Which ones they are can be determined from the information previously collected. The most important processes are those with the highest user-defined priority or those with highest workload, which is a function of the frequency of process occurrence and the amount of data processed. This level of description specifies how the process can accomplish its designated function. Processes are described by a series of data-manipulation operations. A data-manipulation operation shows the interrelationships of the data used in the operation. The data in an operation has one of two roles, criterion or operand. Data is a *criterion* when it is used as the basis of retrieval of the information required to successfully complete the operation. The data that is manipulated or operated on is an *operand*. A given operation may utilize one item, a collection of items, or aggregates of data. A piece of data may be used as both criterion and operand. The following format of a data-manipulation operation can be used:

DERIVE

UPDATE   Operand-data USING criteria-data

REQUIRE

("Operand-data" and "criteria-data" represent a list of data items and/or data aggregates.)

1.2.4 Contents of the Requirements Document

The subsequent phases of the database design process use input from both information and processing requirements. The relative amount of information and processing requirements contained in a requirements document depends upon the system characteristics—the levels of management served, system type(s), and amount of system structure. High-level systems are usually unstructured. To gather requirements for this type of system, high-level management is consulted. As the level of system becomes lower and more structured, the requirements become more detailed. Figure 1.6 documents the interrelationship between level of detail and contents of the requirements documents and system characteristics.

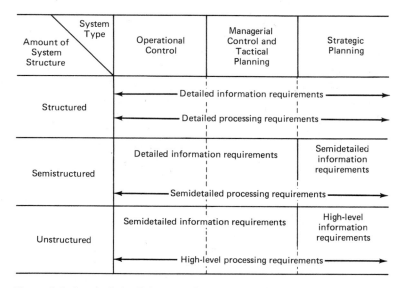

Amount of System Structure \ System Type	Operational Control	Managerial Control and Tactical Planning	Strategic Planning
Structured	← Detailed information requirements →		
	← Detailed processing requirements →		
Semistructured	Detailed information requirements		Semidetailed information requirements
	← Semidetailed processing requirements →		
Unstructured	Semidetailed information requirements		High-level information requirements
	← High-level processing requirements →		

Figure 1.6 Level of detail in a requirements document with respect to system characteristics.

1.3 PREPARING A REQUIREMENTS DOCUMENT

Each pertinent individual in the organization should provide input which becomes the basis of a requirements document. The mode of preparation depends upon organizational policies. The document can be prepared directly by an individual or be produced indirectly by a system analyst who interviews the pertinent individuals. Before an individual is interviewed, pertinent documentation, such as the individual's job description and the reports he or she uses, should be reviewed. In most cases, user participation and analyst endeavors are combined in the production of a requirements document.

The analyst has a number of sources available on which to base the requirements document. The major information-extraction techniques are:

1. To review existing documentation.
2. To observe the operation environment.
3. To administer questionnaires.
4. To interview pertinent individuals.

1.3.1 Documentation Review

Many information systems developed today are based, partially or fully, on existing systems, be they manual or computerized. For this reason, the review of existing system documentation and data is a good place for analysis to begin. It allows the analyst to pinpoint which other techniques are applicable and their scope of applicability. Care must be taken to ensure that the documentation studied is correct and current. As wrong influences can be disastrous, studying incorrect documentation must be avoided. To avoid information overload, system documentation should not be studied all at once.

General documentation should be reviewed first. General documentation includes management overviews, description of the organization's structure, and statements of system goals and objectives and functional tasks. General documentation provides direction for the rest of the analysis process. More detailed documentation should be reviewed on an as-needed basis. Figure 1.7 summarizes the types of documentation available for study. The review of documentation and data can be done with the aid of sampling techniques. A method for sampling data is shown in [57].

1.3.2 Observation

Observation of the operating environment can indicate how individuals participate in the operation of a system. Observation provides the means for the analyst to see firsthand how people in the system handle documents and how practices and

Documents Describing How the Organization Is Organized	Documents Describing What the Organization Plans to Do	Documents Describing What the Organization Does
Policy statements	Statement of goals	Financial statements
Methods and procedure	and objectives	Performance reports
manuals	Budgets	Staff studies
Organizational charts	Schedules	Historical reports
Job descriptions	Forecast	Transactional files
Performance standards	Plans (long- and	(including purchase
Delegations of authority	short-range)	orders, customer
Chart of accounts	Corporate minutes	orders, invoices,
(All other coding		time sheets, expense
structure references)		records, customer
		correspondence, etc.)
		Legal papers
		(including: copy-
		rights, patents,
		franchises, trade-
		marks, judgments,
		etc.)
		Master reference files
		(including customers,
		employees, products,
		vendors, etc.)

Figure 1.7 Illustration of the various types of documents available to the analyst in an organization from which information may be obtained pertaining to systems analysis. John G. Burch Jr., Felix R. Strater, and Gary Grudnitski, *Information Systems: Theory and Practice*, 2/e, John Wiley and Sons, Inc. 1979, p. 252.

procedures are followed under different conditions. The determination of system bottlenecks and problems can be aided through observation. Those individuals from whom others seek advice can also be identified, and informal organizational communication paths and structure can be determined.

The process of observation is difficult to accomplish correctly and effectively. The observer may influence the processes being observed and therefore make inaccurate conclusions. An analyst cannot be completely impartial and may bias observations. Because the analyst can focus attention only on a small number of activities at a time, pertinent facts can be missed. Observation skills cannot be easily learned; they require special training and much practice.

1.3.3 Questionnaires

Interviewing is a time consuming and labor-intensive process and therefore is restricted to a representative sample of individuals. An effective way of gathering information from a large population is to use a questionnaire. A *questionnaire* is a set of written questions to which respondents give written replies, often choosing from a group of preestablished answers. Questionnaire design is a science, and the design of the questionnaire affects its validity and its worth as an information-collection tool. Questionnaires should be set up so that responses are brief, easily recorded, and unambiguous. To ensure that a high percentage of completed questionnaires are returned, questionnaires should be sent to specific individuals, be short, and not be excessively time-consuming to complete. A follow-up distribution to nonrespondents can increase the number returned. In systems analysis typically, 70 to 80 percent of questionnaires are returned.

1.3.4 Interviewing

Interviewing is the most used data-collection technique. The interviewing process consists of five sequential phases:

1. Determining the interviewees.
2. Preparing for the interview.
3. Conducting the interview.
4. Recording interview results.
5. Following-up the interview.

The process of sampling is used to determine the interviewees. The term *sampling* can be defined as a process of obtaining information about the whole of something by examining only a representative portion of it. Sampling makes it possible to collect and summarize information more quickly and economically than by examining the complete population. In gross systems analysis, the complete population of potential interviewees was determined. This population size is usually too large to allow interviewing all the individuals, and therefore sampling must be utilized to select the interviewees.

Before sampling commences, its objectives must be identified and documented. One objective is the degree of precision required. The results of sampling are subject to uncertainty, since only part of the population is measured and errors may be made in measurement. However, uncertainty can be reduced by using a larger sample population and by improving the processes of conducting, recording, and following up the interview. The size of the interviewed population depends more on the amount of interviewing time allocated to the system development project than on achieving a statistical consensus with a high level of certainty. Therefore, scientific sampling techniques are not usually applied. *Nonscientific sampling* procedures are those which do not follow statistical principles. *Judgment sampling*, a type of nonscientific sampling, can be used to select the interviewees. In judgment sampling, the sample is selected by analyst(s) who subjectively choose individuals whom they feel are representative of the total population. There are two problems with judgment sampling. First, the sample interviewees are subject to the personal bias of the analyst(s) doing the selection. Second, the reliability of the nonobjective sample cannot be determined. Owing to personnel availability, the interviewees identified through sampling will not constitute the group actually interviewed. When a selected individual is not available, a person with commensurate organizational characteristics is usually selected as a substitute.

In order to conduct an efficient and effective interview, the analyst must be well prepared. As the number of times increases, the cooperation of the respondent decreases; therefore the number of distinct times an individual is interviewed should be minimized. To be prepared for the interview, the analyst must know the following in advance:

1. The information that needs to be collected.
2. The information that can be collected from this interview.
3. The technique for recording the interview results.
4. The interviewee's role in the organization, including position, responsibilities, and activities.
5. The "language" of the interviewee.

The time, duration, and location of the interview should be established in advance and approval obtained from the interviewee's superiors.

The analyst should conduct the interview in a manner that facilitates gathering the necessary information in as little time as possible. The analyst must maintain control of the interview and not spend a lot of time on minor topics. The analyst should begin by first explaining the purpose of the interview, summarizing the purpose of the system development project, and describing the expected contribution of the interviewee. The analyst should first verify that his or her perception of the interviewee's role in the organization is correct. The analyst should ask specific questions, avoid using jargon, and elicit honest and knowledgeable responses. The analyst should ascertain the sureness of response, pursue for clarity of response, and distinguish between fact and opinion. Before concluding the interview, the analyst should determine whether the interviewee has any additional ideas and then verbally summarize the main points of the meeting.

Accurately documenting the data obtained in the interview is very important. Documenting the interview usually is a two-phase process. First, information is recorded during the interview; second, it is transcribed into a standard, usable form. It is surprising how much of what is heard and understood during the interview becomes a mystery and blank the very next day. A sound analytic practice is to review notes right after the interview and fill in the holes while the information is fresh. Note-taking during the interview is traditional, accepted, and the most commonly used technique. An alternative is the use of a recorder, which eliminates the problems associated with note-taking but may make the interviewee nervous and overly cautious. Specialized forms with standard information and expected response alternatives can be prepared and used by the analyst. These forms must be sufficiently flexible to allow for recording all relevant information obtained.

The first activity in following up an interview is sending a copy of the written interview results to the respondent and requesting confirmation of their correctness by a specific date. The analyst should graciously receive and utilize the interviewee's feedback. Often subsequent interviews are required.

1.4 ALTERNATIVE APPROACHES TO THE REQUIREMENTS PROCESS

Many levels and kinds of information are collected in the requirements process. Information requirements range from high-level data aggregates to low-level elementary pieces of information (i.e., data items, attributes). Processing requirements range from those at system level to low-level data-manipulation operations. It is impossible to simultaneously collect all possible kinds of information and all levels of requirements. A requirements approach is a way to stratify all the possible contents of a requirements document and provide structure for the requirements process. The major requirements approaches are:

1. Top-down.
2. Bottom-up.
3. Backward-forward (output driven).
4. Activity analysis (process driven).

Each of these approaches will be described and its advantages and disadvantages presented. In practice, a combination of approaches is used.

1.4.1 Top-Down Approach

A *top-down approach* views the organization as a whole and decomposes it by some predetermined criteria. The objective of top-down analysis is to develop a model of the information flow and all types of requirements throughout the organization. This approach can be used to collect information and processing requirements either independently or simultaneously.

The following describes the scenario for using this approach for collecting information requirements. Basic functions, major decisions, and objectives of the organization are first identified, then the entities required to support these are determined. Each entity is then decomposed into a collection of attributes and/or nondecomposable groups which characterize it. The identifier of each entity is also determined.

To utilize top-down analysis for the collection of processing requirements, the analyst begins with the identification of "superprocesses" which support organizational decisions or a department's function. These superprocesses correspond to a system and should be decomposed into "seven plus or minus two" [38] subsystems. Each subsystem is then divided into a hierarchy of processes. Eventually each process is subdivided into its constituent modules, which are subdivided into data-manipulation operations.

1.4.2 Bottom-Up Approach

The *bottom-up approach* is based on the assumption that modules or programs are the basic elements of any information processing system. The information processing system is assumed to grow or evolve in response to needs in the organization. The sources of this reactive analysis and evolution are those individuals in the organization who are concerned with the efficient processing of data. Growth is stated in terms of adding new processing requirements or programs. Thus, such analysis is based solely on the definition of the known processing requirements needed to support the information processing system.

Bottom-up analysis depends on the availability of a complete statement of processing requirements at the most detailed level. After the lowest-level processing requirements have been identified, then the data requirements of each process are determined. These data requirements define data-process interactions and are expressed in terms of the units of information or data items required to complete a specific task. These processes are then clustered into subsystems and then systems. Because it is difficult to accurately associate the low-level processes with the high-level organizational functions and decisions, it is difficult to determine if all management functions and decisions are adequately covered by the processes identified.

In the bottom-up approach, information requirements are initially viewed as a set of elementary pieces of data (attributes) that the system is concerned with; then these elementary pieces are aggregated into larger information clusters or entities by some criteria. A bottom-up approach for determining information requirements has been proposed by Taylor and Frank [50]. In this technique, a list of applicable attributes and groups must be derived. This list usually results from knowing the data-process interactions of all processes that were determined in the documentation of processing requirements. Additional attributes are determined by asking pertinent individuals to identify the pieces of data of concern to them. This can be accomplished in a meeting where a group of individuals collectively list data of concern. Since it is the processes that primarily determine the data list, it is impossible to determine if this list is complete. Also, the lack of good aggregation criteria leads to nonreproducible results. In this and in other bottom-up approaches, no acceptable criteria for forming entities are given, and the results of the aggregation process depend totally on the skills of the designer and analyst. Other bottom-up techniques, such as Bracchi [6], are based on a binary view of requirements. In experience with users the author determined that such functional dependencies are an unnatural primitive for users to employ in attempting to directly express and specify their requirements specification.

There appear to be more disadvantages than advantages to the bottom-up approach to analysis. The completeness of the requirements cannot be verified. The assumption that processing requirements are easily identifiable is valid for operational control systems but becomes less so as the system becomes less structured and supports higher-level functions. Therefore, this method is not appropriate for semistructured or unstructured systems. Owing to the reactive nature of this approach, it cannot be easily adapted to accommodate change; hence, it is not applicable to unstable and dynamic systems such as decision support and strategic planning systems. A system tailored to a given set of requirements is not designed to handle change; thus, the time required to accommodate a new processing requirement is usually quite extensive. As the system grows, existing programs and the database will have to be redesigned. Additionally, requirements, both processing and information, are not easily integrated.

1.4.3 Backward-Forward Approach

The *backward-forward approach* views an information system as follows:

$$input \rightarrow process \rightarrow output$$

$$\updownarrow$$

$$internal\ data$$

This approach is called backward-to-forward because it begins with the identification of outputs. For each output, the processes required for its generation are determined. Then, for each process, the data utilized, both data from inputs and internal data, is identified. This is usually accomplished in a top-down manner. First, the high-level output-process-data stream is determined. Then the output is decomposed into its constituent data items and a backward flow is determined for these items. These data items are related to processes, and the processes and data are related to the process' source of the data. It is generally more effective to use this approach in conjunction with another approach, usually top-down.

Because the approach can lead to incomplete systems requirements, it is appropriate only for systems whose outputs are known and definable. It is most applicable to operational control and structured systems.

1.4.4 Activity Analysis

Activity analysis is also based on the input-process-output model of an information system. The analysis begins with the identification of processes, both manual and automated. A process is synonymous with a system activity. For each process, the input(s) required to accomplish each process and the source of each input are determined. Additionally, the output(s) produced by the process and its destination are identified. This approach forms a picture of the information flow of an existing system. This information is at only a single level and therefore can be used to augment either a top-down or bottom-up systems analysis effort.

1.5 CLASSES OF TECHNIQUES FOR THE REQUIREMENTS PROCESS

There are two types of techniques to accomplish the requirements process: manual and computer-aided. These techniques are a means of recording and analyzing the system requirements. They are used to produce a document known as the System Requirements Report, Logical System Design Report, or the like.

In manual methods, the analyst(s) collects the data required, collates, continually organizes, and analyzes the data, and then produces tables, diagrams, flowcharts, and decision tables. The basic tools are pencil, paper, and forms. Usually the analyst must spend a large amount of time doing clerical tasks.

Manual methods that can be used for the specification of requirements usually consist of sets of forms, charts, graphs, and narrative that can be used by an analyst or user to record requirements. Six general problems are associated with manual techniques:

1. The resulting requirements documents may be difficult to understand, usually because of inadequate organization.
2. The documents may be ambiguous because of nonmeaningful names and imprecise statements of relationships between names.
3. The documents are usually quite voluminous and contain redundant information, so that difficulties in finding related information may result.
4. The documents usually contain inconsistencies such as contradictory statements and multiple names for the same object.
5. The documents may not be complete.
6. It is difficult to keep the documents up-to-date and there is no way to determine the currency of the information.

In the computer-aided techniques, the computer is used as a mechanism to facilitate the use of (existing) manual technique(s). In these techniques the computer is used in place of the human to accomplish many of the clerical tasks and some of the analysis. The application of a computer results in more efficient and more accurate processing of requirements. Automating existing techniques proved to be a workable, but suboptimal approach [14]. More interesting methods are designed specifically for computer application. These computer-aided requirement techniques are commonly called computerized. This misnomer leads individuals to incorrectly believe that the technique completely automates the requirements process.

A computer-aided requirements technique consists of three basic components:

1. A *language* for stating requirements which is appropriate for the user and analyst and at the same time sufficiently structured for computer processing and analysis.
2. A *software package* which will store, analyze, retrieve, and display the information recorded in the language.
3. A *database* for storing the requirements in a form that facilitates analysis and the presentation of information required by the analyst and user.

All computerized techniques consist of these three components. The techniques differ with respect to the syntax and scope of the structured language and the capabilities and reports generated by the software. Functions performed by these techniques include:

1. Language processing:
   (a) Syntax checking.
   (b) Consistency and correctness analysis with respect to previously defined requirements.
2. Requirements database management:
   (a) Storage of the requirements specification.
   (b) Modification of the requirements database.
3. Report generation:
   (a) Standard reports.
   (b) Mechanism for developing organization-specific reports.
4. Command language processing:
   (a) Controlling and initiating the other functions of the technique.

When any organization is considering a move from a manual to a computer-aided requirements technique, the costs and benefits must be considered.

The costs include:

> Technique acquisition.
>
> Computer costs for installation and operation.
>
> Personnel training.
>
> Personnel for installation, software maintenance, and operational support.
>
> Documentation, including the development of formalized procedures for effective technique utilization.

The benefits include:

> A higher-quality requirements document which is more complete, consistent, precise, and current.
>
> Improved user involvement which may decrease any resistance to the introduction of the new system.
>
> Improved coordination of the activities of the requirements process.
>
> Better access to requirements and the ability to document specific information.
>
> Improved system development process, costing less and taking less time.

1.6 EXAMPLE TECHNIQUES OF THE REQUIREMENTS PROCESS

1.6.1 Manual Techniques

There are basically two categories of manual techniques. The first is narrative and prose-oriented, utilizing either natural or formal language. The prose is usually augmented by tables and charts. Examples of this category are AUXCO method, Accurately Defined System (ADS) and Analysis, Requirements Determination, Design and Development, Implementation and Evaluation (ARDI) [21]. Techniques in the second category are graphically oriented; requirements are documented pictorially and prose is sparingly used to augment these diagrams. Examples of graphical techniques are Hierarchical Input Process Output (HIPO), Structured Analysis and Design Technique (SADT), and Data Flow Diagrams (DFD). A short description of each of these manual techniques follows.

Additionally, there are an increasing number of manual techniques in use that concentrate on high-level and organization-wide requirements. The outputs produced are not of sufficient detail to support the database design process. Example techniques, commonly called enterprise analysis tools, include IBM's Business System Planning (BSP) and Business Information Control Study (BICS). These techniques produce overall organizational system plans and high-level requirements for potential system projects. These outputs are suitable as input to the other requirements techniques described in this chapter.

1.6.1.1 Prose-Oriented Manual Technique

The AUXCO method is a generalized systems approach to developing and maintaining computerized information systems. This method covers the whole system development process and divides each phase into many minute activities. For each activity, appropriate techniques are explained, decision points denoted, and possible alternatives discussed. Techniques to accomplish each task are supplied, although not always in sufficient detail to allow their use by the analyst. This method has many of the problems associated with manual methods: large volume of possibly redundant data, inconsistencies in the document, incomplete information, outdated information, plus others.

Accurately Defined System (ADS) is a backward-forward analysis technique developed by NCR. ADS is form based and was considered an improvement over other (prior) manual techniques because it provided a well-organized and correlated approach to system definition and specification [14]. ADS provides a means to determine and depict the flow of information throughout the system. NCR did not provide the means for computer processing of ADS, although others have done so.

Hartman et al. [21] organized the description of the system development process in the form of a planning network. Their guide for system development is based on four phases: *Analysis, Requirements determination, Design and development,* and *Implementation and evaluation* and is referred to as ARDI. The system development process is divided into phases. Each phase is described as a collection of the activities which may be further subdivided into steps. Documentation standards for each design activity are providing, including the application project file. The ARDI method is a manual procedure and has problems similar to those associated with the AUXCO method. When comparing ARDI to AUXCO, one finds that ARDI is a superior methodology; it is easier to use, is better organized and more explicit, and contains better design aids.

1.6.1.2 Hierarchical Input Process Output (HIPO)

HIPO is a graphical design aid and documentation technique developed and supported by IBM [28, 33]. This technique lends itself to the top-down, process-oriented approach to systems analysis. It is intended primarily for use by software designers and programmers, since it concentrates on process definition. There are two components of the HIPO diagram: (1) the top-level overview called the Visual Table of Contents and (2) the Input-Process-Output (IPO) Diagrams.

The Visual Table of Contents is a treelike hierarchical decomposition of the system into its constituent processes and modules, each called a function. Each function on the hierarchy is represented as a box and can be described within that box as a verb (action) and an object (data affected). There may be a collection of diagrams of this type. In this collection, one diagram divides a system into its constituent subsystems. Subsequent ones break down these subsystems into their components, then break down these components, and so on, until all subfunctions have been defined. Determining the main function of the system, decomposing it into a hierarchy of subfunctions, and naming the subfunctions are not trivial tasks. They require a great deal of insight, creativity, and experience on the part of the analyst/designer.

For each box on a Visual Table of Contents there is an IPO Diagram documenting the function as a process with its inputs and ouputs. The procedural elements can be described at various levels of detail. To describe these procedures, some organizations use a structured language similar to COBOL.

An example of the Visual Table of Contents for a merchant information processing system is shown in Figure 1.8. This diagram points out that the highest-level process, Merchant-Info-Processing (denoted by 0.0), is made up of four main processes. One of these is Generate-Outputs, which is further subdivided into five processes, and finally at the lowest level Answer-Inquiries is broken into three subprocesses.

The detailed IPO Diagrams are shown in Figures 1.9, 1.10, and 1.11. Figure 1.10 is the IPO for the highest-level process. The subsequent IPOs are process-specific. The IPO shows the downward-hierarchical relationships between processes and the inputs/outputs directly used or generated by it. Notice that HIPO does not provide a method for portraying internal data sets, so Merchant-Master-Info is shown as both input and output.

HIPO is probably the most widely used graphical analysis technique. The Visual Table of Contents provides a simple, uncluttered view of what the system does. It is of value in analyzing systems which are composed of a complex hierarchy of processes, especially for clarifying system structure and locating inconsistencies. HIPO is well documented and well supported: user manuals, coding pads, and templates are readily available.

However, there are some drawbacks to using the HIPO method. It is not helpful in showing interdependencies between processes. Interfaces (i.e., other systems, documents, or organizational units providing information to or receiving information from the system being developed) are ignored, and there is no capability to show explicitly internal data. Like all manual techniques, it is difficult to keep the documentation up-to-date and to locate similarly-structured functions. The flow of data is difficult to determine, especially since it is almost impossible to enforce naming conventions. The decomposition and structure of data are, at best, determined as a byproduct when using the HIPO technique.

1.6.1.3 Structured Analysis and Design Technique (SADT)

SADT is a trademarked technique developed by SofTech, Inc. [13, 43, 44, 45, 47]. It consists of techniques for performing systems analysis and design, as well as a process for applying these techniques in the requirements and design phases of the system development process. SADT provides methods for structured thinking in a top-down manner, requirements documentation, project planning, managing, and

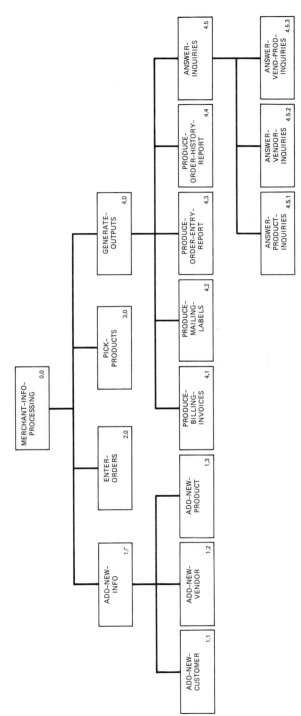

Figure 1.8 Hierarchy chart (called Visual Table of Contents in HIPO) for merchant system.

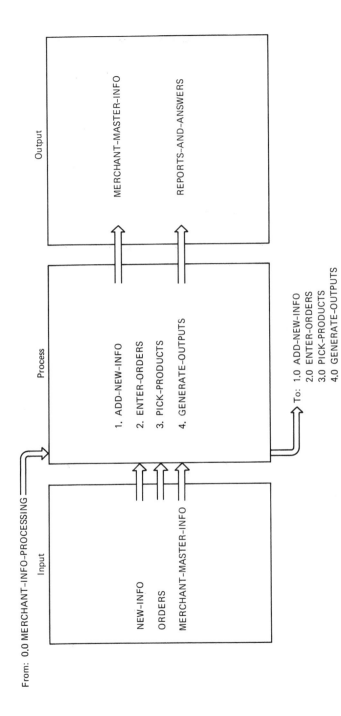

Figure 1.9 Detailed HIPO diagram for highest-level process, Merchant-Info-Processing.

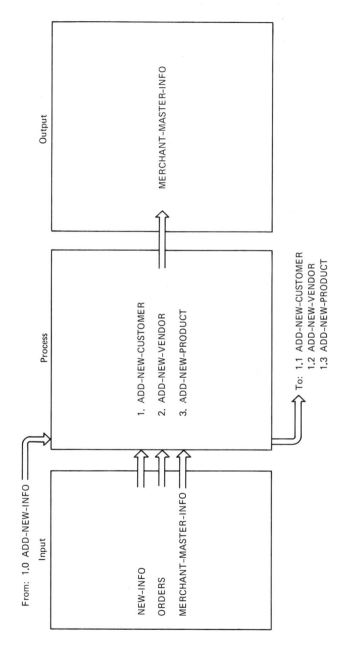

Figure 1.10 Detailed HIPO diagram for Add-New-Info.

Output

MERCHANT–MASTER–INFO

Process

1. ADD–NEW–CUSTOMER
2. ADD–NEW–VENDOR
3. ADD–NEW–PRODUCT

To: 1.1 ADD–NEW–CUSTOMER
     1.2 ADD–NEW–VENDOR
     1.3 ADD–NEW–PRODUCT

From: 1.0 ADD–NEW–INFO
Input

NEW–INFO
ORDERS
MERCHANT–MASTER–INFO

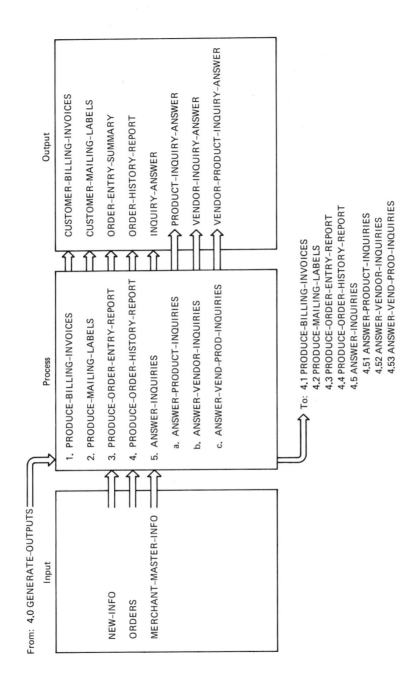

Figure 1.11

evolution, and a team approach for utilizing these methods. The two most important aspects of SADT are the graphic documentation technique and the definition of personnel roles.

Diagrams in SADT correspond to the top-down approach using box-and-arrow notation. There is an organized sequence of diagrams, each with concise supporting text. A whole subject is represented in a high-level overview diagram. Portions of the overview document are each documented in a lower-level diagram representing a limited amount of detail. Two types of diagrams, activity (actigrams) and data (datagrams), provide a dual view of the system. In an *actigram*, activities are represented by boxes named by verbs and data is represented by arrows named by nouns. The arrows interconnect boxes and represent three classes of data: input, output, and control. In a *datagram*, data is represented by boxes and activities by arrows. Horizontal arrows represent input and vertical arrows indicate control variables. Datagrams provide a top-down view of the information requirements, while the actigrams are for processing requirements.

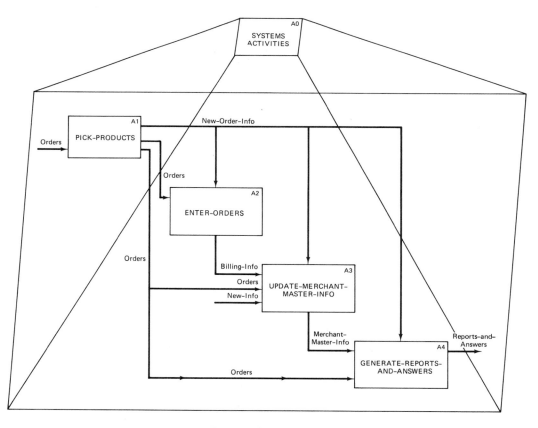

Figure 1.12   Systems Activity Model.

SADT will be applied to the merchant information processing system. The general system description focusing on processes is shown in the Systems Activity Model (Figure 1.12). Generate-Reports-and-Answers, a process, uses Orders and Merchant-Master-Info as input and Reports-and Answers as output. Generate-Reports-and-Answers (Figure 1.13) is, in turn, divided into four processes, and one of those processes, Answer-Inquiries, is further broken down into three processes in (Figure 1.14).

SADT Activity Models provide a detailed and structured description of the process hierarchy. Additionally, they show the relationships between these processes and the data they use; however, this data is not distinguished as input, output, or internal data.

A focus on data is given in Figure 1.15, the overview Systems Data Model. Each block represents a group of data: New-Info and Orders (inputs), Merchant-Master-Info (internal data), and Reports-and-Answers (output). From analyzing this diagram, it is evident that the database Merchant-Master-Info is dependent

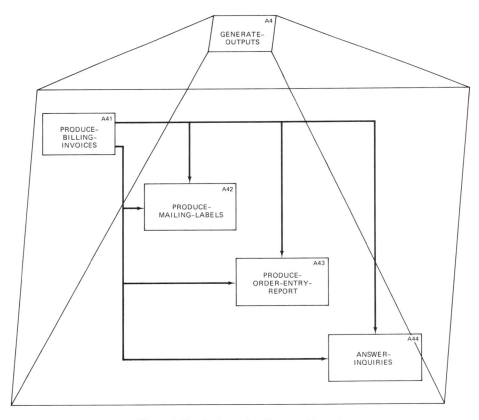

Figure 1.13   Actigram for Generate-Outputs.

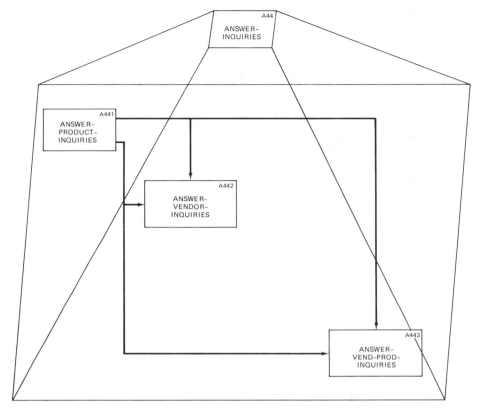

Figure 1.14   Actigram for Answer-Inquiries.

upon Update-Merchant-Master-Info. In turn, this internal data is necessary for the successful operation of Generate-Reports-and-Answers. Merchant-Master-Info is described in more detail in Figure 1.16, where we see that it is composed of the internal data sets Customer-Info, Product-Info, and Vendor-Info.

Relationships between input, process, and output are shown directly in the SADT Activity Model. SADT proves to be an extremely informative method to describe systems with a complex process hierarchy, even more so than HIPO, because it has a means of expressing nonstructural relationships between processes as well as depicting the top-down process hierarchy.

The Data Model of SADT focuses on data, and it documents the source and sink of data (these are usually processes). This focus facilitates the documentation of systems, which often use the output of one process as input to another. Through this feature, data redundancy can be reduced. However, the diagrams do not include any differentiation between input, output, and internal data. This narrow focus limits the applicability of these diagrams in both systems analysis and maintenance.

1.6.1.4 Data Flow Diagrams

The use of data flow diagrams is a general technique based on describing the system by a directed graph. Today, the name "data flow diagram" connotes a specific technique developed by Gane and Sarson [17, 18] and DeMarco [16]. This is a top-down technique which can be utilized in conjunction with a process-oriented, data-oriented, or backward-forward approach.

A general Data Flow Diagram (DFD) is drawn first for the highest level of system (information) flow. It usually has only one process representing the system. An example DFD for a merchandising information system is shown in Figure 1.17. As the system is decomposed into a hierarchy of processes, more detailed DFDs are drawn, which aid in subdividing the system further and in presenting each level of system flow. A detailed DFD with the system decomposed into its major subsystems is shown in Figure 1.18.

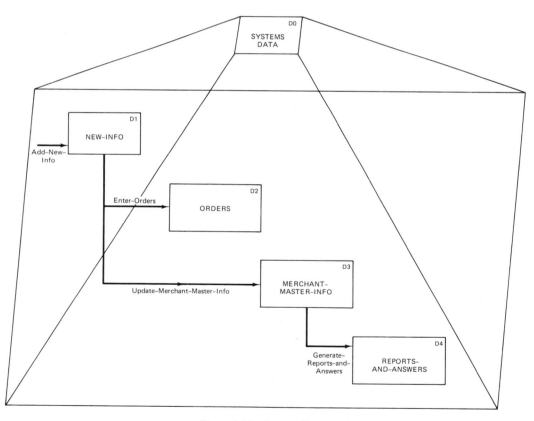

Figure 1.15 Systems Data Model.

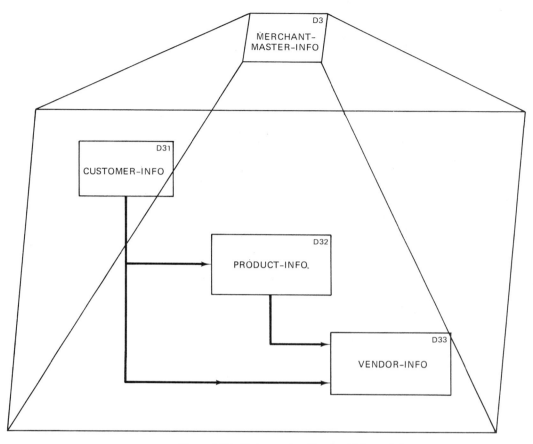

Figure 1.16   Datagram for Merchant-Master-Info.

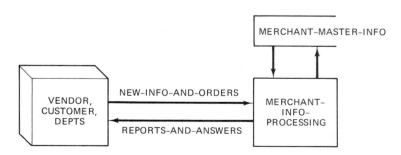

Figure 1.17   Logical Data Flow Diagram—general level I.

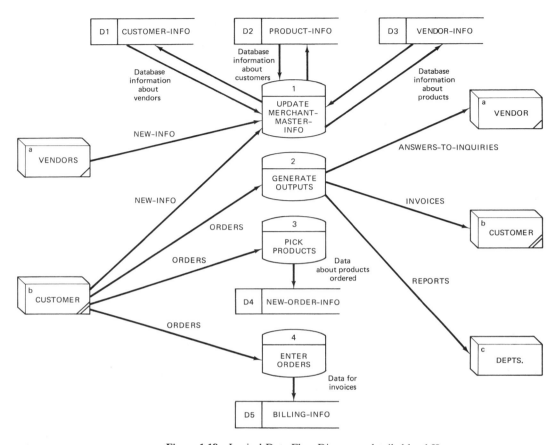

Figure 1.18   Logical Data Flow Diagram—detailed level II.

Data Flow Diagrams are composed of four primitives, each having its own graphical form: interface called an *external entity* (square), *process* (rectangle with rounded corners), internal data called a *data store* (open-ended rectangle), and data flowing to and from processes called *data flow* (arrow). A process is called a *function* and is described by an identification number, a short verb-oriented description, and the organizational location where the function is performed. An external entity represents logical classes of objects (i.e., organizational unit, system, etc.) or people who are the source or destination of data. A data flow represents the movement of data between the other three components. A data store, uniquely numbered, is a place where data resides internal to the system, and is a source and sink for data flows.

Figure 1.17 shows that the highest-level process, Merchant-Info-Processing, uses the input New-Info-and-Orders, which is generated by the interfaces Vendor and Customer. The internal data set, Merchant-Master-Info, is also used by the highest-level process to send an output, Reports-and-Answers, to the Vendor, Customer, and Departments interfaces. Figure 1.18 shows the hierarchical breakdown of the primitives and the interrelationships between these components on a more detailed level. Update-Merchant-Master-Info uses New-Info from Vendor and Customer as input, as well as the three data stores, Customer-Info, Product-Info, and Vendor-Info, which comprise the internal data of the system. The two-way arrows indicate that the information in these data stores is used by the process and also is modified by the same process. Another process, Generate-Outputs, employs no data stores and produces three outputs, Answers-to-Inquiries, Invoices, and Reports, all of which are sent to different interfaces.

Processing and information requirements are integrated into a single diagram. Data flows, inputs, and outputs are used to show the flow of data from and to processes. A DFD provides a means to distinguish between data entering and leaving the system (i.e., inputs and outputs) and internal data (i.e., data stores and data flows). In contrast, HIPO does not differentiate internal data from input, and SADT treats all three data types as being the same. This feature of DFD is especially valuable for systems with intermediate steps because it shows the data stores and data flows rather than showing the output of one process as input to another process; it thereby reduces duplication in the drawing. On the other hand, it may be difficult to use the diagrams in system maintenance, especially when the system designer needs to convert a data store into an input or an output. Modifying the diagrams is much more difficult than the initial drawing, and major modifications usually require completely redrawing a diagram. Another disadvantage of DFD is that, although they are drawn at each level of system flow, there is no direct hierarchy for any of the primitives. This could present problems for a system composed of a complex hierarchy of processes, inputs, or outputs. This problem could be rectified by using DFD in conjunction with HIPO or another technique.

1.6.1.5 Comparison of Graphical System Analysis Techniques

The graphical system analysis techniques are used to document system structure and to aid in analysis. These techniques differ in the amount and type of information presented on the diagrams, and the types of analysis provided and facilitated. A comparison of HIPO, SADT, and Data Flow Diagrams is summarized in Figure 1.19.

For a graphical technique to be a good documentation tool, it should present all required primitives, show interrelationships between these primitives, and be easy to draw and maintain. HIPO, SADT, and Data Flow Diagrams present the primitives Input, Process, and Output, the relationships between these primitives, and the decomposition of processes. Only Data Flow Diagrams explicitly present internal data and interfaces. In HIPO and SADT internal data can be shown but no

Technique	Type of Diagram	Primitives Presented	Relationships Presented	Important Information Missing	Analysis Provided
HIPO	Visual Table of Contents	Process	Hierarchical structure of processes	Interfaces Distinction between internal data and input/outputs Nonstructural process relationships	Hierarchical structure of processes Data flow
	Input-Process-Output	INPUT PROCESS OUTPUT	Inputs used by processes Outputs derived by processes		
SADT	Actigram	INPUT PROCESS OUTPUT	Inputs used by processes Outputs derived by processes	Interfaces Clear distinction between internal data/inputs/outputs	Classes of relationships between primitives Hierarchical structure of primitives Control variables
	Datagram	INPUT PROCESS OUTPUT	Data Data source Data destination		
Data Flow Diagram (DFD)	DFD	INTERFACE INPUT PROCESS OUTPUT INTERNAL DATA: DATA FLOW DATA STORES	Interface produces input(s) used by a process Data flows used by processes Data store/data flow Process derives output received by interface	Direct hierarchical structure of input, process, and output	Flow of data Aid in designing internal data Aid in reducing duplication

Figure 1.19 Comparison of graphical analysis techniques.

distinction is made between internal data, inputs, and outputs. Interfaces are not documented in HIPO and SADT diagrams; therefore it is difficult to determine how systems interact.

The types of relationships presented in these diagrams are quite limited. The flow of data through the system is directly shown in DFDs and SADT Datagrams. The decomposition of processes into a structure is best portrayed in HIPO. In SADT and DFD, multiple diagrams are required to show process structure. Additionally, SADT actigrams present non-structural relationships between processes, and SADT datagrams and DFDs present the structure of data.

The complexity of a diagram directly affects the ease of drawing and maintaining the diagram. HIPO diagrams are the easiest to draw and maintain, SADT and DFDs less so. In documenting system changes, HIPO diagrams do not usually need to be completely redrawn, while SADT and DFD diagrams will be.

The data flow throughout the system is depicted in all the techniques through common naming and the use of multiple diagrams. The development of a data structure is facilitated by SADT datagrams and DFDs, while the determination of the process structure is facilitated in all these techniques. In a manual technique it is difficult to enforce naming standards. In HIPO, data flow is based solely on names; therefore, without the enforcement of standards, data flow cannot be determined. Database design is somewhat facilitated by both DFDs and SADT datagrams. None of the techniques provides a great deal of analysis. For this reason, more and more organizations are using computer-aided system analysis techniques.

1.6.2 Computer-Aided / Computerized Techniques

The application of the computer to the system analysis process has led to the development of many tools and techniques. These techniques provide a formal language for specifying requirements and a method for generating standard reports. The standard reports range from narratives to lists and tables to pictorial presentations. Some of the techniques provide the means for developing and generation organization-specific reports. Some of these techniques are primarily documentation tools rather than system analysis tools. One of these, the Problem Statement Language and Problem Statement Analyzer (PSL/PSA) developed at The University of Michigan, will be described in more detail and applied to an example in Section 1.7.

1.6.2.1 Examples of Computer-Aided Techniques

Computer-Aided Design of Information Systems (CADIS) is a research project at the Department of Information Processing at the Royal Institute of Technology of Stockholm, Sweden [7] concentrating on the improvement of analysis and design of information systems. The CADIS project has developed methodologies and computer-aided tools for systems analysis and design. Software packages CADIS System

1 through 4 and ISAC were developed as tools for system documentation and analysis. These tools include an information storage and retrieval system, a binary language for defining the information system, a language syntax checker, and a report generator. The language is based on the model of an information system developed by Longefors [36] and can be extended with more object types and reports.

The Computer-Aided Systems Construction and Documentation Environment (CASCADE) project [1, 3] at the University of Trondheim, Norway, is concerned with developing tools and methods for the analysis and design of information systems. CASCADE is based on the information systems theory developed by Longefors. In addition to computer-aided tools, a graphic technique for describing system requirements and design has been developed. The CASCADE computer-aided tool includes the basic components of all other similar tools. The language is based on the definition of tasks (i.e., process driven). A task of a system can be documented at any level by a description of input, output, exits, and entries. Syntactical and consistency checks are provided by the system. The design of the system, determined by CASCADE, can be automatically documented with flowcharts, lists, and matrices. CASCADE also provides partial automatic program generation.

Computer-Aided Design and Evaluation System (CADES) is a software package developed by International Computers Limited (ICL). Its goal is to bridge the gap between design and implementation in the system-building process. This is accomplished through design facilities which automatically generate both the implementation code and the tests for that code from the design specifications. The technique uses a data-driven approach to design, whereas CASCADE and CADIS are process driven; that is, information requirements are the primary but not the only input to CADES. This system utilizes the multilevel structured approach based on three definitions. The proposed system description is stored in two databases: design-information system database and implementation code database, while the other computer-aided techniques have only a design database. CADES utilizes the technique of structural modeling, which is a top-down modular design and implementation technique. CADES includes an information retrieval system that includes reports which analyze the entire software design. Other capabilities include a performance evaluation facility and implementation code generator from formal design specifications.

Time Automated Grid (TAG) [22, 56] is an example of the backward-forward (output-driven) approach. The TAG techniques work primarily from the specification of system outputs and produce a variety of output reports which show specification inconsistencies, interrelationship of the data, statement of requirements (system and output), and document analysis. TAG is based on the premise that it is necessary to separate "what" is to be done from the "how," thereby distinguishing the results to be achieved from the means. TAG provides the user with a disciplined technique by which he can define his requirements in his own language without regard for conventional boundaries and implementation considerations.

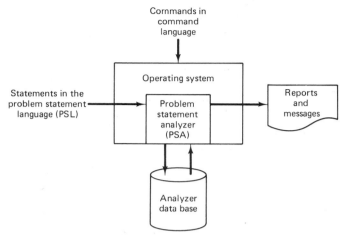

Figure 1.20 The PSL/PSA System and its relationship to the host computer system.

1.7 PROBLEM STATEMENT LANGUAGE AND PROBLEM STATEMENT ANALYZER

The ISDOS (Information System Design and Optimization System) project [24–27, 52–54] at the University of Michigan has developed a computer-aided system analysis and logical design methodology called Problem Statement Language (PSL) and Problem Statement Analyzer (PSA). PSL is a structured language which allows the requirements definer(s) to state their requirements in a human- and machine-readable form. A requirements definer can be a user, analyst, or designer. The language is designed to allow the definer to document requirements at any level of detail. The definer can concentrate on stating *what* the system requirements are without being concerned with *how* these requirements will be satisfied. The components of the PSL are analyzed and placed in a computerized database by the Problem Statement Analyzer. Subsequently, this information is accessed by PSA to be updated, modified, and used to generate standard reports. The capabilities of PSA are described in Section 1.7.2. Figure 1.20 depicts the interrelationship between the PSL/PSA System and its host computer system. There are many versions of the PSL/PSA System; Version 4.2 will be exemplified in this section.

1.7.1 Problem Statement Language (PSL)

The Problem Statement Language is based on a simple and general model of an information system. The basic model is:

interface → input → process → output → interface

↕

internal data

PSL is based on three primitives that are used to describe this basic model: *object type*, *properties* of object type, and *relationships* between object types. An *object type* corresponds to a component of the model of an information system. The spectrum of object types allows the definer to specify both static and dynamic characteristics of an information system. The major types of objects in PSL are:

Object	Classification
Interface	External to the system
Input (external) Output Entity (internal)	Data aggregates (data value containers)
Set Relation	Collection of data aggregates Relationship among internal data aggregates
Group (aggregates) Element	Data
Process	Data-manipulation activity
Event Condition	Dynamic behavior

In addition to these major types of objects, property-oriented objects allow special properties of certain objects to be defined: Synonym, Keyword, Attribute, Attribute-Value, Memo, Source, Security, Mailbox, and Problem-Definer. Mailbox and Problem-Definer can be used for project management.

The classification of an object gives its role in the definition of the information system. Four areas of classification are included in the preceding chart. The first classification is the PSL objects used to describe some part of the organization or environment with which the information system interacts. The object type is called an *interface* and can be used to represent departments in an organization and other information systems. The second classification is data-oriented objects. High-level data aggregates are collections of information. *Inputs* and *outputs* carry information between the system and its environment (i.e., interfaces), while *entities* represent internal information. *Sets* are collections of either inputs, outputs, or entities. *Relations* document structural connections between entities. *Elements* and *groups* are low-level data. Elements can be assigned a value. Collections of elements and groups form inputs, outputs, and entities. The third classification is the processor and manipulator of data. A *process* is defined by specifying the information upon which it operates and the information which it produces. The fourth classification is the definition of the dynamic behavior of the information system, which presents how the operation of the system is affected by particular *conditions* and *events*.

An instance of a PSL name is a specific object in a given information system that is being described. As an example, our merchandise information system takes customer, vendor, and product information which comes from customers and vendors and produces outputs which go to departments in the company, customers, and vendors. The system also maintains internal information about customers, vendors, and products called *merchandise master information*. An overview system flowchart of the merchandise information system is shown in Figure 1.21. The object names with corresponding object types are denoted on the system flowchart according to PSL naming conventions. Each object has a unique name and is assigned a unique object type.

PSL includes a collection of statements that can be used to describe the types of objects. There are two classes of statements: one class is used to connect objects and the second class is the definition of properties of objects.

In the example, merchandise-processing is a process that is related to inputs (i.e., customers, product and vendor information) and outputs (i.e., merchandising outputs). This description can be specified in the following PSL syntax:

PROCESS   merchandise-processing;

RECEIVES   customer-product-vendor-info;

GENERATES   merchandising-outputs;

The PSL syntax includes complementary statements. In the above PSL statements, the definition is centered around the description of the process, merchandise-processing. The same definition could be stated from the input and output perspective, using the complementary statements: the output is generated by the process and the input is received by the process.

The relationships in PSL can be classified by the aspect of the system being represented. System descriptions may be divided into the following major aspects [53, 54].

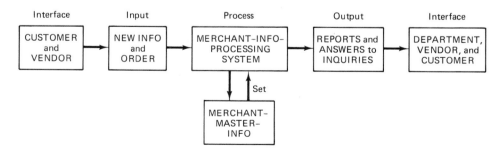

Figure 1.21   System flow of the merchant information processing system.

The system input/output flow aspect of a system description deals with the system's interactions with its environment. This involves describing those inputs supplied by interfaces (its environment), the outputs produced by the system and accepted by the environment, and the collection of internal information (i.e., PSL SET) operated upon by the system.

System structure is concerned with the hierarchies among objects of the same object type in a system. Structures may be introduced to facilitate a specific design approach, such as top-down. In this context, all information may be initially grouped together and given one high-level name, then successively subdivided.

The *data structure* aspect describes the relationships among data used and/or manipulated by the system as seen by the "users" of the system.

The *data deviation* aspect specifies the data and the manner in which it interacts with the processes of the system: what data are used, updated, and/or derived, how this is done and by which processes. These relationships are concerned with data internal to the system's environment.

The *system size and volume* aspect presents the anticipated system workload.

The *system properties* aspect is concerned with the specific characteristics of objects defined. These characteristics distinguish one object from others of the same type.

The *project management* aspect documents characteristics of the project group involved in the design and analysis of the information system.

1.7.2 Problem Statement Analyzer

The Problem Statement Analyzer (PSA) is the software that supports the Problem Statement Language (PSL). PSA provides a means for maintaining a description of an information system and provides a way to analyze and display those requirements. This description of requirements is stored and maintained in a computerized requirements database.

PSA is divided into four major subsystems: command language interface, database update facility, report generation facility, and name selection (retrieval) facility. The interrelationships between these subsystems are shown in Figure 1.22.

PSA commands can be divided into two functional categories: commands that modify the information in the database, called Modifier Commands, and commands that retrieve information and present it in a report format, called Report Commands.

The *Modifier Commands* perform two functions: add new requirements expressed in PSL and modify existing requirements. Before entering new requirements into the database, PSA checks for consistency with respect to the contents of the requirements database and for compliance with the semantics of PSL. After the new requirements are deemed correct and consistent, PSA adds them to the requirements database. Subsequent changes to the requirements made by a modifier command are documented in a report which is used by an analyst to continually log requirements changes.

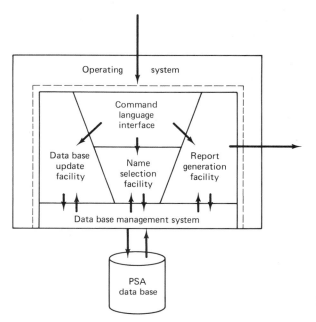

Figure 1.22 Interfaces among parts of PSA and operating system.

Report Commands generate reports for system documentation and to aid in system analysis. There are seventeen different report commands, each of which creates a separate report and does not change the contents of the requirements database. The four types of reports presentation used are lists, tables, matrices, and pictures. Reports can be classified as reference reports, summary reports, and analysis reports. *Reference reports* present selected information in the database in various formats. These formats are intended to be usable to users, analysts, designers, and programmers. For example, the Dictionary Report presents data dictionary information such as name, synonym, name type, description and keywords, and the Formatted Problem Statement Report shows all properties and relationships. *Summary reports* present collections of information in summary form gathered from several different defined relationships. For example, the Structure Report presents hierarchies and the Extended-Picture Report shows the data flows in a graphical form. *Analysis reports* give the results of various types of analysis in a form that facilitates the job of the analyst. For example, the Contents-Comparison Report analyzes the similarity of inputs, output, and internal data, and the Data-Process-Interaction Report can be used to detect gaps in the information flow and process definitions and to identify unused data.

A PSA report can be generated for a specific object or collection of objects whose names must be in a file before the report command is issued. The Name-Selection (NS) command can be used to create this file. The Name-Selection creates a file with a subset of names from the requirements database, according to a specified boolean selection criterion using one or more operators. Types of boolean selection available include name-types strung together by "OR" or "+", such as INPUT or OUTPUT or GROUP or ELEMENT or ALL + UNDEFINED, to extract from the database all names meeting any one of the selection criteria. Another boolean selection involves the use of "AND" or "&" to extract only names which meet more than one selection criterion. An example is OUTPUT AND KEY = SYSTEM1, which would apply only to outputs with SYSTEM1 as the keyword. The "NOT" operator will extract all name-types other than those specified.

1.7.3 An Example Using PSL / PSA

When PSL is applied in top-down design approach, system flow is documented first. System flow gives a general system overview, with one global input, one system process, one global output, usually one set (collection of internal data), and interfaces at either end. This would constitute the top level of top-down design. A flowchart of the system flow of the merchant information processing system is shown in Figure 1.21. This is documented in PSL as:

INPUT NEW-INFO-AND-ORDERS;

    SUBPARTS ARE NEW-INFO, ORDER;

    USED BY MERCHANT-INFO-PROCESSING;

PROCESS MERCHANT-INFO-PROCESSING;

    GENERATES REPORTS-AND-ANSWERS;

    USES MERCHANT-MASTER-INFO;

    UPDATES MERCHANT-MASTER-INFO;

    SUBPARTS ARE ADD-NEW-INFO, ENTER-ORDERS,

        PICK-PRODUCTS, PRODUCE-BILLING-INVOICES,

        PRODUCE-MAILING-LABELS, PRODUCE-ORDER-ENTRY-REPORT,

        PRODUCE-ORDER-HISTORY-REPORT, ANSWER-INQUIRIES;

OUTPUT REPORTS-AND-ANSWERS;

    SUBPARTS ARE CUSTOMER-BILLING-INVOICES,

        CUSTOMER-MAILING-LABELS, INQUIRY-ANSWER,
        ORDER-ENTRY-SUMMARY, ORDER-HISTORY-REPORT;

```
SET MERCHANT-MASTER-INFO;

    CONSISTS OF CUSTOMER-INFO, VENDOR-INFO, PRODUCT-MODEL-INFO;

INTERFACE VENDOR;

    GENERATES NEW-INFO-AND-ORDERS;

    RECEIVES REPORTS-AND-ANSWERS;

INTERFACE DEPARTMENTS;

    RECEIVES REPORTS-AND-ANSWERS;

EOF
```

The Formated-Problem-Statment (FPS) report documents the complete requirements database. An FPS depicting the highest-level flow of the merchant information processing system is shown in Figure 1.23.

In top-down design, the high-level objects (defined in system flow) are further subdivided, forming the structure of the system. Inputs, outputs, interfaces, and processes are decomposed into a hierarchy of objects of the same type. The system structure of the merchant information system is shown in Figure 1.24.

For example, the outputs of the system were broken down into this hierarchy:

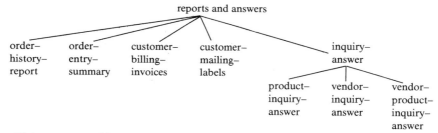

This was stated in PSL as:

```
OUTPUT REPORTS-AND-ANSWERS;

SUBPARTS ARE ORDER-HISTORY-REPORT, ORDER-ENTRY-SUMMARY,

    CUSTOMER-BILLING-INVOICES, CUSTOMER-MAILING-LABELS,

    INQUIRY-ANSWER;

OUTPUT INQUIRY-ANSWER;

SUBPARTS ARE PRODUCT-INQUIRY-ANSWER, VENDOR-INQUIRY-ANSWER,

    VENDOR-PRODUCT-INQUIRY-ANSWER;

EOF
```

```
PAS VERSION A4.2RO
                        BOSTON UNIVERSITY - VPS

                    FORMATTED PROBLEM STATEMENT

PARAMETERS:  DB=  FILE=NPSL  NOINDEX  NOPUNCHED-NAMES  PRINT  EMPTY  NOPUNCH
   SMARG=5  NMARG=20  AMARG=10  BMARG=25  RNMARG=70  CMARG=1  HMARG=40
   NODESIGNATE  ONE-PER-LINE  DEFINE  COMMENT  NONEW-PAGE  NONEW-LINE
   NOALL-STATEMENTS  COMPLEMENTARY-STATEMENTS  LINE-NUMBERS  PRINTEOF
   DLC-COMMENT

  1 INTERFACE                              CUSTOMER;
  2     /*   DATE OF LAST CHANGE -  29OCT81     '          */
  3     SYNONYMS ARE:   CUST;
  4     DESCRIPTION;
  5 CUSTOMERS PURCHASE PRODUCT-MODELS FROM ABC COMPANY;
  6     GENERATES:      NEW-INFO,
  7                     ORDER,
  8                     NEW-INFO-AND-ORDERS;
  9     RECEIVES:       CUSTOMER-BILLING-INVOICES,
 10                     REPORTS-AND-ANSWERS;
 11
 12 INTERFACE                              VENDOR;
 13     /*   DATE OF LAST CHANGE -  29OCT81     '          */
 14     SYNONYMS ARE:   VEND;
 15     DESCRIPTION;
 16 VENDORS SELL PRODUCT-MODELS TO ABC COMPANY;
 17     GENERATES:      NEW-INFO,
 18                     ORDER,
 19                     NEW-INFO-AND-ORDERS;
 20     RECEIVES:       INQUIRY-ANSWER,
 21                     PRODUCT-INQUIRY-ANSWER,
 22                     VENDOR-INQUIRY-ANSWER,
 23                     VENDOR-PRODUCT-INQUIRY-ANSWER,
 24                     REPORTS-AND-ANSWERS;
 25
 26 INTERFACE                              DEPARTMENTS;
 27     /*   DATE OF LAST CHANGE - 29OCT81      '          */
 28     SYNONYMS ARE:   DEPTS;
 29     DESCRIPTION;
 30 THESE ARE THE DIFFERENT DIVISIONS OF ABC COMPANY TO WHICH
 31 INFORMATION IS SENT FROM THIS SYSTEM;
 32     RECEIVES:       CUSTOMER-BILLING-INVOICES,
 33                     CUSTOMER-MAILING-LABELS,
 34                     ORDER-ENTRY-SUMMARY,
 35                     ORDER-HISTORY-REPORT,
 36                     REPORTS-AND-ANSWERS;
 37
 38 INPUT                                  NEW-INFO-AND-ORDERS;
 39     /*   DATE OF LAST CHANGE -  29OCT81     '          */
 40     DESCRIPTION;
 41 THIS IS THE COLLECTION OF ALL THE INPUTS RECEIVED BY THE
 42 MERCHANT INFORMATION PROCESSING SYSTEM;
 43     GENERATED BY:   CUSTOMER,
 44                     VENDOR;
```

Figure 1.23 FPS report on top level of the merchant information processing system.

```
45      SUBPARTS ARE:    NEW-INFO,
46                       ORDER;
47      USED BY:         MERCHANT-INFO-PROCESSING;
48
49 PROCESS                                  MERCHANT-INFO-PROCESSING;
50      /*   DATE OF LAST CHANGE -  29OCT81        '          */
51      DESCRIPTION;
52 THIS IS THE COMPLETE MERCHANT INFORMATION PROCESSING SYSTEM
53 AND IS THE HIGHEST LEVEL PROCESS;
54      GENERATES:       REPORTS-AND-ANSWERS;
55      SUBPARTS ARE:    ADD-NEW-INFO,
56                       ENTER-ORDERS,
57                       PICK-PRODUCTS,
58                       PRODUCE-BILLING-INVOICES,
59                       PRODUCE-MAILING-LABELS,
60                       PRODUCE-ORDER-ENTRY-REPORT,
61                       PRODUCE-ORDER-HISTORY-REPORT;
62      USES:            NEW-INFO-AND-ORDERS,
63                       MERCHANT-MASTER-INFO;
64      UPDATES:         MERCHANT-MASTER-INFO;
65
66 SET                                      MERCHANT-MASTER-INFO;
67      /*   DATE OF LAST CHANGE -  29OCT81        '          */
68      DESCRIPTION;
69 THIS IS THE COLLECTION OF ALL INFORMATION ABOUT CURRENT CUSTOMERS,
70 VENDORS, AND PRODUCT-MODELS;
71      CONSISTS OF:
72                           CUSTOMER-INFO,
73                           VENDOR-INFO,
74                           PRODUCT-MODEL-INFO;
75      USED BY:         ADD-NEW-INFO,
76                       ADD-NEW-CUSTOMER,
77                       ADD-NEW-VENDOR,
78                       ADD-NEW-PRODUCT,
79                       MERCHANT-INFO-PROCESSING;
80      UPDATED BY:      ADD-NEW-INFO;
81      UPDATED BY:      ADD-NEW-CUSTOMER;
82      UPDATED BY:      ADD-NEW-VENDOR;
83      UPDATED BY:      ADD-NEW-PRODUCT;
84      UPDATED BY:      MERCHANT-INFO-PROCESSING;
85
86 OUTPUT                                   REPORTS-AND-ANSWERS;
87      /*   DATE OF LAST CHANGE -  29OCT81        '          */
88      DESCRIPTION;
89 THIS IS THE COLLECTION OF ALL OUTPUTS PRODUCED BY THE MERCHANT
90 INFORMATION PROCESSING SYSTEM;
91      GENERATED BY:    MERCHANT-INFO-PROCESSING;
92      RECEIVED BY:     DEPARTMENTS,
93                       VENDOR,
94                       CUSTOMER;
95      SUBPARTS ARE:    CUSTOMER-BILLING-INVOICES,
96                       CUSTOMER-MAILING-LABELS,
97                       INQUIRY-ANSWER,
98                       ORDER-ENTRY-SUMMARY,
99                       ORDER-HISTORY-REPORT;
100
101 EOF   EOF   EOF   EOF   EOF
```

Figure 1.23   (*continued*)

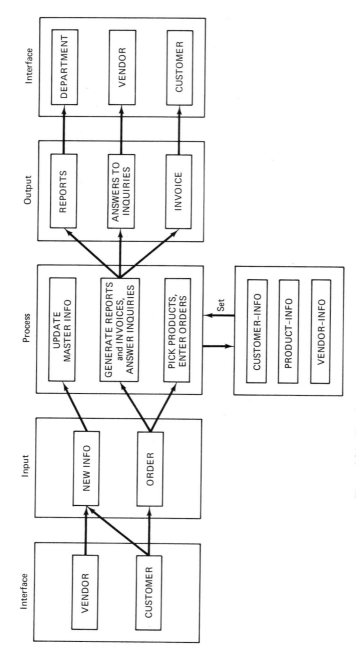

Figure 1.24 Flowchart of system structure of merchant information system.

```
PSA VERSION A4.2RO


                          BOSTON UNIVERSITY - VPS

                            STRUCTURE REPORT

    PARAMETERS:  DB=  NAME=MERCHANT-INFOR-PROCESSING  INDENT=3   NOINDEX
       NONPUNCHED-NAMES  LEVELS=ALL   LINE-NUMBERS   LEVEL-NUMBERS   STATISTICS
       NONEW-PAGE   PRINT

  COUNT    LEVEL    NAME

     1        1     MERCHANT-INFO-PROCESSING                   PROCESS
     2        2        ADD-NEW-INFO
     3         3          ADD-NEW-CUSTOMER
     4         3          ADD-NEW-VENDOR
     5         3          ADD-NEW-PRODUCT
     6        2        ENTER-ORDERS
     7        2        PICK-PRODUCTS
     8        2        PRODUCE-BILLING-INVOICES
     9        2        PRODUCE-MAILING-LABELS
    10        2        PRODUCE-ORDER-ENTRY-REPORT
    11        2        PRODUCE-ORDER-HISTORY-REPORT


  STATISTICS    LEVEL  COUNT    LEVEL  COUNT    LEVEL  COUNT   LEVEL  COUNT   LEVEL  COUNT
                  1      1        2      7        3      3
```

Figure 1.25   Structure report on processes.

PSA documents system structure in many reports. One of these is the Structure Report (STR). The Structure Report is based on the PSL SUBPARTS verb and the hierarchical decomposition of inputs, outputs, processes, and interfaces. The Structure Report on the highest-level process of the example system, merchant-info-system, is shown in Figure 1.25. This Structure Report shows that the system is composed of seven subordinate subsystems (processes), one of which (ADD-NEW-INFO) is further broken down into three more processes:

PROCESS ADD-NEW-INFO;

SUBPARTS ARE ADD-NEW-CUSTOMER, ADD-NEW-CUSTOMER,

  ADD-NEW-VENDOR,ADD-NEW-PRODUCT;

A report that graphically documents system flow, system structure, and data structure is the Picture Report (PICT). This report provides a detailed view of one part of the system by showing all the direct relationships that one particular name has with all other names in the requirements database. A Picture Report on merchant-info-processing depicting system flow and structure is shown in Figure 1.26. This Picture Report presents that both the input new-info-and-order and the set-merchant-master-info are used by this process, with the results of updating

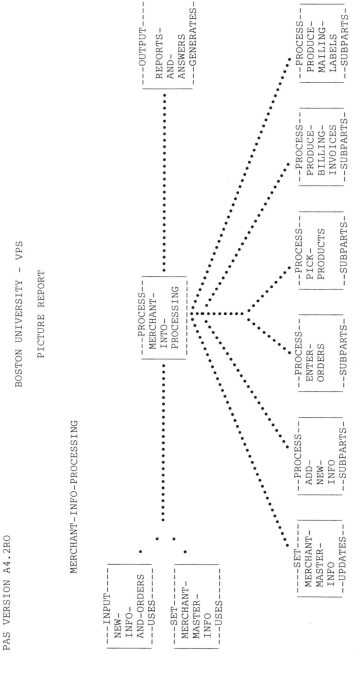

Figure 1.26 Picture report on system process, Merchant-Info-Processing.

PAS VERSION A4.2RO

BOSTON UNIVERSITY – VPS

PICTURE REPORT

MERCHANT-INFO-PROCESSING (continued)

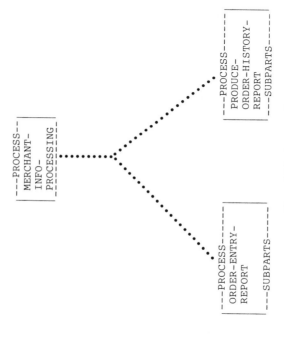

Figure 1.26 (*continued*)

merchant-master-info and producing the output reports-and-answers. This is a pictorial representation of the following PSL:

PROCESS-MERCHANT-INFO-PROCESSING;

USES NEW-INFO-AND-ORDERS, MERCHANT-MASTER-INFO;

UPDATES MERCHANT-MASTER-INFO;

GENERATES REPORTS-AND-ANSWERS;

The structural relationships on the Picture Report indicate that merchant-info-processing is actually composed of seven subordinate processes. This is documented in PSL as:

PROCESS MERCHANT-INFO-PROCESSING;

SUBPARTS ARE ADD-NEW-INFO, ENTER-ORDERS, PICK-PRODUCTS,

    PRODUCE-BILLING-INVOICES, PRODUCE-MAILING-LABELS,

    PRODUCE-ORDER-ENTRY-REPORT, PRODUCE-ORDER-HISTORY-REPORT;

As top-down design progresses, the data items comprising inputs, outputs, and entities are determined and documented. For example, the output customer-billing-invoices was defined in PSL as follows:

OUTPUT CUSTOMER-BILLING-INVOICES;

ATTRIBUTE MEDIA PAPER;

CONSISTS OF CUSTOMER-NUMBER, CUSTOMER-ADDRESS, AMOUNT-BALANCE,

    INVOICE-NUMBER, ORDER-DATE-ENTERED, INVOICE-AMOUNT, ADJUSTMENT-DATE,

    ADJUSTMENT-CODE, ADJUSTMENT-DESCRIPTION, AMOUNT-OF-ADJUSTMENT,

    DATE-PAYMENT-RECEIVED, AMOUNT-OF-PAYMENT-RECEIVED;

PART OF REPORTS-AND-ANSWERS;

PSA reports that document and analyze data structure are Contents, Contents-Comparison, and Consists-Analysis. Data structure is documented primarily in the CONSISTS, CONTAINS, and BETWEEN PSL verbs. A Contents Report on all inputs is shown in Figure 1.27. This report shows that new-customer-info consists of new-customer-name, new-customer-location, which in turn consists of new-customer-address and new-customer-zip-code. It does not show any SUB-PARTS relationships.

Next, the interactions between processes and data are defined. The interactions between processes and data can be analyzed using the Data Process Interactions (DPI) Report. The DPI on Processes in Figure 1.28 uses only process names as input, and it represents all data with which the input process names interact; they are documented using the RECEIVE, GENERATE, USE, DERIVE, and/or UPDATE PSL verbs. In the case of the merchant information processing system, the

```
PSA VERSION A4.2RO


                         BOSTON UNIVERSITY - VPS

                            CONTENTS REPORT

PARAMETERS:   DB=   FILE=   NOCOMPLETENESS-CHECK   NOINDEX   NOPUNCHED-NAMES
      LEVELS=ALL   LINE-NUMBERS   LEVEL-NUMBERS   NAME-TYPES   PRINT   NONEW-PAGE
      1*   (INPUT)      1    NEW-CUSTOMER-INFO
      1    (ELEMENT)      2      NEW-CUSTOMER-NAME
      2    (ELEMENT)      2      NEW-CUSTOMER-NUMBER
      3    (ELEMENT)      2      NEW-CUSTOMER-CREDIT-CODE
      4    (ELEMENT)      2      NEW-CUSTOMER-CREDIT-LIMIT
      5    (GROUP)        2      NEW-CUSTOMER-LOCATION
      6    (ELEMENT)        3      NEW-CUSTOMER-ADDRESS
      7    (ELEMENT)        3      NEW-CUSTOMER-ZIP-CODE

      2*   (INPUT)      1    NEW-INFO

      3*   (INPUT)      1    NEW-INFO-AND-ORDERS

      4*   (INPUT)      1    NEW-PRODUCT-MODEL-INFO
      1    (ELEMENT)      2      NEW-PRODUCT-MODEL-NAME
      2    (ELEMENT)      2      NEW-PRODUCT-MODEL-NUMBER
      3    (ELEMENT)      2      NEW-PRODUCT-MODEL-BIN-NUMBER
      4    (ELEMENT)      2      NEW-PRODUCT-MODEL-PRICE
      5    (ELEMENT)      2      NEW-PRODUCT-MODEL-QTY-EST
      6    (ELEMENT)      2      NEW-PRODUCT-MODEL-QTY-LIMIT
      7    (ELEMENT)      2      NEW-PRODUCT-MODEL-QTY-ONHAND

      5*   (INPUT)      1    NEW-VENDOR-INFO
      1    (ELEMENT)      2      NEW-VENDOR-NAME
      2    (ELEMENT)      2      NEW-VENDOR-ADDRESS
      3    (ELEMENT)      2      NEW-VENDOR-CATALOG-NUMBER
      4    (ELEMENT)      2      NEW-VENDOR-CATALOG-PRICE
      5    (ELEMENT)      2      NEW-VENDOR-NUMBER

      6*   (INPUT)      1    ORDER
      1    (ELEMENT)      2      ORDER-DATE-ENTERED
      2    (ELEMENT)      2      ORDER-DATE-ORDERED
      3    (ELEMENT)      2      ORDER-SHIP-LOCATION
      4    (ELEMENT)      2      ORDER-BILL-LOCATION
      5    (ELEMENT)      2      ORDER-REF-NUMBER
      6    (ELEMENT)      2      ORDER-LINE-NUMBER
      7    (ELEMENT)      2      ORDER-QTY-ORDERED
      8    (ELEMENT)      2      ORDER-NUMBER
```

Figure 1.27   Contents report on inputs.

PAS VERSION A4.2RO

BOSTON UNIVERSITY - VPS

DATA PROCESS INTERACTION REPORT

PARAMETERS: DB= FILE= PROCESS DATA-PROCESS-INTERACTION-MATRIX
DATA-PROCESS-INTERACTION-ANALYSIS PROCESS-INTERACTION-MATRIX PROCESS-INTERACTION-ANALYSIS
EXPLANATION

THE ROWS ARE DATA NAMES, THE COLUMNS ARE PROCESS NAMES.

ROW NAMES

1	MERCHANT-MASTER-INFO	SET
2	NEW-CUSTOMER-INFO	INPUT
3	NEW-INFO	INPUT
4	NEW-PRODUCT-MODEL-INFO	INPUT
5	NEW-VENDOR-INFO	INPUT
6	PRODUCT-INQUIRY-ANSWER	OUTPUT
7	VENDOR-INQUIRY-ANSWER	OUTPUT
8	VENDOR-PRODUCT-INQUIRY-ANSWER	OUTPUT
9	PRODUCT-MODEL-NUMBER	ELEMENT
10	PRODUCT-MODEL-QTY-ONHAND	ELEMENT
11	VENDOR-NUMBER	ELEMENT
12	VENDOR-CATALOG-NUMBER	ELEMENT
13	VENDOR-CATALOG-PRICE	ELEMENT
14	PRODUCT-NUMBER	ELEMENT
15	CUSTOMER-NUMBER	ELEMENT
16	CUSTOMER-NAME	ELEMENT
17	ORDER-SHIP-LOCATION	ELEMENT
18	ORDER-BILL-LOCATION	ELEMENT
19	ORDER-NUMBER	ELEMENT
20	ORDER-DATE-ORDERED	ELEMENT
21	ORDER-DATE-ENTERED	ELEMENT
22	ORDER-REF-NUMBER	ELEMENT
23	ORDER-LINE-NUMBER	ELEMENT
24	ORDER-QTY-ORDERED	ELEMENT
25	PRODUCT-MODEL-QTY-ORDERED	ELEMENT
26	PRODUCT-MODEL-PRICE	ELEMENT
27	NEW-INFO-AND-ORDERS	INPUT
28	REPORTS-AND-ANSWERS	OUTPUT
29	PRODUCT-MODEL-NAME	ELEMENT
30	PRODUCT-MODEL-BIN-NUMBER	ELEMENT
31	CUSTOMER-BILLING-INVOICES	OUTPUT
32	CUSTOMER-ADDRESS	ELEMENT
33	CUSTOMER-LOCATION	GROUP
34	INVOICE-NUMBER	ELEMENT
35	CUSTOMER-MAILING-LABELS	OUTPUT
36	CUSTOMER-ZIP-CODE	ELEMENT
37	ORDER-ENTRY-SUMMARY	OUTPUT
38	ORDER-HISTORY-REPORT	OUTPUT

COLUMN NAMES

1	ADD-NEW-CUSTOMER	PROCESS
2	ADD-NEW-INFO	PROCESS
3	ADD-NEW-PRODUCT	PROCESS
4	ADD-NEW-VENDOR	PROCESS
5	ANSWER-INQUIRIES	PROCESS
6	ANSWER-PRODUCT-INQUIRIES	PROCESS
7	ANSWER-VEND-PROD-INQUIRIES	PROCESS
8	ANSWER-VENDOR-INQUIRIES	PROCESS
9	ENTER-ORDERS	PROCESS
10	MERCHANT-INFO-PROCESSING	PROCESS
11	PICK-PRODUCTS	PROCESS
12	PRODUCE-BILLING-INVOICES	PROCESS
13	PRODUCE-MAILING-LABELS	PROCESS
14	PRODUCE-ORDER-ENTRY-REPORT	PROCESS
15	PRODUCE-ORDER-HISTORY-REPORT	PROCESS

Figure 1.28 DPI report on processes.

```
PAS VERSION A4.2RO
                        BOSTON UNIVERSITY - VPS
                      DATA PROCESS INTERACTION REPORT
DATA PROCESS INTERACTION MATRIX

(I,J) VALUE      MEANING

      R          ROW I IS RECEIVED OR USED BY COLUMN J (INPUT)
      U          ROW I IS UPDATED BY COLUMN J
      D          ROW I IS DERIVED OR GENERATED BY COLUMN J (OUTPUT)
      A          ROW I IS INPUT TO, UPDATED BY, AND OUTPUT OF
                   COLUMN J (ALL)
      F          ROW I IS INPUT TO AND OUTPUT OF COLUMN J (FLOW)
      1          ROW I IS INPUT TO AND UPDATED BY COLUMN J
      2          ROW I IS UPDATED BY AND OUTPUT OF COLUMN J


                                        111111
                              123456789012345
                              +--------------+
                         1 :1111:     1      :
                         2 :R   :     :      :
                         3 :RRRR:     :      :
                         4 :  R :     :      :
                         5 +---R+----+-----+
                         6 :    DD   :      :
                         7 :    D  D :      :
                         8 :    D  D :      :
                         9 :    RR  1:1  RR:
                        10 +----RR---+1--R-+
                        11 :    RR   :      :
                        12 :    R R  :      :
                        13 :    R R  :    R :
                        14 :    R  R :   RR:
                        15 +----+---1+-R-RR+
                        16 :    :   1:  RRR:
                        17 :    :   1:      :
                        18 :    :   1:      :
                        19 :    :   1:1  RR:
                        20 +----+---1+---RR+
                        21 :    :   1: R R :
                        22 :    :   1:   RR:
                        23 :    :   1:1  RR:
                        24 :    :   1:1  R :
                        25 :    :   1:      :
                           +----+----+-----+
                        26 :    :   1:      :
                        27 :    :    R      :
                        28 :    :    D      :
                        29 :    :    :1     :
                        30 +----+----+1----+
                        31 :    :    : D    :
                        32 :    :    : RR R:
                        33 :    :    : R R :
                        34 :    :    : R   :
                        35 +----+----+--D--+
                        36 :    :    : R   :
                        37 :    :    :  D  :
                        38 :    :    :   D:
                           +----+----+-----+
```

Figure 1.28   (*continued*)

PSA VERSION A4.2R0

BOSTON UNIVERSITY – VPS

DATA PROCESS INTERACTION REPORT

DATA PROCESS INTERACTION MATRIX ANALYSIS

DATA

MERCHANT-MASTER-INFO	(SET)	(ROW 1)	NOT DERIVED BY ANY PROCESS
NEW-CUSTOMER-INFO	(INPUT)	(ROW 2)	NOT RECEIVED BY ANY PROCESS
NEW-INFO	(INPUT)	(ROW 3)	NOT RECEIVED BY ANY PROCESS
NEW-PRODUCT-MODEL-INFO	(INPUT)	(ROW 4)	NOT RECEIVED BY ANY PROCESS
NEW-VENDOR-INFO	(INPUT)	(ROW 5)	NOT RECEIVED BY ANY PROCESS
NEW-INFO-AND-ORDERS	(INPUT)	(ROW 27)	NOT RECEIVED BY ANY PROCESS
REPORTS-AND-ANSWERS	(OUTPUT)	(ROW 28)	NOT DERIVED BY ANY PROCESS

Figure 1.28 (*continued*)

56

BOSTON UNIVERSITY - VPS

DATA PROCESS INTERACTION REPORT

PROCESS INTERACTION MATRIX (INCIDENCE)

THE ROWS AND COLUMNS ARE PROCESS NAMES FROM ABOVE. AN ASTERISK IN (I,J) MEANS THAT
SOMETHING DERIVED OR UPDATED BY PROCESS I IS USED BY PROCESS J.

```
              111111
     123456789012345
    +---------------+
 1  :****    *    :.
 2  :****    *    :.
 3  :****    *    :.
 4  :****    *    :.
 5 +-------------+
 6  :.        .:
 7  :.        .:
 8  :.        .:
 9  :.  ** *:******:.
10 +****---*----+
11  :.  ** *:* **:.
12  :.        .:
13  :.        .:
14  :.        .:
15  :.        .:
    +---------------+
```

PROCESS INTERACTION MATRIX ANALYSIS

ANSWER-INQUIRIES   (ROW/COL 5)   NO SUCCESSORS FOR THIS PROCESS
ANSWER-PRODUCT-INQUIRIES   (ROW/COL 6)   NO SUCCESSORS FOR THIS PROCESS
ANSWER-VEND-PROD-INQUIRIES   (ROW/COL 7)   NO INTERACTION, BUT IS PART OF ANOTHER PROCESS
ANSWER-VENDOR-INQUIRIES   (ROW/COL 8)   NO INTERACTION, BUT IS PART OF ANOTHER PROCESS
PRODUCE-BILLING-INVOICES   (ROW/COL 12)   NO SUCCESSORS FOR THIS PROCESS
PRODUCE-MAILING-LABELS   (ROW/COL 13)   NO SUCCESSORS FOR THIS PROCESS
PRODUCE-ORDER-ENTRY-REPORT   (ROW/COL 14)   NO SUCCESSORS FOR THIS PROCESS
PRODUCE-ORDER-HISTORY-REPORT (ROW/COL 15)   NO SUCCESSORS FOR THIS PROCESS

Figure 1.28 (*continued*)

Data Process Interaction Matrix shows that the process produce-billing-invoices USES or RECEIVES customer-number, customer-location, order-date-entered, customer-address, and invoice-number and DERIVES customer-billing-invoices. The Process Interaction Matrix (Incidence) states that produce-billing-invoices uses as input something which was UPDATED or DERIVED by add-new-customer and enter-orders. The statement in Process Interaction Matrix Analysis, "No successors for this process," means that no other processes use data produced by this process. The DPI report can also be run using data as input.

Several aspects of the merchant information processing system have been presented in PSA reports. These reports exemplify the flexibility and breadth of PSA. Additional reports are available, so that each system aspect is presented in more than one report.

1.8 DATA DICTIONARY SYSTEMS

A *data dictionary* is a repository of metadata—the information about an organization's data resource including the definition, structure, and use of data. A *data dictionary system* (DDS) includes the data dictionary and a means for entering, modifying, and reporting its contents. DDSs are also called data dictionary/directory systems. DDSs can play a central role in the requirements phase of system developement by providing a mechanism for central control and management of the organization's data. In fact, a data dictionary system can be considered a requirements technique. There are computerized and manual DDSs which possess similar benefits and costs associated with manual and computer-aided requirements techniques as described in Section 1.5. Today when one speaks of a DDS, the reference is only to a computerized data dictionary system and, therefore, this section will discuss only computerized DDSs.

A data dictionary system consists of:

1. The data dictionary—the database of the metadata, which is commonly referred to as the dictionary database or just the dictionary;
2. A facility for entering data into and maintaining the dictionary;
3. A facility for generating reports and answering ad-hoc queries.

DDSs usually include:

1. A bridge facility between DBMS and non-DBMS applications, and optionally,
2. An ability to interface with DBMS applications at run time.

The last two characteristics distinguish a DDS from other types of requirements techniques. A *bridge facility* is a nonrun-time interface between the DDS, and DBMS, and non-DBMS applications. This interface may be in one or two directions. In one direction, input for the DDS may be drawn from the data definition and the procedures from existing application programs and databases. In the other direction, data definitions and portions of procedures for new applications can be generated directly from the data dictionary. Most DDSs provide the interface in both of these directions. Given that a data dictionary system is required to interface with the organization's DBMS(s), these two systems must be compatible.

The last characteristic, DBMS/DDS run-time interface, divides DDSs into two groups: active and passive (nonactive). In an active DDS, the dictionary is an integral part of the DBMS—the data definitions used while executing DBMS applications come from the dictionary database. The majority of commercial DDSs are passive, although the trend is towards the active.

The most common first use of a data dictionary system is building a (corporate) data inventory. A *data inventory* is the basic description of (all) data used by the organization. At a minimum, this description presents the name, abbreviation, and definition for all objects inventoried. These characteristics of data objects are called object attributes. Creating a data inventory can be a time-consuming effort. The time and cost required for its creation is dependent upon the number of data objects to be defined, the number of attributes (required) to describe each object and the availability and the form of this information. The benefits obtained from a data inventory are directly related to its completeness. The more corporate data defined and the more robust the definitions, the greater the benefits.

A data dictionary system facilitates the collection and recording of the information obtained during the requirements phase. The dictionary is a repository for the documentation of requirements identified. The amount of information collected is usually voluminous and from numerous users. The use of a DDS can reduce the effort of manually aggregating and cross-referencing this information. Requirements can be stated in the form of the dictionary primitives: object types, relationships, and descriptive statements of the DDS syntax. This results in better standardization. Analysts can use the DDS reports for reference and direction during the requirements-collection activities. Clerical burdens are relieved through easy-to-use DDS facilities providing:

- data recording and entry,
- change of requirements (as stored in the dictionary) with the automatic log of these modifications, and
- report generation.

Data entry techniques can be provided through fixed-format and free-format transactions in either on-line or batch mode. Batch mode is used to process large volumes of input and is usually facilitated by pre-printed dictionary input forms.

The dictionary input preparation tasks can be shortened through bridge facilities which generate DDS input for existing programs, and data and database definitions.

A data dictionary system facilitates the specification of requirements by supporting the system analysis technique used and by generating reports suitable for review by users. The DDS's primitives (e.g., object types and relationships) form an underlying model of requirements and should be consistent with and support the system analysis methodology being employed by the analyst. At a minimum, the dictionary primitives should include both process object types (e.g., system, application, function, transaction, process, etc.) and data object types (e.g., database, file, record, item, relationship, etc.), as well as provide the means to describe and interrelate objects. The blending of DDS and requirement technique is often accomplished through a dictionary *extensibility facility*. This facility provides the means to define new object types and new statements about objects. This facility is useless without either standard reports that present this extended information or the ability to easily write special reports to document the augmented information.

A DDS can provide certain basic types of analysis and its dictionary can serve as a database for more sophisticated analytical tools. A DDS is an aid for analysis and not a substitute for the analyst. A data dictionary system facilitates the analysis of requirements by providing:

- easy access to up-to-date information,

- a variety of easy-to-generate reports,

- controls to assure the integrity and security of the dictionary, and

- facilities to identify redundancies and inconsistencies.

The currency of the dictionary is maintained through simple and comprehensive maintenance utilities. Both on-line and batch access to the dictionary should be available for queries and report generation. The commands for report/query generation should be concise, simple-to-use, and have flexible parameter specifications. The reports should be comprehensible to both technical and nontechnical users. At a minimum, the DDS must be capable of generating cross-reference reports on the objects defined in the dictionary and, where used, reports for specific objects. Data redundancy can be reduced through the use of a data inventory and can be detected using keyword-in-context reports. Inconsistencies can be identified by using reports.

The loss of dictionary data integrity can be minimized by multiple dictionary versions; that is, a production version and one or more test versions where only the test version(s) can be changed. Dictionary integrity can be improved by the automatic logging of all dictionary changes, the recording and automatic maintenance of information about responsibility of data, and a comprehensive dictionary security system.

The benefits obtained from using a data dictionary system are not just in the requirements phase but in all phases of the system development process. The trustworthy, correct, and consistent information in the dictionary database is available for all development activities. Therefore, this information provides:

- improved communication between analysts, designers, and users,

- the capability to employ computer-aided development tools such as automated normalization,

- the ability to easily produce current, correct, and understandable system documentation (usually in $8\frac{1}{2} \times 11$ format),

- ability to do change impact analysis, and

- the ability to audit the use of data.

Additionally, the DDS may result in reduced development cost, reduced elapsed time for development, and reduced time for database creation [35]. When organizations acquire a DDS, the major costs are assumed to be its acquisition and software/hardware support. After using a DDS, one finds that these costs are minimal and that the major costs can be attributed to the formation of two new organizational functions, data and database administration, to support the DDS and promote its effective use; organizational disruption caused by new and different system development practices; user, system analysis, and developer training and support; and most importantly, the building and maintaining of the corporate data dictionary. The last task is difficult, time-consuming, personnel-intensive, and never-ending.

Today, organizations do not use a DDS to the complete extent of its capabilities and benefits. In organizations with a DDS, usually less than 25% of all applications are defined in the dictionary and there is no corporate data inventory [Kahn, 1983]. The DDS is only used as an application documentation tool and schema generator and not as a mechanism for effective information resource management and control.

DDS selection is a difficult and important task. Once a DDS is installed and used, it is difficult or perhaps impossible to switch to another without having to repeat all the work done. DDS selection is the topic of Kahn [31] and Plagman [41]. Data dictionary systems are usually acquired on a lease or purchase basis from a software/hardware vendor. Occasionally, organizations internally develop their own DDS when commercial systems do not satisfy their needs. Today, this alternative is rarely selected. The DDS selected must be compatible with the organization's hardware and software environment, especially the database management system(s). Organizations can select from a spectrum of commercial DDSs. The following is a list of the most used commercial DDSs:

Data Dictionary System	DBMS Interface	Vendor
ADABAS Data Dictionary	ADABAS	Software AG of North America Inc.
Data Catalogue 2	ADABAS, IDMS, IMS (DL/1), System 2000, TOTAL	Synergetics Corporation
Data Dictionary	DATA COM/DB, TOTAL, IMS (DL/1)	Applied Data Research, Inc.
Data Manager	ADABAS, IDMS, IMS (DL/1), System 2000, TOTAL	MSP Inc.
DB/DC Data Dictionary	IMS (DL/1)	IBM Corporation
IDMS Integrated Data Dictionary (IDD)*	IDMS	Cullinet Corporation
System 2000 Extended Data Dictionary (EDD)*	System 2000	Intel Systems Corporation
Total Data Dictionary	TOTAL	CINCOM Systems, Inc.
UCC-TEN	IMS	University Computing Company

*Active Data Dictionary System.

REFERENCES

1. Aanstad, P.S., G. Skylstad, and A. Solvberg, "CASCADE—A Computer-Based Documentation System," in Bubenko, Langefors, and Solvberg, eds., *Computer-Aided Information Systems, Analysis and Design*, pp. 93–112, Lund, Sweden, 1972.

2. ANSI/X3/SPARC, "Interim Report from The Study Group on Data Base Management Systems," *FDT (Bulletin of ACM SIGMOD)*, Vol. 7, No. 2 (1975).

3. Auglaend, K., and A. Solvberg, "A Technique for Computerized Graphical Presentation of Information Systems," in Boot, ed., *Approaches to System Design*, pp. 95–104, Manchester, England: NCC Publications, 1973.

4. Auxton Computer Enterprises, Inc., *Auxco Project Management Systems: User Reference Manual*, Section I, 1972.

5. Benci, H., F. Bodart, H. Bodaert, and A. Cabanes, "Concepts for the Design of a Conceptual Schema," in G.M. Nilssen, ed., *Modeling in Data Base Management Systems*, pp. 181–200, New York: North-Holland Publishing Co., 1976.

6. Bracchi, G., P. Paolini, and G. Pelagatt, "Binary Logical Associations in Data Modeling," in G.M. Nilssen, ed., *Modeling in Data Base Management Systems*, pp. 125–148, New York: North-Holland Publishing Co., 1976.

7. Bubenko, J., and O. Kollhammer, "CADIS—Computer-Aided Design of Information Systems," in Bubenko, Langefors, and Solvberg, eds., *Computer-Aided Information Systems, Analysis and Design*, pp. 119–140, Lund, Sweden, 1972.

8. Burch, J.G., F.R. Strater, and G. Grudnitski, *Information Systems: Theory and Practice*, 2d ed. New York: John Wiley & Sons, Inc., 1979.

9. Canning, R.G., ed., "The Data Dictionary/Directory Function," *EDP Analyzer*, Vol. 12, No. 10 (November 1974).

10. Canning, R.G., "Getting the Requirements Right," *EDP Analyzer*, Vol. 15, No. 7 (July 1977).

11. Carlsen, Robert D., and James A. Lewis, *The Systems Analysis Workbook: A Complete Guide to Project Implementation and Control*, pp. 25–26, 78–84, Englewood Cliffs, N.J.: Prentice-Hall, Inc., 1976.

12. Condon, Robert J., *Data Processing Systems Analysis and Design*, pp. 151–157, 162–166, Reston, Va.: Reston Publishing Company, 1978.

13. Connor, Michael A., "Structured Analysis and Design Technique—SADT," Portfolio 32-04-02, System Development Management. Princeton, N.J.: Auerbach Publishers, 1980.

14. Cougar, Daniel J., "Evolution of Business System Analysis Techniques," *Computing Surveys*, Vol. 5, No. 3 (September 1973), pp. 167–198.

15. Davis, Gordon B., *Management Information Systems: Conceptual Foundations, Structure, and Development*, New York: McGraw-Hill, 1974.

16. De Marco, Tom, *Structural Analysis in System Specification*. Englewood Cliffs, N.J.: Prentice-Hall, Inc., 1979.

17. Gane, C.P., and T. Sarson, *Structured Systems Analysis: Tools and Techniques*. Englewood Cliffs, N.J.: Prentice-Hall, Inc., 1979.

18. Gane, C.P., "Data Design in Structured Systems Analysis," in P. Freeman and A.J. Wasserman, eds., *Tutorial on Software Design Techniques*, 3d ed., IEEE Computer Society, 1980.

19. Gilb, T., "Some Principles of System Design," *Management Datamatics*, Vol. 5, No. 1, pp. 45–48.

20. Grad, Burton, et al., *Management Systems*, pp. 41, 95. New York: Dryden Press, 1979.

21. Hartman, W., H. Matthes, and A. Proeme, *Management Information Systems Handbook—ARDI*. New York: McGraw-Hill, 1968.

22. Time Automated Grid System, IBM (Form No. G-Y 20-0358), 2d ed. White Plains, N.Y.: IBM, 1971.

23. International Computer Limited (ICL), *CADES—Computer-Aided Design and Evaluation System*. Undated.

24. ISDOS, Project Staff, *Problem Statement Language (PSL): Introduction and User's Manual*, PSA Version 4.2. Ann Arbor: The University of Michigan, May 1977.

25. ISDOS, Project Staff, *Problem Statement Language (PSL): Language Reference Manual*, PSA Version 4.2. Ann Arbor: The University of Michigan, May 1977.

26. ISDOS, Project Staff, *Problem Statement Analyzer: User's Manual*, Version 4.2. Ann Arbor: The University of Michigan, May 1977.

27. ISDOS, Project Staff, *PSL/PSA Example*, Version 4.2. Ann Arbor: The University of Michigan, January 1978.

28. Jones, M.N., "HIPO for Developing Specifications," *Datamation*, March 1976, pp. 112–125.

29. Juergens, H.F., "Attributes of Information System Development," *MIS QUARTERLY*, June 1977, pp. 31–41.

30. Kahn, Beverly K., "A Review of Systems Analysis and Data Base Design Techniques,"

ISDOS Working Paper No. 129, Ann Arbor: The University of Michigan, November 1975.

31. Kahn, Beverly K., and Eunice W. Lumsden, "User-Oriented Framework for Data Dictionary Systems," *Data Base*, Fall 1983.

32. Kahn, Beverly K., "A Structured Logical Database Design Methodology," Ph.D. Dissertation, The University of Michigan, 1979.

33. Katzan, H., Jr., *System Design and Documentation: An Introduction to the HIPO Method*. New York: Van Nostrand Reinhold Co., 1976.

34. Koudry, Herbert J., "Techniques of Interviewing," *Journal of Systems Management*, May 1972, pp. 22–23.

35. Lefkovits, Henry C., *Data Dictionary Systems*, Wellesley, MA.: Q.E.D. Information Sciences, Inc., 1977.

36. Langefors, B., *Theoretical Analysis of Information Systems*, 3d ed., Student Literature, Lund, Sweden, 1971.

37. Lucas, Henry C., *The Analysis, Design, and Implementation of Information Systems*, pp. 122–125. New York: McGraw-Hill, 1981.

38. Miller, George A., "The Magical Number Seven, Plus or Minus Two: Some Limits on Our Capacity for Processing Information," *The Psychological Review*, Vol. 63, No. 210 (March 1956), pp. 81–97.

39. Nolan, Richard L., "Systems Analysis for Computer Based Information Systems Design," *Data Base*, Vol. 3, No. 4 (Winter 1971), pp. 1–10.

40. Novak, Donald O., and James P. Fry, "The State of the Art of Database Design," Technical Report 76 DE 7, Ann Arbor: The University of Michigan, August 1976.

41. Plagman, Bernard K., "Criteria for the Selection of Dictionary/Directory Systems," Auerbach Publication 22-04-01. Princeton, N.J.: Auerbach Publishers, 1977.

42. Rampe, G., "An Approach to Data Base Design," White Plains, N.Y.: AT & T Longlines, 1975. Unpublished.

43. Ross, D.T., and J.W. Brackett, "An Approach to Structured Analysis," *Computer Decisions*, September 1976, pp. 40–44.

44. Ross, D.T., "Structured Analysis (SA): A Language for Communicating Ideas," *IEEE Transactions on Software Engineering*, January 1977.

45. Ross, D.T., and K.E. Schoman, Jr., "Structured Analysis for Requirements Definition," "*IEEE Transactions on Software Engineering*," January 1977.

46. Senn, James A., *Information Systems in Management*, pp. 473–478. Belmont, Calif.: Wadsworth Publishing Company, 1978.

47. SofTech, Inc., "An Introduction to SADT—Structured Analysis and Design Technique." Waltham, Mass., February 1976.

48. Solvberg, A., "Formal Systems Description in Information Systems Design," in Boot, ed., *Approaches to System Design*, pp. 85–93. Manchester, England: NCC Publications, 1973.

49. Sprowls, R. Clay, *Management Data Bases*. New York: John Wiley & Sons, Inc., 1976.

50. Taylor, Robert W., and Randall L. Frank, "The CODASYL Database Management System," *Computing Surveys*, Vol. 8, No. 1 (March 1976), pp. 67–103.

51. Teichroew, D. and H. Sayani, "Automation of System Building," *Datamation*, August 1971, pp. 25–30.

52. Teichroew, D., E.J. Rataj, and E.A. Hershey, III, "An Introduction to Computer-Aided Documentation of User Requirements for Computer Based Information Processing Systems," *ISDOS Working Paper No. 72.* Ann Arbor: The University of Michigan, March 1973.

53. Teichroew, D., and E. Winters, "Recent Developments in Systems Analysis and Design," *Atlantic Economic Review*, November-December 1976, pp. 39–46.

54. Teichroew, D., and E.A. Hershey, III, "PSL/PSA: Analysis of Information Processing Systems," *IEEE Transactions on Software Engineering*, January 1977.

55. Uhrowczik, P.P., "Data Dictionary/Directories," *IBM Systems Journal* (December 1973), pp. 332–350.

56. Weisbard, M.F., "A Computer-Aided System Study Methodology T.A.G.—Time Automated Grid," in Boot, ed., *Approaches to System Design*, pp. 163–165. Manchester, England: NCC Publications, 1973.

57. Yao, S.B., and V. Waddle, "Database Design by Sampling," Working Paper. College Park, MD: University of Maryland, 1981.

ADDITIONAL READINGS

1. Anthony, Robert N., *Planning and Control Systems: A Framework for Analysis*, Graduate School of Business Administration, Harvard University, 1965.

2. Athey, Thomas, *Systematic Systems Approach: An Integrated Method for Solving Systems Problems*, Englewood Cliffs, N.J.: Prentice-Hall, Inc., 1982.

3. Awad, Elias M., *Systems Analysis and Design*, Homewood, IL: Richard D. Irwin Inc., 1979.

4. British Computer Society Data Dictionary Systems Working Party, "The British Computer Society Data Dictionary Systems Working Party Report," *Data Base*, Vol. 9, No. 2 (Fall 1977), pp. 2–24.

5. Cougar, D. J., M. A. Colter, and R. W. Knapp, *Advanced System Development/Feasibility Techniques*, New York: John Wiley & Sons, 1982.

6. Davis, G. B., "Strategies for Information Requirements Determination," *IBM System Journal* (1982), Vol. 21, No. 1, pp. 4–30.

7. Fehder, Paul L., "The IBM DB/DC Data Dictionary, A Brief Overview—With Special Emphasis on the Extensibility & Program Access Facilities," IBM General Products Division, 1980.

8. Gorry, G. A. and M. S. Scott Morton, "A Framework for Management Information Systems," *Sloan Management Review*, Fall 1971, pp. 55–70.

9. IBM Corporation, "Business Systems Planning—Information Systems Planning Guide, Application Manual," *IBM Manual GE20-0527*, July 1981.

10. Kahn, B. K., "Some Realities of Data Administration," *Communications of the ACM*, October 1983, pp. 794–799.

11. Lefkovitz, Henry C., Edgar H. Sibley, and Sandra L. Lefkovitz, *Information Resource/Data Dictionary Systems*, Wellesley, MA: Q.E.D. Information Sciences, Inc., 1982.

12. Zackman, J. A., "Business System Planning and Business Information Control Study: A Comparison," *IBM System Journal*, Vol. 21, No. 1 (1982), pp. 31–53.

2

Data Models and the
ANSI/SPARC Architecture

Eric K. Clemons
University of Pennsylvania

2.1 INTRODUCTION: COMPETING DATA MODELS AND THE ANSI / SPARC ARCHITECTURE

This chapter describes the three principal data models—hierarchical, network, and relational—and their basic similarities and differences, strengths and limitations. Each model will be introduced and used in a small database design problem, after which a brief example will be presented to illustrate programming of retrieval against the database. Since we will evaluate each model in the context of the ANSI/X3/SPARC database architecture, we begin with a discussion of this architecture.

The network and hierarchical data models were introduced in the early 1960s, and the relational model can be traced to an article published by Codd in 1970 [14]. By 1972 each had proponents and detractors, since each had relative advantages and disadvantages. Claims were made for each in terms of ease of use, naturalness of data representation or query language, efficiency, data independence, and a host of other criteria; these claims were often unsupported and sometimes unsupportable. These arguments among proponents of "the one true data model" were usually entertaining, sometimes acrimonious, and of course futile in their attempt to agree on a common data model. They culminated in the Great Debate of 1974 [30].

The ANSI/X3/SPARC Proposal of 1975 [1] highlighted the reasons for the irreconcilable differences and explained the failure of most attempts to select a best model. It demonstrated the existence of multiple classes of users with dramatically different requirements. Under different sets of assumptions, or with attention restricted to a single class of user, a preferred data model might be selected; this data model, while serving one class well, usually left other classes served poorly. The key contribution of the ANSI/SPARC proposal was the introduction of a *multischema* or multilevel architecture. Each level had its own data representation, or schema, and mapping functions were provided to transform data from the representation of one schema to that of another. Each schema could employ a different data model, permitting all data models to be used in a single database system if this appeared useful. Recent work by proponents of different data models has demonstrated the viability of multischema architectures [2, 9, 29].

2.1.1 Terminology

The following concepts will be useful in the remainder of this chapter, when the ANSI/SPARC architecture and the major data models are treated in more detail. No attempt is made at a formal definition, and for many of these terms only partial consensus is available among database professionals.

A *schema* provides a description of the data contained in the database. This description is more complete than that provided in file-based environments. It includes a description of structure, such as data types and items grouped together, and a description of linkages or relationships. Often semantic descriptions are also included, such as integrity constraints restricting data values, relationships, or behavior over time. The schema is written in its own *data-description language*, or *DDL*, and is common across a large number of application programs; it is invoked by these programs and not written by each programmer.

Use of the data for retrieval or update requires a *data manipulation language*, or *DML*. This language may be stand-alone, such as a query language, used without any other programming language, or it may be a *data-sublanguage*, used to provide a database interface for a procedural *host language*.

Data independence is frequently used as a criterion in evaluating data models or comparing database products. Unfortunately, there is no generally accepted definition for this term, nor is any accepted metric available to measure it [4]. Any definition adopted in the future is likely to contain the following ideas: data independence is a measure of a database system's ability to provide for change in representation or in content of the database without affecting programs. In the limit, under perfect data independence, a change that does not explicitly remove data needed by an application program will not affect the operations of a program or its production of correct results, except perhaps for changes in performance efficiency.

Extensibility is another term for which no precise definition is available. It is intended to measure the ease with which new application programs can be added to the set of applications supported by a database. Some changes—for example, the addition of new attributes, extending the description of some entity already in the database—may require simply extending the schema to include these new attributes. Other additions may alter the nature of relationships between or among entities, and thus they may require minor or major restructuring of the schema and of the database. We ignore here the cost of restructuring the database because, while it can be considerable, it is almost always far less than the cost of revising application code. Some changes may require minor or major modification of programs, at considerable expense. Since the amount of program revision required is related to data independence, data independence and extensibility may be seen to be closely related.

We will defer detailed description of the terms *data model* and *database system architecture* to the end of the chapter; the reader will probably not be surprised to learn that no generally accepted definitions for these terms exist either. For now, we note that data models are distinguished principally through the manner in which they treat relationships among objects in the database. And, for now, we accept a database architecture as a simplified description of a database system that presents major system components and their function, omits details and specifics of these components, but does present details of interfaces between components.

2.2 THE ANSI / SPARC ARCHITECTURE

As noted earlier, an important contribution of the ANSI/SPARC proposal was the observation that there were three distinct classes of users to be served by a database management system:

1. The organization, firm, or enterprise as a whole, treated as a single user.
2. The application programmers and query-language interface users—that is, the individual database users.
3. The database management system and the machine that must actually retrieve or update the data.

Each class of user will have different requirements.

2.2.1 Classes of User

The enterprise will require logical completeness. Data description for the enterprise will include:

1. Enumeration of the entity types of interest, which will be captured in the database.
2. Description of these entities—that is, attributes of interest.
3. Relationships among entities.
4. Some degree of semantics, such as restrictions on relationships or restrictions on data values, to assure conformity of the data to behavior observed in the enterprise or its world.

In brief, the enterprise requires a description of a data processing world view sufficient to support the entire collection of data processing applications; if possible, this description should also contain restrictions sufficient to assure a correct and consistent database.

The application programmers and query language users will require logical simplicity intended to assure ease of use. Users require a user view of the database, which may be different from the view provided for the enterprise. Data structures provided to a user in his user view ideally should be similar to cognitive structures employed solving programming problems. These cognitive structures are not necessarily similar to those described in the enterprise's world view or to those physically stored in the database; moreover, the structures employed in two different applications may be quite dissimilar.

The machine that must actually access, retrieve, and update data requires device-level detail. This will include:

1. Data formats, such as word length and numeric encoding.
2. Device addresses.
3. Access methods.
4. Access paths: indices, inversions, pointer chains, or list structures.

2.2.2 Multilevel Architectures

The ANSI/SPARC proposal introduced multilevel database systems with multiple schemas and associated mapping functions. The architecture includes three levels:

1. External.
2. Conceptual.
3. Internal.

The external level supports applications programmers and query-language users. The *external schemas* provide the user interface to the database management system. There may be one or several external schemas provided, each supporting a distinct user view designed for a specific application or set of applications and each exploiting an appropriate data model.

The conceptual level supports the enterprise and contains a single *conceptual schema* presenting the enterprise's world view. This conceptual schema contains both structure and semantics.

The internal level supports the database management system and the machine itself. A single *internal schema* permits efficient access and permits performance tuning.

The database profession exhibits different degrees of understanding of the three levels. The internal, or performance, level is best understood, and a wide range of material from analysis of algorithms, data structure, and file processing is directly applicable. Physical design and performance is the subject of the second volume of this book. Considerable progress has been made in the understanding of the conceptual level, though our knowledge here still falls far short of our knowledge of the internal level. Relevant publications include those of Hammer and McLeod [19, 20, 21], Kent [22, 23, 24], and the Smiths [31, 32]. There has been a considerable European effort reported in the conference proceedings of IFIP TC2, WG 2.6 [17, 27, 28] and by ISO/TC97/SC5/WG3. Semantic modeling is the subject of the next chapter. The external level is the least thoroughly investigated and the least understood. As there is not yet enough material for a volume, or even for a chapter, it will be treated in Section 2.3.

2.2.3 ANSI / SPARC Example

We will illustrate with a simple example the ANSI/SPARC architecture, the contents of the various schemas, and their interactions. The example will focus on the academic functions of a university, such as student registration, classroom scheduling, and the recording of grades. Nonacademic functions, such as payroll and purchasing, will be supported by other databases, not considered here; similarly, interactions between the university and its surrounding community will not be considered.

The first step in designing the database is, of course, to determine requirements —that is, to decide what data are to be captured, based on current and projected needs. After that we select a collection of entities—people, objects—to include in the database. Next we decide which of the attributes and characteristics that might be used to describe an entity should actually be captured in the database. Relationships among entities are examined to determine which to include and how to describe them. Finally, integrity constraints—restrictions on data values or relationships—must be added.

Based on our understanding of the problem environment, we may decide that the following entity types and attributes will be important:

1. Department: name, department number, school, chairman.
2. Faculty: name, department, social security number, rank, tenure status.
3. Student: name, social security number, grade-point.
4. Course: number, department, credits.
5. Section: department, course number, section number, term, room, time.

Many problems or limitations of this arrangement are obvious. Where should grade information be kept—as an attribute of the student receiving the grade or as an attribute of the course in which the grade was received? Since neither alternative is adequate, we add a sixth entity—almost a pseudoentity: grade:

6. Grade: letter grade, student number, section, term.

Next we list relationships:

1. Students major in departments.
2. Departments have faculty members.
3. Departments offer courses.
4. Faculty members are reponsible for courses.
5. Faculty members teach sections.
6. Faculty members advise students.
7. Students receive grades in sections.
8. Courses meet in sections.

Lest this process appear more systematic than is actually the case, we note the following objections. Often the distinction between an entity and an attribute will seem arbitrary. Why, for example, is school listed as an attribute of department (e.g., Arts and Sciences for Physics, Engineering for Computer Science); if we maintained more information on the school, such as the faculty member serving as dean, wouldn't school be elevated to the status of entity? Similarly, the distinction between attributes and relationships is less clear than is often claimed: should department be listed as an attribute of faculty, or should this relationship be captured solely as an explicitly declared relationship between departments and faculty members? Should chairman be an attribute of department or a relationship between department and another entity; if the second alternative is preferred, should the other entity be a chairman entity or a member of a collection of faculty entities?

It may be comforting to note that often the database designer need not consider the numerous ways of representing entities, attributes, and their relationships, as the particular data model chosen and its data-description language will severely limit the set of alternatives. That is, once the decision has been made to use a particular data model or a single database management system, this decision may determine how certain attributes or relationships will be represented. Thus, bias in world view is often imposed upon the designer.

After making some design decisions and adding a few constraints, we could summarize the conceptual schema as in Figure 2.1.

Note that many attributes included in our preliminary design are now maintained solely through relationships. For example, only the actual grade received is now shown as an attribute of grade; the student receiving the grade and the course in which it was received may be inferred from relationships in which grade participates.

Once the conceptual schema is designed to support the set of applications, the internal schema may be designed to provide desired performance. Several classes of decisions must be made:

1. Representation of elementary data items.
2. Placement of attributes.
3. Placement of records.
4. Provision of access to records.
5. Representation of relationships.

Since this material is described in detail elsewhere in this book, we will simply illustrate here the types of decisions to be made. For representation of data items we decide such things as the length of the character string used to store a student's name and whether social security number should be stored as a numeric or as a character string. For placement of attributes we decide whether all attributes are to be stored together or whether seldom-used attributes are to be stored in secondary records; since grade-point is derivable from grades and course credits, we may actually decide not to store it at all. Record placement includes such alternatives as hashing, clustering related records together, or partitioning frequently and infrequently used records on different devices. Record access options include primary and secondary key inversions. Finally, linkages among related records may be made using physical address pointer or symbolic key, by pointer chain or lists of keys.

Entities	*Attributes*
DEPARTMENT:	NAME, DEPT–NO, SCHOOL
FACULTY:	NAME, SSN, RANK, TENURE–STATUS
STUDENT:	NAME, SSN, GRADE–POINT
COURSE:	NUMBER, NAME, CREDITS
SECTION:	SECTION #, TERM, ROOM, TIME
GRADE:	GRADE–RECVD

Relationships	*Entities Related*
CHAIRMAN	DEPARTMENT, FACULTY
AFFILIATION	DEPARTMENT, FACULTY
MAJOR	DEPARTMENT, STUDENT
OFFERS	DEPARTMENT, COURSE
COURSE–SECTION	COURSE, SECTION
ADVISOR	FACULTY, STUDENT
STUDENT–GRADE	STUDENT, GRADE
SECTION–GRADE	SECTION, GRADE
TEACHES	FACULTY, SECTION
RESPONSIBLE	FACULTY, COURSE

Integrity Restrictions

1. No more than one section may meet in a given room at any time.
2. Department chairman must be a faculty member affiliated with the department.

Figure 2.1 Entities, attributes, and relationships in a university academic database.

The external schema functionality is discussed in some detail in Section 2.3; here we provide only illustrative examples of external schemas defined over the conceptual schema just developed. Consider a course and room roster of the type published each spring and fall to enable students to select and register for their courses. Each entry in the roster includes department code, course number, section number, faculty name, room, and time. This could be provided by a single record in an external schema, combining data from department, course, section, and faculty records defined in the conceptual schema. As a more complex example, consider an external schema entry to define student transcript records. Each such record will have data on each term for which the student took courses and, for each term, data on each course—its number, name, and credits, and the grade received.

2.2.4 Strengths of the Architecture

Two advantages are claimed for the ANSI/SPARC multischema architecture. The first is ease of use. Contrast the ease of retrieval specified against the external schema with that of retrievals directed against the conceptual level, or the ease of specifying integrity control restrictions in the conceptual schema instead of in the internal schema.

The second advantage of a three-schema over a two-schema architecture is enhanced data independence. Enhancing or extending the conceptual schema to capture additional information need not affect any application code; we need merely respecify conceptual-to-external maps to reflect any changes made at the conceptual level. Moreover, the conceptual level serves as a stable platform for the definition of these external schemas: any restructuring of the internal level that does not remove information from the database can be treated without modifying any external schemas of conceptual-to-external maps; we need only change a single internal-to-conceptual map. Since the number of external schemas may become quite large, this isolation of the numerous external schemas and their maps from changes to the internal level offers a considerable saving over architectures where the internal and external levels are directly linked.

2.3 THE EXTERNAL SCHEMA

The external schema facility is intended to serve as a user interface to a database management system. Each external schema provides a simple user view, tailored to the requirements of a specific application or set of applications and to a specific user or user population. The role of the external level is to provide a general and powerful mapping facility, to transform data between the representation of the enterprise view or conceptual schema and the representation of the user view or external schema.

Prior to the ANSI/SPARC proposal, database systems frequently provided little or no mapping capability to support user views. The subschema facility of the original CODASYL network proposal, for example, enabled records, data items, or linkages to be omitted; it provided neither for major changes in representation nor for alternative data models. The ANSI/SPARC proposal made popular the concept of general-purpose mappings to construct external schemas but provided no details for these maps and made no recommendations for the external schema facility.

In the absence of formal direction from ANSI/SPARC, no consensus has emerged on the form of the external schema facility or on requisite functionality. One opinion, with which we agree, advocates user views that provide for the simplest possible use and the minimum possible interrecord navigation; it is this opinion that we shall present first. Other positions on external schema facilities are included in subsequent sections on data models.

The term *database navigation* was first used by Bachman [3] and refers to the process of following relationships between records in the database. As we have noted, data models differ principally in the type and complexity of relationships permitted between records and in the linkages used to support them; thus the form of navigation differs considerably among different data models. While it might be expected that the complexity of navigation and its susceptibility to errors would also differ among data models, it has been shown in controlled experimentation that in all three principal data models navigation is the most significant source of errors and that these error rates are surprisingly similar across data models [25]. For this reason, the bulk of the process of traversing interrecord relationships should be subsumed in the external schema facility and, wherever possible, data from different conceptual level records should be related, restructured, and combined by the external schema facility to produce a single record in the user view.

Ideally, the difficulty of writing programs against a complex, shared database should be no greater than that of writing programs in a file-oriented COBOL language environment with files tailored to the needs of the particular application. Thus the external schema facility can be used to hide the complexity of the conceptual schema, much as the conceptual schema hides the implementation detail of the internal level.

For example, an external schema user record might correspond to a student transcript in a traditional file-based system. A statement like READ TRANSCRIPT would then correspond to several, perhaps hundreds, of database accesses: the student record, grade records, and course records associated with the transcript would all be accessed. Moreover, in supporting this request for a transcript, the system would also be required to sort course and grade information by semester and to compute semester grade-point averages and composite average.

Two additional observations also serve to determine the form of the external schema facility. First, note that each external schema has little need for the completeness or generality that is required of the conceptual schema: while one conceptual schema must provide a world view general enough to support the needs of all applications and complete enough to impose necessary semantic restrictions upon all data in the database, each external schema need support only a single application, requiring only a single view. Also, the external schema can in fact ignore respecification of validity restrictions, since these restrictions will still be imposed by the system. Second, note that the collection of external schemas may appear contradictory or inconsistent: it matters not if the view of one external schema can be mapped into the view of a second, provided that the conceptual schema is sufficiently general to support mappings between itself and each external schema.

These observations probably imply a simple hierarchical basis for the external schema facility used by most traditional commercial programmers. Necessary functionality for a hierarchical external schema facility [10] and mappings to provide an interface to nonhierarchical database systems [12] are reviewed in the literature. This external schema facility makes possible relatively easy use of a database; the key database design problems then will be:

1. Design of a complete conceptual schema for effectiveness and for extensibility; that is, design of a conceptual schema that will support the development of needed application programs and provide for future application requirements.
2. Design of a detailed internal schema for efficiency; that is, design of an internal schema that provides the necessary system performance.

With this architecture it is anticipated that:

1. External schemas may be added when desired, at little cost.
2. Changes to the conceptual schema will be infrequent, may be moderately complex to effect, since many conceptual-to-external maps may need to be altered; and will not affect application programs unless needed information is removed.
3. Changes to the internal schema may be made whenever it is desired to tune performance, and they will not change the conceptual schema or the maps from the conceptual schema to the external schemas.

It may appear that this use of the external schema facility to reduce programmer navigation merely shifts responsibility within the organization, requiring considerable navigation from the database systems personnel who prepare the external schemas and define the supporting maps, and leading to increased navigation errors by the systems staff. This is not likely to be the case, because each external schema is likely to support the requisite view of several related applications. The view that supports printing of final transcripts for graduating seniors can, for example, readily be modified to produce term-by-term average grade-points, and thus to detect students who are having unexpected difficulty. Thus the external schema facility can be viewed as a data-access macro facility; use of external schemas will permit several programs to use the same specification of interrecord navigation and thus should reduce the total amount of navigation code and of navigation errors.

2.4 RELATIONSHIPS IN DATABASE SYSTEMS: A BRIEF INTRODUCTION

It may be argued that the principal differences among data models are differences in the types of relationships that may be represented and in the restrictions they impose upon them. Certainly, understanding these restrictions is central to understanding the major data models. For this reason, we present here a classification of relationships and a summary of how different types of relationships may be represented.

2.4.1 Some Major Classifications of Relationships

Several characteristics serve to classify the relationships represented in a database management system. Among these are:

1. Degree.
2. Complexity.
3. Optionality.
4. Reflexivity.
5. Behavior over time.

To illustrate these concepts we will use another familiar example—that of suppliers, warehouses, and parts. Numerous relationships can exist among these entities: an inventory of a part, supplied by a specific supplier, is present at a warehouse; a supplier can supply a part; a warehouse has dealt with a supplier.

If a supplier can supply a particular part, then a binary relationship exists between supplier and part. If a relationship exists among a supplier, a part, and a warehouse, then their relationship is of degree 3. Note that this relationship of degree 3 may not necessarily be factorable into two binary relationships, one between supplier and part and another between part and warehouse; the fact that Clemons supplies fountain pens and that there are indeed fountain pens in a Philadelphia warehouse does not always mean that Clemons has supplied the particular items in Philadelphia. Combining two binary relationships to infer a more complex, false relationship has been called by Codd the *connection trap* [14]. To avoid setting this trap for database users who follow after the designer, navigating through the data as best they can, the database designer must have some means of representing the desired relationships of higher degree.

If each warehouse may be supplied by a collection of suppliers, but each supplier serves only a single warehouse, then we say that a one-to-many relationship exists between warehouse and supplier. If, however, many suppliers may serve each warehouse and each warehouse may be served by many suppliers, then a many-to-many relationship exists between the entity types supplier and warehouse. Relationships that are many-to-many are *complex*; others are considered *simple*.

Let a binary relationship, can-supply, exist between a supplier and a part. The relationship is said to be *optional* if an instance of either entity is permitted to be present in the database while not participating in the relationship: for example, it is probably meaningful to carry in the database parts for which there currently are not suppliers or suppliers who currently do not supply any parts. There also exist relationships that are *mandatory*. Such a mandatory relationship is necessary to permit interpretation of the entities that participate in it, and one or more of the entities that form this relationship may not have a valid meaning and thus may not exist in the database unless they do participate in it. Returning briefly to the conceptual schema of Section 2.2.3 the relationships between student and grade and section and grade are mandatory for the grade entity; a grade is earned by a particular student in a course section and cannot be given any reasonable interpretation without the student and the course.

Some relationships are permitted to vary over time, while others must remain fixed. In a *time-varying* relationship, an entity may be related to some other entity at one time and to yet another entity at a later time. Thus, if a supplier may supply at most one warehouse at a time, Clemons may supply Philadelphia today and the District of Columbia at a later time. If the time-varying relationship is also optional, then Clemons may supply Philadelphia today and no warehouse tomorrow. In a *fixed* or permanent association, a relationship between entities cannot be altered as long as the entities continue to exist. The relationship between student, course section, and grade is fixed over time: a student who received a grade of A in a first database course may not trade or sell the grade to another student, nor can he exchange the grade for an A in another course. Some models do not permit time-varying relationships; others do permit them but provide no language feature for specifying which relationships are fixed and which may vary.

Reflexive relationships are those that relate entities of the same type. If one supplier may in fact supply not only warehouses but other suppliers, then a reflexive relationship exists between suppliers; if a warehouse is served not only by suppliers but by other warehouses, then a reflexive relationship exists between warehouses.

Data models and even implementations may differ in their treatment of relationships and in the representations directly supported. Thus, as we shall see, some data models permit direct representation only of binary relationships; others prohibit direct representation of many-to-many relationships. Some implementations do not support the declaration of reflexive relationships.

In addition to differences in their support of relationships that are based on this set of five characteristics, several other differences exist among data models in their treatment of relationships. One such difference is the ability to capture attributes that describe relationships rather than describe entities. For example, it may sometimes be desirable to characterize the can-supply relationship between supplier and part by the attribute *quote*, the price at which the supplier is in fact willing to supply the item. In a data model that does not permit a relationship to have attributes, we must "elevate" the attribute to the status of entity; the relationship can-supply between supplier and part is then replaced by two relationships, quoted-by between supplier and quote and quoted-at between part and quote. In this particular example, quote may in fact be reasonably viewed as an entity possessing other attributes, such as date-offered and date-to-be-withdrawn; in other cases, restructuring the relationship, making it into an entity and adding additional relationships, may be somewhat contrived.

A final difference noted here is that some data models will permit more than one relationship between two entities while others permit at most one. For example, for the relationship between department and chairman, three representations are possible:

1. Chairman is an attribute of the department entity, not a separate entity in the conceptual schema.
2. Chairman is a separate entity, participating in a relationship with department.
3. Chairman is simply a special instance of the faculty entities; the chair relationship between faculty and department relates two entities already participating in the faculty affiliation relationship.

Some data models prohibit this third possibility. Some make the first appear more natural, or less natural, than the second. All these representations are equivalent in the sense that the same data are present and the same operations can be supported; they differ in that some are better or worse, resulting in greater or lesser difficulty in obtaining information from the database.

2.4.2 Design of the Conceptual Schema under Restrictions on Relationships

It appears useful to treat here the design of the conceptual schema under various restrictions placed upon relationships that can be directly declared and supported under various data models, within various data-description languages, or using limitations or features specific to individual implementations. Of course, much of the material presented here will guide development of conceptual schemas in the following section, and for convenience some may be repeated. However, it will be valuable to introduce these design considerations before the data models and in the absence of the unnecessary and arbitrary detail of their DDLs.

We first present the *data-structure diagram*, or Bachman diagram, used to illustrate graphically the design of a conceptual schema. In its full form it is associated principally with only one data model, the network model, and is used little or not at all by proponents of another data model, the relational model. We have found that a simplified version of the data-structure diagram works reasonably well for the portrayal of relationships during the development of a conceptual schema, regardless of the data model and DDL ultimately to be employed. Partisans and advocates of other data models will, we trust, bear with us.

A data-structure diagram employs rectangular boxes to denote entity types described in the conceptual schema and connects them with line segments to indicate the presence of a relationship to be captured between the entities. Thus, if, in the example introduced in the previous section, we have SUPPLIER entities,

WAREHOUSES entities, and a relationship between them, we may represent this as follows:

Actually, two more features are frequently used. Since in a complex conceptual schema two or more relationships may exist between entity types, it is necessary to permit placing a name on the line segment to identify the relationship being illustrated. And it is customary also to place an arrowhead at the end of the line segment where many instances of the entity may be related to a single instance of the other entity. Thus, if many suppliers may SERVE each warehouse, but each warehouse may be SERVED only by a single supplier, our diagram will be as follows:

In the remainder of this section we will use arrowheads in diagrams to indicate complexity of the relationships; we will omit naming the line segments to avoid biasing choice of data model or offending the relational users.

2.4.2.1 Representing Many-to-Many Relationships

For a first restriction, consider representing a many-to-many relationship between supplier and warehouse in a system that does not permit direct representation of many-to-many relationships. The relationship must somehow be factored into two simpler one-to-many relationships, as shown in Figure 2.2.

Sometimes these link entities will be dummies, introduced only to circumvent the limitations of the system and containing no data; as long as they are required by the system and will indeed be present in the database, users find useful attributes to include in the links. Others, making virtue of necessity, claim that many-to-many relationships will always require such *intersection data*; intersection data describes not either of the principal entities, but both, in the context of the relationship in which they participate. We will not claim that intersection data are always necessary; we will, however, illustrate their use in this example. Let us assume that, for whatever reasons of company policy, warehouse operators are required to place orders with their suppliers at least once each quarter; the link will therefore possess a single attribute, date of last order.

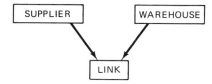

Figure 2.2 Indirect representation of a many-to-many relationship between SUPPLIER and WAREHOUSE.

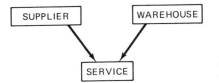

Figure 2.3 Indirect representation of an attribute that describes a relationship.

2.4.2.2 Representation of Attributes of Relationships

The form of a conceptual schema that is developed to capture attributes of a relationship, when the data model or implementation will not permit the direct representation of these attributes, will also employ link entities. For example, quality of service is an attribute that characterizes the SERVE relationship between supplier and warehouse; if restrictions upon the conceptual schema forbid direct representation, the alternative design of Figure 2.3 may be used.

The use of this linking entity to capture attributes of the relationship may be avoided if the relationship is not many-to-many. For example, if a supplier may serve at most one warehouse, the quality of service can be captured as an attribute of the supplier. A purist might argue that this is truly disguising the semantics to fit limitations of the model. Moreover, the representation of the attributes of a relationship warehouses-served-by-a-supplier is altered; the change to capture data about relationships is related to, but somehow semantically different from, the use of links for intersection data—the problems are different, but the forms of the solution are very similar.

2.4.2.3 Representation of Ternary and Higher-Degree Relationships

The inability of some data models to represent ternary or higher-order relationships directly in the conceptual schema poses different problems, for which we employ a somewhat different solution. A ternary relationship exists among part, supplier, and warehouse if a quantity of the part, supplied by the supplier, is in inventory at the warehouse. One way of representing this relationship is to factor it into two binary relationships, as shown in Figure 2.4.

Unfortunately, this factoring possesses several limitations. First, it is, in a sense, not semantically reasonable: it places the part entity in a subordinate role, although part is of interest comparable to that of supplier and warehouse. Part may

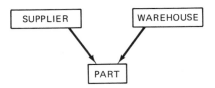

Figure 2.4 An unsatisfactory representation of a relationship among SUPPLIER, PART, and WAREHOUSE.

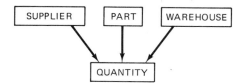

Figure 2.5 A robust representation of a ternary relationship in a system that directly supports only binary relationships.

exist as an entity even if it currently is in no warehouse and has no supplier. The quantity on hand in a warehouse perhaps belongs in a lower-level entity as shown; name and description will be of interest and should be available irrespective of participation in relationships with supplier and warehouse. Second, this factoring introduces problems similar to those encountered in unnormalized relations, as shown in Section 2.7. Storing the part description in the part entity occurrence for each quantity of the part in each warehouse or for each supplier makes consistency almost impossible to assure. Finally, as these part occurrences really correspond more closely to inventory occurrence, they make it difficult to formulate queries or processes based on parts—for instance, total quantity on hand in one warehouse or across all warehouses. In fact, to the extent that the form of the conceptual schema suggests its function, the very possibility of queries based on part is obscured and thus such queries become less likely.

The preferred factoring involves four entities and three relationships, if the conceptual schema is restricted to binary relationships. This is illustrated in Figure 2.5.

As we shall see in Section 2.7, this factoring corresponds to a normalized relational representation.

2.5 HIERARCHICAL SYSTEMS

Historically, hierarchical systems are the oldest of the database systems in use, and the hierarchical data model is the oldest of the three major data models. Unlike network systems, hierarchical systems do not trace their ancestry to a common specification like the CODASYL Data Base Task Group April 71 Report [6], and no ongoing CODASYL or ANSI committee exists to develop languages. And, unlike relational systems, there is no landmark paper such as Codd's original publication [14] to relate diverse implementations and provide a common theoretical basis. The hierarchical model was intended to capture one-to-one and one-to-many relationships and can directly represent only such relationships; upon first examination, hierarchical systems appear to have little beyond this in common.

Lack of a common heritage, and lack of common syntax and semantics among hierarchical implementations, has prevented progress in the development of ANSI standards for hierarchical systems. At present, there is no ANSI committee working on such standards, and no migration path for users wishing to move from one hierarchical database product to another.

2.5.1 Characterization of the Hierarchical Data Model

A data model may be described by its capabilities for representing and manipulating relationships. The following are generally true of hierarchical systems:

1. Only one-to-one and one-to-many relationships may be represented directly; in order to capture many-to-many relationships, it is necessary to use additional constructs.
2. Only binary relationships may be represented directly.
3. No more than one relationship may exist between two entity types, either directly or indirectly, eliminating the need to name relationships in the schema or select among access paths when programming retrievals or updates.
4. One entity type is selected as special, serving as the *root* when instantiating the database, and all other entities must be related to an occurrence of the root type.
5. The above imply that the schema will be tree-structured and that data instances will be tree-structured.
6. Relationships are frequently mandatory, as in IBM's IMS, in that no entity other than the root can exist in the database unless it participates in the relationships linking it to the root. Thus, any database instance will comprise entity types that compose a forest of rooted subtrees of the schema.
7. Relationships are generally permanent rather than time-varying, although this is a property more of the languages used to operate on hierarchical databases than of the underlying hierarchical data model; that is, the changing of an association will usually be accomplished by deleting and reinserting entities rather than by moving them.
8. There is an almost total absence of semantic information recorded in the conceptual schema and thus an almost total absence of integrity constraints, although this too is more a property of available languages than of the data model.

2.5.2 Hierarchical Terminology

The following terms are frequently used to describe the hierarchical data model:

Root: The entity that forms the start of a data instance and that can exist in the database even when participating in no relationships is a root.

Child: An entity or node that participates in a relationship with a second node N, and that is subordinate to N, is said to be a child of node N.

Descendant: The descendants of node N are the child nodes of N, and their descendants.

Parent: If node N is a child of node M, then M is the parent of N.

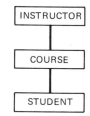

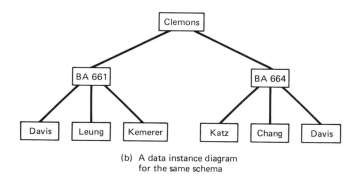

(a) The data structure diagram for
    a simple hierarchical schema

(b) A data instance diagram
    for the same schema

Figure 2.6 A data structure diagram and a data instance diagram for a hierarchical schema relating INSTRUCTOR, COURSES, and STUDENTS.

Ancestor: If node N is a descendant of M, then M is an ancestor of N.

Sibling: All nodes with a common parent are siblings.

Thus, in the data instance shown in Figure 2.6, Clemons is the root, BA 661 and BA 664 are siblings and children of the root, and Davis, Leung, Kemerer, Katz, Chang, and Davis are all descendants.

Note that in the hierarchical model we cannot be certain that the two Davis nodes are intended to reference the same student, and we cannot therefore enforce consistency between the two entries.

2.5.3 A Simple Hierarchical Design Problem — The Academic Database

We illustrate the nature of the hierarchical data model, its use, and its limitations through the academic database example. In theory, the simplicity of the hierarchical data structures appears quite attractive. In practice, combining this simplicity with the completeness of the relationships required in the conceptual schema often proves cumbersome, producing designs that are complex, restrictive, or unnatural. In this section, we will successively refine a database design until we develop a schema that has most of the properties we desire.

2.5.3.1 A Preliminary Design

We start with the conceptual schema shown in Figure 2.7. This schema captures many of the relationships that we want to maintain. For example, we can tell which faculty members are associated with which courses and which courses are taught by a department, who teaches a particular section, which students are in a course, and which students have majors in a department. Unfortunately, many queries cannot readily be answered using the database schema; the following, for example, present problems:

1. Student schedules—for all students, list schedule: courses assigned, section, and time.
2. Faculty course loads—for each faculty member, list courses taught as either section instructor or course head.
3. Department affiliation—for each faculty member associated with more than one department, list all associated departments.

Let us see why these difficulties arise. We note that, in this schema, no record corresponds to the entity *student*. That is, there is no record of type STUDENT whose occurrences represent a complete description of each student and exist in one-to-one correspondence with these students. Rather, each occurrence of the STUDENT record records a single specific fact—that a given student is assigned to a given section of a course. If a student is taking six courses, there will be six STUDENT records, each engaged in a relationship with one course. It may be our intention that these six records all correspond to the same student, but there is no way of specifying this in this schema and no way of requesting that the database management system enforce it. More significantly, there is no way of noting when

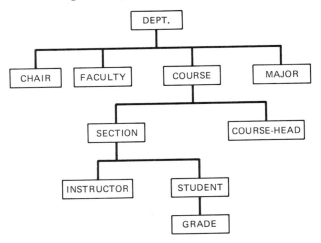

Figure 2.7 A preliminary design of a hierarchical conceptual schema for the academic database.

STUDENT records in different courses of various departments actually correspond to the same student; thus there is no easy way to note when a STUDENT record and a MAJOR record reference the same student.

Similarly, each instructor is assigned to a section of a course, but in this schema it is difficult to determine that several such INSTRUCTOR records correspond to the same faculty member. Likewise, it is difficult to detect when instructor, faculty, and chair records all are intended to reference the same individual.

Our problem, then, arises from the fact that in this schema records are used to record facts and do not exist in one-to-one correspondence with their associated entities. This problem is exacerbated by the hierarchical model and its limitation on the number and complexity of relationships in which a record may participate. While the model makes more difficult the problem of effective schema design, it does not make it impossible. We shall see this as we continue to work on this example.

2.5.3.2 A Design to Treat Problems of Redundancy — The Academic Database Continued

The first problem we must face, which results from the need for more than one record corresponding to a single entity, is that of data redundancy and the accompanying difficulty in maintaining consistency. If there are six entries for a student, one for each course assigned, and four for a faculty member, one for each section taught, then we have no way of being certain that each student or faculty entry is the same as others for the same person, and that inconsistent or contradictory information is not recorded. Figure 2.8 shows a schema design for the academic database of Figure 2.7, but with the record named MAJOR being used for all student information rather than STUDENT and MAJOR, and with FACULTY being used for all faculty information, rather than FACULTY, INSTRUCTOR, COURSE-HEAD, and CHAIR. Records corresponding to the same entity are linked in this schema with dashed lines.

The multischema architecture offers a straightforward solution to this problem of data redundancy. If we assume for the moment that every faculty member will be associated with exactly one department, and that every student will have a major in exactly one department, then we can elevate in importance the records originally marked MAJOR and FACULTY: these two records will actually contain student data and faculty data. The other, related records—STUDENT, INSTRUCTOR, COURSE-HEAD, and CHAIR—will not actually contain data. In the internal schema, these latter records will be represented only by pointers to the MAJOR and FACULTY records that contain their data, while the conceptual schema remains much as shown in Figure 2.7.

This distinction between internal and conceptual schemas, based on the IMS distinction between logical and physical databases, is sufficient to eliminate much of the problem of data redundancy. In some systems, such as IMS, there are limits on the number of pointers that can be used to connect to a single record. More

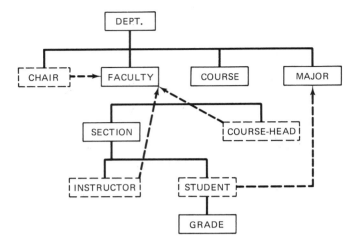

Figure 2.8   The schema of Figure 2.7, modified to treat the problems of data redundancy. No data are actually stored in the dashed boxes. An attempt to get such data follows the dashed arrows and retrieves data from either FACULTY or MAJOR.

significantly, if some student has not yet designated a major department, or some faculty member has two or more departmental affiliations, this solution begins to come apart.

Unfortunately, the problem queries listed in Section 2.5.3.1 remain as problems.

2.5.3.3 The Final Hierarchical Design — The Academic Database Concluded

The experienced and creative database designer may eventually produce a schema like that shown in Figure 2.9. Here we can answer the queries posed against our original hierarchical design for the academic database. Numerous additional queries, including those in the problem list of Section 2.5.3.1, can now be treated as well. We accomplished this as follows:

1. Student and faculty records were broken out of the hierarchical schema; they are now treated as alternate root nodes or as root nodes in separate, distinct hierarchical databases. These nodes are indicated as records above the dashed line in Figure 2.9.

2. Records referring to student and faculty in the original schema are represented in Figure 2.9 as dashed boxes. They do not actually contain data, but rather are linked by address pointers or symbolic pointers back to the new nodes described above. These pointers are shown in Figure 2.9 as heavy lines with arrows.

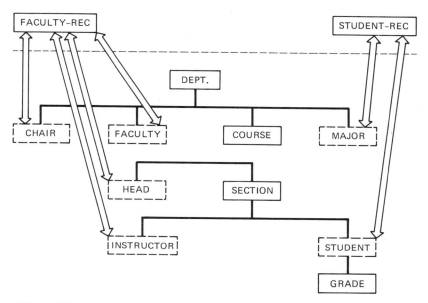

Figure 2.9 The hierarchical academic database concluded. The conceptual schema of Figure 2.7 has been extended and modified to capture additional relationships.

3. The new nodes, FACULTY-REC and STUDENT-REC, are also linked back to the records in dashed boxes. These pointers permit the problem queries—student schedules, faculty course loads, and department affiliation—to be answered.

It should be clear that we have avoided many of the restrictions supposedly placed by the hierarchical model upon the representation of relationships, and that by so doing we have also avoided many of the limitations inherent in our first hierarchical schema of Figure 2.7. We appear to have used a hierarchical schema to capture information that initially seemed beyond the hierarchical model's capabilities. But we cannot infer from this that hierarchical and network systems are equivalent.

Clearly the design we have selected is outside the hierarchical data model. We have three root nodes. We have many relationships, some of them many-to-many, between certain entities in the schema. We have distorted and contorted the hierarchical model so that it can reasonably be used for a complex application environment, but it is now difficult to argue convincingly that we have concluded with a hierarchical design.

Since this design contorts the hierarchical data model, we may be not only outside the confines of that model but outside particular hierarchical systems implementations as well. We have been forced to resort to the use of patches—addresses or symbolic pointers. These pointers are frequently outside the provided

DML, requiring that we use traditional data access rather than database navigation. And by exploiting patches to capture nonhierarchical data structures, we move outside the DDL as well, making difficult or impossible the declaration of integrity constraints or schemas declared upon the structures.

Despite the objections raised in these last paragraphs, we trust it is clear that many restrictions and limitations generally associated with the hierarchical data model can be avoided. The cost is complexity in the schema, some nondatabase navigation in the applications code, and some ingenuity on the part of the database designer.

2.5.4 Concluding Remarks on the Hierarchical Data Model

All hierarchical implementations have in common their use of the hierarchical data model, with its simple data structures representable as rooted trees. All possess some mechanism for escaping the limitations placed on relationships that can be represented in the hierarchical model. They have little else in common.

We note that there is no real consistency among the various data-description languages used to describe hierarchical databases and declare hierarchical schemas and that these inconsistencies extend to the interpretation of hierarchies that may be represented in different systems with the same data-structure diagrams. Similarly, there is no real similarity among the data manipulation languages. In consequence of this, there are no ANSI or CODASYL committees presently working on drafting specifications of standards for hierarchical DDL or DML. We choose, therefore, not to attempt to provide an integrating DDL-DML example for hierarchical systems; while this example might well illustrate the syntax and semantics of one system, it would be at best suggestive, and at worst misleading, when applied to another system. We conclude by noting that theoretical discussions of a data model's power, generality, or extensibility must not be confused with a true measure of a database management system's adequacy. There are many thoroughly satisfied users of commercial hierarchical systems, far more than actually use relational systems. Since many applications do not require extensive collections of complex relationships, the various patches offered by most systems will provide sufficient power and generality.

2.6. SECOND MAJOR DATA MODEL — CODASYL NETWORK APPROACH

The CODASYL network data model attempts to be more robust than hierarchical systems. It can directly represent both one-to-one and one-to-many relationships. Many-to-many relations can also be captured indirectly through the use of multiple relationships.

The current CODASYL data model is defined by the CODASYL Data Description Language Committee (DDLC) and COBOL Committee (CC) *Journals of Development* [5, 7]. The work on which the model is based was first done by the Data Base Task Group (DBTG); the publication in 1971 of the Data Base Task Group Report [6] placed the network model in the public domain, and commercial implementation began shortly thereafter. Development has continued and standardization efforts by ANSI are proceeding, resulting in numerous related but conflicting documents. Except where otherwise indicated, our base document in this chapter will be the DDLC 1981 *Journal of Development*.

The architecture introduced by the DBTG is characterized by two levels and two types of schemas. The main level includes a single main schema, called simply the *schema*, which describes the database. The schema describes records, relationships, and attributes; it includes some semantic detail and originally included some implementation specifics as well. The *subschemas* describe that portion of the database needed for individual applications; each application will employ a single subschema that describes a subset of the schema, the records, relationships, and attributes to be used by the application. Three languages were also introduced by the DBTG. A Data Description Language (DDL) is required to describe the schema and a Subschema Data Description Language (SDDL) is required to describe the subschemas. Additionally, a Data Manipulation Language (DML) should be embedded in a host language; the host language is used for nondatabase actions such as arithmetic operations, traditional input and output, and logical control, while the DML is used to transfer data between the database and the application program. The DBTG originally prepared only one DML, now the basis for the CODASYL COBOL DML.

The single characteristic that most distinguishes the CODASYL network model from hierarchical and relational approaches is the reliance upon named information-bearing sets to capture relationships. This concept is treated in detail in the next section.

2.6.1 Characterization of the Network Data Model

The material introduced in Section 2.4 will be used to characterize more fully the network data model by describing the mechanisms available for representing relationships and the different characteristics of relationships that may be represented.

Entities are represented by named *records*, which have as attributes elementary and grouped *data items*, much as in COBOL records. Relationships among entities are represented by named *sets* among record types. A single record type is designated as the *owner* of a set type, and one or more record types are designated as *members*. Only a single occurrence of the owner type is permitted in a set occurrence, but there may be any number of member records present. Thus, a set is used to capture relationships between the owner and one or more members.[1]

---

[1]Where there is no possibility of confusion, we will now refer to owner occurrence, member occurrence, record occurrence, and set occurrence simply as owner, member, record, and set.

We can now characterize the network model as follows:

1. Only binary relationships are directly represented.
2. Only one-to-one or one-to-many relationships are directly represented.
3. Members may be specified as optional or mandatory; there is no way of specifying that an owner record type cannot be stored in the database unless it participates in some set.
4. Reflexivity is handled differently in different specifications.
5. Behavior of the relationship over time can be specified only for the members in a set, not for the owner.

The restrictions imposed by the first two points above do not actually limit the relationships that can be captured by a CODASYL database, although they do sometimes impose design difficulties or result in schemas that do not initially appear clear or natural. A ternary relationship among three entities can be represented in the CODASYL model by three binary relationships. As shown in Figure 2.5, a ternary relationship among parts, suppliers, and warehouses may be represented using three binary relationships and an additional entity type. Similarly, a many-to-many relationship can be represented as two binary one-to-many relationships. Thus, if it is necessary to relate a member record occurrence to two or more owner occurrences, we do not place it in two or more sets. Rather, we restructure the schema and employ a link record as shown in Figure 2.2.

Member record types are specified as mandatory or optional. A record that is optional in a set type can exist in the database even if it participates in no set occurrence, while a record that is mandatory cannot exist in the database unless it participates in exactly one set occurrence. It is not possible to specify that an owner's participation in a relationship is mandatory. It is not possible in the CODASYL model to specify that an owner record cannot exist unless it participates in a set in which member records are actually present.[2]

Reflexivity is treated differently in various specifications of the network model. The original DBTG report prohibited a record type from being owner and member in the same set type. This restriction was dropped in the 1978 DDLC *Journal of Development*, permitting direct representation of reflexive relationships as single-type cycles, also called recursive sets. Recursive sets are still prohibited in COBOL and the proposed ANSI standard, and are not supported by many implementations. The reason for precluding recursive sets in some current specifications is not technical but historical. When a record can be linked to members in both one set occurrence in which it is an owner and another set occurrence in which it is a member, the DML must be modified to permit specification of which set occurrence is being traversed.

---

[2]Unfortunately, the actual details of optionality are somewhat more complex than this paragraph would suggest. They are linked also to insertion specifications, which are more correctly viewed as DML-related than as part of the underlying semantics. They are linked also to behavior over time, since both are included in RETENTION specification.

Such modification would make programs that used the old DML obsolete. When not captured directly, a reflexive relationship can be represented by two simple sets, in a manner analogous to the representation of many-to-many relationships using two sets. (Many-to-many relationships are described in Section 2.6.2.)

Behavior of the relationship over time can be specified for member records in sets. A member may be specified as *fixed*, meaning that it must always be related to the same owner, as *mandatory*, meaning that it must always be related to some owner, or as *optional*, meaning that on occasion it may be associated with no owner. No such restrictions can be stated for owners. The similarity of this specification to that of the optional or mandatory nature of a relationship should be clear.

2.6.2 Design of a CODASYL Schema — The Academic Database

We now develop the CODASYL schema for the academic database presented in Section 2.2. The principal entities are as before: department, faculty member, student, course, section, and grade. Relationships exist between pairs of entities. An initial design is shown in Figure 2.10. This design unfortunately has several flaws, which are addressed and corrected later in this section.

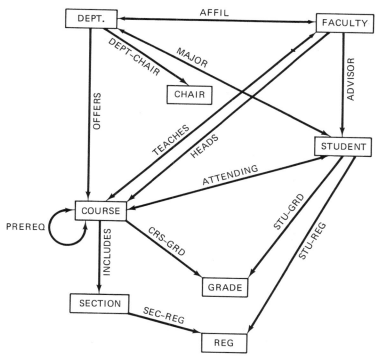

Figure 2.10 A preliminary Bachman diagram for the academic database, in a format not fully consistent with the CODASYL model.

2.6.2.1 Design to Remove Many-to-Many Relationships

Four direct many-to-many relationships are present in the schema of Figure 2.10. However, since such relationships cannot be directly represented by CODASYL sets, alternate representations will be required. Some such relationships—e.g., Major, Affiliation—are transformed into two relationships and represented as two sets. Thus the relationship Major is transformed from one relationship between student and department as follows: a linking record, called MAJOR, is introduced, and this record participates in sets owned by STUDENT and DEPT. Other many-to-many relationships represent design errors: the relationship Teaches, between faculty and course, results in the loss of information, since it is not possible to determine who teaches a particular section or student; Teaches is replaced by a relationship between faculty and section.

It is often claimed that *whenever a many-to-many* relationship is requested, it is best replaced by two sets and the introduction of a link record. This seems to be a post-facto rationalization. Often this link record will contain useful intersection data, data describing neither entity but common to them by virtue only of their relationship. Grade so links a STUDENT to a COURSE; the association between DEPARTMENT and FACULTY may also be described by useful data. Sometimes this link record will contain no useful data; use of this artifice may not appear natural, but with practice we can accept it.

2.6.2.2 Design to Remove Recursion

The relationship Prerequisite, which exists among courses, is reflexive, because it relates entities of a single type. This relationship is represented in Figure 2.10 as a recursive set. Since recursive sets are not supported by all implementations, it may be necessary to remove them from the schema. This is done in a manner analogous to the elimination of many-to-many relationships. We note that a course may have many prerequisites or may be a prerequisite for many other courses; thus a many-to-many relationship exists. Since both owner record types are the same, the representation differs from that employed for other many-to-many relationships and is as shown in Figure 2.11.

2.6.2.3 The Search for a Natural Design

Our attempts to determine an appropriate way to represent a department chairman will illustrate the difficulty of producing a natural design. Initially, in Figure 2.10, we showed the chair as a separate entity type. Such designs are, in a sense, atavistic:

Figure 2.11 Support of a recursive set using two sets and a linking record.

they frequently are carried-over designs from predatabase applications, or they reflect lack of understanding of database capabilities. The chairman is a faculty member; though a special, distinguished case; the chairman will teach sections, head courses, advise students, and perhaps participate in all other types of relationships in which faculty engage. The simplest alternative is simply to include an additional set CHAIR between DEPT and FACULTY, as shown in Figure 2.12(a).

Unfortunately, this provides us no natural place to store intersection data describing the relationship, such as the start date and termination date of the current chairman's appointment. We can quickly see that a link record would be helpful, since these data are not truly attributes of either department or chairman. The next possibility is shown in Figure 2.12(b). Here a departmental chair can have any

(a) A simple representation of the relationship
      between department and its chairman

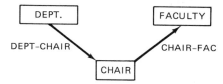

(b) A representation that permits attributes of the
      relationship, but fails to assure integrity

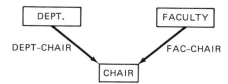

(c) A representation most commonly used to provide
      attributes of relationships, which also fails to
      assure integrity

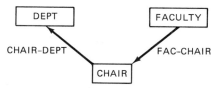

(d) A representation that permits attributes of
      relationships, and that provides some of the
      desired semantics

Figure 2.12 Four alternative representations for a simple binary relationship between a department and its chairman.

number of faculty occupants. We cannot even assure that the chair is occupied: making FACULTY a required member only requires that every faculty member serves as chairman of some department but does not require that there be faculty participants for every CHAIR-FAC set. The next possibility, shown in Figure 2.12(c), is the one most commonly used to capture attributes of relationships. This assures that there is exactly one faculty member and exactly one department associated with an appointment as chairman; since this CHAIR link record has precisely the appearance of a link record used to represent a many-to-many relationship, we are certain that we cannot impose the requirement that every department have exactly one chairman. The final alternative is shown in Figure 2.12(d). It, too, is imperfect. However, if DEPT is mandatory in set CHAIR-DEPT and CHAIR is mandatory in set FAC-CHAIR, then we are assured every department has exactly one chair, and that this chair is occupied by exactly one faculty member. We are not certain that everything works correctly: a faculty member could still be listed as the chair of several departments, perhaps even of one with which he had no affiliation. Further integrity restrictions would be helpful. But we have greatly increased our expectations that the database performs as intended.

2.6.2.4 The Final Network Design — The Academic Database Concluded

The experienced and creative network database administrator would produce a database design like that shown in Figure 2.13. This design would have been produced without explicitly considering some of the obviously bad choices that we examined and rejected. We note that the stated restrictions of the CODASYL model have not limited our ability to represent desired entities, relationships, or attributes.

2.6.3 Data Description Language and Data Manipulation Language: A Short Introduction

A comprehensive treatment of DDL and DML is clearly beyond the scope of this chapter. We provide a very brief introduction in order to illustrate the nature and appearance of the languages. Full treatment is, of course, available in the DDLC and COBOL Committee *Journals of Development*.

   The DDL has elements to describe the schema itself, the records, and the sets that relate records. Record descriptions include description of attributes and indication of which attributes or combinations can serve to identify unique record occurrences. Set descriptions can be quite complex. They include specification of owner record type, mechanism to be used to select an owner occurrence when storing a member record, and specification of members. Member specification in turn will include insertion characteristics. Additional CHECK clauses may be appended to data item, record, or set entries in the DDL. They describe the legitimate data values for a data element or more complex conditions that must hold

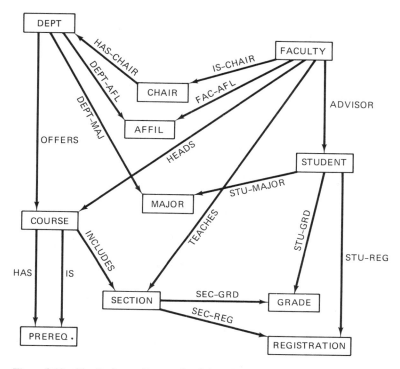

Figure 2.13   The Bachman diagram for the academic database, after adjustments to reflect CODASYL requirements.

among data elements in a record or between owner and member records in a set. CHECK clauses are semantic, rather than structural, and serve to permit central definition of some integrity restrictions. Finally, an order may be specified for the member records of a set. The DDL for the records FACULTY, CHAIR, and DEPT and for the sets HAS-CHAIR and IS-CHAIR is shown in Figure 2.14.

Our treatment of the DML is also very brief. A key concept of the CODASYL DML is the *currency indicator*, a sort of place-marker or pointer into the database. The most recently accessed record of the database will be current of the program (current of run unit). Additional currency indicators are maintained for each record type and for each set type. Effects of most actions are influenced by currency; e.g., ERASE can be used only to delete the record that is current of run unit. Many verbs implicitly alter currency, so that navigation may sometimes be tedious or confusing.

A second important concept is the *error status indicator*. If a requested action cannot be completed a nonzero error code is returned by the database control system; the value returned in the error status indicator can be used to determine the nature of the exception condition. Once a nonzero value has been returned in the error status indicator, no additional requests will be executed until the error value has been cleared.

```
RECORD NAME FACULTY
      KEY FAC-ID IS SSN
             DUPLICATES ARE NOT ALLOWED.

01    SSN              TYPE CHARACTER 11.
01    NAME             TYPE CHARACTER 25.
01    RANK             TYPE CHARACTER 6.
01    TENURE-STATUS    TYPE CHARACTER 3.

RECORD NAME CHAIR.

01    START-DATE       TYPE CHARACTER 8.
01    UNTIL            TYPE CHARACTER 8.

RECORD NAME DEPT
      KEY DEPT-ID IS DEPT-NO
             DUPLICATES ARE NOT ALLOWED.

01    DEPT-NO          TYPE CHARACTER 4.
01    NAME .           TYPE CHARACTER 20.
01    SCHOOL           TYPE CHARACTER 15.

SET NAME IS-CHAIR
      OWNER IS FACULTY
      ORDER IS SYSTEM-DEFAULT

      MEMBER IS CHAIR

      INSERTION IS AUTOMATIC
             RETENTION IS MANDATORY

      SET SELECTION IS THRU IS-CHAIR IDENTIFIED BY
             KEY FAC-ID.

SET NAME HAS-CHAIR
      OWNER IS CHAIR
      ORDER IS SYSTEM DEFAULT

      MEMBER IS DEPT

      INSERTION IS AUTOMATIC
             RETENTION IS FIXED

      SET SELECTION IS THRU HAS-CHAIR IDENTIFIED BY
             APPLICATION.
```

Figure 2.14 Part of the schema DDL describing the FACULTY, CHAIR, and DEPT records and the sets that relate them.

```
*       DML PLUS COBOL HOST-LANGUAGE PROGRAM TO PROVIDE
*       GRADE REPORT FOR A SINGLE REQUESTED COURSE.
*       DATA IN COURSE-LINE, SECTION-LINE, AND STUDENT-LINE
*       ARE FROM WORKING STORAGE; REMAINING DATA ARE FROM
*       DATA BASE, AS DESCRIBED IN A SUBSCHEMA.
*
GRADES-DISPLAY.
        MOVE WHICH-DEPT TO DEPT-NO OF DEPT.
        MOVE WHICH-COURSE TO COURSE-NO OF COURSE.
        FIND COURSE.
        GET COURSE.
        IF DB-STATUS NOT EQUAL ZERO
             DISPLAY 'COURSE ERROR'
        ELSE
             MOVE DEPT-NO OF DEPT TO DEPT-NO OF COURSE-LINE;
             MOVE COURSE-NO OF COURSE TO COURSE-NO OF COURSE-LINE;
             WRITE COURSE-LINE;
             FIND FIRST SECTION WITHIN INCLUDES;
             PERFORM SECTION-LOOP UNTIL DB-STATUS
                  NOT EQUAL ZERO.
        MOVE ZERO TO DB-STATUS.

SECTION-LOOP.
        GET SECTION.
        MOVE SECTION-NO OF SECTION TO SECTION-NO OF SECTION-LINE.
        FIND OWNER WITHIN TEACHES.
        GET FACULTY.
        MOVE NAME OF FACULTY TO NAME OF SECTION-LINE.
        WRITE SECTION-LINE.
        FIND FIRST GRADE WITHIN SEC-GRD.
        PERFORM STUDENT-LOOP UNTIL DB-STATUS.
                  NOT EQUAL ZERO.
        MOVE ZERO TO DB-STATUS
        FIND NEXT-SECTION WITHIN INCLUDES.

STUDENT-LOOP.
        FIND OWNER WITHIN STU-GRD.
        GET GRADE.
        GET STUDENT.
        MOVE NAME OF STUDENT TO NAME OF GRADE-LINE.
        MOVE GRD-RECVD OF GRADE TO GRD-RECVD OF GRADE-LINE.
        WRITE GRADE-LINE.
        FIND NEXT GRADE WITHIN SEC-GRD.
```

Figure 2.15   COBOL DML and host language code to list grades and students for a single course (arranged by section).

Perhaps arbitrarily, we divide the DML verbs into three classes:

1. Navigation: FIND.
2. Data transfer: GET, STORE, ERASE, MODIFY.
3. Set manipulation: CONNECT, DISCONNECT, RECONNECT.

FIND comes in several varieties and can be used to navigate up, down, or across a set; it is used only to alter currency and does not transfer data from the database. GET brings data from the database to the program, STORE inserts a new record in the database, ERASE deletes a record, and MODIFY changes data values. CONNECT puts a record occurrence in a set, DISCONNECT removes a record if permitted, and RECONNECT is used to change set associations. In Figure 2.15 we illustrate a portion of a COBOL program used to list all the grades for students in a single course.

2.6.4 Limitations and Enhancements

Several limitations were perceived and documented when the 1971 DBTG Report was released. Many of these were addressed by subsequent enhancements to the *Journal of Development*. Some flaws remain.

Almost immediately after the publication of the DBTG Report there were objections to the implementation orientation of the CODASYL model and to the intrusion of physical performance detail into both the DDL and the DML [18]. Navigation was perceived as exceedingly difficult [15, 16, 35]; the subschema facility was tied too closely to the main schema, forcing the programmer to contend with a schema not designed for his application [13, 26]. Some observers felt that the restrictions of the CODASYL model limited the ability to model the underlying universe of discourse realistically and called for multiple owner occurrences (many-to-many sets), multiple owner types, or single-type cycles [26]. After publication of the ANSI/SPARC report the basis for some of these complaints became more widely recognized.

Several enhancements were introduced in the 1978 *Journal of Development*. Principal among these was a draft Data Storage Description Language (DSDL) to remove much of the explicit implementation orientation and performance detail. Recursive sets were added, and integrity restrictions were extended. The process of revising and enhancing the *Journal* continues. The 1981 DDL includes additional semantic modeling capabilities, such as conditional data elements for record sub-types.

Several remaining difficulties were detected by the ANSI committee during attempts to prepare a network DDL standard:

1. Simplification: The DDL specification is close to a hundred pages long. In places the interaction among DDL and DML options is illogical; in other places it is undefined.

2. Access control: A better facility is required for defining the security restrictions placed upon a shared database.

3. Integrity control: A more complete and more consistent facility is needed to define valid database states and transitions.

4. User interface: It is necesary to improve the DML. It may be desirable to extend the subschema facility.

2.6.5 Concluding Remarks on the Network Data Model

How shall we evaluate the network model, using our earlier criteria of generality, extensibility, and data independence? It is frequently claimed that the network model is fully general, meaning that if the necessary relationships are all fully known, an appropriate schema can be designed to support them. While it is difficult to devise a proof for such a claim, it seems likely that it is true. It also seems likely that it is irrelevant: requirements are never fully known in advance, nor are they ever fully static. Therefore, we are concerned with extensibility and data independence.

Sometimes the addition of new applications will require changes to the schema, replacing a simple hierarchy with a confluency to represent a many-to-many relationship. On other occasions, a similar change may be required by a change to the nature of the underlying relationship, or simply by our desire to capture attributes describing the relationship. Since the schema and subschema are so closely linked, changes to the schema will be apparent to the existing applications; since the subschema and explicit navigation are closely linked, changes will probably disable most existing applications using the affected portion of the schema. We conclude that data independence is limited: change to records may be permitted, but change to sets will have serious adverse effects on existing programs. Since data independence is limited, we must conclude that extensibility of the application set is limited as well.

We note that these limitations are not properties inherent to the network model but rather are characteristics of the present CODASYL architecture. Limitations of the CODASYL architecture have been presented before [11, 12, 26]. An alternative subschema facility, while not changing the basic data model, would enhance both data independence and extensibility.

It should also be noted that the network specification is proceeding toward standardization more rapidly than the other data models.

Despite the cautionary notes, we must conclude that the CODASYL model and architecture perform well in practice. Numerous vendors supply network database management systems, offering at least some degree of compatibility with a

CODASYL specification; many satisfied users have employed these systems to put up databases and build application programs.

2.7 FINAL MAJOR DATA MODEL — THE RELATIONAL APPROACH

The relational model was introduced in 1970 by E. F. Codd in the now classic paper, "A Relational Model of Data for Large Shared Data Banks" [14]. All subsequent work on relational theory and implementation clearly has its origins in this paper. The relational model was immediately adopted by fervent supporters throughout the academic community.

Objectives of the model include:

1. Ease of use.
2. Mathematical rigor in definition of data representation and operators.
3. Simplicity of data structures.
4. Generality.
5. Absence of performance detail and implementation clutter.

Although there is some dispute over whether all these objectives are satisfied, there is little disagreement that all are worthwhile goals.

Relational systems store all information as normalized relations. There is no explicit description of the means of implementing links for relationships, or of implementing anything else. Relations are the only means for storing data and are used both for entities and relationships.

2.7.1 Characterization of the Relational Model

Relations are used for the storage of all information, and relational operators are provided for the manipulation of these relations. A relation can be viewed as essentially a fixed-format table or matrix. A column of the matrix, called an *attribute*, is drawn from the set of permitted values in an underlying *domain*. A row in the matrix, which will often correspond to an entity description, is called a *tuple*, or, if the matrix has *n* columns, it may be called an *n-tuple*. It is not permitted that two or more rows be identical; it is required that a subset of columns be designated as *primary key*, sufficient to differentiate among all tuples in the relation.

In the CODASYL model there were predefined access paths among records, corresponding to relationships known to be present. If a relationship betwen two record types was important, a set was declared to associate them; if necessary, because the relationship was many-to-many, for example, then two sets might be required. In the relational model it is not necessary to exploit explicit links of this

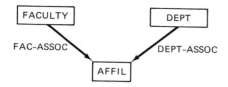

FACULTY: (<u>SSN</u>, NAME, RANK)
DEPT: (<u>D#</u>, NAME, CHAIR, FROM, UNTIL)
AFFIL: (<u>SSN</u>, <u>D#</u>)

Figure 2.16 A portion of a CODASYL schema relating FACULTY and DEPT records.

Figure 2.17 A portion of the relational schema corresponding to Figure 2.16.

form: in theory we can associate any tuples in any relations by comparing values of attributes drawn from the same underlying domain.

In the relational model it is not common to focus explicitly upon relationships. If we wish to ignore this and continue our design process as in previous models, we note that tuples in two relations can be related simply by defining a third relation to associate them; attributes in this new relation could be simply the keys of the first two relations. As our first relational example, we show in Figure 2.16 a portion of a CODASYL schema relating two record types in a many-to-many relationship. The corresponding relational definition, ignoring domain definition, is shown in Figure 2.17.

Relations are generally normalized. First normal form is a structural or syntactic normalization. It implies the absence of repeating groups, resulting in flat tables, all of whose rows have the same number of columns. It also implies the absence of complex or nonelementary attributes: no relational attribute will be composed of subattributes. An attribute NAME, comprising FIRST and LAST as in a COBOL group, would not be permitted; FIRST and LAST might still be attributes, but they cannot be combined to form a superattribute. Higher normalizations, which are semantic rather than structural, are discussed in a later chapter.

We can now characterize the capabilities of the relational model for describing relationships:

1. Binary and higher-order relationships are captured with equal facility.
2. One-to-one, one-to-many, and many-to-many relationships may all be directly represented.
3. Reflexive relationships are handled as any other relationships.
4. Optional or mandatory nature of relationships is considered outside the scope of the model.
5. Time-varying behavior of relationships is considered outside the scope of the model.

The first three points are obviously strengths of the model; the last two are obviously limitations. The relational model uses the same structure and the same syntax to describe both entities and relationships. This structure is almost devoid of semantics. Since the model does not include provision for specifying that a relation is in fact describing relationships rather than entities, there is neither need nor means to prohibit many-to-many associations; similarly, attributes of relationships are as easily represented as attributes of entities.

This lack of semantics would be a serious obstacle to easy and effective use of relational systems in practice. Therefore, when the model is converted from a theoretical exercise to a complete and usable product, facilities are generally added to enhance the ability of the conceptual schema to represent the underlying semantics of entities and relationships. Although these facilities are outside the formal definition of the model, it should be understood that they are provided when the model is implemented. Both System R and Ingres [2, 8, 33] provide mechanisms for declaring assertions or integrity restrictions; these can be used to declare the complexity of a relationship (e.g., many-to-many), the mandatory or optional nature of the relationship, and considerably more.

2.7.2 Design of a Relational Schema: The Academic Database

We will design the schema for the academic database in a manner analogous to the design of network and hierarchical databases. We will determine the necessary entities and relationships and encode each in the appropriate relation.

Entities are readily defined as relations. For example, to indicate that each student is identified by social security number and is described by a name, address, and grade-point we include the following entry in our schema:

STUDENT: (SSN, NAME, ADDRESS, GRADE-POINT)

Similarly, departments may be described as follows:

DEPT: (D#, NAME)

Relationships are also readily described by relations. Students are associated with their departmental majors in a many-to-many relationship. This is *not* well represented simply by adding the department numbers of major departments to student tuples because of the redundancy that would result; for example, if the student Clemons were to major both in Physics and Economics, the following two tuples would be required:

STUDENT:	(SSN	NAME	ADDRESS	MAJOR)
	123-45-6789	CLEMONS	HANCOCK	D8
	123-45-6789	CLEMONS	HANCOCK	D14

We note that a similar problem would have been encountered had we attempted to list student majors directly in the department relation. Instead, we associate students and departmental majors in an additional relation. Since this relationship is captured in a relation like any other, we may add attributes; in this case we add an attribute called status, which indicates whether departmental requirements for graduation have been completed. The tuples for Clemons might then be as follows:

```
MAJOR:      (SSN            D#        STATUS)
             123-45-6789    D8        COMPLETE
             123-45-6789    D14       INC
```

As with the other data models, there will be alternative representations for some relationships. Not all representations will prove to be equally appropriate, and design decisions will have to be made on the basis of expected use, convenience for users, and expected change in the nature of the relationships. For example, the association between department and chairman is one-to-one. We can represent this relationship using a separate relation, CHAIR, much like the relation MAJOR used above. Alternatively, since the relationship is one-to-one, we could place the social security number of the chairman in each department tuple, or we could place in each faculty tuple the number of the department chaired. Since most faculty members are not chairmen, this last choice is artificial. Since placing the chairman's number directly in the department will make navigation between department and chairman more direct, we choose this representation. The representation chosen here was rejected for the CODASYL schema; this inconsistency reflects differences in the emphasis placed by the two data models upon relationships.

The relationship among advisors and students poses different problems. This relationship is one-to-many. Normalization will not permit us to record students advised in the faculty relation, but we still must decide whether to record advisor in the student relation or to employ an additional relation to associate students with their advisors. If we are certain that students will continue to have at most one advisor, then placing advisor in the student relation will facilitate navigation. If we expect that in the future students may be advised by committee or that a student with additional majors will require additional advisors, then we expect this relationship to become many-to-many. A many-to-many relationship would require an additional linking relation, like MAJOR above. Since the change from representation of the relationship directly in the STUDENT relation to the introduction of an ADVISOR relation would change navigation, it would potentially affect all programs that used the relationship. If we expected this change to the relationship, we would probably employ the ADVISOR relation now, to avoid subsequent program conversion.

Reflexive relationships are handled like any others. The relationship among courses and prerequisites is many-to-many and thus is captured in a separate relation:

```
PREREQ:(CRS#, PRE-CRS#)
```

DEPT	(D#,NAME,SCHOOL,CHAIR,FROM,UNTIL)
FACULTY	(SSN,NAME,RANK,TENURE_STATUS)
STUDENT	(SSN,NAME,GRADE_POINT,ADVISOR)
COURSE	(CRS#,D#,NAME,CREDITS,HEAD_SSN)
SECTION	(SECT#,CRS#,D#,ROOM,TIME,TEA_SSN)
GRADE	(SECT#,SSN,GRADE_RECVD)
REGISTRATION	(SECT#,SSN)
AFFIL	(SSN,D#)
MAJOR	(SSN,D#,STATUS)
PREREQ	(CRS#,PRE-CRS#)

Figure 2.18 A relational schema for the academic database.

In Figure 2.18 we illustrate the relational schema for the academic database, corresponding to the network schema of Figure 2.13. Our approach to relational schema design in this chapter was of necessity brief and informal, based on the familiar concepts of entities and relationships. Relational schema design is more frequently based upon the concepts of functional and multi-valued dependencies. Schema design based on these concepts will be found in a subsequent chapter of this book.

2.7.3 Data Description and Data Manipulation

Unlike CODASYL-type database systems, which all trace their ancestry to common specifications published in the *Journals of Development*, relational system do not enjoy common syntax and semantics. We choose to illustrate typical data description and data manipulation languages by showing small examples that would be used in System R, a widely publicized experimental implementation now in commercial use as DB2.

To describe relations we should first describe the underlying domains and then combine them. FACULTY, STUDENT, DEPT, and MAJOR relations are shown in Figure 2.19.

System R's query language, SQL, is block structured. A simple query to retrieve the names of all students would look as follows:

```
SELECT NAME FROM STUDENT
```

A more complex query, to select only students majoring in physics, would have blocks added:

```
SELECT NAME
FROM STUDENT
WHERE SSN IN
        SELECT SSN
        FROM MAJOR
        WHERE D# IN
                SELECT D#
                FROM DEPT
                WHERE NAME = 'PHYSICS'
```

```
CREATE TABLE FACULTY
      (SSN                (CHAR   (11),NONULL),
      (NAME               (CHAR   (25)),
      (RANK               (CHAR   (6)),
      (TENURE_STATUS      (CHAR   (3))
CREATE TABLE DEPT
      (D#                 (CHAR   (4),NONULL),
      (NAME               (CHAR   (20)),
      (SCHOOL             (CHAR   (15)),
      (CHAIR              (CHAR   (11)),
      (FROM               (CHAR   (8)),
      (UNTIL              (CHAR   (8))
CREATE TABLE STUDENT
      (SSN                (CHAR   (11),NONULL),
      (NAME               (CHAR   (25)),
      (GRADE_POINT        (FLOAT),
      (ADVISOR            (CHAR   (11))
CREATE TABLE MAJOR
      (SSN                (CHAR   (11),NONULL),
      (D#                 (CHAR   (4),NONULL)
      (STATUS             (CHAR   (14))
```

Figure 2.19   SQL definitions in System R for four of the relations of Figure 2.18.

The example shown in Figure 2.15, in which all students and grades were listed for a single course, is repeated in SQL as Figure 2.20.

It is important that the power, level, or capability of the data model be distinguished from the attributes of its programming languages. It is clear that the program of Figure 2.20, written in SQL, is much shorter than the COBOL plus CODASYL DML program originally shown in Figure 2.15. It is obvious that SQL provides facilities for iteration and navigation that are far terser than the corresponding language structures of CODASYL. None of this indicates that the rela-

```
SELECT    FACULTY.NAME,COURSE.CRS#,COURSE.D#,
          SECTION.SECT#,FACULTY.NAME,STUDENT.NAME,
          GRADE.GRADE_RECVD
FROM      FACULTY,COURSE,SECTION,STUDENT,GRADE
WHERE     FACULTY.SSN  =  SECTION.TEA_SSN
AND       COURSE.D#  =  SECTION.D#
AND       COURSE.CRS#  =  SECTION.CRS#
AND       SECTION.SECT#  =  GRADE.SECT#
AND       GRADE.SSN  =  STUDENT.SSN
AND       COURSE.CRS#  =  WHICH_COURSE
AND       COURSE D#  =  WHICH_DEPT
ORDER BY SECTION.SEC# ASC,ORDER BY STUDENT.NAME ASC
```

Figure 2.20   SQL code to list students and grades by course and section, as shown in Figure 2.16 using COBOL plus DML.

tional model has representational capabilities beyond those of the network model, or that a better network DML could not be developed.

2.7.4 Limitations of the Model and Enhancements of the Implementations

There are three perceived limitations to the relational model. While all are, in fact, omissions from the original statements of the model, all are actually remedied in existing implementations.

1. A lack of explicit attention to implementation makes it impossible to tune a database to attain necessary levels of performance.
2. A lack of explicit semantics makes it difficult to assure the integrity of the database as it evolves through the actions of numerous users.
3. The uniformity of structure and the fragmentation into normalized relations makes for queries that are long, repetitive, and tedious.

This first observation was the most frequent objection to the relational model during the great debate of 1974. The fact that the model did not address implementation and performance was taken by some observers to mean that it could not, and thus it was claimed that relational implementations could not be used in practice. Since relational implementations employ the same hardware as other database systems, they employ the same data structures as well. Indexes provide rapid access to tuples when keys are known. Lists permit rapid navigation from one tuple to a collection of related tuples. Such structures are invisible, in that the user cannot reference them when writing a query and need not know which lists and indexes have been defined. One might conclude that relational implementations have an internal schema definition.

As we saw earlier, the relational model does not capture a great deal of the underlying semantics of entities and their relationships. Since the same data structure is used for both entities and relationships, the system is unaware of which relations represent relationships. Properties easily captured in the CODASYL model —e.g., every student must have an advisor, and the advisor must be a member of the faculty—must be stated. Of course, these semantics must be part of a workable implementation; therefore, they are generally included when the model is converted into a product. In System R the restriction that every student must have an advisor could be expressed as follows:

```
ASSERT STU _ ADVISOR:
        (SELECT ADVISOR FROM STUDENT)
                IS IN
        (SELECT SSN FROM FACULTY)
```

Additional restrictions can as easily be imposed. To assure that no faculty advisor advises more than five students, we write:

```
ASSERT MAX_ADVIS:
        (SELECT (COUNT SSN)
        FROM STUDENT
        GROUP BY ADVISOR)
            ≤ 5
```

Finally, to assure that the chairman of the department is a full or associate professor affiliated with the department, we write:

```
ASSERT CHAIR_RULES ON DEPT D:
        (SELECT CHAIR FROM D)
            IS IN
        (SELECT SSN FROM FACULTY
        WHERE (RANK = 'ASSOC'
        OR      RANK = 'FULL')
        AND SSN IS IN
                SELECT SSN FROM AFFIL
                WHERE D# = D.D#)
```

Again, one might conclude that relational implementations have a facility for the definition of conceptual schemas.

The fragmentation of data into normalized relations unfortunately makes it necessary to write tedious and lengthy queries to obtain useful information. For example, to obtain the schedule for a student named Clemons we would have to navigate among courses, sections, and registrations, as shown in Figure 2.21. In contrast, if the registration were maintained as a COBOL record with repeating groups, a single ISAM read would suffice. The view facility of System R offers a useful compromise: virtual relations are defined that eliminate the need for much navigation. These virtual relations are in first normal form, which means that repeating groups are not offered; the fragmentation resulting from further normalization is reversed. Using the view definition of Figure 2.22, which is very similar to the query of Figure 2.21, we can now obtain the schedule for Clemons as follows:

```
SELECT (*) FROM EXTENDED_REGISTRATION WHERE NAME = 'CLEMONS'
```

```
SELECT STUDENT.NAME,STUDENT.SSN,SECTION.SECT#,
        SECTION.TIME,COURSE.CRS#,COURSE.D#,COURSE.NAME
FROM STUDENT,REGISTRATION,SECTION,COURSE
WHERE STUDENT.SSN = REGISTRATION.STU–SSN
        AND REGISTRATION.SECT# = SECTION.SECT#
        AND SECTION.CRS# = COURSE.CRS#
        AND SECTION.D# = COURSE.D#
        AND STUDENT.NAME = 'CLEMONS'
```

Figure 2.21   An SQL query to provide registration information for a student named Clemons.

```
DEFINE VIEW EXTENDED_REGISTRATION AS
SELECT STUDENT.NAME,STUDENT.SSN,SECTION.SECT#,
        SECTION.TIME,COURSE.CRS#,COURSE.D#,COURSE.NAME
FROM STUDENT,REGISTRATION,SECTION,COURSE
WHERE STUDENT.SSN = REGISTRATION.STU–SSN
        AND REGISTRATION.SECT# = SECTION.SECT#
        AND SECTION.CRS# = COURSE.CRS#
        AND SECTION.D# = COURSE.D#
```

Figure 2.22 An SQL definition of a virtual relation to facilitate queries about registration.

Although this may not be a full external schema facility, with all the generality anticipated in the ANSI/SPARC proposal, it does successfully reduce the user's effort.

2.7.5 Concluding Remarks on the Relational Model

It is still premature to attempt to evaluate the success of relational systems in commercial use. Despite the extravagant claims of potential advantages made by some relational advocates, and despite the opportunistic assertions of some vendors of inverted file systems that their products offer relational capabilities, relational systems have seen very little nonlaboratory mainframe use. Still, those relational systems for which user experience has been documented seem to have performed well [34].

Based more on theoretical analysis than upon field experience, generality appears to be excellent. That is, if it is known that certain information will be required, relations can be designed so that this information can be captured. As before, data independence and extensibility are related, and as before, each has limits.

A one-to-one or one-to-many relationship among entities is frequently captured by including additional information in the description of one of the entities; e.g., the relationship between a student and his advisor is represented in the student relation. Many-to-many relationships cannot be represented in this way but require the use of a separate linking relation; e.g., the relationship among students and departments requires the linking relation MAJOR. Since a change from a one-to-many to a many-to-many relationship may require a change to the relations, corresponding to a change to the conceptual schema, we may conclude that both data independence and extensibility are limited. However, changes may be relatively rare, and the experienced schema designer may plan for them in advance. More significantly, the use of a view facility may protect application programs from the need to change navigation when the relations change, enhancing data independence and thus extensibility.

Excessive navigation is required when using relational systems in their pure form, since normalization of relations results in very fragmented representation.

Again, this limitation can be circumvented using the external schema capability implied by a view facility. Ease of use then appears quite acceptable.

The lack of explicit semantics in the relational model also appeared to be a serious limitation. The semantics captured by the explicit declaration of access paths as CODASYL sets facilitates the development of automatic query generators, and the interpretation of these sets as relationships facilitates the definition of integrity restrictions. Enhancements to the relational model again circumvent both limitations. A view facility can be used to precode some navigation that would otherwise be the user's responsibility. And a robust and general facility for integrity restrictions can be provided as part of a relational implementation.

2.8 CONCLUSIONS: COMPARISONS AND EVALUATIONS

By now we should be better able to address questions raised earlier about the definition of an architecture and of a data model. We also should be better able to address the significance of the proposed ANSI/SPARC architecture.

2.8.1 Database Systems Architectures

A database system architecture may be seen to be a functional specification, showing how basic information representation is mapped into an internal performance specification and an external user interface. In the ANSI/SPARC architecture, information representation, including semantic restrictions and interrelations, is contained in the conceptual schema. The maps to performance specification and user interface are via the internal schema and external schemas, respectively. In a particular data model, such as the relational model, design of an architecture and determination of performance and user support features is the first step in the conversion of the model to a marketable product.

Implementations of systems based on data models that lack a common specification, i.e., hierarchical and relational, exhibit varying degrees of conformation to the principles expressed in the ANSI/SPARC proposal. IBM's IMS, perhaps the most widely used hierarchical system, does not fully employ a three-schema architecture. Questions of access method cannot be fully resolved independently of physical data design; similarly, logical database design is closely tied to some physical design decisions. Still, the permitted divergence between logical and physical structures is in the spirit of the conceptual-to-external-schema maps. IBM's System R, perhaps the most advanced relational implementation, exhibits a well-developed three-schema architecture. The definition of the conceptual schema has adequate capability for capturing semantics and is free of implementation detail. The internal level permits performance tuning without affecting what can be represented at the conceptual level or requested by the user; that is, it is fully transparent. While the external level may lack some of the multi-model restructuring capability expected by some advocates of the ANSI/SPARC architecture, it does permit external views that are more than merely edited subsets of the underlying base relations.

While CODASYL systems cannot be considered fully three-schema, their specifications have progressed from "one and a half" schemas to "two and a half." That is, the original DBTG schema corresponded well to the ANSI/SPARC conceptual schema but the schema-to-subschema mapping capability was too limited to qualify the subschema as a full external schema. Addition of a storage schema in 1978, corresponding to the ANSI/SPARC internal schema, was not accompanied by improvement of the subschema.

The original 1971 DBTG Report encompassed a single main schema replete with semantic, performance-related, and user-oriented facilities. The concept of set is an interesting example: it is the definition of a semantic construct and makes clear the presence of a relationship. It is a user-oriented feature, influencing the specification of navigation. And it is a performance specification, indicating preferred access paths that must be supported. Specification of retention rules extends the semantic content; specifying the presence or absence of pointers to prior members or to owner is free of semantics but influences performance, and specifying insertion rules is user oriented. Since this report provided no additional, separate schema for performance tuning, and since the subschema facility provided no restructuring, no predefinition of navigation, and no calculation of additional data items, we cannot consider it fully a second schema. The revised 1978 specification, published as the CODASYL DDLC *Journal of Development*, represents a significant improvement. While the set remains an overworked concept, with implications at the internal, conceptual, and external levels, all explicit references to implementation details such as hashing (CALC) keys and pointers are removed from the main schema. A new data-storage description language and DSDL schema provide the functions of the internal schema. Although proposals have been presented for extending the capability of the subschema facility, to convert it to a more complete external schema, no new capabilities have been added to the subschema since 1971, and we must view the CODASYL specifications as yielding at best a two-and-a-half schema architecture.

2.8.2 Evaluation and Comparison of Data Models

We now appear to be in a position to offer a definition for the term "data model." A data model is a mechanism for representing data and relationships. The three models are almost indistinguishable in their representation of entity descriptions; it is the differences in representing relationships, and the different restrictions these imply, that truly distinguish the three data models.

In the hierarchical model at most one relationship—direct or indirect—can exist between any two entities. There is therefore no need to name relationships, and navigation is accomplished by specifying entity names. No attributes can be directly represented for relationships; other restrictions are as discussed in Section 2.5.

The network model represents relationships as named sets, and the presence of names permits an arbitrary number of direct and indirect relationships between two entities. There are no attributes directly represented for relationships. Some specification of behavior for relationships is supported, and other restrictions are as noted in Section 2.6.

The relational model makes no distinction between the representation of relationships and of entities; both are supported as relations. Therefore relationships, like entities, may have attributes specified. The model, in its pure form, provides very limited semantics, both for the conceptual schema and for aiding in navigation. There are very few restrictions on the declaration of relationships, as noted in Section 2.7.

We do not presume to recommend a single data model, independent of applications requirements and computer installation resources; as noted, theoretical limitations of a data model are sometimes of less importance than the strengths and weaknesses of the products based upon it. Below we summarize for purposes of comparison the evaluations made earlier:

1. Hierarchical:

    (a) Generality: In theory, limited. In practice, the restrictions of the data model can be avoided, but at the expense of somewhat ingenious schema designs and some navigation outside the DML.

    (b) Data independence: In theory, limited. In practice, some schema-to-schema mapping, as in IMS physical and logical database separation, offers improvements.

    (c) Extensibility: In theory, limited. Some extensions cannot be made, because some sets of relationships cannot be represented. In practice, sometimes the restrictions of the model can be circumvented by going outside the model, encoding relationships as in a predatabase environment using ISAM keys. This cannot be encouraged on a large scale, since the advantages of using a database management system for navigation and maintenance become lost.

2. Network:

    (a) Generality: Very good. Although the schema designed may on occasion need to employ structures that do not seem fully natural, as in the use of two sets and a linking record when attributes are required for a relationship, there do not appear to be limitations, either on the types of relationships or on collections of relationships that can be represented.

    (b) Data independence: In theory, some limitations exist. Changes in the description of an entity, resulting in changes to record definition, need not affect application programs. But the limited nature of the schema-to-subschema maps means that changes to relationships, resulting in changes to sets, will affect existing applications.

    (c) Extensibility: In theory, there is no limit to the relationships that can be represented and thus no limit to the extensions that can be made to the set of supported applications. In practice, limits to data independence impose some restrictions on the extensions that can be made, unless the installation is willing to undertake the expensive program-conversion effort required.

3. Relational:

   (a) Generality: Very good. There do not appear to be limitations on the types of relationships or collections of relationships that can be represented.

   (b) Data independence: In theory, there are some limitations to data independence. A change in the complexity of a relationship from one-to-many to many-to-many may require addition of a linking relation and changes to navigation, requiring program conversion. In practice, this program conversion can sometimes be averted through use of a view facility.

   (c) Extensibility: In theory, there is no limit to the relationships that can be represented, and thus no limit to the extensions that can be made to the set of supported applications. In practice, limits to data independence impose restrictions on the extensions that can be made. These restrictions will be slightly less severe than in the network model, largely because of the presence of the view facility.

Thus, the selection of data management system should be made in part on the basis of underlying data model and its appropriateness for the level of complexity and change of the set of applications it is to support. Other factors should include naturalness or ease of use of data structures and languages, on which there is unfortunately very little scientific evidence. Finally, the decision should entail vendor-specific features such as available query languages, product reliability, and of course suitability for the existing hardware configuration.

REFERENCES

1. ANSI/X3/SPARC, "Interim Report from the Study Group on Data Base Management Systems," 75-02-08, *FDT* (*Bulletin of the ACM SIGMOD*), Vol. 7, No. 2 (1975).

2. Astrahan, M.M., et al., "System R: Relational Approach to Database Management," *ACM Transactions on Database Systems*, Vol. 1, No. 2 (June 1976), pp. 97–137.

3. Bachman, C.W., "The Programmer as Navigator," *Communications of the ACM*, Vol. 16, No. 11 (November 1973), pp. 653–658.

4. Berg, J.L., M. Graham, and K. Whitney, eds., "Database Architectures—A Feasibility Workshop Report," NBS Publication SP 500–76, NBS, Washington, D.C., April 1981 (available through N.T.I.S.).

5. CODASYL COBOL Committee, *Journal of Development*, 1981.

6. CODASYL Data Base Task Group April 71 Report. New York: ACM, 1971.

7. CODASYL Data Description Language Committee, *Journal of Development*, January 1981.

8. Chamberlin, D.D., et al., "SEQUEL 2: A Unified Approach to Data Definition, Manipulation, and Control," *IBM Journal of Research and Development*, Vol. 20, No. 6 (November 1976), pp. 560—575.

9. Chamberlin, D.D., et al., "A History and Evaluation of System R," *Communications of the ACM*, Vol. 24, No. 10 (October 1981).

10. Clemons, E.K., "Design of a Prototype ANSI/SPARC Three-Schema Data Base System," *Proceedings of National Computer Conference*, New York, 1979, pp. 689–695.

11. Clemons, E.K., "The External Schema and CODASYL," *Proceedings of the Fourth International Conference on Very Large Data Bases*, Berlin, 1978, p. 130.

12. Clemons, E.K., "An External Schema Facility for CODASYL 1978," *Proceedings of the Fifth International Conference on Very Large Data Bases*, Rio de Janeiro, 1979, pp. 119–128.

13. Clemons, E.K., "Rational Data Base Standards: An Examination of the 1978 DDLC Report," *Information Systems*, Vol. 4 (1979), pp. 235–239.

14. Codd, E.F., "A Relational Model of Data for Large Shared Data Banks," *Communications of the ACM*, Vol. 13, No. 6 (June 1970), pp. 377–387.

15. Codd, E.F., and C.J. Date, "Interactive Support for Non-Programmers: The Relational and Network Approaches," in *Data Models: Data-Structure-Set versus Relational (Proceedings of the ACM SIGMOD Workshop on Data Description)*, ed. R. Rustin, May 1974, pp. 11–14.

16. Date, C.J., and E.F. Codd, "The Relational and Network Approaches: Comparison of the Application Programming Interfaces," in *Data Models: Data-Structure-Set versus Relational (Proceedings of the ACM SIGMOD Workshop on Data Description)*, ed. R. Rustin, May 1974, pp. 83–113.

17. Douque, B.C.M., and G.M. Nijssen, eds., *Data Base Description (Proceedings of the IFIP TC2 Working Conference, Wepion, Belgium, January 13–17, 1975)*. New York: North-Holland, 1975.

18. Engels, R.W., "An Analysis of the April 1971 Data Base Task Group Report," *Proceedings of the ACM SIGFIDET Workshop, 1971*, pp. 69–92. New York, ACM.

19. Hammer, M.M., and D.J. McLeod, "Semantic Integrity in Relational Database Systems," *Proceedings of the First International Conference on Very Large Data Bases*, Framingham, Mass., September 1975.

20. Hammer, M.M., and D.J. McLeod, "A Framework for Database Semantic Integrity," *Proceedings of the Third International Conference on Software Engineering*, Atlanta, May 1978.

21. Hammer, M.M., and D.J. McLeod, "The Semantic Data Model: A Modeling Mechanism for Data Base Applications," *Proceedings of the ACM SIGMOD*, Austin, Tex., May 1978.

22. Kent, W., "Entities and Relationships in Information," in *Architecture and Models in Data Base Management Systems (Proceedings of the IFIP TC2 Working Conference, Nice, France, January 3–7, 1977)*, pp. 67–91. New York: North-Holland, 1977.

23. Kent, W., "Limitations of Record Oriented Information Models," IBM Technical Report TR03.028, May 1977.

24. Kent, W., *Data and Reality*. New York: North-Holland, 1978.

25. Lochovsky, F., and D. Tsichritzis, "User Performance Considerations in DBMS Selection," *Proceedings of the ACM SIGMOD Workshop*, Toronto, August 1977.

26. Nijssen, G.M., "Set and CODASYL Set or Coset," in B.C.M. Douque and G.M. Nijssen eds., *Data Base Description*, pp. 1–70. New York: North-Holland, 1975.

27. Nijssen, G.M., ed., *Modeling in Data Base Management Systems (Proceedings of the IFIP*

TC2 Working Conference, Freudenstadt, W. Germany, January 5–9, 1976). New York: North-Holland, 1976.

28. Nijssen, G.M. ed., *Architecture and Models in Data Base Management Systems. (Proceedings of the IFIP TC2 Working Conference, Nice, France, January 3–7, 1977*). New York: North-Holland, 1977.

29. Nijssen, G.M., "Experience with a Three-Schema Architecture DBMS," Presented at NBS Workshop, "A Family of Database Management Standards," NBS, Gaithersburg, Md., September 8–10, 1980.

30. Rustin, R., ed., *Data Models: Data-Structure-Set versus Relational. (Proceedings of the ACM SIGMOD Workshop on Data Description, Access and Control, May 1–3, 1974*).

31. Smith, J.M., and D.C.P. Smith, "Database Abstractions: Aggregation," *Communications of the ACM*, Vol. 20, No. 6 (June 1977).

32. Smith, J.M., and D.C.P. Smith, "Database Abstractions: Aggregation and Generalization," *ACM Transactions on Database Systems*, Vol. 2, No. 2 (June 1977).

33. Stonebraker, M., "Implementation of Integrity Constraints and Views by Query Modification," *Proceedings of the ACM SIGMOD*, San Jose, Calif., November 1975, pp. 65–78.

34. Stonebraker, M., "Retrospection on a Database System," *ACM Transactions on Database Systems*, Vol. 5, No. 2 (June 1980).

35. Taylor, R.W., "Data Administration and the DBTG Report," *Proceedings of the ACM SIGMOD Workshop 1974*, pp. 431–444. New York, ACM.

36. Tsichritzis, D., and A. Klug, eds., "The ANSI/X3/SPARC DBMS Framework, Report of the Study Group on Database Management Systems." Montvale, N.J.: AFIPS Press, 1977.

3

Semantic Data Models

Roger King and Dennis McLeod
University of Southern California

3.1 INTRODUCTION

A *database model* (*data model*) is a mechanism for specifying the structure of a database and the atomic operations that may be performed on the data in that database. Thus, a database is an *instance* of a specific database model. A specification of such an instance of the database model is the database's *schema*, which is a structural description of the database. The typical mode of specifying a schema is to utilize a *data-definition language*, which embodies the database model constructs. A data-definition language typically defines the *statics* of the database in terms of the record structures used to model the application environment. Equally important are the *dynamics* of the database: the operations provided in a database model are general-purpose and can be used to access and update any database defined using the database model. And the general-purpose operations of a database model are used to support database *transactions* specific to a given application environment; transactions are usually expressed using a *data-manipulation language*.

Conventional database models, such as the *hierarchical*, *network*, and *relational* database models, provide facilities for describing the logical structure of a database using trees, collections of nodes and links, and relations (tables), respectively. Conventional models provide general-purpose access and update operators (language facilities) for manipulating these data structures.

Semantic database models carry the database modeling process one step further by attempting to logically structure the information in a database in a manner that captures more of the meaning of the data than conventional database models. That is, semantic database models attempt to provide a richer set of modeling constructs, which are more expressive of data meaning and thus are closer to the way users think about data. Logically organizing data with a semantic database model greatly facilitates the design, access, and evolution of a database: a designer can organize a database by directly specifying his knowledge[1] of the application environment. Also, a semantic schema is more evolvable than a conventional one when the nature of the application environment activities changes.

The purpose of this chapter is to acquaint the reader with semantic database models and, for concreteness, to detail a unified semantic database model (the event model). In order to provide specific examples and a source of typical database modeling situations, a particular application environment is used throughout the chapter. This environment concerns insurance claims processing. Essentially, the insurance claims processing application environment is concerned with subscribers of health insurance plans, groups of subscribers (unions, corporations, etc.), health insurance claims, and providers of medical services (doctors, hospitals, laboratories, etc.). Typical activities in this environment include the addition and deletion of subscribers, the formation of groups with specific types of coverage, and the submission and payment of claims.

3.2 CONVENTIONAL DATABASE MODELS

The conventional database models, which dominate the database systems in common use today, include the *hierarchical*, *network*, and *relational* models. Although there is considerable variation among these models concerning specific modeling constructs, each presents the user-level view of a schema in terms of record structures.

For our purposes here, a *record* consists of a number of *fields*, each field having an associated *value*. In a record-based database model, record types are the classes of particular kinds of records. Each record in a database is an instance of a single record type. All the records of a given type have the same basic structure—that is, the same fields (of course, the field values in various records of a type differ).

While typically presented in the literature in the context of rather intricate data definitions and manipulation facilities, the essential approach of the hierarchical and network models is to model data using records and interrecord connections. In the data-definition languages of these models, the designer specifies the record types and *link types*; link types define interrecord connections. While in principle the sole purpose of the link types is to connect semantically related records, in practice they most commonly indicate physical access paths as well. In contrast with the hierarchical and network models, the relational model accommodates only record types and not explicit links; logical interrecord connections are expressed implicitly via com-

---

[1] The personal pronoun "he" and adjectives such as "his" are used in this chapter to denote an arbitrary person of either sex.

mon field values. In what follows, the conventional database models are further reviewed, in order to provide a basis for the subsequent discussion of semantic database models.

3.2.1 The Hierarchical and Network Models

A hierarchical schema (a database description specified with the hierarchical database model) consists of a number of trees, each of which in turn consists of:

> A collection of record types.
>
> A collection of link types, which specify connections between the record types; each record type in a given tree (with the exception of the root type) must be the child type of a single parent record type.

A hierarchical database consists of a forest of trees, conforming to the structure defined in the schema. An additional constraint imposed on a hierarchical database is that each instance of a record type (i.e., each physical record) must have exactly one parent record of the parent type; this constraint applies to all records except those of a type that is a root of a tree defined in the schema.

Using the definitions given above, Figure 3.1 illustrates a portion of a hierarchical schema for the claims-processing application environment. In the figure, nodes represent record types and arcs represent link types; the names of the fields associated with a given record type are shown in parentheses. In this example there are two kinds of policyholders: groups and lone subscribers; group subscribers are individual members of groups who carry insurance.

The network database model supports the specification of schemas that can differ in two fundamental ways from those permitted by the hierarchical model:

> Multiple link types between record types are permitted.
>
> A given record can have multiple parent records.

In consequence, the network database model is more flexible than the hierarchical model; a given record type can have many parent record types, and a given record

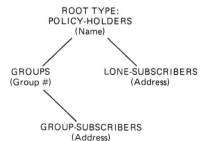

Figure 3.1   A section of a hierarchical schema.

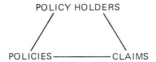

Figure 3.2 A section of a network schema.

instance can have many parent record instances of a given record type. Thus, many-to-one and many-to-many relationships can be represented.

Figure 3.2 illustrates a portion of a network schema. Nodes in the diagram denote record types, and arcs denote link types; for simplicity, the names of the fields associated with each record type have been omitted. Here, a given policyholder may have several policies, a number of claims can be associated with a given policy, and a policyholder may have many claims. Since this schema is not a tree, it would not be definable as such using the hierarchical model.

Virtually all existing database management systems based on the hierarchical and network models utilize variations on the "pure" models described here. For example, IBM's IMS is an implementation of a variation on the pure hierarchical model. Similarly, the predominant variation of the pure network model described above is the CODASYL DBTG database model [13]. The CODASYL model is, in some respects, a restriction of the network model; for example, many-to-many links are not directly supported.

3.2.2 Limitations of the Hierarchical and Network Models

One of the most significant problems of the hierarchical and network database models is that they encourage a direct correspondence between physical access paths and logical interrecord links. Thus, data-manipulation languages associated with commercial versions of these models tend to be "navigational" in the sense that a user must access a database by explicit traversal through a tree or network, rather than by stating the properties of the data of interest. It is important to remember that this phenomenon is not truly an inherent problem of the hierarchical and network models; rather, it is a result of language designers' exploiting the fact that tree and network structures are conducive to navigational access. In addition, the data and network database systems typically do not allow the easy definition of new transactions. The reason is that the set of legal transactions is very tightly constrained by the structure of the record links, and interrecord links tend to be expressed at a very low level; thus an experienced software engineer is needed to correctly specify new transactions.

The hierarchical and network models also tend to force a single active (view) of data. The problem is that the data is arranged in a rigid, inflexible structure; fixed structural interconnections among data items are not easily molded into a variety of semantic interpretations. As an example, Figure 3.3 illustrates an alternative view of the information on policyholders shown in Figure 3.1. If it were desired to accommodate both perspectives (that in Figure 3.1 and that in Figure 3.3), it would be

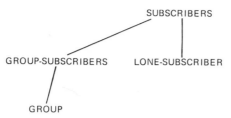

Figure 3.3 A section of a hierarchical schema.

Figure 3.4 An instance of the hierarchical schema of Figure 3.1.

necessary to define a schema with two separate hierarchical structures (and the relationship among these alternative views could not be specified within the model).

A related problem is that it is sometimes necessary to logically duplicate data values. Duplication is generally needed to model multiple hierarchies or networks and to support many-to-many relationships in the hierarchical model. This is due to the inability to indicate that two separate record instances correspond to the same object in the application environment. As an example, Figure 3.4 illustrates two instances of the Groups to Group-Subscribers subhierarchy (as shown in Figure 3.1); if a group subscriber, "Mary Ellen" must be a child of two records of type Groups.[2] The essential problem here is that an important fact is unexpressed: the two "Mary Ellen" records designate the same subscriber.

3.2.3 The Relational Model

A relational database consists of a number of (*n*-ary) *relations* and a collection of underlying *domains*. A relation may be viewed as a table containing a fixed number of named columns and a variable number of rows. The values that may appear in a given column of a relation are those that are members of the underlying domain of that column. Figure 3.5 illustrates an example relational database; relation names are listed with their corresponding tables, column names are placed above the columns they identify, and the names of underlying domains are listed in parentheses (below the columns to which they apply.)

Data-manipulation languages for the relational model are typically derivatives of a *relational calculus* or a *relational algebra* [14]. These types of languages basically allow a database use or application program to select and modify values in relational tables and to relate entries in different tables by matching column values. These languages are highly flexible, in that they allow dynamic definition of new transactions.

---

[2] The quotes in the figure are used to informally indicate that a record corresponds to a given object in the application environment.

POLICYHOLDERS		CLAIMS	
SUBSCRIBER (person–names)	GROUP # (group #s)	CLAIM # (claim #s)	SUBMITTED BY (person–names)
MARY ELLEN	1	101	MARY ELLEN
JEFFREY	1	102	JEFFREY
MARY ELLEN	2	103	MARY ELLEN
ANNETTE	NIL		

Figure 3.5   A portion of a relational database.

A fundamental characteristic of the relational database model is that relationships among data items are formed at access time. That is, relational data-manipulation facilities can be used to dynamically define logical interrelation relationships. Although this is typically not a feature of commercial relational databases, it may be desirable for reasons of semantics to require that only like data values be compared in defining such relationships, e.g., that two relations can be logically "joined" only on columns that have a common underlying domain. In Figure 3.5 this would mean that Policyholders and Claims could be logically linked on equal value of Subscriber and Submitted-By but that these two relations could not be joined on Group# = Claim#. The essential point here is that the user can dynamically impose a logical structure on the data as he manipulates a database, and this freedom can lead to meaningless results.

An important contribution of research on the relational database model and its use has been the concept of *normalization*. The basic idea of normalization is to provide guidelines to the structuring of a relational schema. One aspect of normalization involves the elimination of multivalued columns (columns that allow more than one entry per row), so as to make relations as simple and easy to manipulate as possible. Further principles of normalization involve the avoidance of *anomalies*; an anomaly occurs when a given database update transaction has unintended effects.

As an example of normalization to avoid anomalies, Figure 3.6(a) illustrates a relation that contains information on claims; for each claim the relation gives its Claim#, the name of the subscriber who submitted it (Submitted-By), and the subscriber's address.[3] A significant problem with this structure is that if "Mary Ellen's" address changes, it will be necessary to change two values in the Claims relation. To avoid this type of update anomaly, relations should be structured so they contain:

One column (or column group) that uniquely identifies rows of the relation; this identifying column of column group serves as a logical *key*.

A set of mutually independent columns that describe the object modeled by a row.

[3] In Figure 3.6, domain names have been omitted for simplicity.

CLAIMS

CLAIM #	SUBMITTED–BY	ADDRESS
101	MARY ELLEN	LOS ANGELES
102	JEFFREY	LOS ANGELES
103	MARY ELLEN	LOS ANGELES

(a)

CLAIMS   SUBSCRIBERS

CLAIM #	SUBMITTED–BY	NAME	ADDRESS
101	MARY ELLEN	MARY ELLEN	LOS ANGELES
102	JEFFREY	JEFFREY	LOS ANGELES
103	MARY ELLEN		

(b)

Figure 3.6   An example of normalization.

There is thus a *dependency* between the column (or column group) that serves as a key and the other columns; that is, the value of the key for any given row determines uniquely the values of the other columns. For example, in Figure 3.6(a), Submitted-By is dependent upon Claim#, while Address is dependent upon Submitted-By. The normalized version of the schema segment shown in Figure 3.6(a) is provided in Figure 3.6(b).

In sum, the relational database model provides an added degree of data independence and flexibility over the hierarchical and network database models. Further, owing to its symmetric structure, the relational model favors data-manipulation languages that are "nonprocedural" rather than "navigational." And, since relational data-manipulation languages are based upon the idea of defining logical record links at access time, an added degree of flexibility to dynamically define new database transactions is provided. Many of these advantages could in fact be realized with pure forms of the hierarchical and network models as well; but in practice they are not realized, due to the existence of fixed logical connections and the tendency of hierarchical and network database language designers to exploit this phenomenon.

3.2.4 The Lack of Semantic Expressiveness in Record-Based Models

A fundamental problem of the hierarchical, network, and relational database models is their limited *semantic expressiveness* [25]. As noted above, the conventional database models are all fundamentally record-oriented. The mapping of an application environment into low-level, record-oriented structures implies substantive modeling limitations [20, 25, 28, 29, 35]. Thus, these models employ overly simple data structures to model an application environment. In consequence, the application of a conventional model inevitably involves the loss of information and therefore provides for the expression of only a limited portion of a database designer's knowledge of the application environment [4, 51, 65].

The essential modeling limitation involved with mapping an application environment into a conventional database model is that record-based database models fail to distinguish different generic kinds of relationships among application objects. Specifically, the same construct (i.e., the hierarchy of records, the network of records, or the relational table) is used to describe attributes of objects in the application environment, to specify the type of an object, and to relate the types themselves.

Three fundamental generic kinds of semantic relationships should be expressible via a database model [40]:

1. The *has-subtype* relationship logically links an object type with another object type; the latter is a subtype of the former. For example, Lone-Subscribers is a subtype of Subscribers.

2. The *has-attribute* relationship logically connects an object with another object or objects; the latter object(s) describes some aspect of the first. For example, a policy has subscribers.

3. The *has-instance* relationship links a type to an object that is an instance of that type. For example, "Mary Ellen" is an instance of Subscribers.

As an example of the failure to distinguish these different generic kinds of semantic relationships, note that in Figure 3.1, hierarchic links are used to model both a has-subtype and a has-attribute relationship. The problem here is that the semantics of the relationships is unexpressed.

There are a number of important ramifications of the limited semantic expressiveness of the hierarchical, network, and relational database models. The most significant of these ramifications are detailed below. The purpose here is to set the stage for the discussion of semantic database models in Section 3.3 and to motivate the particular features that semantic models provide.

3.2.4.1 Statics Limitations

A significant problem with conventional database models is that the database designer is faced with a large number of arbitrary degrees of freedom in modeling. For example, when using the hierarchical or network models, the designer can choose to model relationships by common field values (as is done in the relational model) or by using interrecord links. In practice, the dominating factors that tend to dictate this choice involve physical implementation considerations; this is totally counter to the notion of physical data independence.

The designer of a conventional database is also given very little guidance in the design process. Mapping an application environment into record structures is a tedious task that requires a significant amount of software-engineering expertise and experience. The result is that conventional database schemas often are expensive to design and much less semantically expressive than is desirable.

3.2.4.2 Dynamics Limitations

Perhaps one of the most fundamental problems of record-based models is their lack of a notion of an abstract object. That is, the correspondence between an object in the application environment and records in the database is indirect and complex [29]. For example, the concepts of attribute and instance of a type are needed in order to identify and directly relate application objects as abstract objects in a database.

In conventional databases, application objects are represented as record structures and are related indirectly through common identifiers, which are character strings that serve as (not necessarily unique) keys to individual records. Thus, in a conventional database, a subscriber and his claim would typically be associated through either of two identifiers representing a claim number. In either case, the subscriber record and the claim record would each contain a copy of the identifier.

Allowing objects to represent themselves instead of using some identifier to stand for them makes it possible to directly reference an object from a related one. In record-oriented database models, it is necessary to explicitly cross-reference between related objects by means of their identifiers; this causes data manipulation to be intricate and semantically confusing. While it is, of course, necessary to eventually represent "abstract" objects as symbols inside a computer, the point is that users (and application programs) should be able to reference and manipulate abstractions as well as symbols; internal representations to facilitate computer processing should be hidden.

As an example, suppose that a claims processing database user desires to travel from a policyholder object to the objects that model the claims that were filed by that policyholder. To accomplish this, it would be desirable to define an attribute "Claims-Filed" that applies to every policyholder, and whose value consists of one or more claims. As indicated above, to model this information using a record-oriented database model, we need to select some identifier of claims records to connect them to policyholder records. (In the hierarchical and network models, the user is given assistance in determining which record types may logically be related, but he must still select the correct identifier on which to match.) Figure 3.5 contains an example of this approach, wherein rows in the Policyholders relation are logically linked to rows in the Claim relation by the matching of Subscriber in Policyholders with Submitted-By in Claims. Explicit cross-referencing is required of the user here, which forces him to deal with an extra level of indirection. In contradistinction, a semantic database would model both the subscriber and the claim as objects and allow them to be associated without making identifier matching visible to the user.

Normalization in the relational model further inhibits the notion of an abstract object. Normalization was developed for the relational model to help guide the

SUBSCRIBERS

NAME	ADDRESS
MARY ELLEN	LOS ANGELES
JEFFREY	LOS ANGELES
ANNETTE	BOSTON

CLAIMS

CLAIM #	ADDRESS
101	BOSTON
102	LOS ANGELES
103	BOSTON

Figure 3.7 An example of a relational database.

designer, but it is only a partial aid and exhibits some significant[4] problems. In particular, normalized schemas tend to be unnatural: the splitting of relations to avoid anomalies may introduce relations whose rows do not correspond to objects in the application environment, thus making the resulting database even harder to use. For example, the user-level view of the claims-processing environment may include the abstract object Claim-Submission, consisting of the following fields: Subscriber #, Claim #, Dependent-Of (indicating if the subscriber is actually included on someone else's policy and has no individual policy of his own), and Date-of-Submission. However, as Date-of-Submission is dependent on Claim # and Dependent-Of is dependent on Subscriber #, normalization would break the atomic concept of Claim-Submission into two relations, one involving Subscriber # and Dependent-Of and one involving Claim #, and Date-of-Submission into two relations, one involving Subscriber # and Dependent-Of and one involving Claim # and Date-of-Submission.

A significant ramification of the lack of semantic expressiveness in the conventional database models is that a user can easily misinterpret a schema. For example, Figure 3.7 illustrates a portion of a relational schema that is intended to capture the fact that both subscribers and claims have an address. A user unfamiliar with the database may not realize that the address of a claim is the address of the insurance company location where the claim was received, rather than the address of the subscriber. The user may, for instance, try to associate all claims submitted in Boston with people who live in Boston. The problem here is that the schema simply does not express enough of the semantics of the application environment to facilitate sensible interpretation and manipulation. Specifically, with the concept of attribute,

---

[4] It should be noted that while normalization was developed for the relational model, it also applies to the hierarchical and network models, as they can be viewed as including relationlike record structures plus interrelation links.

the designer would be able to indicate to the user that the address property of a claim is not a function of the attributes of any subscriber. Furthermore, as a claim address and a subscriber address are of a very different semantic nature, the attribute concept would generally provide a means of indicating to the user that they are not even comparable (i.e., they have different underlying domains).

Conventional models also require a rigid structure to be imposed on the data in a database. This often implies that data in a record-based database may be in a form that is difficult for some applications to utilize. For example, hierarchies tend to make easy those manipulations that match the hierarchic structure, while those that cross branches of the hierarchy are typically more difficult to express.

A related problem is that most semantic integrity constraints on a database structured with a record-based model must be defined and enforced externally. Additional mechanisms must be provided to supplement conventional database models for this purpose, such as those described in [8, 18, 22, 23, 59]. The problem with this approach is that these supplemental constraints are at best ad hoc and do not integrate all available information into a simple structure. This situation is at least partially corrected in a semantically expressive model, as such a model naturally embodies certain integrity constraints: as a semantically expressive database is much easier to understand, it is much less likely to be misinterpreted and updated incorrectly.

3.2.4.3 Limitations of Evolvability

Record-oriented models are also limited in their ability to allow the structure of a database to support alternative ways of looking at the same information. The capability of expressing such alternate views may be termed *relativism*. In order to accommodate multiple perspectives on the same data and to enable the evolution of new views of existing data, a database model must support schemas that capture the relationships and similarities between multiple ways of viewing the same information —for example, if one wished to express the fact that an individual has submitted a claim, one could define Claims as an attribute of Subscribers, or Submitter as an attribute of Claims, or Submissions as a type with two attributes (Claims and Submitters), or perhaps all three. The first modeling technique may be useful for insurance company employees who maintain subscriber records; the second view may be useful for processing claims. Another example is that suspicious subscribers could have a boolean-valued attribute called "Suspicious?" (set to yes), or suspicious subscribers could be placed in a subtype of Subscribers called Suspicious-Subscribers.

The primary motivation for relativism is that slightly different views of the same information should be conceptualized as a semantic unit (i.e., all the above definitions may coexist in the same user view). In conventional models, it is generally necessary to impose a single structural organization on the data, one which inevitably carries along with it a particular interpretation of the data's meaning. This meaning may not be appropriate for all users of the database and may furthermore become entirely obsolete with time [26].

Conventional schemas are also, in a sense, structurally intricate. This has ramifications on the evolution of both database statics and dynamics: statics expressed in record-based structures are difficult to understand and are therefore risky to alter. Further, dynamics expressed in navigation or algebraic languages are so intimately tied to the specifics of the statics that evolutionary changes in the latter are liable to upset the workings of the former. For example, splitting a relation into two due to a change in a dependency is likely to destroy the algebraic operation of any transaction using the original relation. Also, changes in processing requirements, when mapped into record-based languages, often result in significant reprogramming effort.

3.2.5 Semantic Model Requirements

A semantic database model must attack the limitations of record-based models; to do this it must meet the goals described below.

Modeling and evolving statics. The model must view the statics of an application environment as consisting of abstract objects. The model must support and differentiate semantic primitives, such as has-attribute, has-instance, and has-subtype. Further, the model must be conducive to maintaining alternate and evolving views of application environment statics (relativism). This implies that the model must be versatile, have a high degree of data independence, and provide a mechanism for controlling logical data redundancy.

Modeling and evolving dynamics. The model must supply an object-oriented mechanism for the specification of database dynamics: the designer must be able to clearly specify the manipulation of database objects in terms of high-level transactions. Further, integrity and consistency constraints must be integrated into the semantic constructs of the model.

Integration. Finally, the static and dynamic aspects of the model must be integrated into a usable tool. This means that the model must be simple enough (while still being versatile and semantically expressive) to apply and implement.

3.3 SEMANTIC DATABASE MODELS

Having analyzed in some detail the properties and limitations of conventional database models in expressing semantics and supporting the database life-cycle, we now turn to a review of specific semantic database models. The emphasis here is on the unique contributions of various models, and their impact on database design, access, and evolution. Of course, any brief summary of a data model cannot capture all its aspects, and redundant features among models are typically described here with respect to only one model.

3.3.1 Database Statics

A typical set of statics constructs would provide for the definition of types that are atomic, printable strings of numbers (e.g., Names, Positive-Integers) and types that are built recursively out of other types, and are not directly printable (e.g., Subscribers may have attributes called Name from the type Names and Age from the type Positive-Integers). Typically, a mechanism for deriving subtypes is also supported (e.g., Elderly-Subscribers may be all subscribers over the age of 85). A complete set of database static constructs might include mechanisms for representing any relationship between two or more objects (e.g., has-unique identifier, has-descriptive property), any relationship between two or more types (e.g., has-subtype, are-modified-by-common-transaction), and any relationship between one or more types and one or more objects (e.g., current-count-of-number-of-instances, has-instance). Thus far the discussion has been (based on intended uses of semantic models) limited to one very general object/object relationship (has-attribute), one specific kind of type/type relationship (has-subtype), and one specific kind of type/object relationship (has-instance). However, even though these latter constructs seem to be the standard, not all semantic models limit themselves to them. Below, the statics capabilities of various models are examined in detail.

3.3.1.1 Related Research

Many of the concepts found in semantic database statics mechanisms derive from research in the area of *knowledge representation* that has been undertaken by artificial intelligence (AI) researchers. In general, this research assumes that knowledge consists of objects and relationships among them. A knowledge base may be viewed as consisting of a network of objects (nodes) connected by relations (directed edges). The directed edges are labeled with the type of each relation (e.g., has-attribute, has-subtype, has-instance). These networks are called *semantic networks*. Figure 3.8 gives a generalized semantic network representation of part of the Claims Processing database. Note that semantic networks often contain terminology such as "is a" ("is a subtype of"), "is" ("is an instance of"), and "is part of" ("is an attribute of").

The fundamental difference between semantic network research and semantic database modeling research is that AI researchers are concerned with representing abstract information, not information structured in a manner oriented toward database applications. Specifically, as instances of types appear in semantic network definitions, schema and data are unified. One implication of this unification is that large amounts of data cannot be handled conveniently as the network grows with the

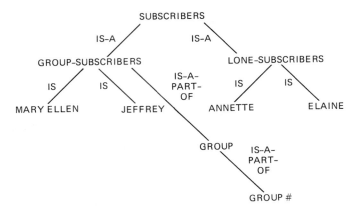

Figure 3.8 An example of a semantic network.

addition of new data (even when no new types or attributes are added). Further, the lack of the concept of a distinct schema means that semantic networks tend to suffer from the same "navigational" problems of record-based models: a semantic network does not adequately accommodate access facilities that are independent of the network structure.

The ADD data definitional model [48] utilizes the semantic network model as its basic structure, but augments it considerably with constructs that allow more semantics to be incorporated into a schema. Thus, ADD has made the semantic network approach to information modeling a practical method for database design. As an example, a typical semantic network might only state with a directed edge that Large-Groups is a subtype of Groups, while an ADD schema would state that Large-Groups is a subtype of Groups and provide the derivation stating that Large-Groups consists of all groups where the number of members is greater than 100.

3.3.1.2 Basic Statics

The *entity-relationship model* [11] *captures the concept* of an abstract object having an identity in a database. This model provides for four levels of specification, which are used to support logical and physical database design. The first level is the semantic level, in which information concerning the "entities" (objects) and "relationships" among objects that are being modeled in the schema is recorded. (The concept of a relationship in the entity-relationship model thus supports a generalized interobject association similar to "has attribute," with the significant differences that the relationships are not directional and any number of objects may serve in a relationship. A similar concept is that of a "role" in the object-role model of Falkenberg [19]). The second level of specification breaks the abstract concepts developed in level one into relations, while the third and fourth levels are concerned with physical design (in terms of underlying storage structures).

ENTITIES

ENTITIES	ATTRIBUTES	VALUES
SUBSCRIBERS	NAME	SUBSCRIBER–NAMES
GROUPS	GROUP #	GROUP # 'S

RELATIONSHIPS:

ENTITIES		RELATIONSHIPS	ATTRIBUTES	VALUES
SUBSCRIBERS	GROUPS	GROUP–MEMBERSHIP	SIZE–OF–GROUP	POSITIVE INTEGERS

Figure 3.9   A section of an entity-relationship schema.

The first (semantic) level of the entity-relationship model in effect supports the notion of abstract objects and the has-instance primitive: each entity or relationship is viewed as an abstract object of some type. (There is, however, no concept of a subtype.) The has-attribute primitive is also partially supported; the word "attribute" in the entity-relationship model refers only to an atomic identifier that describes a property of an entity or relationship. On the other hand, a "role," which also defines an object-object association, refers to an abstract object involved in a relationship (as opposed to an attribute of that relationship). Thus, as attributes in an entity-relationship schema cannot be abstract objects, a true has-attribute primitive is supported only with respect to the roles of a relationship.

An entity-relationship version of part of the claims-processing schema is shown in Figure 3.9.[5] In the figure, two entities are described: Subscribers and Groups; Subscribers have the attribute Name with values in the set of symbols named Subscriber-Names, and Groups have a Group# selected from the set of Group#s. A single relationship is defined in the figure, namely Group-Membership; it relates Subscribers and Groups and has the attribute Size-of-Group with values taken from the set Positive-Integers.

The *semantic hierarchy model* (*SHM*) [55, 56, 57] directly supports the has-attribute (called "aggregation") and has-subtype (called "generalization") semantic primitives. As a type is considered to contain a number of "individuals," the "has-instance" primitive is also supported. (See Figure 3.10 for an SHM example.) Subtypes of a given type are assumed to be nonoverlapping; thus, subtypes partition the instances of the parent type. And subtypes may themselves be further subtypes. Furthermore, the attributes of a subtype are inherited from its parent types, and the subtype may introduce additional attributes as well. For example, Group-Subscribers have all the attributes of Subscribers, plus possibly some additional ones.

---

[5] In this figure as well as all figures illustrating semantic models, some liberties have been taken with syntax and form in order to simplify the description.

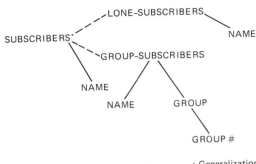

```
                    ┌─LONE-SUBSCRIBERS┐
                    │                  │
SUBSCRIBERS─────────┤                NAME
                    └─GROUP-SUBSCRIBERS
           │            ╱        ╲
         NAME         ╱           ╲
               NAME           GROUP
                                 ╲
                              GROUP #
```

─ ─ ─ ─ : Generalization   **Figure 3.10** An example of aggregation
───────── : Aggregation   and generalization.

3.3.1.3 Additional Statics

The *semantic database model* (*SDM*) [24, 26, 35] views a database as consisting of disjoint "classes" of objects (classes are essentially types), and it directly accommodates the has-instance and has-attribute relationships. And SDM distinguishes between nonatomic abstract objects (called "entities") and atomic identifiers ("names"). SDM also supports a has-subtype semantic primitive ("subclasses"); in SDM, subclasses may be overlapping.

SDM includes several unique statics features, such as grouping types: a *grouping type* is formed by considering instances of a type to be subtypes, rather than individual objects. Using the grouping concept, a designer may form and name a relationship between any set of subtypes that have a common parent type. As an example, the two subtypes Major-Claims and Standard-Claims of the type Claims could be considered instances of the grouping type Claim-Types. SDM also allows attributes to be assigned to a relationship mechanism. As an example, Claims as a type may have the attribute Maximum-Allowable-Amount.

SDM also provides an extensive predicate language for specifying derived information. This mechanism allows a significant amount of data that would normally have to be derived at access time to be made a permanent part of the schema; thus, as will be discussed in the section on database dynamics, statics and dynamics often are not entirely independent. In SDM, subtypes may be derived from properties of parent types, and attributes may be derived in terms of other attributes. Also, attributes may be defined as being "inverses" of each other; for example, the type Group may have the attribute Subscribers (members of the group), and its inverse may be the attribute Group of the type Subscribers. Other methods of deriving subtypes and attribute values exist, including the capacity of stating that a subtype is an arbitrary, user-chosen group of values, and that the value of an attribute is to be assigned directly by the user.

Finally, certain additional semantic integrity constraints are integrated into SDM. For example, an attribute defined on an object may be specified as being "single-valued" or "multivalued"; an attribute may also be specified as being "nonoverlapping" (i.e., two members of the type to which the attribute applies may not have the same value for the attribute).

Taxis [43] is a programming language that supports the semantic constructs has-subtype, has-attribute, and has-instance. Taxis also has a statics construct similar to SDM's grouping construct: *metaclasses* in Taxis are types where each instance of the type is a type itself. For example, one special metaclass is Variable-Class, which consists of all types where the user may directly assign membership to the types. The designer may define an arbitrary number of metaclasses; a metaclass is defined by specifying bounds on the properties and property-values of its instances (which are, of course, types).

In [44] an approach that may be characterized as an *extended entity-relationship model* was proposed. As in the entity-relationship model, a distinction is made between attributes of an object and the relationships in which it is involved. Thus, a database consists of "entities," which may be either atomic or formed of a set of other entities; these objects are related through "associations," and associations may involve entities, associations, or both. Further, a variety of specific associations is defined, which allows each association type to be bound by special update characteristics; this allows important integrity constraints to be embodied naturally. (Some update characteristics are, of course, implicit in constructs already discussed; for example, if a type is deleted, so are all its instances and subtypes, and if an object is deleted, the values of any attributes of which the deleted object served as the value are changed to nil.) A variety of associations may be defined, such as the following: identifier association defines a high-level identifier; a dependent subscriber may be identified by his name and his parents' name; if an identifier is deleted, so is the object that it identified.

Just as SDM distinguishes between name and entities, the *semantic association model* (*SAM*) [60, 61] supports schemas that are networks of "atomic concepts" and "nonatomic concepts." Atomic concepts are representable by character strings, while nonatomic concepts are built recursively using one or more "associations" among atomic concepts. These associations allow for the definition of a variety of relationships among types and objects. Thus, a nonatomic concept can model objects, relationships among objects, types, subtypes, and instances of types. Each specific type of relationship may have associated with it certain integrity constraints and update characteristics. (This latter property was seen in the model proposed in [44].) An important contribution of SAM is its detailed classification of relationships among objects; for example, the following specific kinds of "semantic associations" are supported:

Membership association is used to specify that a number of objects belong to a set; this directly supports the has-instance primitive.

Characterization association defines the attributes of an object; this directly supports the has-attribute primitive.

Interaction association is used to define an abstract interaction of objects; for example, Claim-Investigation may involve the interaction of a claim, a subscriber, an amount, and an investigator. (As an example of association type-dependent constraints, one-to-one, one-to-many, and many-to-many constraints may be placed on interaction association.)

Set-relationship association defines subsets, thereby supporting the has-subtype primitive. The set relationships provided are intersection, set equality, and set exclusion.

Composition association is used to model a type that has a single occurrence and that consists of a number of independent concepts. For example, the composition association construct can be used to form a type Subscribers, which consists of Lone-Subscribers and Group-Subscribers; the instances of Lone-Subscribers are independent of the instances of Group-Subscribers in that changes to the instances of one of the two types do not affect instances of the other type.

Cause-effect association is used to model the cause-and-effect interaction of various types; for example, Claim-Payment may be caused by Valid-Claim and result in Subscriber-Paid-Amount.

Action-means association specifies the type involved in accomplishing a particular transaction; for example, Claim-Payment may be accomplished by Payment-Reserve-Account, which provides payment funds.

Action-purpose association associates the types that represent an action and the purpose of that action; for example, Sales-Visit may have the purpose of creating an instance of Adding-a-Subscriber. (As another example of an association-specific constraint, if a date is associated with each instance of Sales-Visit, and a date is associated with each instance of Adding-a-Subscriber, the date of each sales visit can be constrained to be less than or equal to the date of its corresponding subscriber addition.)

Logical-relation-of-implication association is used to specify that the existence of an instance of one type implies the existence of a specific instance of another type; for example, a Payment-Reserve-Deduction instance may imply the existence of a Subscriber-Paid-Amount instance.

3.3.1.4 Extended Semantics for the Relational Model

Rather than directly capturing the various static constructs necessary for semantic modeling, some researchers have examined the possibility of providing mechanisms for mapping semantic constructs directly into record-based structures. The designer is well aware that he is dealing with a record-based model, but he is given the opportunity to expand its semantic capabilities. As an example, the "extended" relational model of Codd (RM/T) [16] incorporates a rich set of semantic constructs into the relational database model. A type is represented by a relation (an "entity relation") that contains a single column that specifies the "surrogate" (internal unique identifier) for every instance of the type. Attributes are represented by a relation ("property relation") that associates surrogate values with property values.

ENTITY RELATION:
SUBSCRIBERS

"JEFFREY"
"MARY ELLEN"
"ANNETTE"
"ELAINE"

PROPERTY RELATION:
SUBSCRIBER–ADDRESS

SUBSCRIBER	ADDRESS
"JEFFREY	LOS ANGELES
"MARY ELLEN"	LOS ANGELES
"ANNETTE"	BOSTON
"ELAINE"	BERKELEY

Figure 3.11 A portion of an extended relational database.

Figure 3.11 provides a brief claims-processing example, specified with RM/T, that illustrates these points.

A significant contribution of RM/T is to demonstrate that it is indeed possible to directly represent a large spectrum of semantic constructs in relational form. Specifically, the model unifies a number of semantic primitives of various other models, such as single-valued and multivalued attributes, application events, and grouping (as in SDM). Perhaps the most significant problem with RM/T is that it uses symbolic identifiers to simulate constructs that are more naturally accommodated with a direct notion of abstract objects.

The *structural model* [66] is also an extension of the relational model. In this model, objects ("entities") and attributes of entities are represented with relations. Also, specialized relations exist of describing "existence dependencies" between objects (e.g., a claim no longer exists if the submitter cancels his policy), "lexicons," which describe one-to-one correspondence between names (e.g., the name of a subscriber-group and the group#), and "associations" (many-to-many relationships among objects). The structural model also specifies rules for the enforcement of integrity during the insertion and deletion of tuples.

The structural model contains fewer specific semantic constructs than the extended relational model; as a result, it is less expressive. However, it is quite a bit simpler than RM/T. This illustrates an important trade-off between semantic expressiveness and simplicity in database models.

3.3.2 Database Dynamics

A complete set of semantic database dynamics constructs typically includes mechanisms for manipulating objects, attributes, and types; for example, attribute values must be updated, types instances may be inserted and deleted, etc. Also, standard programming language control and arithmetic constructs are typically provided, so that standardized transactions may be defined within a schema. Most semantic modeling researchers have been concerned largely with statics; significantly less emphasis has been placed on developing semantically expressive dynamics capabilities. Below, the dynamics mechanisms of a variety of semantic models are discussed.

3.3.2.1 Related Research

Much of the motivation and direction of database statics research derives from work in the abstract-data-type and programming language realms. In particular, abstract-data-type research is concerned with embedding behavioral semantics within the notion of an abstract object; thus there is a strong similarity between the notions of database dynamics and abstract data types. Specifically, abstract-data-type mechanisms (such as those provided in the languages CLU and Alphard) were the first facilities to embody the important semantic notion of the abstract object: an instance of an abstract data type is viewed as an object with distinct properties. And an abstract data type has associated with it certain operations; the operations defined with a type are the only ones that may be applied to the type. One major difference between semantic modeling techniques and abstract data types is that an abstract-data-type operator is generally associated with a single type of object; thus, special facilities must be provided to allow objects of different types to be semantically related.

The integration of structural and behavioral semantics is the impetus of a significant amount of recent research in programming languages. These languages are designed to provide convenient tools for specification of complex information systems. Two specific database languages are Plain [64] and Rigel [49]; both support the relational model. Thus, these languages are complete programming languages that also treat a relation as a variable type and support relational operators. In short, Plain and Rigel provide an integrated programming environment where standard programming language constructs can be used to structure database manipulations. However, they are limited in their semantic expressiveness—essentially because they are based on the relational model.

3.3.2.2 Information Systems Programming Languages

The languages detailed in this section were developed in an attempt to isolate the static and dynamic properties a language must have in order to support semantically expressive information systems; thus, such a language is not a standard programming language augmented with database constructs (as Plain and Rigel are), but rather a language that views a program as consisting of a semantic data schema and the procedures that act upon that schema. The result is a language with dynamic capabilities oriented specifically toward high-level database manipulations, and not including full general-purpose programming language capabilities.

One such language is Taxis, mentioned earlier in our discussion of database statics; this language supports a complete semantic model, in terms of dynamics and statics. In fact, the basic contribution of Taxis is that it provides a unified treatment of structural and behavioral constructs: Taxis breaks the application environment into a number of types, including tokens (atomic objects), classes (types), properties (attributes of tokens and classes), transactions, and exceptions; it places them all in a has-subtype hierarchy. Thus, dynamics constructs, like statics constructs, may be thought of as being organized into subtypes. The transaction specification facilities of Taxis allow for the definition of parameters, "locals" (variables), "prerequisites" (transaction preconditions), "actions" (transaction body), and "returns" (return values). Actions may include (among others) statements that insert and remove objects from types, iterate through all the instances of a type, retrieve instances of a type that meet a specified property, and delete an instance from the database.

As an example of a Taxis application, Claims and Subscribers may be defined as types and Pay-Claim may be defined as a transaction that checks to see if the person submitting the claim is a subscriber (a "prerequisite"), deletes a claim tuple if the individual meets the prerequisite, returns a pay/no pay boolean, and calls an exception handler called Earmark-Claim if the amount claimed is in excess of $10,000. A subtype of Pay-Claim may be the transaction Pay-VIP-Claim, which is initiated if the subscriber submitting the claim meets some predicate. Thus, Taxis is a very powerful database design and maintenance tool: it supports a high-level data model and provides a mechanism for building complex retrieval and update operations.

DIAL [21] is a language that supports a full semantic model: a modified version of SDM. Each DIAL program consists of two sections—a database description (in modified SSDM) and a set of procedures that operate on the database. The procedures are built out of procedures that manipulate types and instances of types. DIAL supports an assignment statement, a procedure call statement, a "case-procedure" statement for choosing one of a number of actions, an "iterator" statement for processing aggregates of objects one at a time, a conditional statement, and exception-handling control structures.

3.3.2.3 The Dynamics of Semantic Models

The boundary between database programming languages and semantic models is tenuous; for example, many database researchers would consider Taxis to be a semantic model. The difference seems to be one of emphasis: a database programming language is a set of constructs for specifying the objects and procedures involved in an information system, whereas a semantic model is a set of constructs for building a representation of the structure of a real-world environment, along with the dynamics necessary to manipulate that representation. Thus, semantic models tend to stress more rudimentary dynamics such as operations that manipulate types and attributes, rather than mechanisms for defining complete procedures.

The *semantic hierarchy model* (*SHM*) was described in the section on statics; it has associated with it a set of constructs for defining atomic database transactions. SHM also provides for the definition of "functions" and "procedures." The model also includes primitives to support the creation, deletion, and modification of objects; a predicate language for identifying individuals to update; and control structures (such as an if-then-else construct) from which to build functions and procedures.

Other database models have taken the approach of basing a database's statics capabilities on its dynamics. Such models view data definition and data manipulation from an integrated point of view. Generally, any such model is called a *functional database model*. The significant contribution of this model is its unique way of viewing objects, properties of objects, and interobject relationships. In the functional model, attributes of an object are viewed as mappings from that object to other objects. Derived information (usable at schema definition or access time) is then viewed as compositions and restrictions of these mappings. This allows data retrieval to be viewed as derived functions, which adds to semantic modeling a mathematically precise manner of viewing data manipulation. As an example, Claims of Subscribers may be viewed as a mapping from Subscribers to Claims, and Claim#s of Claims may be viewed as a mapping from Claims to Claim#s; then, Claim#s of Subscribers is the direct composition of these two mappings. Also, function constraints (single-valued or set-valued, total or partial, one-to-one, etc.) are a means of ensuring update consistency.

Three main functional database models have been recently developed. In the functional model *DAPLEX* [54], zero-argument functions are used to define types, and single- and multiargument functions are used to define relationships among objects. For example, Claims and Subscribers could be defined as types, Submitters could be defined as a mapping from Claims to Subscribers, Name could be a mapping from Subscribers to Strings, and Claim-Decisions could be defined as a mapping from Claims and Subscribers to Dates, which are Strings. In the data-manipulation language of DAPLEX, functions can be manipulated by using predicates. Functions may also be inverted, and a set of control statements is also provided; they include a for-each (instance of a type or subtype) statement and a print statement that accepts a subtype of Strings as an argument. For example, a user of a DAPLEX database could request the date of all claims where the subscriber is an individual with a specific name. Also, there is a special operator in DAPLEX, "define," that is used to incorporate such user-derived mappings into the schema.

FQL [7] is based on the functional model but is principally a query language. It encompasses a set of data-retrieval primitives that are very similar to those of DAPLEX; they allow the database user to invert functions, form compositions of mappings, derive mappings that return tuples of objects (these are called "constructions"), and restrict mappings using predicates. An example of a construction would be a function that, given a claim, will derive the submitter of the claim and the date it was submitted. Finally, FQL includes arithmetic and boolean operators for use in query formulation.

The *functional data model* (*FDM*) [27] (previously called the "conceptual data model" and the "functional dependency model," and not to be confused with the generic functional model) is another functional database model. A FDM schema consists of nodes and mappings between the nodes. Nodes are essentially types. Functions may be many-to-one, one-to-one, or identity mappings between nodes. Mappings may also be defined as being either partial or total, and onto or into, and the domains of functions may be ordered. Other specialized function properties exist, such as the ability to define the degree of partialness of a function. The has-subtype primitive is also supported.

FDM provides data-manipulation facilities that are based upon treating mappings between nodes as logical access paths. Thus, there are three retrieval primitives: "item," which maps an element of a domain to the range of the corresponding function; "set," which performs the inverse; and "entry," which identifies nodes that are to be manipulated with range and domain operations. There are also four data-manipulation primitives: "create," which adds a value to a node (i.e., adds an instance to a type); "link," which adds a pair of values to the domain and range of a function; "unlink," which performs the inverse; and "delete," which deletes a value from a node. Furthermore, control structures such as "for loop's" may be used to build procedures.

3.3.3 An Integrated Model

In this section we define the *event database model*. The goal is to integrate and build upon the important aspects of the modeling mechanisms described above in order to construct a simple, yet versatile model. The model presented here is actually a simplified version of the event model as defined in [30, 31]. The event model was originally developed as the underpinning of a structured logical database design methodology. The event methodology is omitted here, and the discussion that follows is concerned solely with describing the essentials of a semantic database model with integrated statics and dynamics constructs.

The event model includes basic statics capabilities, including a simple, yet reasonably powerful predicate mechanism for defining subtypes. For example, the model does not include mechanisms for deriving attribute values but does include type attributes as in SDM. The dynamics capabilities of the event model are similar to both the SHM and the functional database model approach. (A different set of dynamics capabilities that are influenced by both of these approaches and also encompass several original mechanisms is under development [5, 6]). In sum, the event model was designed as an essentially generic semantic model; virtually every model described in this chapter has influenced its development.

3.3.3.1 Statics

An event database consists of *objects*. Objects are classified into *types*, and a given object is an *instance* of one or more types. The set of all types for a given database is structured as a collection of type trees, each of which has a single *root type*. Each node in the tree represents a type, and the node's children represent *subtypes* of the *parent type*; the instances of a subtype constitute a subset of the instances of the parent type. A complete tree of subtypes is called a *family* (Figure 3.12 contains the object definitions for the insurance environment). There are two varieties of objects, as follows:

Descriptor objects. *Descriptor objects* are atomic strings of characters or numbers and generally serve as symbolic identifiers in the database. There are two family-level descriptor object types, called Numbers and Strings. All database-specific

```
Type:Subscribers, Submitters
   Primary Attributes
        [ID from Subscriber-IDs (single-valued, exhausts)]
      or [Name from Names (single-valued)
        with Address from Addresses (single-valued)]
   Dependent Attributes
        [Claims from Claims (multivalued, exhausts),
        (inverse of Submitter of Claims)]
        [Group from Groups (single-valued),
        (inverse of Members of Groups)]
        [Deductible from Deductibles (single-valued)]
   Multiplicity—yes

Type:Providers
   Primary Attributes
        [Name from Names (single-valued)
        with Address from Addresses (single-valued)]
   Dependent Attributes
        [Services from Claims (multivalued, exhausts),
        (inverse of Provider-of-Service of Claims)]
   Multiplicity—yes

Type:Claims
   Primary Attributes
        [Submitter from Submitters (single-valued),
        (Inverse of Claims of Subscribers)
        with Date from Dates (single-valued)]
   Dependent Attributes
        [Amount from Amounts (single-valued)]
        [Provider-of-Service from Providers (single-valued)
        (inverse of Services of Providers)]
   Type Attributes
        [Maximum-Allowable-Amount from Amounts
        (single-valued)]
   Multiplicity—yes

Subtype:Major-Claims
   Claims where [Claims.Amount > 100 00]
```

Figure 3.12 Insurance-processing object type definitions.

Subtype:Standard-Claims:
  Claims where [Claims.Amount < = 100 00]

Subtype:Payable-Claims:
  arbitrary of Claims

Subtype:Bad-Claims:
  arbitrary of Claims

Type:Groups
  Primary Attributes
[ID from Group-IDs (single-valued, exhausts]
  Dependent Attributes
[Address from Addresses (single-valued)]
[Members from Subscribers (multivalued),
 (inverse of Group of Subscribers)]
[Policy from Policies (single-valued),
 (inverse of Holders of Policies)]
  Multiplicity—yes

Type:Policies
  Primary Attributes
    [Type from Coverage-Types]
  Dependent Attributes
    [Effective-Date from Effective-Dates
    (single-valued)]
    [Renewal-Date from Renewal-Dates
    (single-valued)]
    [Members from Groups (single-valued),
    (inverse of Policy of Groups)]
  Multiplicity—yes

Type:Payment-Reserve-Account
  Type Attributes
    [Current-Value from Amounts
    (single-valued)]
  Multiplicity—no

Type:Policy-Assignments
  Dependent Attributes
    [Group from Groups (single-valued)]
    [Policy from Policies (single-valued)]

Type:Group-Assignments
  Dependent Attributes
    [Group from Groups (single-valued)]
    [Members from Subscribers (multivalued)]

Note: Subscriber-IDs, Names, Addresses, Deductibles, Dates, Effective-Dates, Renewal-Dates, Amounts, Groups-IDs, and Coverage-Types are all descriptor object subtypes.

Figure 3.12 (*continued*)

descriptor types are defined as eventual subtypes of Strings of Numbers. For example, Integers is a subtype of Numbers, Ages is a subtype of Integers, etc.

Each descriptor object subtype is specified by a definition containing a subtype name, a statement specifying the instances of the subtype, and an optional ordering statement defining a total order on the instances of the subtype. The statement specifying the instances may enumerate the instances, derive them in terms of string operations (length, arithmetic bounds, etc.), or derive them in terms of other objects in the database; for example, a subtype of Strings could be defined as the names of all current subscribers (Subscriber-Names). The ordering statement is of use in applying predicates on subtypes in order to form other subtypes; for example, if the instances of Subscriber-Names were ordered lexicographically, the subtype Subscriber-Names could be partitioned into a set of subtypes, each   representing the subscriber names beginning with a specific letter.

Abstract objects.   *Abstract objects* are nonatomic entities, which are formed of descriptors and other abstract objects. While all database-specific descriptor types are eventual subtypes of Strings or Numbers, an arbitrary number of top-level abstract object types can be defined.

Each abstract object type or subtype definition contains a type name, a predicate specifying the properties of its instances (only if it is a subtype definition), zero or more sets of *primary instance attributes* (each set acts as a unique identifier for the type or the subtype), zero or more *dependent instance attributes* (these describe properties of the types), zero or more *type attributes*, and a *multiplicity indicator* stating whether or not the type or subtype may naturally contain more than one instance.

An example abstract object type is Claims, with the primary attribute set Submitter (value type Subscribers) and Date (value type Dates), dependent attribute Amount (value type Positive-Integers), and type attribute Maximum-Allowable-Amount (value type Positive-Integers). An example subtype is Major-Claims, which consists of all Claims such that Amount exceeds 10,000. As an example of a type with a false multiplicity indicator, Payment-Reserve-Account is a type that represents an atomic object; it has only one attribute, the type attribute Current-Value (value type Nonnegative-Integers).

A number of simple integrity constraints may be specified with each attribute. The *value* of an attribute is specified as consisting of either strictly one instance (*single-valued*) or a set of instances (*multi-valued*) from the value type. For example, a subscriber may submit more than one claim but may have only one name. It may be required that all instances of a value type be used as values of the corresponding (primary or dependent) attribute by stating that the attribute must *exhaust* the value type. For example, a given claim must belong to somebody. An attribute may be required to be *nonnull*. For example, it is most likely true that all groups have policies, even though policy would not be the primary attribute of Groups.

All primary and dependent attributes between two abstract objects must be bidirectional. For example, a claim has a submitter and a subscriber has claims. A subtype *inherits* all instance attributes of the parent type but may have instance and type attributes that the parent type does not have. Further, the value type of an attribute of a subtype may be a subtype of the value type of a corresponding attribute of the parent. For example, Major-Claims may be a subtype of Claims, have all the attributes of Claims, and also have the extra dependent attribute Investigator. And the value type of Amount of Major-Claims may be Integers > 10000 (the value type of Amount of Claims is Positive-Integers).

The event subtype predicate mechanism.   The subtype predicate mechanism is designed with the goal of allowing the power of compound universal and existential quantifiers and string comparison operators in a user-oriented manner. Variables and compound structures are avoided by using operations that act only on simple predicates. A given descriptor or abstract object subtype is thus formed by defining a series of intermediate subtypes, each of which contains a simple predicate in its definition. A predicate may also state that the subtype is *arbitrary*, in that the user explicitly assigns instances to the subtype at data-access time.

The general form of an abstract-object subtype derivation statement consists of a left side defining the parent type and a name for the new subtype, and a right side consisting of a predicate expression that restricts the instances of the subtype by placing restrictions on the allowable values of its attributes. Example predicates follow:

A common inquiry into a database consists of asking for the identifiers (descriptors) of specific application objects; for example, the user may require the names of all subscribers. This would be specified as:

Subscriber-Names: Subscribers.Name

The names of all people who have submitted claims may be obtained by isolating all subscribers who have claims; this demands the use of the "where" clause and the nonempty intersection operator:

Active-Names: Subscribers.Name   where
[Subscribers.Claims intersects Claims]

The subtype of subscribers consisting of all subscribers serviced by Dr. Oh may be derived by following two levels of attributes and isolating the subscribers who have submitted claims serviced by Dr. Oh:

Dr.-Oh-Patients: Subscribers where ["Dr.Oh" intersects Subscribers.Claims.
Provider-of-Services]

The names of all patients of Dr.Oh such that all of their claims are major claims requires the definition of the subtype Dr.-Oh-Patients and the definition of a subtype of Claims:

Major-Claims: Claims where [Claims.Amount > 10000]

Major-Dr.-Oh-Patients: Dr.-Oh-Patients.Name where [Dr.-Oh-Patients.Claims included in Major-Claims]

The "and" operator may be used to define the subtype of descriptors consisting of the names of all subscribers serviced by both Dr. Oh and Dr. No:

Drs.-Oh-No-Patients: Subscribers.Names where [Subscribers.Claims.Provider-of-Service intersects "Dr.Oh"] and [Subscribers.Claims.Provider-of-Service intersects "Dr.No"]

The special value "nil" may be used to derive the subtype of subscribers that consists of all subscribers who are not yet assigned to a group:

Groupless-Subscribers: Subscribers where
[Subscriber.Group = nil]

3.3.3.2 Dynamics

In addition to the structures described above to accommodate the statics of an event database, the event model supports database dynamics through the concept of an *event*. Each time an event database is accessed, an event is *initiated*. There are two kinds of events, *application* and *perusal* events. Both are built out of primitive *operations*. (Figure 3.13 gives the application events corresponding to the insurance processing environment.)

Data operations.   *Data operations* are used to define application and perusal events (perusal events, as detailed later in this subsection, may use only the first and last data operations). Data operations assign variable values, add instances to types and subtypes, delete instances from types and subtypes, insert instances in arbitrary subtypes, update attributes values, and display the values of descriptor-valued attributes; they are used in application of perusal events. There are seven event data operations:

1. *Assign variable*: Variables are defined and assigned values with this operation. As variables are assigned values with a predicate that may match the properties of more than one instance of the type, a variable may refer to more than one instance at any one time.
2. *Add instance*: This operation adds an instance of a subtype to the subtype and all (eventual) parent types.
3. *Delete instance*: This operation deletes an object from the database.
4. *Insert instance*: This operation inserts an existing instance of some (eventual) parent type into an "arbitrary" subtype of that type.

Receiving-a-Claim [external]
    (Submitter-ID from Subscriber-IDs,
    Amount from Amounts, Date from Dates,
    Provider-of-Service from Providers)
    Working subtypes
    Valid-Submitter: Subscribers where [Subscribers.
    ID = Submitter-ID]
    Action box
      Add instance [C: Claims]
      C.Submitter: = Valid-Submitter
      C.Amount: = Amount
      C.Date: = Date
      C.Provider-of-Service: = Provider-of-Service

Processing-a-Claim [external]
    (Submitter from Subscriber-IDs,
    Date from Dates)
    Working subtypes
    Valid-C: Claims where [[Claims.Submitter = Submitter]
      and [Claims.Date = Date]]
    C: Payable-Claims where
      [Valid-C intersects Payable-Claims]
    Action box
      Evaluating-a-Claim (Valid-C)
      If C then Paying-a-Claim (Valid-C) else
        Rejecting-a-Claim (Valid-C)

Subtype: Processing-a-Major-Claim [external]
    (Submitter from Subscriber-IDs, Date from Dates)
    Working subtypes
    Major-Claims: Claims where [Claims.Amount > 100 00]
    Valid-M-C: Major-Claims where
      [[Major-Claims.Submitter = Submitter]
      and [Major-Claims.Date = Date]]
    C: Payable-Claims where
      [Valid-M-C intersects Payable-Claims]
    Action box
      Evaluating-a-Claim (Valid-M-C)
      Auditing-a-Major-Claim (Valid-M-C)
      If C then Paying-a-Claim (Valid-M-C) else
      Rejecting-a-Claim (Valid-M-C)
    Subtype: Processing-a-Standard-Claim [external]
        (Submitter from Subscriber-IDs, Date from Dates)

Figure 3.13   Insurance-processing application event type definitions.

Preconditions
    Standard-Claims: Claims where [Claims.Amount ⇐ 10000]
    Valid-S-C: Standard-Claims where
    [[Standard-Claims.Submitter = Submitter]
    and [Standard-Claims.Date = Date]]
C: Payable-Claims where
    [Valid-S-C intersects Payable-Claims]
Action box
    Evaluating-a-Claim (Valid-S-C)
    If C then Paying-a-Claim (Valid-S-C) else
      Rejecting-a-Claim (Valid-S-C)
Evaluating-a-Claim [internal]
    (Claim from Claims)
    Working subtypes
      Payable-Claim: Claim where [(Claim.Policy intersects
      Policies)] and [(Claim.Amount
      < Claims.Maximum-Allowable-Amount)]*
    Payable-Claims
    Bad-Claims
Action box
    If P then insert [Claim in Payable-Claims]
    else insert [Claim in Bad-Claims]
Paying-a-Claim [internal]
    (Claim from Claims)
    Working subtypes
C: Payable-Claims where [Claims intersects
    Payable-Claims]
    Payment-Reserve-Account
Action box
    Payment-Reserve-Account: Payment-Reserve-Account where
    [Payment-Reserve-Account.Current-Value =
    Payment-Reserve-Account.Current-Value-C.Amount]
    Delete instance (C where [C intersects Payable-Claims])
    Auditing-a-Major-Claim, Placing-a-Subscriber-in-a-Group, Assigning-a-Subscriber-to-a-Group, Deleting-a-Subscriber, Creating-a-Group, Creating-a-Policy, and Rejecting-a-Claim are also application events. Also, all references to, and the definition of, Calculate-Group-Profit/Loss-Status have been omitted for simplicity.

    *For simplicity, an algorithmic implementation of Evaluating-a-Claim has not been used here; thus, Payable-Claims and Bad-Claims could actually have been derived, not arbitrary, subtypes. For the same reason, many of the IDs and properties of Groups and Policies have been omitted from the design schema, as they are of use only in an algorithmic implementation of Evaluating-a-Claim.

Figure 3.13   (*continued*)

5. *Remove instance*: This operation removes an instance of some (eventual) parent type of an "arbitrary" subtype from the subtype.

6. *Update attribute*: The update attribute operation is used to update attribute values of existing instances. Attributes whose value types are abstract objects may be assigned new values by isolating the proper attributes of other objects with predicates. Or a number-valued attribute may be added to, subtracted from, divided by, or multiplied by another number-valued attribute (isolated with a predicate) or a number constant or any attribute of the object being manipulated. A string-valued attribute may be concatenated with another string-valued attribute or a string constant or any attribute of the object being manipulated.[6]

7. *Output*: Given an abstract object (isolated with a predicate), a composite of attribute mappings is used to locate a descriptor to output.

Application events.   An event database schema consists of abstract and descriptor objects and of *application events*. Each application event definition specifies a particular transaction and consists of an event name, a set of parameters that are of descriptor or abstract object types, and a set of *actions*. Actions may consist of other application events, data operations, or a programming language control structure (if then else, while do, or iterate through type).

Application events are arranged in families in a manner very similar to object family trees. An application event is a subtype of another event if the value types of its parameters are subtypes of the parameters of the second event, and if the actions of the first event are intuitively a special case of the actions of the second event. Also, an event that serves only as an action of other events, and thus is not accessed directly by a database user, is termed an *internal* event; any event that may be initiated directly by a user or application program is an *external* event. When application events are embedded as actions within another application event, the outermost application event (an external event) must have parameters that are descriptor types in order for the database user to be able to initiate the event from an input device. However, in order to enhance the semantic expressiveness of the schema, it is a good idea to consider the parameters used in embedded application events as representing application objects; thus, these parameters shoud normally be of abstract object types.

Perusal events.   A perusal event is initiated when a one-time, nonproduction query must be made on the database. A perusal event is implemented as a series of assign variable and output data operations. For example, to find the names of all providers who have treated subscribers in group 1, the user would first form Group-1-Subscribers, which is a subtype of Subscribers (all subscribers who are in group 1), then output Group-1-Subscribers.Claims.Provider-of-Service. Thus, as data access and subtype creation are strongly related, the event database model allows the

---

[6] The event model may easily be augmented with other arithmetic and string operators.

casual user to peruse the database with semantically expressive, nonnavigational constructs; in fact, subtypes created by perusals may be viewed as temporary extensions to the database.

Thus, the dynamic capabilities of the event model are similar to those of Taxis, DIAL, and SHM in that they contain standard programming language control statements and special operators that manipulate objects and types. Further, the functional notation of the event model enables the designer of subtypes and application events and the originator of perusals to employ a unified, conceptually clean predicate mechanism for describing deriver data.

3.4 SUMMARY

This chapter has shown that semantic models provide a versatile and powerful mechanism for representing data manipulations of data by embedding the semantics of the data in the schema definition and by providing associated access facilities. Furthermore, recent semantic modeling research has exhibited the importance of integrating application-specific operations into the schema. Semantic models thus facilitate the easy design and access of a database, allow a schema and the corresponding data to evolve gracefully, and provide constructs that allow certain integrity and consistency constraints to fit naturally into a schema. In particular, this chapter has examined a number of semantic database models and has detailed a simplified version of a unified database model: the event model.

REFERENCES

1. Abrial, J.R., "Data Semantics," *Database Management*, eds. J. Klimbie, and K. Koffeman. New York: North-Holland, 1974.
2. ANSI/X3/SPARC 1975 (Standards Planning and Requirements Committee), "Interim Report from the Study Group on Database Management Systems," *FDT (Bulletin of ACM SIGMOD)*, Vol. 7, No. 2 (1975).
3. Bachman, C.W., "The Role Concept in Data Models," *Proceedings of International Conference on Very Large Databases*, Tokyo, October 6–8, 1977.
4. Biller, H., and E.J. Neuhold, "Semantics of Databases: The Semantics of Data Models," *Information Systems*, Vol. 3, No. 1 (1978), pp. 11–30.
5. Brodie, M.L., "On the Conceptual Modeling of Behaviour," University of Maryland, Department of Computer Sciences Technical Report, 1980.
6. Brodie, M.L., "On Modeling Behavioural Semantics of Data," submitted to The Seventh International Conference on Very Large Databases, Cannes, France, 1981.
7. Buneman, P., and R.E. Frankel, "FQL—A Functional Query Language," *Proceedings of ACM SIGMOD International Conference on the Management of Data*, Boston, May 30–June 1, 1979.

8. Buneman, P., and H.L. Morgan, "Implementing Alerting Techniques in Database Systems," *Proceedings of COMPSAC '77*, Chicago, November 8–11, 1977.

9. Chamberlin, D.D., "Relational Database Management Systems," *Computing Surveys*, Vol. 8, No. 1 (March 1976).

10. Chang, C.L., *A Hyper-Relational Model of Databases*, IBM Research Report RJ1634, San Jose, Calif., August 22, 1975.

11. Chen, P.P.S., "The Entity-Relationship Model: Toward a Unified View of Data," *ACM Transactions on Database Systems*, Vol. 1, No. 1 (March 1976), pp. 9–36.

12. Chen, P.P.S., *The Entity-Relational Approach to Logical Database Design*, Monograph No. 6. Wellesley, Mass.: QED Information Sciences, 1978.

13. CODASYL Committee on Data System Languages, *CODASYL Database Task Group Report*. New York: ACM, 1971.

14. Codd, E.F., "A Relational Model for Large Shared Data Banks," *Communications of the ACM*, Vol. 13, No. 6 (June 1970).

15. Codd, E.F., "Further Normalization of the Database Relational Model," *Database Systems*, ed. R. Rustin. Englewood Cliffs, N.J.: Prentice-Hall, Inc., 1971.

16. Codd, E.F., "Extending the Database Relational Model," *ACM Transactions on Database Systems*, Vol. 4, No. 4 (December 1979).

17. Date, C.J., *An Introduction to Database Systems*. Reading, Mass.: Addison-Wesley Publishing Co., 1977.

18. Eswaran, K.P., and D.D. Chamberlin, "Functional Specifications of a Subsystem for Database Integrity," *Proceedings of International Conference on Very Large Databases*, Framingham, Mass., September 22–24, 1975.

19. Falkenberg, E.D., "Conceptualization of Data," *Infotech State-of-the-Art Report*, 1980.

20. Hammer, M., "Research Directions in Database Management," *Research Directions in Software Technology*, ed. P. Wegner. Cambridge, Mass.: MIT Press, 1979.

21. Hammer, M., and B. Berkowitz, "DIAL: A Programming Language for Data Intensive Applications," *Proceedings of ACM SIGMOD International Conference on the Management of Data*, Santa Monica, Calif., June 1980.

22. Hammer, M., and D. McLeod, "Semantic Integrity in a Relational Database System," *Proceedings of International Conference on Very Large Databases*, Framingham, Mass., September 22–24, 1975.

23. Hammer, M., and D. McLeod, "A Framework for Database Semantic Integrity," *Proceedings of Second International Conference on Software Engineering*, San Francisco, Calif., October 13–15, 1976.

24. Hammer, M., and D. McLeod, "The Semantic Data Model: A Modeling Mechanism for Database Applications," *Proceedings of ACM SIGMOD International Conference on the Management of Data*, Austin, Tex., May 31–June 2, 1978.

25. Hammer, M., and D. McLeod, "On the Architecture of Database Management Systems," *Infotech State-of-the-Art Report on Data Design*, 1979.

26. Hammer, M., and D. McLeod, "Database Description with SDM: A Semantic Database Model," *ACM Transactions on Database Systems*, Vol. 6, No. 3 (September 1981), pp. 351–386.

27. Housel, B.C., V. Waddle, and S.B. Yao, "The Functional Dependency Model for Logical Database Design," *Proceedings of the Fifth International Conference on Very Large Data Bases*, Rio de Janeiro, Brazil, October 3–5, 1979.

28. Kent, W., *Data and Reality*. New York: North-Holland, 1978.

29. Kent, W., "Limitations of Record-Based Information Models," *ACM Transactions on Database Systems*, Vol. 4, No. 1 (March 1979), pp. 107–131.

30. King, R., "The Event Database Specification Model," Ph.D. thesis, Computer Science Department, University of Southern California, Los Angeles, Calif., in preparation (1981).

31. King, R., and D. McLeod, "The Event Database Specification Model," *Proceedings of Second International Conference on Databases: Improving Usability and Responsiveness*, Jerusalem, Israel, June 1982.

32. Lee, R.M., and R. Gerritsen, "Extended Semantics for Generalization Hierarchies," *Proceedings of ACM SIGMOD International Conference on the Management of Data*, Austin, Texas, May 31–June 2, 1978.

33. Liskov, B., et al., "Abstraction Mechanisms in CLU," *Communications of the ACM*, Vol. 20, No. 8 (August 1977), pp. 564–576.

34. McLeod, D.J., "High Level Definition of Abstract Domains in a Relational Database System," *Journal of Computer Languages*, Vol. 2, No. 3 (1977).

35. McLeod, D., *A Semantic Database Model and Its Associated Structured User Interface*, Technical Report, MIT Laboratory for Computer Science, Cambridge, Mass., 1978.

36. McLeod, D., *A Database Transaction Specification Methodology for End-Users*, Technical Report 79-6, Computer Science Department, University of Southern California, Los Angeles, 1979.

37. McLeod, D., "An Approach to Conceptual Database Modeling," *Proceedings of Workshop on Data Abstraction, Databases, and Conceptual Modeling*, Pingree Park, Col., June 23–26, 1980.

38. McLeod, D., and D. Heimbigner, "A Federated Architecture for Database Systems," *Proceedings of National Computer Conference*, Anaheim, Calif., 1980.

39. McLeod, D., and R. King, "Applying a Semantic Database Model," *Proceedings of International Conference on the Entity-Relationship Approach to Systems Analysis and Design*, Los Angeles, December 10–12, 1979.

40. McLeod, D., and J.M. Smith, "Abstraction in Databases," *Proceedings of Workshop on Data Abstraction, Databases, and Conceptual Modeling*, Pingree Park, Col., June 23–26, 1980.

41. Michaels, A.S., et al., "A Comparison of the Relational and CODASYL Approaches to Data-Base Management," *Computing Surveys*, Vol. 8, No. 1 (March 1976).

42. Mylopoulos, J., "An Overview of Knowledge Representation," *Proceedings of Workshop on Data Abstraction, Databases, and Conceptual Modeling*, Pingree Park, Col., June 23–26, 1980.

43. Mylopoulos, J., P.A. Bernstein, and H.K.T. Wong, "A Language Facility for Designing Interactive Database-Intensive Applications," *ACM Transactions on Database Systems*, Vol. 5, No. 2 (June 1980), pp. 185–207.

44. Navathe, S.B., and M. Schkolnick, "View Representation in Logical Database Design," *Proceedings of ACM SIGMOD International Conference on the Management of Data*, Austin, Tex., May 31–June 2, 1978.

45. Palmer, I., "Record Subtype Facilities in Database Systems," *Proceedings of the Fourth International Conference on Very Large Databases*, West Berlin, September 13–15, 1978.

46. Paolini, P., "Abstract Data Types and Data Bases," *Proceedings of Workshop on Data Abstraction, Databases, and Conceptual Modeling*, Pingree Park, Col., June 23–26, 1980.

47. Pirotte, A., *The Entity-Property-Association Model: An Information-Oriented Database Model*, Technical Report, M.B.L.E. Research Laboratory, Brussels, Belgium, 1977.

48. Roussopoulos, N., "ADD: Algebraic Data Definition," *Proceedings of Sixth Texas Conference on Computing Systems*, Austin, Tex., November 14–15, 1977.

49. Rowe, L.A., and K.A. Shoens, "Data Abstraction, Views and Updates in Rigel," *Proceedings of ACM SIGMOD International Conference on the Management of Data*, Boston, Mass., May 30–June 1, 1979.

50. Schank, R.C., "Identification of Conceptualizations Underlying Natural Language," *Computer Models of Thought and Language*, eds. R.C. Schank and K.M. Colby. San Francisco: W.H. Freeman, 1973.

51. Schmid, H.A., and J.R. Swenson, "On the Semantics of the Relational Data Model," *Proceedings of ACM SIGMOD International Conference on the Management of Data*, San Jose, Calif., May 14–16, 1975.

52. Senko, M.E., "Information Systems: Records, Relations, Sets, Entities, and Things," *Information Systems*, Vol. 1, No. 1 (1975), pp. 3–14.

53. Senko, M.E., "Conceptual Schemas, Abstract Data Structures, Enterprise Descriptions," *Proceedings of ACM International Computing Symposium*, Belgium, April 1977.

54. Shipman, D., "The Functional Data Model and the Data Language DAPLEX," *ACM Transactions on Database Systems*, Vol. 6, No. 1 (March 1981).

55. Smith, J.M., and D.C.P. Smith, "Database Abstractions: Aggregation," *Communications of the ACM*, Vol. 20, No. 6 (June 1977), pp. 405–413.

56. Smith, J.M., and D.C.P. Smith, "Database Abstractions: Aggregation and Generalization," *Proceedings of NYU Symposium on Database Design*, New York, May 18–19, 1978.

57. Smith, J.M., and D.C.P. Smith, *A Database Approach to Software Specification*, Technical Report CCA-79-17, Computer Corporation of America, Cambridge, Mass., April 1979.

58. Solvberg, A., "A Contribution to the Definition of Concepts for Expressing Users' Information System Requirements," *Proceedings of International Conference on the Entity-Relationship Approach to Systems Analysis and Design*, Los Angeles, December 10–12, 1979.

59. Stonebraker, M.R., *High Level Integrity Assurance in Relational Database Management Systems*, Electronics Research Laboratory Report ERL-M473, University of California, Berkeley, August 16, 1974.

60. Su, S.Y.W., and D.H. Lo, "A Semantic Association Model for Conceptual Database Design," *Proceedings of International Conference on the Entity-Relationship Approach to Systems Analysis and Design*, Los Angeles, December 10–12, 1979.

61. Su, S.Y.W., H. Lam, and D.H. Lo, "Transformation of Data Traversals and Operation in Application Programs to Account for Semantic Changes of Database," *ACM Transactions on Database Systems*, Vol. 6, No. 2 (June 1981).

62. Taylor, R.W., and R.L. Frank, "CODASYL Database Management Systems," *Computing Surveys*, Vol. 8, No. 1 (March 1976).

63. Tsichritzis, D.C., and F.H. Lochovsky, "Hierarchical Database Management: A Survey," *Computing Surveys*, Vol. 8, No. 1 (March 1976).

64. Wasserman, A.I., "The Data Management Facilities of Plain," *Proceedings of the ACM SIGMOD International Conference on the Management of Data*, Boston, Mass., May 30–June 1, 1979.

65. Wiederhold, G., *Database Design*. New York: McGraw-Hill, 1977.

66. Wiederhold, G., and R. El-Masri, "Structural Model for Database Design," *Proceedings of International Conference on the Entity-Relationship Approach to Systems Analysis and Design*, Los Angeles, December 10–12, 1979.

67. Wong, H.K.T., and J. Mylopoulos, "Two Views of Data Semantics: A Survey of Data Models in Artificial Intelligence and Database Management," *Infor.*, Vol. 15, No. 3 (October 1977), pp. 344–382.

68. Woods, W.A., "What's in a Link: Foundations for Semantic Networks," in *Representation and Understanding*, eds. D.G. Bobrow and A.M. Collina. New York: Academic Press, 1975.

4

Processing-Requirement Modeling and Its Applications in Logical Database Design

Stanley Y. W. Su
Database Systems Research and Development Center
University of Florida

4.1 INTRODUCTION

Logical database design involves the collection, specification, analysis, modeling, and integration of many possibly conflicting application requirements of an enterprise to derive the conceptual schema and the external schemas of a DBMS. It is a complex and difficult task. Conventional database design methods do not provide adequate guidance to the database administrator (DBA) in his or her design. Few powerful design tools are available that contribute to the systematic design of complex databases. Often a design is guided by the DBA's intuition and understanding of the enterprise's application requirements. The resulting database often fails to meet the enterprise's real application needs.

An optimal design of a database is difficult to achieve. It requires that a thorough and careful requirement analysis be undertaken to determine how users' different and conflicting information needs can best be satisfied. Application requirements can be classified into three general categories of information: corporate constraints, information requirements, and processing requirements. *Corporate constraints* describe such things as the operational policies and rules of an organization, the related government regulations and laws, the spatial, temporal, and financial constraints, etc. *Information requirements* describe data attributes, entities, associations, and semantic integrity constraints which form the users' views of the database. *Processing requirements* describe three types of processing: planning (principally by top management), control (principally by middle management), and operations (principally by end users). They deal mainly with the expected use of the database and the operations to be performed on the database to satisfy the users' information needs.

The analysis, specification and modeling of these three categories of information is an essential step in database design, since the data obtained in this step can be used as a basis to select a proper design from various alternatives and to guide the steps in both logical and physical database design processes, as described in Chapter 1. The three categories of information are very much interrelated. For example, an organization's policy of allowing each employee to work on only one project can determine the way in which information requirements are modeled. The operations described in processing requirements have to be meaningful or semantically consistent (not conflicting) with the semantic properties of data described in information requirements. For example, it would not be meaningful to relate two data entity types in an operation (such as a relational JOIN) if they were not semantically related through some association or comparable attributes. The completeness of information requirements can be verified, based on the processing requirements. For example, a description of a user's view of the database (information requirements) is incomplete if the corresponding user's processing requirements contain retrieval or storage operations on data which are not defined in the information requirements. Furthermore, there often exist several alternative ways of modeling users' information requirements, and different models used at the logical level may affect the efficiencies of their physical implementations. The processing requirements specify the expected use of the database and thus can be used to select an optimal model.

In the process of integrating the users' views to form the conceptual model of a database, differences in views need to be accommodated and conflicts resolved. The integration process can again be guided by the users' processing requirements, so that a conceptual model which can best represent the community users' view of the database can be constructed.

Processing requirements are important for the design of DBMS-processible schemas (external schemas and the conceptual schema in ANSI SPARC's terminology). A DBMS may be based on any of the popular data models such as the relational model, the hierarchical model, or the DBTG's network model. In this case, the schemas to be designed may be very different from the conceptual schema. Since the conceptual model represents the semantic descriptions of the users' view and the enterprise's view of the database, an automatic generation of DBMS-processible external and conceptual schemas is possible as demonstrated in the existing works on data models [1, 2, 4, 22]. No matter whether it is by automatic generation or by manual design, the objective of this design step is to produce DBMS-processible schemas which are optimal under the given constraints and requirements. The major issues of DBMS-processible schema design are involved with the minimization of the response time or cost for database operations specified in the processing requirements.

Processing requirements can also be used to guide the physical database design process. The purpose is to produce a design which is (1) implementable on the given hardware and the DBMS and (2) efficient and capable of meeting the predefined processing requirements of the present and projected applications. Processing requirements are very important, since the analysis of primary file structures, record placement, and secondary file structures and the design of performance evaluation mechanisms undertaken in this step are dependent on these data.

There have been many publications in the area of specification, analysis, and modeling of information requirements. Some examples of works in this area are the database design methodologies [5, 6, 14, 29], the specification of the requirements in general information systems [26], the theoretical works on data models [4, 17, 22, 24], the schema analysis and restructuring [17], and the description of information requirements [11, 21]. However, little work has been done on the specification, analysis, and modeling of corporate constraints and processing requirements.

In this chapter we shall concentrate on the specification, analysis, and modeling of processing requirements and the applications in logical database design. Some basic constructs useful for modeling processing requirements will be introduced, and performance variables which are useful for evaluating alternative database designs will be identified. A process-definition language (PDL) will be used to define processing requirements. Examples will be given to illustrate the applications of processing-requirement modeling to the various steps of logical database design. Whenever possible, the existing methodologies will be incorporated in the presentation. While reading this chapter, the reader should bear in mind that there is not a large body of existing literature on this subject. The ideas presented here, both those of the author and others, are research ideas and are highly speculative. They should not be taken as the results of an established field of study. The purpose of this chapter is to aid the reader's understanding of the role and the importance of processing- requirement modeling in logical database design and to stimulate further research in this area.

This chapter is organized in the following way. Section 4.2 presents a technique of modeling processing requirements at the data-item level and its application in different logical design steps. Section 4.3 presents a technique of modeling processing requirements at the query level and its application. Section 4.4 presents modeling techniques at the transaction level. A summary is given in Section 4.5.

4.2 PROCESSING-REQUIREMENT MODELING AT THE DATA-ITEM LEVEL

To design a model of processing requirements (or process model) for logical database design, two things are essential: a set of constructs which represent the operational characteristics of processes and a language for specifying the processing requirements of database users in terms of these constructs. The inclusion of a construct in a process model has to be justified by its intended use in the design of external models and the conceptual model of a database. The language for processing-requirement specification should be a high-level language easy for the users and database designers to employ. We shall call this language a *process-defini-*

TABLE 4.1   TERMINOLOGIES FOR INFORMATION- AND PROCESSING-REQUIREMENT MODELING

Information-Requirement Modeling	Processing-Requirement Modeling
External (data) schema	External process schema
Conceptual (data) schema	Conceptual process schema
External (data) model	External process model
Conceptual (data) model	Conceptual process model
Data-definition language (DDL)	Process-definition language (PDL)

tion language (or *PDL*) and the definition and description of processing requirements using a PDL a *process schema*. We can therefore talk about external process
schemas and a conceptual process schema, which correspond to external data
schemas (or external schemas) and conceptual data schema (or conceptual schema)
of a database. Table 4.1 shows the corresponding terminologies in information-
requirement modeling and processing-requirement modeling.

The PDL is different from a *data manipulation language (DML)* of a database
management system. The former is used to specify the abstraction of database users'
expected data retrieval and manipulation requirements and is used for database
design. The latter is used to specify the specific data retrieval and manipulation
commands to be operated against the database. A process schema represents a rough
estimation of database usage rather than the precise queries or application programs
issued by the database users.

In this and the following sections we systematically present the modeling
techniques at the data-item level, the query level, and the transaction level. Each
consecutive level contains more information about database users' processing requirements than the preceding one. The use of this information in the design and
implementation of external and conceptual data models is illustrated. A PDL is
introduced to define and describe the process models.

From an application viewpoint, a *data item* can be considered as the smallest
unit of named data useful to database users. The information requirement of an
application can be defined in terms of entities and associations, which are described
by a collection of data items. The processing requirement of the application can be
defined in terms of the operations expected to be performed on the entities and
associations. A good example of this modeling approach is the work by Mitoma and
Irani [15]. They model the processing requirement of an application in terms of a set
of *run units*, each of which is an abstract representation of an application program.
A run unit is modeled by a set of *database operations*, each of which has a number of
operands (the data-item values involved in the operation), a *key item* for specifying
the search constraint, a *relation* involved in the operation, and the *frequency* of each
operation. The approach can be generalized so that a set of data items can be used to
specify the conditions under which a second set of data items which describe entities
or associations are to be processed by some operation. We shall call the first set a
qualification set, *Q*, and the second set a *target set*, *T*. The set of database

operations, such as retrieve, insert, delete, update, lock/unlock, and protect, will be the operation set, O. We observe that $T \cap Q$ may or may not be empty and T may be identical to Q. In a database operation, the values of data items in Q have to be accessed from the database before an operation can be performed on the values of data items in T.

One method of modeling the processing requirements is to use Q, T, and O to define the requirements of various applications. Corresponding to an external data model which defines the information requirements of a user (or a user group) in an application, we can use a set of triplets $(Q_1, T_1, O_1), (Q_2, T_2, O_2), \ldots (Q_n, T_n, O_n)$ to characterize the expected usage of the database as seen by the user. (Q_i, T_i, O_i) means that a set of data items in Q_i is used in the application to determine whether a set of data items in T_i should be operated upon by the operation O_i. A frequency count can be assigned to each of the triplets to indicate the number of times the particular type of processing is expected to be performed. The use of the frequency information will be explained below. We shall first give an example of an external process schema using a PDL. Assume that the information requirements of a user are described by the user. Each employee can be described by his EMP#, NAME, AGE, RACE, WEIGHT, SALARY, YEAR-OF-SERVICE. The name and salary of an employee cannot be accessed simultaneously.

An example of a process schema is as follows:

1. ({RACE, AGE}, {EMP#, NAME, AGE, RACE, HEIGHT, WEIGHT}, RETRIEVE) (20)
2. ({SALARY}, {EMP#, NAME, YEAR-OF-SERVICE}, RETRIEVE) (30)
3. ({AGE}, {NAME, SALARY}, RETRIEVE) (1)
4. ({ $\varnothing$ }, {SALARY}, UPDATE) (20)

The schema contains four unrelated processes. Each triplet is followed by a frequency count. An empty set $\varnothing$ in the last statement means that no qualification condition is placed on the selection of EMPLOYEE occurrences, thus all employee salaries are to be updated. A frequency of use can be assigned to each process schema to specify the frequency of an application run.

The processing-requirement modeling at the item level has several applications:

1. *Completeness and consistency checking of information requirements*: One requirement in logical database design is that the information requirements of a user (or user group) be complete and semantically consistent (not conflicting) with the processing requirements. A process model can be used to verify the completeness and consistency of information requirements. For example, the information requirement in our previous example is not complete because the HEIGHT information, which is one of the data items to be retrieved by statement 1 above, is left out. It is also semantically inconsistent with the processing requirement specified in statement 3. Incompleteness and inconsistency need to be detected and corrected in the early stage of logical database design. The process model provides a good source of information for this task.

2. *Identification of proper data entities*: As described in Chapter 1 and reviewed in the introduction to the present chapter, one design activity involves defining the users' views of the database and integrating these views to form the conceptual model. In both the users' views and the conceptual model, proper data entities need to be identified and defined to best reflect not only the users' individual views but also the community of users' compromised view of the database. Processing requirements are an important source of information for this design task. For instance, the information requirement in the above example can be modeled in terms of one or many entity types in a user's view or in the conceptual model. It can be modeled by a single entity type EMPLOYEE (EMP#, NAME, AGE, RACE, WEIGHT, HEIGHT, SALARY, YEAR-OF-SERVICE), or by two entity types EMP1 (EMP#, NAME, AGE, RACE, WEIGHT, HEIGHT) and EMP2 (EMP#, NAME, SALARY, YEAR-OF-SERVICE), or by a number of entity types. The selection of a good design of entity types is very important and should be guided by the process model.

A number of heuristic rules can be established to guide the information-requirement modeling. For example, one plausible rule is to find the minimal number of entity types which can support all the processing requirements stated in the process model. The assumption here is that the smaller the number of entity types, the simpler the design is. Another rule is to use a minimal set of data items to describe an entity type and to have the set contain the elements in the union of Q and T, $Q \cup T$, of a processing-requirement specification. Thus, when the stored record corresponding to an occurrence of the entity type is accessed, the values of those data items in Q and T can be verified, processed, and retrieved. Data items in an entity type which are not members of $Q \cup T$ can be considered as added costs, because they are accessed but are not contributing either to the qualification condition or to the target set. Thus, the number of such data items should be kept minimal in an entity type. This rule will tend to cause sets of data items to be broken up into smaller sets, thus increasing the number of entity types in a database. Owing to the conflicting processing requirements of users, the access and manipulation of data items in more than one entity type may be unavoidable. Thus, a third obvious rule is to reduce the number of operations required to access and combine data items from two or several different entity types to form the Q's and T's of the process model. It is obvious that the above rules conflict with one another. They alone are not adequate for guiding the selection of a good design. Cost functions need to be introduced to estimate the costs of database operations associated with each alternative design.

We shall first define two parameters for cost computation of retrieval operations. Let c_1 be the cost for accessing the value of a data item which is not a member of $Q \cup T$ set. We note that c_1 may represent the added time for accessing the value and/or the added storage (buffer) for storing the value. Let N_1 be the number of such items accessed. Let c_2 be the cost of relating and concatenating the data items of two entity types and N_2 be the number of such pairs of entity types traversed, in order to form the data items in $Q \cup T$. A linear cost function can be defined as

$$F_{\text{retrieve}}(N_1, N_2) = c_1 N_1 + c_2 N_2$$

A design can be evaluated against each of the retrieval statements in a process schema. The cost of retrieval for the design would be

$$C_{\text{retrieval}} = \sum_{i=1}^{k_1} (c_1 N_{1i} + c_2 N_{2i}) \times f_i$$

where k_1 is the number of retrieval triplets in the process schema, f_i is the frequency of the ith retrieval triplet, N_{1i} is the number of data items accessed by the ith triplet which are not the members of $Q \cup T$, and N_{2i} is the number of pairs of entity types traversed to form the data items in $Q \cup T$.

The cost involved in operations other than retrieval, such as insertion, deletion, and update, can be quite different and should also be considered in designing the proper entity types. We shall use a simple example to illustrate this point. A more general example is given in Wang [27].

Assume that we are interested in evaluating the following two alternative schemas:

Schema 1: R1 $(\underline{K_1 K_2 K_3 K_4 K_5} A_1 A_2)$
              R2 $(\underline{K_1 K_2 K_3} B_1 B_2 B_3)$
Schema 2: R12 $(\underline{K_1 K_2 K_3 K_4 K_5} A_1 A_2 B_1 B_2 B_3)$

The underscored data items in parentheses form the unique identifiers of the respective entity types. The expected insertion operations defined in a process schema may be used as one of the sources of information for selecting a good schema. For example, the insertion of the occurrences shown in Figure 4.1 demonstrates that insertion into Schema 2 would be better because it involves inserting 30 data items versus 33 items in the case of Schema 1. The amount of work involved in updating data in these two schemas can differ, depending on the data to be updated.

R_1	K_1	K_2	K_3	K_4	K_5	A_1	A_2
	K_{11}	K_{21}	K_{31}	K_{41}	K_{51}	A_{11}	A_{21}
	K_{11}	K_{21}	K_{31}	K_{42}	K_{52}	A_{12}	A_{22}
	K_{12}	K_{22}	K_{32}	K_{42}	K_{52}	A_{13}	A_{23}

R_2	K_1	K_2	K_3	B_1	B_2	B_3
	K_{11}	K_{21}	K_{31}	B_{11}	B_{21}	B_{31}
	K_{12}	K_{22}	K_{32}	B_{12}	B_{22}	B_{32}

R_{12}	K_1	K_2	K_3	K_4	K_5	A_1	A_2	B_1	B_2	B_3
	K_{11}	K_{21}	K_{31}	K_{41}	K_{51}	A_{11}	A_{21}	B_{11}	B_{21}	B_{31}
	K_{11}	K_{21}	K_{31}	K_{42}	K_{52}	A_{11}	A_{22}	B_{11}	B_{21}	B_{31}
	K_{12}	K_{22}	K_{32}	K_{42}	K_{52}	A_{13}	A_{23}	B_{12}	B_{22}	B_{32}

Figure 4.1 Different number of data items involved in the same insertion.

For example, if one updates B_1 B_2 B_3 values, Schema 1 will be better than Schema 2 because less redundancy of B_1 B_2 B_3 values exists in R2 than in R12. But if one updates K_1 K_2 K_3 K_4 K_5, then Schema 2 will be better because only one entity type is involved and no redundant values of K's exist.

To incorporate the costs associated with insertion, update, and deletion into the cost computation for a process schema, we shall call the cost of inserting a single data item into a database c_3, the cost of updating one data item c_4, and the cost of deleting a data item c_5. Since insertion, update, and deletion operations generally require searching the database for the point of insertion or for the data items to be updated or deleted, the cost function for these three operations should, therefore, involve the parameters for retrieval as follows:

$$F_{\text{insert}}(N_1, N_2, N_3) = c_1 N_1 + c_2 N_2 + c_3 N_3$$

$$F_{\text{update}}(N_1, N_2, N_4) = c_1 N_1 + c_2 N_2 + c_4 N_4$$

$$F_{\text{delete}}(N_1, N_2, N_5) = c_1 N_1 + c_2 N_2 + c_5 N_5$$

where N_3, N_4, and N_5 are, respectively, the numbers of data items to be inserted, updated, and deleted by the triplets of a process schema.

A schema design can be evaluated based on the costs for implementing the triplets in a process schema. The cost for the design would be the sum of the costs computed for all the triplets as shown below:

$$C_{\text{total}} = \sum_{i=1}^{k_1} F_{\text{retrieve}}(N_{1i}, N_{2i}) \times f_i + \sum_{j=1}^{k_2} F_{\text{insert}}(N_{1j}, N_{2j}, N_{3j}) \times f_j$$

$$+ \sum_{l=1}^{k_3} F_{\text{update}}(N_{1l}, N_{2l}, N_{4l}) \times f_l + \sum_{m=1}^{k_4} F_{\text{delete}}(N_{1m}, N_{2m}, N_{5m}) \times f_m$$

where k_1, k_2, k_3, and k_4 are, respectively, the number of retrieval, insertion, update, and deletion triplets in a process schema, the f's are the frequencies, and the N's are the number of data items processed by the triplets. If an operation is missing from the process schema, its corresponding term will become zero. The costs of other primitive database operations, such as locking an item, a record, or a file for integrity control or opening a file for processing, can also be added to the cost computation. Among a set of alternative schemata, the one with minimal total cost would be the best schema for the design.

In our previous example, there are three retrieval triplets and one update triplet in the process schema. For the single entity types EMPLOYEE (EMP#, NAME, AGE, RACE, WEIGHT, HEIGHT, SALARY, YEAR-OF-SERVICE), the total estimated cost would be

$$C_{\text{total}} = (2c_1 \times 20) + (4c_1 \times 30) + (5c_1 \times 1) + (7c_1 + c_4) \times 20$$

$$= 305c_1 + 20c_4$$

For the two entity types EMP1 and EMP2, the estimated cost would be

$$C_{total} = 0 + 0 + c_2 \times 1 + (3c_1 + c_4) \times 20$$
$$= 60c_1 + c_2 + 20c_4$$

The design of the two entity types would be better than a single entity type if $245c_1 > c_2$. The values of c_1 and c_2 should be based on a particular implementation. The physical database design parameters and the hardware system characteristics and constraints will have to be taken into consideration.

4.3 PROCESSING-REQUIREMENT MODELING AT THE QUERY LEVEL

If a database is defined by a network of interconnected entity types and relationship (association) types, a *query* is a user's interaction with the database. It can be defined by a traversal of the network starting from one node (entity or relationship type) to another until reaching a destination node to perform a database operation. At each node a set of occurrences is accessed and is used to restrict the access of the next node. Therefore, one can use the data traversal path and the data operation to describe a general query type to be used by the database user. Several works have taken this approach to model processing requirements. Gerritsen uses a set of anticipated queries expressed in a language called HI-IQ [7, 8] in an automatic process to determine record contents and the hierarchical relationships of record types. The work by Raver and Hubbard [19] presents a technique for automated logical database design which uses the frequency of path traversal to determine the physical parents of data segments in an IMS hierarchical model. The work by Housel, Waddle, and Yao [9] introduces a language called TASL for describing the processing requirements for a functional data model proposed for logical database design. The use of TASL will be described in Chapter 9. The works by Su et al. [12, 16, 23, 24] use a number of high-level, nonprocedural access patterns for describing data traversals for the purpose of program description and database design. In the following presentation, this latter approach will be used to illustrate the principles of modeling processing requirements at the query level.

The path of data traversal can be described using a small number of primitive access patterns, each of which involves the data of one or two nodes. Four basic access patterns exist and are believed adequate for traversing the network of entity types and relationships [23]. They are explained below using a simple model of PART and SUPPLIER and their association SUPPLY, as shown in Figure 4.2.

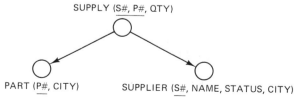

SUPPLY (S#, P#, QTY)

PART (P#, CITY)   SUPPLIER (S#, NAME, STATUS, CITY)

Figure 4.2 A SUPPLIER-PART data model.

In the network representation, all associations between entity types are represented by explicit nodes. The directed edges connect entity nodes to the association node. The underlined data items in Figure 4.2 are unique identifiers (keys).

Pattern 1 Examples:

```
ACCESS PART (*: CITY)
ACCESS SUPPLY (QTY: S#, P#)
ACCESS SUPPLIER (NAME, STATUS: S#, NAME)
```

Each of the examples above establishes an entry in the network. It accesses the occurrences of either an entity type or an association type based on some qualification condition defined over the set of data items enclosed in parentheses. The first access pattern causes a set of PART occurrences to be accessed which satisfy the CITY condition. The asterisk denotes the entire occurrence. The second access pattern accesses the quantity QTY of some specified S#-P# pair. The third access pattern accesses suppliers' names and status using S# and NAME as qualification conditions. Thus, the items on the left of the colon form the target set and the items on the right form the qualification set.

Pattern 2 Examples:

```
ACCESS SUPPLY VIA PART
ACCESS SUPPLY (*: P#) VIA SUPPLIER
```

Pattern 2 allows upward traversal from an entity type to an association type in which the entity type is involved. Each of the examples above accesses a set of occurrences from an association type node. The access is restricted by the occurrences of PART and SUPPLIER. For example, the first pattern accesses those occurrences of SUPPLY whose P# is the same as the P#s of the occurrences of PART. Since no other qualification is used to further restrict the selection of the occurrences, the specification of the target and qualification sets for SUPPLY would not be necessary. Access of entire occurrences is thus implied. The second pattern accesses those occurrences of SUPPLY whose S#s are the same as the S#s of the occurrences of SUPPLIER and whose P# is subject to some qualification condition. This pattern of data access allows a set of association occurrences to be accessed based on a set of entity occurrences involved in the association.

Pattern 3 Examples:

```
ACCESS SUPPLIER (*: STATUS) VIA SUPPLY
ACCESS PART (*: CITY) VIA SUPPLY
```

Pattern 3 allows downward traversal from an association type to a participating entity type of the association. The explanation of the examples above is similar to that for those of Pattern 2.

Pattern 4 Example:

ACCESS PART VIA SUPPLIER THROUGH (PART.CITY, SUPPLIER.CITY)

Pattern 4 allows two arbitrary nodes (entity types and/or association types) to be related (or JOINed in relational terminology) through some comparable data items. This is different from Patterns 2 and 3, which relate two nodes through their unique identifiers (i.e., through their association).

The four basic access patterns above can be used to give a high-level description of query types to be run against a database. Some examples of query types using the network description of a database shown in Figure 4.3 are given below. The network representations of the query types called query graphs are also given.

Query Type Example 1:

English: Get the NAME and STATUS of a supplier who supplies a certain quantity of parts manufactured by a manufacturer with a certain name. This type of query will be run approximately 30 times a day.
Process schema:

```
QUERY (30)
BEGIN
   ACCESS MANUFACTURER (*: NAME);
   ACCESS MADE VIA MANUFACTURER;
   ACCESS PART VIA MADE;
   ACCESS SUPPLY (*:QTY) VIA PART;
   ACCESS SUPPLIER (NAME, STATUS:) VIA SUPPLY;
   RETRIEVE;
END.
```

The query above is modeled by a sequence of access patterns describing the traversal path and the operation (retrieval, in this example) to be performed on the data items reached. The process schema can be simplified as below because each access pattern

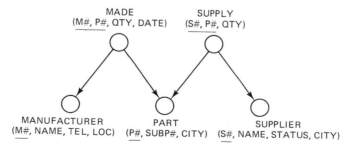

Figure 4.3   A MANUFACTURER-PART-SUPPLIER database.

is using the occurrences accessed by the preceding pattern as the context of access without any further qualification.

```
QUERY (30);
BEGIN
  ACCESS MANUFACTURER ( * : NAME);
  ACCESS MADE;
  ACCESS PART;
  ACCESS SUPPLY ( * : QTY);
  ACCESS SUPPLIER (NAME, STATUS);
  RETRIEVE;
END.
```

Figure 4.4 is a graphical representation of the traversal path and operation described by the process schema. In the figure, the double arrow represents Pattern 1 access, upward arrows represent Pattern 2 access, and downward arrows represent Pattern 3 access. Note here that the semantics of the directed edges in query graphs is different from that of the edges in the network representation of entity and association types such as in Figure 4.3.

Query Type Example 2:

English: Update the QTY of those subparts which are supplied by a certain supplier and which are subparts of a certain given part. Frequency of this type of query is 5.

Process schema:

```
QUERY (5);
BEGIN
  ACCESS SUPPLIER ( * : NAME);
  TI = ACCESS SUPPLY;
  ACCESS PART ( * : P # );
  ACCESS PART VIA PART THROUGH (PART.P # , PART.SUBP # );
  ACCESS TI (QTY:);
  UPDATE;
END.
```

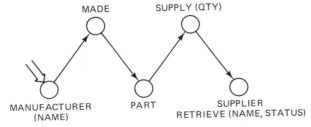

MADE   SUPPLY (QTY)

MANUFACTURER   PART   SUPPLIER
(NAME)   RETRIEVE (NAME, STATUS)

Figure 4.4   A query graph for Example 1.

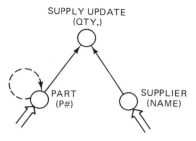

Figure 4.5 A query graph for Example 2.

In the process schema, TI temporarily holds the occurrences accessed for later reference.

This example illustrates that a query may have several entry points to the network; the access loops may occur in some nodes. The dotted-line arrow in Figure 4.5 is used to represent the Type 4 access pattern.

It is possible to use a query graph to summarize the access patterns of a set of query types which are expected to be formulated by a user or a community of users. Taking the PART-SUPPLIER example again, the combined query graph in Figure 4.6 illustrates the traversal of PART and SUPPLIER entity types and their association by a set of queries. The numbers on the arrows indicate the frequencies of path traversal in a set of queries which have different frequencies of use. For example, the set of queries make 70 entry accesses to SUPPLIER, and 30 of these accesses traverse to the SUPPLY node. The frequency number is the product of the number of times a traversal path is taken by the set of queries and the frequencies of each query execution.

In logical database design, the task of the database designer is to derive external data models which will best support users' processing requirements and to derive a conceptual model which will best support the community users' processing needs. Process models at the query level using the paths of traversal and frequencies can be used to guide the design of optimal data models. The following example illustrates their possible applications.

In an external model or a conceptual model, there often is more than one way of modeling an association between two entity types. For example, Figure 4.7 shows

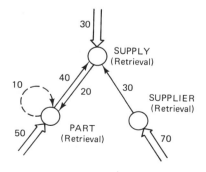

Figure 4.6 A query graph summarizing the frequency of data traversals.

three alternative schemas for defining an association between PART and SUPPLIER with a one-to-one mapping in a relational database (similar examples can be given for the case of the network model and the hierarchical model). In Schema 1, the association between PART and SUPPLIER is explicitly modeled by a separate relation SUPPLY. Figure 4.6 represents a number of data traversals using Schema 1. If Schema 2 is used, the combined query graph shown in Figure 4.6 will become the one shown in Figure 4.8(a). Figure 4.8(b) shows the query graph using Schema 3. Comparing the query graphs in Figures 4.6, 4.8(a), and 4.8(b), we find that if Schema 2 is used, we can eliminate the 40 accesses from PART to SUPPLY and 20 accesses from SUPPLY to PART which are necessary if Schema 1 is used. If Schema 3 is used, we can eliminate the 30 accesses from SUPPLIER to SUPPLY. These accesses represent the "JOIN" of PART and SUPPLY relations over P# and of SUPPLIER and SUPPLY relations over S#. The actual implementation of the JOIN operation is quite time-consuming. If the frequency of access f is the only parameter considered, we can say that Schema 2 is better than Schema 3 and Schema 1.

Besides the access frequency, other parameters for the evaluation of query graphs (thus of schemas) can be introduced and used to determine the estimated work loads associated with the data accesses and operations described by query graphs. Some possible parameters are given on the following page.

Schema 1.

      PART (P#, SUBP#, PNAME, COLOR)
      SUPPLIER (S#, SNAME, CITY)
      SUPPLY (S#, P#, QTY)

Schema 2.

      PART (P#, SUBP#, PNAME, COLOR, S#, QTY)
      SUPPLIER (S#, SNAME, CITY)

Schema 3.

      PART (P#, SUBP#, PNAME, COLOR)
      SUPPLIER (S#, SNAME, CITY,P#, QTY)

Figure 4.7 Alternative schemas for a one-to-one association.

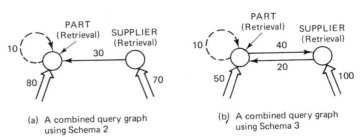

(a) A combined query graph using Schema 2

(b) A combined query graph using Schema 3

Figure 4.8 Combined query graphs using different schemas.

1. $n =$ the estimated number of occurrences associated with an entity type or an association type. The value of n can be used to estimate the amount of processing involved in "joining" an entity type to an association, e.g., ACCESS PART VIA SUPPLY.

2. $p =$ the average size of m in a 1-to-m mapping between two entity types. The value of p can be used to determine the estimated number of occurrences to be produced on an average by a join, e.g., the number of occurrences resulted in ACCESS PART VIA SUPPLY. This number can determine the amount of output or other subsequent storage operations involved, such as deletion, insertion, and update.

3. $k =$ the multiplicity of a non-key data item, which is the number of distinct values associated with the data item. The values of k associated with the non-key data items can be used to determine the number of occurrences to be obtained if the "projection" operation is performed over the data items. The smaller the k values are, the fewer occurrences will result, which often means less storage for holding the results and shorter output time. The value of k can also be used to determine the amount of work associated with an update operation. For example, if there are five different colors of parts existing in the entity type PART ($k = 5$) whose estimated number of occurrences is 100 ($n = 100$), then the update of a color in PART would involve an average of 20 occurrences.

4. $h =$ the number of entity and association types which define an external model or the conceptual model. The value of h is a measure of the complexity of a model. Generally speaking, the smaller the value of h, the better is the design. The reasons are that the design would be simpler for the user or DBA to understand and would involve less storage and processing overhead, because entity and association types are fewer. The value of h can be obtained by simply counting the number of entity and association types defined in the conceptual schema. However, there is a limit to this. If we put everything into a few entity types, the entity types will become complex themselves. An extreme example is the universal relation. Therefore, this parameter has to be weighed against those discussed in the paragraph on "Identification of proper data entities" in Section 4.2.

The list of parameters above might not be complete. However, it should give a fairly good estimation of the work load involved in the access patterns and operations characterizing a set of queries. It should be noted that the parameters are useful for selecting alternative logical designs and are independent of the implementation strategies used in the physical database. However, the relative importance of these parameters and their relationship should be determined based on the physical database design considerations, such as buffer size, secondary storage access time, indexing structure, and storage requirement.

To combine all the parameters described above, we can define for each arrow in a query graph a work load w_i which is a function of n, p, k, and h; i.e., $w_i = F(n, p, k, h)$, where $1 \leq i \leq l$ and l is the number of arrows in the graph. The objective of logical database design is, in one aspect, to select a schema (external or conceptual) whose associated query graph has a minimal total work load, which can be defined as

$$\sum_{i=1}^{l} (f_i \times w_i)$$

where f_i is the frequency of ith traversal path.

The values of n, p, and k are about the data defined in the data model. They should be given in the data schema rather than the process schema. Thus, a conceptual data schema and its associated process schema for the combined query graph of Figure 4.6 can be as shown in Figure 4.9. The process schema defines a set of possible queries which can be combined to form the query graph of Figure 4.6.

The technique of modeling queries described above makes use of the concepts of target set, qualification set, and operation set introduced for modeling at the data-item level. In addition to these concepts, the path traversals expressed in terms of high-level access patterns, their frequencies, and a number of parameters for estimating the work load involved in the path traversals provide additional information about applications' processing requirements. The process schema defined for an application would contain a set of abstract query types, each of which represents an abstraction of a set of similar queries.

Data Schema:

      ENTITY PART ($n = 5000$, KEY $= P\#$)
         P# DEC (3);
         SUBP# DEC (3) ($k = 10$);
         PNAME CHAR (20) ($k = 4000$);
         COLOR CHAR (10) ($k = 40$);

      ENTITY SUPPLIER ($n = 150$, KEY $= S\#$)
         S# DEC (5);
         SNAME CHAR (25) ($k = 15$);
         CITY CHAR (20) ($k = 4$);

      ASSOCIATION SUPPLY ($n = 2000$, KEY $= (S\#, P\#)$, $S\# : P\# = 1 : m$, p $= 100$)
         S# DEC (5);
         P# DEC (3);
         QTY DEC (3) ($k = 2000$);

Figure 4.9 A conceptual schema and its associated process schema.

Process Schema:

```
QUERY (40)
BEGIN
      ACCESS SUPPLIER (SNAME, CITY; S#);
      RETRIEVE;
END;

QUERY (10)
BEGIN
      ACCESS SUPPLIER (*: CITY);
      ACCESS SUPPLY;
      ACCESS PART (PNAME: );
      RETRIEVE;
END;

QUERY (20)
BEGIN
      ACCESS SUPPLIER (*: SNAME);
      ACCESS SUPPLY (QTY: );
      RETRIEVE;
END;

QUERY (20)
BEGIN
      ACCESS SUPPLY (QTY: S#, P#);
      RETRIEVE;
END;

QUERY (10)
BEGIN
      ACCESS SUPPLY (*: S#);
      ACCESS PART (PNAME, CITY:);
      RETRIEVE;
END;

QUERY (40)
BEGIN
      ACCESS PART (*: COLOR);
      ACCESS SUPPLY (QTY: );
      RETRIEVE;
END;

QUERY (10)
BEGIN
      ACCESS PART (*: COLOR);
      ACCESS PART (PNAME: ) VIA PART THROUGH (PART.P#, PART.SUBP#);
      RETRIEVE;
END;
```

Figure 4.9   (*continued*)

4.4 PROCESSING-REQUIREMENT MODELING AT THE TRANSACTION LEVEL

A *transaction* is a sequence of database operations which, when completed, will bring the database to a consistent state. It can be described by an ordered set of "queries" as defined before. The order of query execution can be important in at least the following two cases: First, the sequence of events which occurs in the operation of an enterprise requires that one database operation always be performed after another operation. For example, an enterprise always retrieves data from the PART-IN-STOCK file after the access to the ORDER-MASTER file. Second, a sequence of operations can be triggered by another operation in order to enforce the integrity of a database. For example, an insertion of a record about a part sold to some customer may trigger the update of the number of the parts in stock.

Different from modeling at the query level at which queries are considered as unrelated, modeling at the transaction level provides additional information about the relationship and the order of database operations. This information can be used for selecting alternative logical designs. Some examples are given below:

Assume that a user's view of a database is as shown in Figure 4.10—i.e., two entity types and their association with 1:n mapping. The following transaction shows that the deletion of an employee occurrence is always followed by the deletion of data associated with the employee's dependents. It is estimated that the transaction will be run 200 times a day.

```
TRANSACTION (200/day)

BEGIN
      QUERY
            BEGIN
                  T = ACCESS EMPLOYEE (*:ENAME);
                        DELETE;
            END;

      QUERY
            BEGIN
                  ACCESS EMP_DEP VIA T;
                  ACCESS DEPENDENT;
                  DELETE;
            END;
      END;
```

(a)

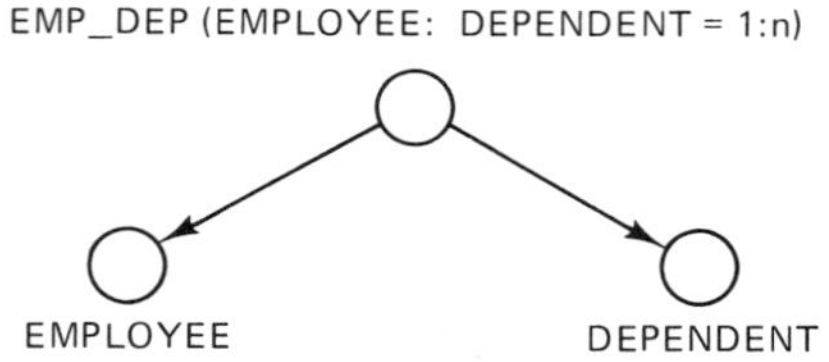

EMP_DEP (EMPLOYEE: DEPENDENT = 1:n)

EMPLOYEE   DEPENDENT

(b)

Figure 4.10 Two entity types and their association.

The semantics illustrated by Figure 4.10 can be modeled in different ways. For example, a relational conceptual schema can be one of the following alternatives:

1. EMPLOYEE (*ENAME*, DEPARTMENT, SALARY)
   DEPENDENT (*DNAME*, DAGE, DSEX)
   EMP_DEP (*ENAME*, *DNAME*)
2. EMPLOYEE (*ENAME*, DEPARTMENT, SALARY)
   DEPENDENT (*DNAME*, DAGE, DSEX, ENAME)
3. EMPLOYEE (*ENAME*, *DNAME*, DEPARTMENT, SALARY, DAGE, DSEX)

Although many redundant ENAME, DEPARTMENT, and SALARY values will occur in the EMPLOYEE relation in the third schema, and the relation is not in the third normal form, it can be the best model for the transaction above, since only one instead of two or three relations is involved and the deletion of a given ENAME will cause the deletion of tuples which contain the dependent information of the employee.

The order of database operations can be an important source of information for logical database design. Assume that the semantics of a database is that there is an association between EMPLOYEE and PROJECT entity types and the mapping between them is many-to-many. If the transactions defined in a process model show that the retrieval of PROJECT data is always followed by the retrieval of EMPLOYEE data associated with the projects, and no other ways of data access are expected, then the hierarchical model (IMS) of Figure 4.11(a) would be better than those of Figures 4.11(b) and 4.11(c).

An application program can be viewed as a structure of queries and/or transactions which manipulate a database to produce desirable results to the database user. To model the processing requirements of an application program, we can take into consideration the structural relationship and performance data of these queries and/or transaction executions, the conditions under which queries and transactions will be executed, and the expected frequency and percentage of time in which they will be executed.

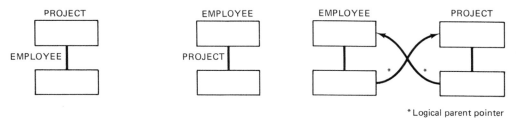

(a) A single physical database with project segment as the root

(b) A single physical database with employee segment as the root

(c) Two physical databases

Figure 4.11

Structural and performance data at the program level can be captured by procedural constructs in a program specification. In Housel, Waddle, and Yao [9, Chap. 9] the specification language TASL is given. Queries in an application program are defined in TASL in terms of operations on sets of values retrieved from the database. The values in these sets are then used to retrieve still other sets of values, similar to the VIA concept described in Section 4.3 on modeling at the query level. A number of functions are used to perform set operations to sort a set of values in ascending or descending order and to eliminate duplicates of a set of values, respectively. A READ statement is used to read in values to variables, and a WRITE statement can be used to output a variable or a list of variables. PL/1-like program control constructs are introduced in TASL to allow the specification of the control structure of an application program. They are "For *variable* IN *set* DO . . . ENDFOR" and "WHILE *expression* DO . . . ENDFOR," which can be used together or separately. A conditional statement IF in the forms of "IF *expression* THEN *statements* ENDIF" and "IF *expression* THEN *statements* ELSE *statements* ENDIF" is also used to specify the conditional branching. There are also operations for the specification of manipulations on the database. CREATE and DELETE allow values to be added to or deleted from a set. LINK and UNLINK are used to connect and disconnect values with a dependency occurrence.

To specify the frequencies with which an application performs data traversals and operations, volume indicators are used in various language constructs to provide the information concerning, for example, the expected number of items which will be in certain sets of values and the expected number of times the branches of IF statements are taken. These indicators are values which indicate either expected numbers or percentages. We shall, in the following example, adopt some of the TASL constructs and performance data to illustrate the modeling of the processing requirements in application programs.

Assume that a user's view of database is as shown in Figure 4.3. A process schema of an application program can be as below:

```
PROGRAM EXAMPLE (20 / month);

/* This program processes manufacturer, part, and supplier information;
   It is expected that the program will be run 20 times a month. */

VARIABLE P1, P2, P3 SET of P#;
         T SET OF PART;
BEGIN
    QUERY /* retrieve P# of parts made by a given manufacturer */
         BEGIN
              ACCESS MANUFACTURER (*: NAME);
         P1 =  ACCESS MADE (P#);
              RETRIEVE;
         END;
    QUERY /* retrieve P# of parts supplied in certain quantities by suppliers with a given
            name and status */
BEGIN
              ACCESS SUPPLIER (*: NAME, STATUS);
```

```
P2=            ACCESS SUPPLY (P#: QTY);
               RETRIEVE;
END;
P3=INTERSECT (P1,P2);/ *intersect P1 and P2 sets * /
IF P3=EMPTY THEN /* check if P3 set is empty * /
DO (10%) /*10% time the intersection will be empty; insert records so that the
         manufacturer will now make some part for the supplier(s) * /
         ACCESS PART (P#, SUBP#, CITY: );
         INSERT;
         ACCESS SUPPLY (S#, P#, QTY: );
         INSERT;
         ACCESS MADE (M#, P#, QTY, DATE: );
         INSERT;
END;
ELSE
DO (90%) /*90% time the intersection is not empty; output the part data * /
         ACCESS PART VIA P3;
         OUTPUT;   /* retrieve and output PART occurrences * /
END;
TRANSACTION
BEGIN
     QUERY/ * delete the parts in a given city * /
            BEGIN
            T = ACCESS PART (*: CITY);
                    DELETE;
            END;
     QUERY /*delete the SUPPLY data associated with the deleted parts* /
            BEGIN
                    ACCESS MADE VIA T;
                    DELETE;
            END;
     QUERY /* delete the MADE data associated with the deleted parts* /
            BEGIN
                    ACCESS MADE VIA T;
                    DELETE;
            END;
     END;
     END; /* end of transaction * /
END. /* end of program * /
```

The program specification above should be self-explanatory with the help of the comments. In addition to the performance data discussed in the previous levels of modeling, the application program specification provides the structural relationship of the queries and transactions and the percentage of times queries are expected to be performed. These data can be used to determine more accurately the sequence and the frequency of operations to be carried out in an application. The process schema above represents a high-level abstraction of the processing requirements of an application without the specificity of an actual application program. For example, in the schema, the specific search conditions about manufacturer's name, part number, supplier name, status, and so on are not given and the data values to be inserted into SUPPLIER, SUPPLY, and MADE relations are not provided. These specific details can be useful for physical database design, which in turn will determine the desirability of alternative logical designs.

4.5 SUMMARY

This chapter presents the techniques of modeling the processing requirements of database application in a systematic way. Processing requirements can be modeled at the data-item, the query, and the transaction levels. Each subsequent level contains more explicit information about processing requirements than the preceding one(s). At each level, a number of basic constructs useful for process modeling are presented, and parameters useful for the evaluation of alternative logical designs of a database are identified. Examples are given to illustrate the applications of process models at various steps of logical database design. These applications include the completeness and consistency checking of information requirements and the identification of proper grouping of data items to form data entities and associations, and the selection of the optimal logical structure from a number of alternative designs for the external and conceptual models of a database. In this chapter no attempt is made to determine and show the relationships among the set of identified performance parameters. The reason is that the relative importance of the performance parameters at the logical level can only be determined when physical database design parameters have been taken into consideration.

REFERENCES

1. Aurdal, E., "A Multi-level Procedure for Design of File Organizations," *CASCADE Working Paper* 36, University of Trondheim, Norway, June 1975.
2. Bernstein, P.A., "Synthesizing Third Normal Form Relations from Functional Dependencies," *ACM Transactions on Data Base Systems*, Vol. 1, No. 4 (December 1976).
3. Bubenko, J.A., S. Berild, E. Lindencronaohlin, and S. Nachmens, "From Information Structures to DBTG Data Structures," *Proc. of Conference on Data*, *SIGMOD FDT*, Vol. 8, No. 2 (1976).
4. Chen, P., "The Entity-Relationship Model—Toward a Unified View of Data," *ACM Trans. on Database Systems*, Vol. 1, No. 1 (March 1976), pp. 9–36.
5. Curtice, R.M., and P.E. Jones, Jr., "Key Steps in the Logical Design of Data Bases," *Proc. NYU Symposium on Database Design*, May 1978.
6. Fry, J.P., and B.K. Kahn, "A Stepwise Approach to Database Design," *Proc. ACM Southeast Regional Conf.*, pp. 34–43. New York: ACM, 1976.
7. Gerritsen, R., "A Preliminary System for the Design of DBTG Data Structures," *CACM*, Vol. 18, No. 10 (1975), pp. 551–557.
8. Gerritsen, R., "HI-IQ (Hierarchical Interactive Query): An Implemented Query Language for DBTG Databases," Technical Report, Department of Decision Sciences, The Wharton School, University of Pennsylvania, 1976.
9. Housel, B.C., V. Waddle, and S.B. Yao, "The Functional Dependency Model for Logical

Database Design," *Proc. Fifth International Conference on VLDB, Oct. 3–5, 1979.*

10. Hubbard, G., and N. Raver, "Automation of Logical File Design," *Proc. First International Conference on VDLB,* 1975, pp. 227–253.

11. Kahn, B.K., "A Method for Describing Information Required by the Database Design Process," *Proc. ACM SIGMOD Conference,* June 1976.

12. Lo, D.H., "A Logical Database Design Process," Technical Report, DSRDC 7901, Database Systems Research and Development Center, University of Florida, 1979.

13. Lum, N.Y., and H. Ling, "An Optimization Problem on the Selection of Secondary Keys," *Proc. ACM National Conference,* 1971, pp. 349–356.

14. Lum, V., et al., "1978 New Orleans Database Design Workshop Report," *Proc. Fifth International Conference on VLDB,* Oct. 1979, pp. 328–339.

15. Mitoma, M.F., and K.B. Irani, "Automatic Database Schema Design and Optimization," *Proc. First Conference on VLDB,* Sept. 1975.

16. Nations, J., and S.Y.W. Su, "Some DML Instruction Sequences for Application Program Analysis and Conversion," *Proc. ACM's SIGMOD Conference,* 1978, pp. 120–131.

17. Navathe, S.B., and M. Schkolnick, "View Representation in Logical Database Design," *Proc. ACM-SIGMOD International Conference on Management of Data,* June 1978.

18. Navathe, S.B., "Schema Analysis for Database Restructuring," *ACM Transactions on Database Systems,* Vol. 5, No. 2 (June 1980), pp. 157–184.

19. Raver, N., and G.U. Hubbard, "Automated Logical Data Base Design: Concepts and Applications," *IBM Systems J.,* Vol. 16, No. 3 (1977).

20. Schkolnick, M., "The Optimal Selection of Secondary Indices for Files," *Information Systems,* Vol. 1 (1975), pp. 141–146.

21. Sheppard, D., "Data Base Design Methodology—Parts I and II," *Auerbach Data Base Management Series,* Portfolios #23-01-01,02, 1977.

22. Smith, J.M., and D.C.P. Smith, "Database Abstractions: Aggregation and Generalization," *ACM Trans. on Database Systems,* Vol. 2, No. 2 (1977), pp. 105–133.

23. Su, S.Y.W., H. Lam, and D.H. Lo, "Transformation of Data Traversals and Operations in Application Programs to Account for Semantic Changes of Databases," *ACM Trans. on Database Systems,* Vol. 6, No. 2 (June 1981), pp. 255–294.

24. Su, S.Y.W., and D.H. Lo, "A Semantic Model for Conceptual Database Design," *Proc. International Conference on Entity-Relationship Approach to Systems Analysis and Design,* Dec. 1979, pp. 147–171.

25. Teorey, T.J., and J.P. Fry, "Logical Database Design: A Pragmatic Approach," Technical Report 78 DE 12, Database Systems Research Group, University of Michigan, Jan. 1978.

26. Teichroew, D., and E.A. Hershey, III, "PSL/PSA: A Computer-Aided Technique for Structured Documentation and Analysis of Information Processing Systems," *IEEE Transactions on Software Engineering,* Jan. 1977.

27. Wang, C.P., and H.H. Wedeking, "Segment Synthesis in Logical Data Base Design," *IBM J. Res. Develop.,* Vol. 19 (1975), pp. 71–77.

28. Yao, S.B., "An Attribute Based Model for Data Base Access Cost Analysis," *ACM Trans. Database Systems,* Vol. 2, No. 1 (March 1977), pp. 45–67.

29. Yao, S.B., S.B. Navathe, and J.L. Weldon, "An Integrated Approach to Logical Database Design," *Proc. NYU Symposium on Database Design,* May 1978.

5

Database Design Based on Entity and Relationship

Peter P. S. Chen
Louisiana State University

5.1 INTRODUCTION

In this chapter we describe a database design technique based on the concepts of entities and relationships. Compared with other techniques in this book, this technique is relatively simple and appears to many people to be quite natural. The reason is that it focuses on a fundamental issue of database design: what does a database represent? A database is a representation of our perceptions of the portion of the real world which is of interest to us. How do we represent our perceptions about the real world? We usually express them in terms of entities, relationships, attributes, and so on. Therefore, the identification of entities and relationships is a straightforward way for database design.

Although the technique is relatively simple, it can be used in the design of several major types of databases such as hierarchical, CODASYL, and relational types [34]. In some cases, the results of applying this technique will be similar to the results of applying a more complicated technique such as the relational normalization process for obtaining third normal forms.

It should be pointed out that similar concepts have been used in several other methods and systems (Falkenberg, PSL/PSA). Work to further extend this type of design approach is currently being conducted by researchers and practitioners. At the end of this chapter we discuss some recent literature concerning the technique presented here.

5.1.1 Problems in Logical Database Design

Logical database design is concerned with organizing data into a form acceptable to the underlying database system (see Figure 5.1). It is a very complicated process, since the database designer has to consider not only how to model the real world, but also the limitations of the database system and the efficiency of retrieval and updating. Examples of the difficulties are:

1. The database designer is constrained by the limited data-structure types supported by the database system. For example, the many-to-many relationships between two types of entities, such as the relationship between employees and projects, cannot be represented directly in many database systems.

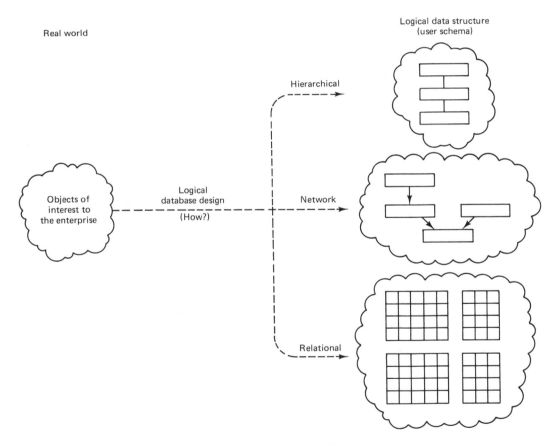

Figure 5.1 Logical database design.

2. The database designer may have to consider the access path of the records (i.e., how to access a particular record type).

3. The database designer may have to consider how to make the retrieval and updating more efficient. Thus the data about an entity in the real world may be put into more than one record for efficiency purposes.

There are two problems in the conventional database design approach:

1. The database designer has to consider many issues at the same time, which makes the database design task very difficult.

2. The final output of the logical database design process is the user schema (i.e., a description of the user view of database). Since the user schema represents the database designer's solution to the complicated issues mentioned above, it is easy to see why user schemata are usually difficult to understand and difficult to change.

5.1.2 The Entity-Relationship Approach

The technique to be described in this chapter is called the *entity-relationship* (*ER*) *approach*. Its key idea is to concentrate on the design of the conceptual schema, which is an intermediate stage in logical database design (see Figure 5.2). The database designer first identifies the entities and relationships which are of interest to the enterprise using the *entity-relationship* (*ER*) *diagrammatic technique*. At this stage the designer should view the data from the point of view of the whole enterprise (not that of a particular application programmer). Therefore, we shall call this description of data the "enterprise conceptual schema" or simply the "enterprise schema." The enterprise conceptual schema should be a "pure" representation of the real world and should be independent of storage and efficiency considerations. The database designer first designs the enterprise conceptual schema and then translates it to a user schema for his database system (see Figure 5.2). The advantages of the two-phase approach are:

1. The division of functionalities and labor into two phases makes the database design process simpler and better organized.

2. The enterprise schema is easier to design than the final user schema, since it need not be restricted by the capabilities of the database system and is independent of the storage and efficiency considerations.

3. The enterprise schema is more stable than the user schema. If one wanted to change from one database system to another, one would probably have to change the user schema but not the enterprise schema, since the enterprise schema is in principle independent of the database system used. What needs to be done is to remap the enterprise schema to a user schema suitable for the new database system. Similarly, if one wanted to change the user schema to

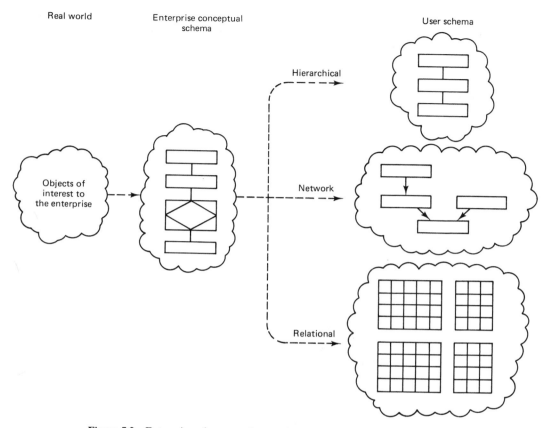

Figure 5.2 Enterprise schema–an intermediate step in logical data base design.

optimize a new application program, one would need not to change the enterprise schema but rather to remap the enterprise schema to a new user schema.

4. The enterprise schema expressed by the entity-relationship diagram is more easily understood by non-EDP people.

5.2 ENTITY-RELATIONSHIP (ER) DIAGRAM

In this section we introduce an entity-relationship (ER) diagrammatic technique. We first discuss how to represent entities and relationships and then explain how to represent their properties.

EMPLOYEE   STOCK-HOLDER

Figure 5.3 Entity types are represented by rectangular-shaped box.

5.2.1 Entities and Relationships

5.2.1.1 Elementary Entity Type

An elementary entity is a "thing" which can be distinctly identified in our minds and is of interest to the enterprise. Entities can be classified into different *entity types*, such as EMPLOYEE and STOCK-HOLDER (see Figure 5.3). In the ER diagram, an entity type is represented by a rectangular-shaped box (see Figure 5.3).

There are many "things" in the real world. Some of them are of interest to the enterprise; the rest are not. It is the responsibility of the database designer to select the entity types which are important to his or her company.

5.2.1.2 Relationship Type

Relationships may exist between entities. For example, "IS-MARRIED-TO" is a relationship between two person entities (see Figure 5.4). Relationships can be classified into different *relationship types*. For instance, "WORK-FOR" and "MANAGE" are two different relationship types between two entity types, PROJ (project) and EMP (employee). There are several versions of ER diagrammatic techniques [13, 22]. In the diagrammatic notation used in this chapter, a relationship type is represented by a line connected to related entity types (see Figure 5.5). The "N" and "1" notions associated with the relationship type "MANAGE" in Figure 5.5 indicate that each project has only one manager, but that an employee can be the manager of many projects. The "M" and "N" associated with the relationship type PROJ-EMP indicate that the relationship is a many-to-many mapping. That is, each project may consist of several employees and each employee may be associated with more than one project. Note that other types of mapping between entities are also possible. For instance, the relationship type IS-MARRIED-TO is a one-to-one mapping between person entities (Figure 5.6).

"IS-MARRIED-TO"

Figure 5.4 IS-MARRIED-TO as a relationship between two person entities.

Figure 5.5 Relationship types are represented by lines.

IS-MARRIED-TO

Figure 5.6 IS-MARRIED-TO as a relationship type between person entities.

PART #	SUPPLIER #	PROJ #
68	3	1
68	5	2
10	3	2
10	3	3
17	2	1
17	5	1

Figure 5.7 Information about PART-SUPP-PROJ relationships.

It is possible to define a relationship type among more than two entity types. For example, PART-SUPP-PROJ, which describes what parts are supplied by particular suppliers to particular projects (Figure 5.7), is a relationship type defined on three entity types: PART, SUPP (supplier), and PROJ (Figure 5.8). Note that a three-way relationship usually cannot be replaced by three binary relationships. As an example, the three-way relationship PART-SUPP-PROJ in Figure 5.7 is replaced by three binary relationships: PART-SUPP, SUPP-PROJ, and PROJ-PART (see Figure 5.9). However, if we want to construct the three-way relationship back from these three binary relationships, we will get some "nonfacts" (see the starred entries in Figure 5.10).

There are many types of relationships between entities, and some of them may not be of interest to the enterprise; the database designer is responsible for the selection of the relationship types relevant to the enterprise. He should also specify the types of mapping of the relationship types (e.g., one-to-one, one-to-many, and many-to-many).

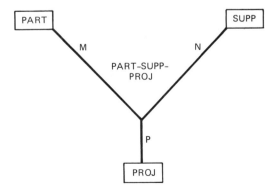

Figure 5.8 PART-SUPP-PROJ as a relationship type.

PART #	SUPP #
68	3
68	5
10	3
17	2
17	5

SUPP #	PROJ #
3	1
3	2
3	3
5	1
5	2
2	1

PROJ #	PART #
1	68
1	17
2	10
2	68
3	10

Figure 5.9 Information about three binary relationships: PART-SUPP, SUPP-PROJ, and PROJ-PART.

	PART #	SUPP #	PROJ #
	68	3	1
*	68	3	2
*	68	5	1
	68	5	2
	10	3	2
	10	3	3
	17	2	1
	17	5	1

Figure 5.10 Information generated from three binary relationships in Figure 5.9.

5.2.1.3 Composite Entity Type

A *composite entity* is an entity formed by other entities (elementary entities or composite entities). For example, "SHIPPING" is a composite entity type formed by two entity types: PRODUCT and CUSTOMER (Figure 5.11). Note that a composite entity type is represented by a special rectangular box. In some sense, a composite entity type is similar to a relationship type. The distinction is that a relationship cannot have properties while a composite entity can. This is different from the notations used in some previous work [6] in which relationships can have properties. By disallowing properties for relationships, we may make the modeling job simpler for some people. That is, the distinction between entities and relationships is clear, since the former will have properties and the latter will not.

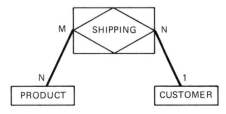

Figure 5.11 SHIPPING as a composite entity type.

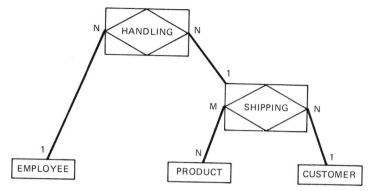

Figure 5.12 A composite entity type can build on top of other composite entity types.

Note that it is possible to build a composite entity on top of other composite entities (and elementary entities). For example, "HANDLING" is a composite entity type formed by an elementary entity type EMPLOYEE and a composite entity type SHIPPING (see Figure 5.12).

In order to identify which entity types are the "components" of a composite entity type, we will connect the "component" entity types to the corners of the diamond-shaped box of the "composite" entity type (see Figure 5.12). When we connect this composite entity type to form another composite entity type, we will use the same convention to make the diagram more readable.

Another suggestion is to use "nouns" for elementary entity types, "verbs" for relationships, and "gerunds" for composite entities. This rule of thumb will also make the modeling job simpler. For further information on the correspondence between the ERD and English sentence structures, please refer to [12].

5.2.2 Properties of Entities

5.2.2.1 Attributes and Values

Elementary entities and composite entities have properties which can be expressed in terms of attribute-value pairs. For example, in the statement "the AGE OF EMPLOYEE x is 24," "AGE" is an "attribute" of employee x, and "24" is the "*value*" of the attribute AGE. Values can be classified into different *value types*, such as NO-OF-YEARS, QUANTITY, and COLOR. In the ER diagrammatic notation, a value type is represented by a circle (see Figure 5.13), and an attribute is represented by an arrow directed from the entity type to the desired value type.

In some cases an attribute may have more than one value for a given entity. For instance, "PHONE-NO" of employee x may have two values: 253-6606 and 253-9999. In this case we put "$1:n$" in the arrow to indicate that it is a multivalued attribute. This is similar to the "repeating group" concept in conventional data

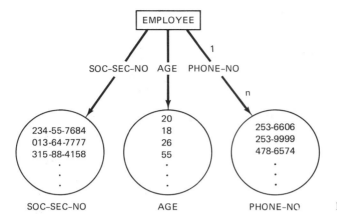

Figure 5.13 Value types and attributes.

processing. However, many attributes, such as "AGE" and "SOC-SEC-NO," are single-valued. For simplicity, we do not associate anything such as "1 : 1" with the arrows in the ER diagram for such attributes.

So far we have considered only the attributes of elementary entities. Now we shall discuss the properties of composite entities. For instance, we may want to know when employee x started working on a particular project. The STARTING-DATE is an attribute neither of EMPLOYEE nor of PROJ, since its value depends on both the particular employee and the project involved. Therefore, STARTING-DATE is an attribute of the composite entity WORKING. Another example is PERCENTAGE-OF-EFFORT, which is the percentage of time that an employee devotes to a particular project (see Figure 5.14). The "attribute of composite entity" is also called the "attribute of relationship." This concept is similar to the "relationship data" in "network" (CODASYL) type database systems, and similar to the "intersection data" in hierarchical-type (IMS-type) database systems.

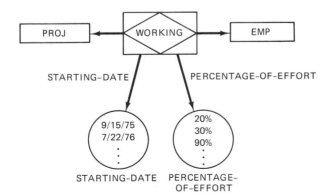

Figure 5.14 Attributes of composite entity.

5.2.2.2 Elementary Entity Identifier

The elementary entities discussed so far are those which exist in our minds or can be identified by pointing our finger at them. When someone asks, "What color is it?", "it" either is understood by both the speaker and the listener or is identified by pointing a finger at the subject. This identification scheme can work for very few objects, and we will run into difficulties when we want to communicate the information about a variety of objects to many different people. Therefore, in both daily conversation and computer data processing, we need another scheme to identify entities.

A commonly used scheme is the use of attribute-value pairs to identify entities. Every entity has many attributes, but which one should be chosen? The answer is that the attributes chosen should be able to uniquely identify the entities. For instance, we may use the attribute NAME to identify the employees in a small company but not in a large company. These chosen attributes of the entity are called the *entity identifiers*. In some cases it may be difficult or inconvenient to use available attributes as the entity identifier. What we may do is to create an artificial attribute which can positively identify the entities. Examples are "SOC-SEC-NO," "EMP-NO," "PART-NO," and "PROJ-NO." The concept of "entity identifier" is similar to that of "primary key" in conventional data processing.

5.2.2.3 Relationship and Composite Entity Identifiers

Relationships are identified by utilizing the identifiers of the entities involved in the relationship. For example, if a project is identified by its PROJ-NO and an employee by EMP-NO, then the WORK-FOR relationship is identified by *both* PROJ-NO and EMP-NO. In some situations a relationship type is defined between two occurrences of the same entity type. For instance, IS-MARRIED-TO is a relationship type defined between occurrences of the same entity type, PERSON. In order to positively identify such relationships, we not only use the entity identifier but also indicate what role the entity plays in the relationship. In the case of MARRIAGE, we shall attach the role names HUSBAND and WIFE to the entity identifier NAME, where HUSBAND and WIFE are the "roles" they play in the relationship MARRIAGE.

Similarly, composite entities are identified by utilizing the identifiers of the "component" entities (which may be composite entities themselves).

5.2.3 Special Entity and Relationship Types

In this section we discuss several special entity types and relationship types which are commonly encountered.

5.2.3.1 Existence Dependency

The existence of an entity may depend on the existence of another entity type. For example, the existence of CHILDREN entities in the database depends on the existence of the associated employees. In other words, if an employee leaves the company, we shall not keep track of his children. Figure 5.15 illustrates the ER diagram for this situation. CHILDREN is represented by a double-rectangular-shaped box, which means that it is a "weak" entity type. The existence of a weak entity depends on the existence of other entities. The "E" indicated that it is an "existence-dependent" relationship; the arrow indicates the direction of the dependency.

It is possible that the "existence-dependent" relationship is a many-to-many mapping. For example, if the father leaves the company, the CHILDREN entities may still exist if their mother is still an employee of the company. This situation is represented in the ER diagram shown in Figure 5.16.

5.2.3.2 ID Dependency

If an entity cannot be uniquely identified by its own attributes and has to be identified by its relationships with other entities, then we say that it has "ID dependency" on other entities. For example, a street is unique only within a city, a city is unique only within a state, and a state is unique only within a country. In order to uniquely identify the address of a location, we have to specify the names of the city, state, and country in addition to the name of the street. The "ID dependency" is indicated by the "ID" along the relationship line, and the direction of the dependency is indicated by the arrow (see Figure 5.17); most ID dependencies are associated with existence dependencies. However, existence dependency does not imply ID dependency. For example, the CHILDREN entities in Figure 5.18 are

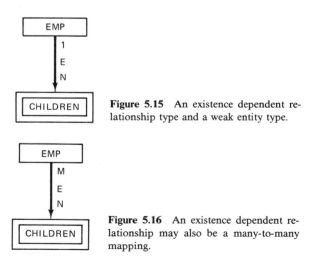

Figure 5.15 An existence dependent relationship type and a weak entity type.

Figure 5.16 An existence dependent relationship may also be a many-to-many mapping.

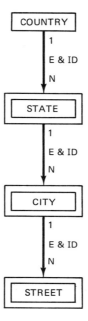

Figure 5.17 Existence dependency and ID dependency.

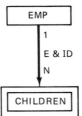

Figure 5.18 Existence dependency and ID dependency.

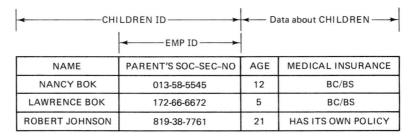

NAME	PARENT'S SOC–SEC–NO	AGE	MEDICAL INSURANCE
NANCY BOK	013-58-5545	12	BC/BS
LAWRENCE BOK	172-66-6672	5	BC/BS
ROBERT JOHNSON	819-38-7761	21	HAS ITS OWN POLICY

Figure 5.19 ID dependency.

←————— CHILDREN ID —————→			
CHILDREN-NO	NAME	AGE	MEDICAL INSURANCE
1011	NANCY BOK	12	BC/BS
1025	LAWRENCE BOK	21	BC/BS
1044	ROBERT JOHNSON	5	HAS ITS OWN POLICY

Figure 5.20   No ID dependency.

identified with their own attribute(s) and their parent(s)' ID (see Figure 5.19), while the CHILDREN entities in Figure 5.15 may be identified by their own CHILDREN-NO (see Figure 5.20).

5.3 TRANSLATION OF ER DIAGRAMS INTO DATA-STRUCTURE DIAGRAMS

5.3.1 Data-Structure Diagrams

The logical data structures of database supported by CODASYL (network) type database systems can be expressed in terms of data-structure diagrams. Figure 5.21 illustrates a data-structure diagram. Each rectangular box represents a record type, such as EMP and DEPENDENT. The arrow represents a data-structure set, which connects two record types together. The record type in which the arrow originates is the *owner record type* of the data-structure set, and the record type in which the arrow ends is the *member record type* of the data-structure set. In Figure 5.21, EMP is the owner record type, and DEPENDENT is the member record type. In a data-structure set, the owner record may have zero, one, or more member records (occurrences). A member record in a data-structure set has exactly one owner record. In our example, each employee record may be connected to many DEPENDENT records, or to none. However, each DEPENDENT record must be associated with exactly one EMP record. This is illustrated in Figure 5.22. Conceptually, the arrow represents a 1:n (one-to-many) association between the owner record type and the member record type. This kind of association can also be represented in table form (Figure 5.23).

Figure 5.24 illustrates a more complicated data structure. The EMPLOYEE record type is the owner record type of a data-structure set in which the

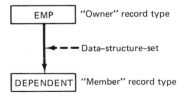

Figure 5.21   A data-structure diagram.

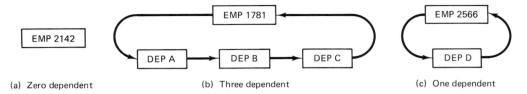

(a) Zero dependent   (b) Three dependent   (c) One dependent

Figure 5.22   An owner record may have zero, one, or more member records.

EMP–NO	DEPENDENT
1781	A
1781	B
1781	C
2566	D
⋮	⋮

Figure 5.23 One-to-many correspondence between EMPLOYEE and DEPENDENTS.

EMPLOYEE-SKILL is the member record type. The record type EMPLOYEE-SKILL is also the member record type of another data-structure set in which the SKILL record type is the owner record. Actually, the EMPLOYEE-SKILL record contains the cross-reference information about EMPLOYEES and SKILLS. This kind of information can be represented in table form as shown in Figure 5.25.

We can see from Figure 5.25 that an employee may have one or more skills and that usually more than one employee has a particular skill. Therefore, the relationship between employees and skills is $m:n$ (many-to-many). This $m:n$ correspondence between employees and skills can be derived from Figure 5.24. The data-structure sets in Figure 5.24 show that there exists a $1:m$ (one-to-many)

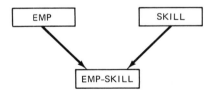

Figure 5.24   Two data-structure sets have the same member record type.

EMP–NO	SKILL
2142	COBOL
2142	PL/1
1781	COBOL
2566	PL/1
⋮	⋮

Figure 5.25 Cross-reference information about EMPLOYEES and SKILLS.

mapping between EMPLOYEE record type and EMPLOYEE-SKILL record type, and that a similar mapping $(1:n)$ exists between SKILL record type and the EMP-SKILL record type. Therefore, the correspondence between the EMP record and the skill record type is $m:n$ (many-to-many).

The data-structure diagram in Figure 5.24 can be implemented using a pointer array as shown in Figure 5.26. The data-structure set between EMP record type and SKILL record type is represented by solid lines and the data-structure set between the SKILL record type and the EMP-SKILL record type by dotted lines.

In Figure 5.26, how do we determine the skills of a particular employee? The first step is to locate the EMP record with EMP-NO = 2142 using a hashing algorithm or some other method. The second step is to find the first EMP-SKILL record related to this employee. After that, via the pointer shown by the dotted line, we can find a skill record with SKILL-NAME = COBOL. We then find the second EMPLOYEE-SKILL record related to the same employee record (via solid-line pointers). From the EMP-SKILL record, we can go through the dotted-line pointer to locate a SKILL record with SKILL-NAME = PL/1. We cannot then find any more EMP-SKILL records related to the same EMPLOYEE records (i.e., we have found the information we require: the employee with EMP-NO = 2142 has two skills: COBOL and PL/1).

How do we find all the employees with a particular skill, say COBOL? First, we locate the SKILL record with SKILL-NAME = COBOL. Then we retrieve all EMP-SKILL records related to the SKILL record. For each EMPLOYEE-SKILL record, we retrieve via the solid-line pointer the corresponding EMP record. By doing this, we know that there are two employees having the skill COBOL, and their employee numbers are 2142 and 1781.

Another way to implement the data-structure diagram in Figure 5.24 is to use "chains" as shown in Figure 5.27. The solid lines connect all the EMP-SKILL records related to the same EMP record. The dotted lines connect all the EMP-SKILL records related to the same SKILL record. Let us see how to find the skills of the employee with EMP-NO = 2142. The first step is to find the first EMP-SKILL record

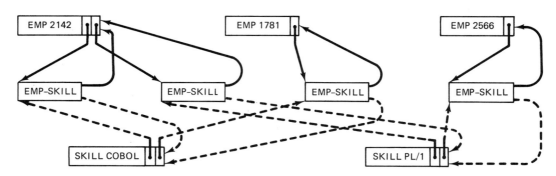

Figure 5.26 Implementation of the data-structure sets in Figure 5.24 as pointer arrays.

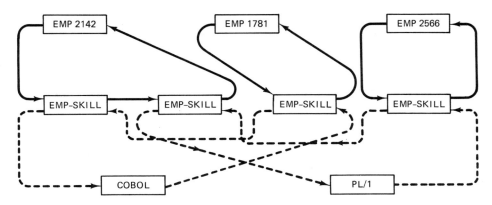

Figure 5.27   Implementation of the data-structure sets in Figure 5.24 as chains.

via the solid-line chain. From this EMP-SKILL record, we can find the corresponding skill record via the dotted-line chain. Then, from this EMP-SKILL record, we move to the next EMP-SKILL record via the solid-line chain. From the second EMP-SKILL record, we can determine the corresponding SKILL record through the dotted-line chain. Now, since we can find no more EMP-SKILL records in the solid-line chain, we have already retrieved all the information about the skills of the employee 2142. Similarly, we can find all the employees with a certain skill by going through the chains.

Another type of data structure, which can usually be found in manufacturing databases, is shown in Figure 5.28. There are two record types: PART and MFG-REL (manufacturing-relationship). Each product to be manufactured consists of many "parts" (components). Each part is in turn made of other parts. The PART record type contains information about the particular "part." The MFG-REL record type contains the information about the relationship between parts. Figure 5.29 illustrates this kind of relationship.The data in Figure 5.29 indicate that each part #1 is made from five part #2's and two part #3's. We can also see that PART #3 is a subpart of both PART #1 and PART #4. There are two data-structure sets in Figure 5.28, and they can be implemented as "chains" as shown in Figure 5.30. The solid lines represent the COMPONENT chain and the dotted-lines the WHERE-USED chain. In order to find out the components of a particular part, we first retrieve all the MFG-REL records via the COMPONENT chain and then retrieve the corresponding subparts via the WHERE-USED chain. By doing this, we can find out that PART #4 consists of one PART #3 and two PART #5's. In

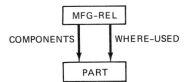

Figure 5.28   Two data-structure sets have the same owner and member record types.

SUPER-PART-NO	SUB-PART-NO	QTY
1	2	5
1	3	2
4	3	1
4	5	2

Figure 5.29 Manufacturing relationship between parts.

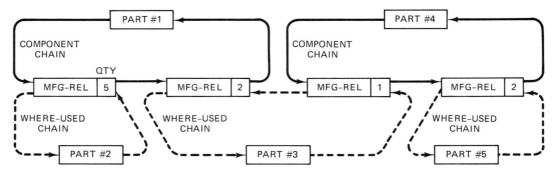

Figure 5.30 Implementation of the data-structure sets in Figure 5.28.

order to find out where a particular part is used to manufacture other parts, we first retrieve all the MFG-REL records related to that particular PART record via the WHERE-USED chain and then retrieve the corresponding PART records via the COMPONENT chain. By doing this, we can find out that two PART #5's are used in the manufacturing of PART #4.

Figures 5.21, 5.24, 5.28 are the basic types of data-structure diagrams. A database can be expressed in a large data-structure diagram based on these three basic building blocks.

5.3.2 Translation Rules

As we have seen from the previous section, the data-structure diagram is closer to the physical organization of the database than the entity-relationship diagram. It is usually difficult to draw a data-structure diagram for the entities and relationships which are of interest to the enterprise. Therefore, we propose that the database designer first draw an ER diagram to represent the enterprise view of data and then translate it to a data-structure diagram. In this section we discuss how to translate an ER diagram to a data-structure diagram. We identify several basic rules for translation, based primarily on the types of relationships between entities. We start with relationships defined by two entity types, then relationships defined by two or more entity types, and finally relationships of the same entity type. At the end, we shall discuss how to handle the composite entity type. The following are the translation rules:

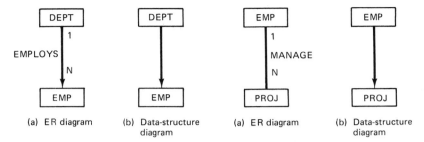

(a) ER diagram   (b) Data-structure diagram   (a) ER diagram   (b) Data-structure diagram

Figure 5.31   **Figure 5.32**

1. *Relationships defined on two different entity types*:

    (a) The relationship is a one-to-many or (one-to-one) correspondence. For example, the relationship type DEPT-EMP in Figure 5.31(a) is a one-to-many mapping and can be transformed into the data-structure diagram in Figure 5.31(b). Note that the entity types such as DEPT and EMP in the ER diagram are treated as record types in the data-structure diagram, while the relationship type EMPLOYS is represented by a data-structure set (an arrow) in the data-structure diagram. Similarly, the relationship type MANAGE in Figure 5.32(a), which restricts to one manager per project but allows multiple projects having the same manager, is represented by an arrow in the data-structure diagram shown in Figure 5.32(b).

    (b) The relationship is a many-to-many mapping. For instance, the relationship type WORK-FOR in Figure 5.33(a) is a many-to-many mapping. The corresponding data-structure diagram is shown in Figure 5.33(b). Note that the relationship type WORK-FOR was not translated into an arrow, but rather into a record type. We may conclude that if a relationship type is a many-to-many mapping, it will be translated into a record type with two arrows pointing from the related entity record types. The PROJ-EMP record type is usually called a "relationship record type" or a "dummy record type." A similar example is shown in Figure 5.34. Since the HAVE relationship type is a many-to-many mapping, it is translated into a (relationship) record type EMP-SKILL in the data-structure diagram.

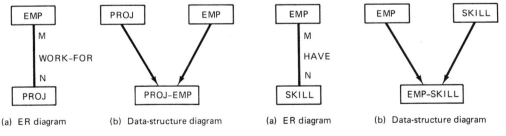

(a) ER diagram   (b) Data-structure diagram   (a) ER diagram   (b) Data-structure diagram

Figure 5.33   **Figure 5.34**

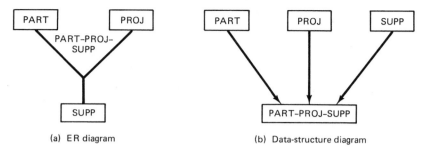

(a) ER diagram   (b) Data-structure diagram

Figure 5.35

2. *Relationships defined on three or more entity types*: In this case, the relationship type in the ER diagram will be translated into a relationship record type in the data-structure diagram, no matter whether the relationship is a one-to-many or other type of mapping. For example, the PART-PROJ-SUPP relationship type in Figure 5.35(a) is a relationship type defined by three entity types and will be translated into a record type in the data-structure diagram as shown in Figure 5.35(b).

3. *Binary relationships defined on the same entity types*: If the binary relationship is a one-to-many mapping, such as the relationship type MANAGES in Figure 5.36(a), it can be transformed into at least two possible data-structure diagrams as shown in Figures 5.36(b) and (c). Since most CODASYL (network) type database systems do not allow the same record type to be used as both the owner record type and the member record type of a data-structure set, Figure 5.36(b) is illegal. Therefore, we shall use Figure 5.36(c) as the data-structure diagram counterpart of the ER diagram in Figure 5.36(a). For binary relationships with other types of mapping, we shall use the same type of data-structure diagram. For example, the CONSISTS-OF (MFG-REL) relationship type is a many-to-many mapping, and its equivalent data-structure diagram is shown in Figure 5.37(b).

4. *Composite entity types*: All composite entity types will be translated into record types. For example, the composite entity types SHIPPING and HANDLING in Figure 5.38(a) are translated into the record types SHIPPING and HANDLING in Figure 5.38(b). The "*component* entity types" will become the "owners" of the data-structure sets, and the *composite* entity types will become

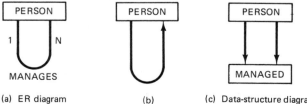

(a) ER diagram   (b)   (c) Data-structure diagram   **Figure 5.36**

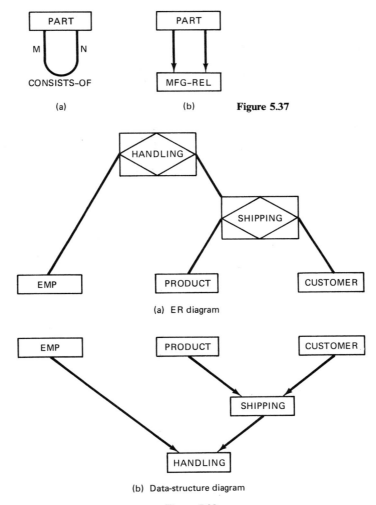

Figure 5.37

(a) ER diagram

(b) Data-structure diagram

Figure 5.38

the "members" of the data-structure sets. For example, PRODUCT and CUSTOMER are owners of the data-stucture sets in which SHIPPING is the member. Similarly, EMP and SHIPPING are the owners of the data-structure sets in which HANDLING is the member [see Figure 5.38(b).]

5.4 STEPS IN LOGICAL DATABASE DESIGN AND AN EXAMPLE

In this section we shall describe the major steps in logical database design and then give an example.

5.4.1 Major Steps in Logical Database Design

The ER approach to logical database design consists of the following steps:

1. Draw an initial ER diagram.
   (a) Identify elementary entity types.
   (b) Identify relationships between elmentary entity types.
2. Refine the ER diagram.
   (a) Convert some relationship types into composite entity types.
   (b) Identify "new" relationship types and high-level composite entity types.
   (c) Repeat subsets (a) and (b) until no more new relationship types and composite entity types can be found.
3. Draw an attribute diagram for entity types.
4. Convert the ER diagram into one of the following:
   (a) A data-structure diagram for CODASYL DBMS's.
   (b) A hierarchical diagram for hierarchical DBMS's.
   (c) A set of relations (tables) for relational DBMS's.

5.4.2 Example: A Manufacturing Company

5.4.2.1 Draw an Initial ER Diagram

Identify elementary entity types.   The initial step is to identify elementary entity types of interest to the company. In a manufacturing company, the major elementary entity types are EMP, PROJ, DEPT, PART, and SUPP (supplier) [see Figure 5.39(a)]. Other elementary entity types may be of interest to a manufacturing company; for simplicity, we shall limit our attention to the entity types mentioned above.

Identify relationship types between elementary entity types.   We start with relationship types defined on only one entity type, then on two entity types, and finally on three or more entity types.

1. *Relationship types defined on one entity type*: The CONSISTS-OF relationship type describes the superparts and subparts of a given part. This is the only relationship type of interest in this category.
2. *Relationship types defined on two entity types*: We can identify five of them:
   (a) The IS-AFFILIATED-WITH relationship type describes the employees affiliated with a given department and is a one-to-many mapping.
   (b) The WORK-FOR relationship type describes the project affiliations of all the employees and is a many-to-many mapping. That is, an employee can work for many projects, and a project can involve many employees.

(c) The MANAGE relationship type identfies the managers of projects and is a one-to-many mapping. That is, a project has at most one manager, but an employee can manage several projects.

(d) The POTENTIALLY-SUPPLY relationship describes the list of potential suppliers for a given part and is a many-to-many mapping.

(e) The IS-STORED-IN relationship type describes which part is stored in which warehouse and is a many-to-many mapping.

3. *Relationship types defined on three or more entity types*: There is only one such relationship type of interest to the hypothetical manufacturing company. That is the PROJ-SUPP-PART relationship type, which describes which supplier supplies which part for a particular project and is a many-to-many-to-many three-way mapping. In other words, for a given part, there may be many suppliers who can supply this part to many projects. Similarly, a project may use many parts from different suppliers. As we discussed before, this kind of three-way relationship usually cannot be replaced by three binary relationships such as SUPP-PART, PART-PROJ, and PROJ-SUPP.

An ER diagram illustrating these entity and relationship types is given in Figure 5.39(a).

5.4.2.2 Refine the ER Diagram

Convert some relationship types into composite entity types.   We now examine each relationship type to see whether we intend to keep data about it. If so, we will convert it into a composite entity type. As discussed before, we shall use a special rectangular-shaped box to represent a composite entity type, and the name for the composite entity type will be a gerund or a noun.

After examining the relationship types in Figure 5.39(a) based on the objectives and interests of the hypothetical manufacturing company, we can identify the following five conversions:

1. The IS-AFFILIATED-WITH relationship type is converted into the DEPT-EMP composite entity type.

2. The WORK-FOR relationship type is converted into the PROJ-EMP composite entity types.

3. The PROJ-SUPP-PART relationship type is converted to a composite entity type with the same name.

4. The CONSIST-OF relationship type is converted into the MFG-REL composite entity type.

5. The IS-STORED-IN relationship type is converted into the INVENTORY composite entity type.

Identify new relationship types and high-level composite entity types.
There are no other relationship types or high-level composite entity types of interest
to the hypothetical manufacturing company.

Repeat the previous two substeps.   Since there are no new relationship
types and composite entity types, we stop here. Figure 5.39(b) is the refined ER
diagram.

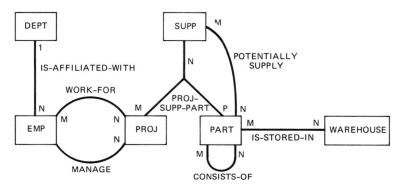

(a) An initial ER diagram for a manufacturing company

(a)

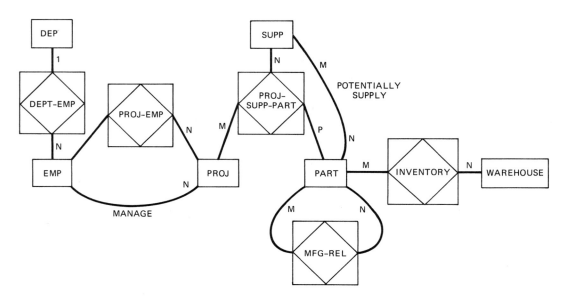

(b) An ER diagram for a manufacturing company

Figure 5.39

5.4.2.3 Draw Attribute Diagrams for Entity Types

The next step is to identify attributes and value types for the elementary and composite entities in Figure 5.39(b). Let us start with the entity types DEPT, EMP, and DEPT-EMP. Figure 5.40 illustrates the attributes and value types for DEPT and EMP. The entity types are in the upper conceptual domains and the attribute and value types are in the lower conceptual domain. In Figure 5.40 we have identified the following value types: DEPT-NO, BUDGET, EMP-NO, DATE, SALARY, and PHONE-NO. DEPT had three attributes: DEPT-NO, THIS-YEAR-BUDGET, and LAST-YEAR-BUDGET. EMP has five attributes: EMP-NO, BIRTH-DATE, SALARY, HOME-PHONE, and OFFICE-PHONE. Note that attributes might not have the same names as the value types, and that it is possible to have more than one attribute relating to the same value type. For example, THIS-YEAR-BUDGET and LAST-YEAR-BUDGET of DEPT use the same value type BUDGET. Another example is the attributes OFFICE-PHONE and HOME-PHONE of EMP, which use the same value type PHONE-NO. In order to simplify the diagram, we shall omit the attribute names if they are the same as the value types. Thus, Figure 5.41 is a simplified version of Figure 5.40.

Next we shall consider the elementary entity types PROJ and EMP and the composite entity type PROJ-EMP. There are five value types: %EFFORT, DATE, PROJ-NO, BUDGET, and PROJ-NAME. There are also five attributes in Figure 5.42 (even though some attribute names are omitted in the diagram): %EFFORT, STARTING-DATE-IN-PROJ, PROJ-NO, BUDGET, and PROJ-NAME. Note that the composite entity PROJ-EMP has two attributes: STARTING-DATE-IN-PROJ and %EFFORT. The STARTING-DATE-IN-PROJ is the date that the employee started working for a particular project, and the %EFFORT is the percentage of time that an employee is expected to spend on a particular project. Note that the value

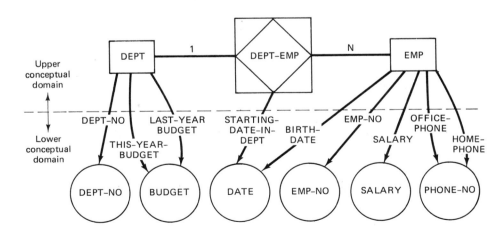

Figure 5.40   Attributes and value types for DEPT, EMP, and DEPT-EMP.

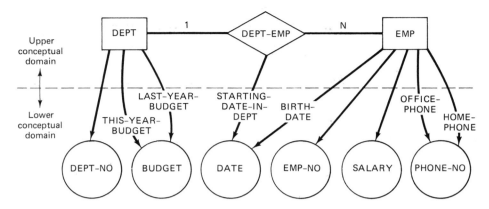

Figure 5.41   A simplified version of Figure 5.40.

type BUDGET is the same as the value type BUDGET in Figure 5.41. Therefore, we may say that attributes can help us to interpret the meaning of values.

Figure 5.43 illustrates the value types and attributes for the elementary entity types SUPP and PART and the composite entity type PROJ-SUPP-PART. The entity SUPP has two attributes: SUPP-NO and ADDRESS. The entity PART has attributes PART-NO, WEIGHT, and COLOR. The composite entity PROJ-SUPP-PART has attribute QTY, which is the quantity of a certain part supplied by a certain supplier to a certain project. The attributes of the entity PROJ have already been shown in Figure 5.42.

Figure 5.44 shows the attributes and value types of the properties of the WAREHOUSE, INVENTORY, and MFG-REL entities. A WAREHOUSE elementary entity has attributes WAREHOUSE-NO and ADDRESS. An INVENTORY composite entity has attribute QTY-ON-HAND, which is the quantity of a part

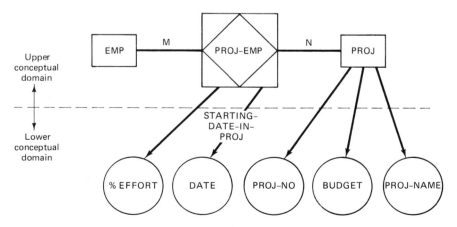

Figure 5.42   Attributes and value types for PROJ and PROJ-EMP.

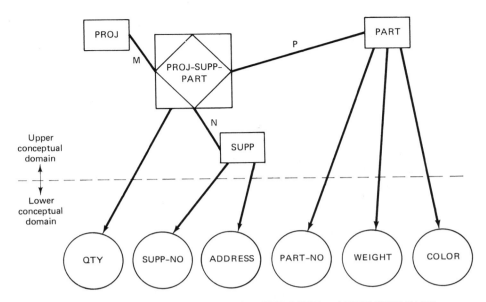

Figure 5.43   Attributes and value types for SUPP, PART, and PROJ-SUPP-PART.

stored in a warehouse. A MFG-REL composite entity has attribute QTY-FOR-MFG, which is the quantity of a subpart needed to make a super-part. Note that QTY-ON-HAND and QTY-FOR-MFG share the same value type QTY.

Figures 5.41 through 5.44 illustrate the attributes and value types needed to describe the properties of entities which may be of interest to a hypothetical manufacturing company.

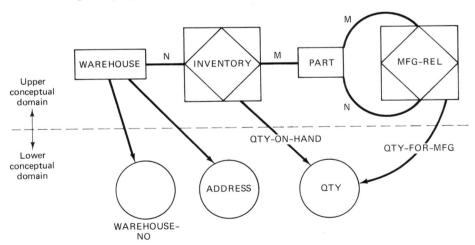

Figure 5.44   Attributes and value types of WAREHOUSE, INVENTORY, and MFG-REL.

5.4.2.4 Translate the ER Diagram into a Data-Structure Diagram (or Other Kinds of Database Structure Diagrams)

The fourth step is to translate the ER diagram into a data-structure diagram using the translation rules discussed in Section 5.3.2.

Consider the ER diagram in Figure 5.39(b). It can be translated into the data-structure diagram shown in Figure 5.45. All the elementary and composite entity types in the ER diagram become record types in the data-structure diagram. There are only two relationship types in Figure 5.39(b). Since the relationship type MANAGE is a one-to-many mapping, it is translated into a data-structure set (i.e., an arrow). Since the relationship type PROJ-EMP is a many-to-many mapping, it is translated into a record type with arrows pointing to it from the related entity record types, EMP and PROJ.

5.4.2.5 Design Record Format

The fifth step is to group attributes of entities into records and to decide how to implement the data-structure sets (using "chains"?, "pointer arrays"?, etc.). The basic guideline for grouping attributes into records is:

> All the attributes of an elementary or composite entity will be put into the same record type. For example, the attributes of DEPT will be treated as the names of fields in the DEPT record type (see Figures 5.41 and 5.46).

After putting all the attributes in the record types, we must next decide how to implement the data-structure sets. In this manufacturing-company example, we shall

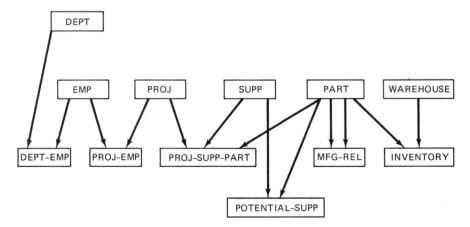

Figure 5.45   The data-structure diagram derived from the ER diagram in Figure 5.39.

Figure 5.46   DEPT record.

use "chains" as the physical implementation of the data-structure sets. That is, we shall use Figures 5.27 and 5.30 as the physical implementation of Figures 5.24 and 5.28, respectively. From these figures, we may make the following observations on how to implement chain pointers:

1. If the record is the owner record type of a data-structure set, it should have a pointer to the first member record occurrence.
2. If the record is a member record type of a data-structure set, it should have a pointer to the next member record occurrence in the chain or, if it is the last record in the chain, to the owner record occurrence.
3. If a record type is involved in multiple data-structure sets, it should contain several pointers, one for each data-structure set.

Using these rules, we can define the pointers in the record type as shown in Figures 5.46 through 5.56. Let us first consider Figure 5.46. Since the DEPT record type is the owner record type of a data-structure set, it has a pointer pointing to the first DEPT-EMP record occurrence related to this department. The EMP record type in Figure 5.47 has three pointers, since it is involved in three data-structure sets. Since EMP record type is the owner record of the data-structure set whose member record type is PROJ, it keeps a pointer to the first PROJ record occurrence managed by this employee. If the employee is not a manager of any project, the value of the pointer is null. Since the EMP record type is also the owner record type of the

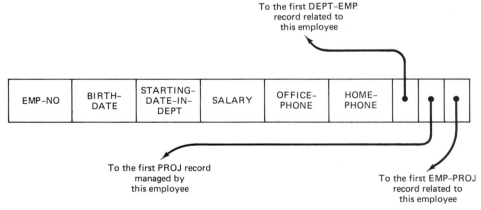

Figure 5.47   EMP record.

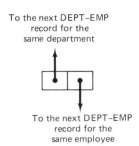

Figure 5.48   DEPT-EMP record.

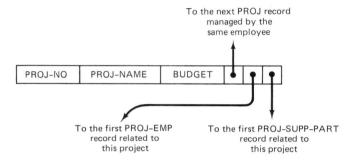

Figure 5.49   PROJ record.

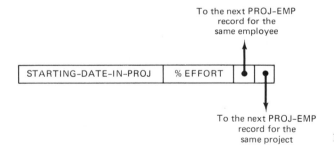

Figure 5.50   PROJ-EMP record.

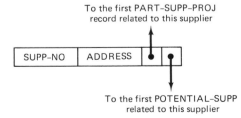

Figure 5.51   SUPP record.

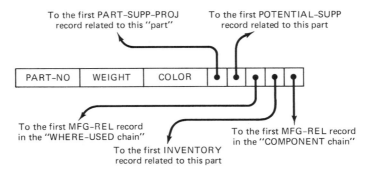

Figure 5.52   PART record.

data-structure type of the data-structure set whose member record type is PROJ-EMP, it maintains a pointer to the first PROJ-EMP record occurrence in the chain.

Since DEPT-EMP is the member record type of two data-structure sets, it maintains two pointers, one pointing to the next DEPT-EMP record occurrence for the same department, and the other pointing to the next DEPT-EMP record occurrence for the same employee (see Figures 5.45 and 5.48).

Consider a more complicated case: the record type PROJ-SUPP-PART in Figures 5.45 and 5.53. Since it is the member record type of three data-structure sets, it has three pointers, one for each chain. Similar explanations can be given for the pointers in other record types.

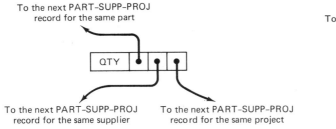

Figure 5.53   PART-SUPP-PROJ record.

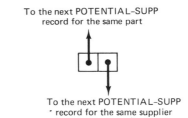

Figure 5.54   POTENTIAL-SUPP record.

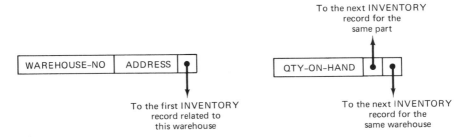

Figure 5.55   WAREHOUSE record.

Figure 5.56   INVENTORY record.

5.5 OTHER CONSIDERATIONS IN LOGICAL DATABASE DESIGN

5.5.1 Other Translation Rules from ER Diagrams to Data-Structure Diagrams

Translation rules from ER diagrams to data-structure diagrams discussed in Section 5.3.2 are not the only rules. For example, we may use a simple rule which translates all relationship types into record types, no matter what types of mapping they are (many-to-many, one-to-many, etc.). Using this rule, the ER diagram in Figure 5.39(b) would be translated into Figure 5.57 instead of Figure 5.45.

Using this simplified rule, the resultant data-structure diagram will be more complicated and may be less efficient in retrieval and updating. However, it may provide a higher level of data independence. That is, programs and database structures need not be changed when a particular relationship type changes from a one-to-many mapping to a many-to-many mapping. This change in types of mappings will convert a data-structure set into a record type or vice versa if the translation rules discussed in Section 5.3.2 are used, but no change is needed if the simplified rule discussed in this section is used.

5.5.2 Modifying the Data-Structure Diagram for Performance and Storage Reasons

After we obtain data-structure diagrams from ER diagrams using the translation rules, we may want to modify them to get better system performance or better utilization of storage space. For example, we may split the EMP record in Figures 5.45, 5.47, and 5.57 into two records. One is the EMP-MASTER record, which contains fields EMP-NO, BIRTH-DATE, and SALARY (see Figure 5.58). The other

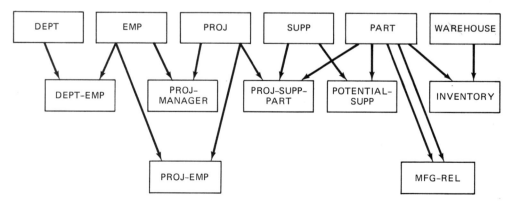

Figure 5.57 Another data-structure diagram derived from the ER diagram in Figure 5.50.

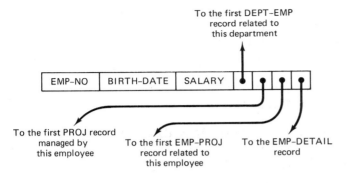

To the first DEPT–EMP
record related to
this department

| EMP-NO | BIRTH-DATE | SALARY | | | | |

To the first PROJ record
managed by
this employee

To the first EMP–PROJ
record related to
this employee

To the EMP–DETAIL
record

Figure 5.58   EMP-MASTER record.

To the EMP–MASTER
record

| OFFICE-PHONE | HOME-PHONE | |

Figure 5.59   EMP-DETAIL record.

is the EMP-DETAIL record, which contains the fields STARTING-DATE-IN-DEPT, OFFICE-PHONE, and HOME-PHONE (see Figure 5.59). Note that a pointer is needed to connect the occurrence of these two record types. The data-structure diagrams in Figures 5.45 and 5.57 will be modified by incorporating Figure 5.60. One of the reasons for splitting a record into two or more records is to improve the retrieval performance. For example, we may expect that the fields in the EMP-MASTER record will be used more often than the fields in the EMP-DETAIL record. Since we do not want to retrieve more data than needed, it may be a good idea to split the record into two records. Another reason to split a record into two records is the limitation of the record size. In some cases, owing to hardware/software limitations, it may be preferable to limit the record size to a fixed length (say 256 bytes). If a "conceptual" record is larger than the maximum length of a record, the "conceptual" record may have to be split into two or more records.

Another common practice is to factor out the repeating groups. For example, if the SHIP-TO-ADDRESSES is a repeating group (i.e., there are many data values for this attribute) in a customer record, we can move this field out and put it into a new record called SHIP-TO-ADDRESS (see Figure 5.61).

| EMP-MASTER |

| EMP-DETAIL |

Figure 5.60   Data-structure diagram for
EMP-MASTER- and EMP-DETAIL.

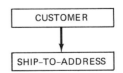

| CUSTOMER |

| SHIP-TO-ADDRESS |

Figure 5.61   A data-structure diagram for
CUSTOMER and SHIP-TO-ADDRESS.

Note that an ER diagram may be translated into many different data-structure diagrams to meet different data processing needs. Therefore, we recommend that the database designer start with an ER diagram and then translate it into a data-structure diagram suitable for his or her environment.

5.6 DESIGN OF HIERARCHICAL DATABASES

In hierarchical database systems such as IBM's IMS, data will be organized into hierarchies of records. In this section we discuss briefly how to use the ER approach for the design of hierarchical databases.

5.6.1 Translation Rules

Since the hierarchical relationship types allow only one-to-many mappings, we have to translate relationship types with many-to-many mappings into hierarchical structures. There are at least five possible logical data structures for the ER diagram in Figure 5.62:

1. The PROJ record type is treated as a "child-record" (or "subordinate-record") for EMP record type (see Figure 5.63). This logical data structure will be efficient for certain types of queries but not for others. For example, if we want to find all the employees associated with a particular project, we may have to do an exhaustive search of the whole database.

2. The EMP record type is treated as a "child-record" for PROJ record type (see Figure 5.64). If we wanted to find all the projects associated with a particular employee, an exhaustive search of the whole database would be needed.

3. Since neither the logical data structure in Figure 5.63 nor the one in Figure 5.64 can be efficient for all types of queries, we may want to maintain two databases as shown in Figure 5.65. But this requires the maintenance of redundant data.

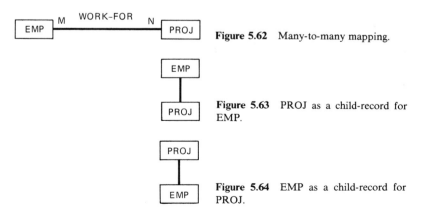

Figure 5.62   Many-to-many mapping.

Figure 5.63   PROJ as a child-record for EMP.

Figure 5.64   EMP as a child-record for PROJ.

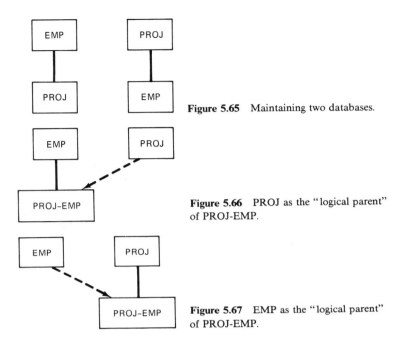

Figure 5.65 Maintaining two databases.

Figure 5.66 PROJ as the "logical parent" of PROJ-EMP.

Figure 5.67 EMP as the "logical parent" of PROJ-EMP.

4. In IMS, we may choose the logical data structure in Figure 5.66 so that EMP record type will be the "physical parent" of PROJ-EMP, and PROJ record type will be the "logical parent."

5. An alternative in IMS is to make the EMP record type the "logical parent" instead of the "physical parent" of PROJ-EMP record type (see Figure 5.67).

5.7 FINAL REMARKS AND FURTHER READINGS

The entity-relationship approach to logical database design has attracted considerable attention in industry and the research community. Many people have used this approach in the real-world environment and have found it easy to understand and easy to use. In addition, the ER diagrammatic technique has been found to be an effective tool between end-users and database designers for the specifications of user information requirements.

Certainly, the theory and techniques of the entity-relationship approach need further development. Recently, many researchers and practitioners have suggested various ways to improve the ER approach [10, 11, 16, 17].

Information concerning the ER approach can be found in various publications. Those interested in its role in data management may refer to a book by Ullman [34]. For modeling techniques, the reader may refer to [1, 4, 5, 7, 8, 24, 31, 32, 35]. Those interested in applications may refer to [9, 21, 26]. For the theoretical foundation the reader can study [2, 14, 20, 28, 29]. Those interested in DBMS implementations may refer to [3, 14, 15, 18, 19, 23, 25, 27, 30, 33, 36, 37].

In conclusion, the ER approach is a practical approach for logical database design. It is a valuable tool for the initial design where simplicity of technique is required. It can be used effectively together with other tools presented in this volume to form an integrated database design approach.

REFERENCES

1. Atzeni, P., C. Batini, M. Lenzerini, and F. Villanelli, "INCOD: A System for Conceptual Design of Data and Transactions in the Entity-Relationship Model," in *Entity-Relationship Approach to Information Modeling and Analysis*, ed. P.P. Chen, North-Holland, Amsterdam/New York, 1983.

2. Atzeni, P. and P.P. Chen, "Completeness of Query Languages for the Entity-Relationship," in *Entity-Relationship Approach to Information Modeling and Analysis*, ed. P.P. Chen, North-Holland, Amsterdam/New York, 1983.

3. Benneworth, R.L., et al., "The Implementation of GERM, an Entity-Relationship Data Base Management System," *Proc. Seventh VLDB Conference*, Cannes, France, 1981. (Available through IEEE Computer Society, Silver Spring, Maryland).

4. Casanova, A.M., "Mapping Uninterpreted Schemes into Entity-Relationship Diagrams: Two Applications to Conceptual Schema Design," *IBM Journal of Research and Development*, Vol. 29, No. 1, IBM, Armonk, New York, January 1984.

5. Ceri, S. ed., *Methodology and Tools for Data Base Design*, North-Holland, Amsterdam/New York, 1983.

6. Chen, P.P., "The Entity-Relationship Model: Towards a Unified View of Data," *ACM TODS*, Vol. 1, No. 1 (March 1976), pp. 9–36.

7. Chen, P.P., *Entity-Relationship Approach to Logical Data Base Design*, Monograph Series, QED Information Sciences Inc., Wellesley, MA, 1977.

8. Chen, P.P., "The Entity-Relationship Model: A Basis for Enterprise View of Data," *Proc. National Computer Conference*, Vol. 46, pp. 77–84. AFIPS Press, 1977.

9. Chen, P.P., "Applications of the Entity-Relationship Model," *NYU Symposium on Database Design*, May 1978.

10. Chen, P.P., (ed.), *Entity-Relationship Approach to Systems Analysis and Design*, New York/Amsterdam: North-Holland, 1980.

11. Chen, P.P., ed., *Entity-Relationship Approach to Information Modeling and Analysis*. New York/Amsterdam: North-Holland, 1983.

12. Chen, P.P., "English Sentence Structure and Entity-Relationship Diagrams," *Information Sciences*, Vol. 29, pp. 127–149, Elsevier Science Pub. Co., New York, 1983.

13. Chen, P.P., "A Preliminary Framework for Entity-Relationship Models," in *Entity-Relationship Approach to Information Modeling and Analysis*, ed. P.P. Chen, North-Holland, Amsterdam/New York, 1983.

14. Chen, P.P., "An Algebra for a Directional Binary Entity-Relationship Model," *Proc. of IEEE 1st International Conference on Data Engineering*, April, 1984, Los Angeles, California.

15. Chiang, T.C., "Design and Implementation of a Production DBMS," *Bell System Technical Journal* (*Computer Science and Systems*), Vol. 61, No. 9, AT & T Bell Lab., Short Hills, New Jersey, 1982.

16. Chu, W.W., and P.P. Chen, (eds.), *Tutorial: Centralized and Distributed Database Systems.* IEEE Computer Society, Los Alamitos, Calif., October 1979.

17. Davis, C., S. Jajodia, P. Ng, and R. Yeh (eds.), *Entity-Relationship Approach to Software Engineering*, North-Holland, New York/Amsterdam, 1983.

18. Dogac, A., and E.A. Ozkarahan, "A Generalized DBMS Implementation on a Database Machine," *Proc. 1980 ACM-SIGMOD Conference*, Santa Monica, May 1980, pp. 133–143.

19. Elmasri, R., and G. Wiederhold, "GORDAS: A Formal High-Level Query Language for the Entity-Relationship Model," in *Entity-Relationship Approach to Information Modeling and Analysis*, ed. P.P. Chen, North-Holland, Amsterdam/New York, 1983.

20. Jajodia, S., P. Ng, and F.N. Springsteel, "The Problem of Equivalence for Entity-Relationship Diagrams," *IEEE Trans. on Software Eng.*, Vol. SE-9, pp. 617–630, Sept. 1983.

21. Ho, Thomas, I.M., "New Perspectives for Information Systems Education," *AFIPS Conference Proceedings*, (1977 National Computer Conference), Vol. 46, pp. 569–574 AFIPS Press.

22. Kent, W., *A Taxonomy for Entity-Relationship Models*, IBM Santa Teresa La., San Jose, California, 1984 (Working Paper).

23. Lien, E.Y., and J.H. Ying, "The Design of Entity-Relationship Distributed Database Systems," *Proc. of 3rd IEEE COMPSAC Conf.*, IEEE Computer Society, Silver Spring, Maryland 1978.

24. Lusk, E.L., R.A. Overbeek, and Parrello, "A Practical Design Methodology for the Implementation of IMS Databases, Using the Entity-Relationship Model," *Proc. 1980 ACM-SIGMOD Conference*, Santa Monica May 1980, pp. 9–21.

25. Markowitz, V. M., and Y. Raz, "A Modified Relational Algebra and its Use in an Entity-Relationship Environment," in *Entity-Relationship Approach to Software Engineering*, ed. C. Davis, S. Jajodia, P. Ng, and R. Yeh, North-Holland, Amsterdam/New York, 1983.

26. McCarthy, W.E., "An Entity-Relationship View of Accounting Models," *The Accounting Review*, Vol. 54 (Oct. 1979), pp. 667–687.

27. Moulin, P.J., M. Randon, S. Scappapietra, H. Tardieu, and M. Teboul, "Conceptual Model as a Database Design Tool," *Proc. IFIP TC-2 Working Conference*, January 1976, Black Forest, Germany, pp. 459–479.

28. Ng, P., "Further Analysis of the Entity-Relationship Approach to Database Design," *IEEE Transactions on Software Engineering*, Vol. SE-7, No. 1 (January 1981), pp. 85–98.

29. Parent, C., and S. Spaccepietra, "An Entity-Relationship Algebra," *Proc. 1st IEEE Int. Conf. on Data Eng.*, IEEE Computer Society, Silver Spring, Maryland, 1984.

30. Poonen, G., "CLEAR: A Conceptual Language for Entities and Relationships," in *Centralized and Distributed Databases*, ed. W. Chu and P.P. Chen, IEEE Computer Society, Silver Spring, Maryland, 1980.

31. Sakai, H., "Entity-Relationship Approach to the Conceptual Schema Design," *Proc. 1980 ACM-SIGMOD Conference*, Santa Monica, May 1980, pp. 1–8.

32. Schiffner, G., and P. Scheuermann, "Multiple View and Abstractions with an Extended Entity-Relationship Model," *Journal of Computer Languages*, Vol. 4, 1979, pp. 139–154.

33. Shoshani, A., "CABLE: A Language Based on the Entity-Relationship Model," Technical Paper, Computer Science and Applied Mathematics Department, Lawrence Berkeley Laboratory, Berkeley, California, 1978. (Available through author).

34. Ullman, J.D., *Principles of Database Systems*. Rockville, Maryland: Computer Science Press, 1982.

35. Wang, S. "Normal Entity Relationship Model—A New Method to Design Enterprise Schema," *Proc. 1st Int. Conf. on Computers and Applications*, IEEE Computer Society, Silver Spring, Maryland, June 1984.

36. Zaniolo, C., "The Database Language: GEM," *Proc. 1983 SIGMOD Conf.*, ACM, New York, May 1983.

37. Zhang, Z.Q., and A.O. Mendelzon, "A Graphical Query Language for Entity-Relationship Databases," in *Entity-Relationship Approach to Software Engineering*, eds. C. Davis, S. Jajodia, P. Ng, and R. Yeh, North-Holland, Amsterdam/New York, 1983.

6

Relational Database Design

Y. E. Lien
Bell Laboratories
Murray Hill, New Jersey

6.1 INTRODUCTION

The past decade has witnessed a widespread interest among database practitioners and researchers in Codd's relational model [11]. One reason for this model's popularity is that, while it provides conceptual simplicity, it rests upon a rich theoretical foundation—the theory of sets and relations—and therefore makes database problems amenable to formal treatment.

At the heart of the relational model is the theory of data dependencies. Codd recognized very early the presence of certain anomalies in complex databases, and to characterize the absence of these anomalies he introduced the concepts of functional dependency and normal forms. As the theory gradually evolved, higher forms of dependencies were introduced and more sophisticated varieties of anomalies identified [16, 17, 19, 27, 28, 29, 34, 35, 36]. Although this hierarchy of dependencies is becoming more and more abstract, the intention has always been to yield better designs for relational databases.

Intuitively, the objective of relational database design is to decide how many relations should be in the database and what their underlying attributes should be. This chapter surveys the existing design methods for relational systems. We shall concentrate on design *algorithms* as opposed to informal design guidelines. In other words, this chapter considers only those methods that are readily reduced to computer software. It was written in the summer of 1980 and represents the state of the art of the relational database design up to then.

We will first propose a formal framework in which database design can be viewed as a database translation process. Several design principles will be stated as formal properties of translation processes. Existing algorithms will then be presented and examined in the light of these properties.

One key assumption underlies all the algorithms described in this chapter: the *universal relation assumption*. This assumption says that an enterprise or a database can be described by a single relation. A strong implication is that given any two types of entities in the database, there can only be one kind of relationship between them. When more than one relationship has to be represented, new types of entities are often introduced to satisfy the assumption. For example, if we want to model two relationships among projects, parts, and suppliers where one relationship is "this supplier is supplying these parts to those projects" and the other is "this supplier could supply these parts to those projects," we may have to classify suppliers into two types of entities: "active suppliers" and "potential suppliers." Therefore, database design is basically a task of constructing smaller relations from this universal relation. This universal relation assumption can be made valid by choosing a large enough relation and by renaming some of the attributes in it. However, this approach may not be practical in large operational databases.

In the next section we review the basic definitions and relational terminology. Database design viewed as a translation process is explained in Section 6.3, along with several design principles. Section 6.4 describes the major design algorithms and examines them according to the design principles expounded in Section 6.3. Section 6.5 summarizes the properties of the existing design algorithms.

6.2 THE RELATIONAL MODEL

This section reviews the main concepts in the relational model. The contents will be a sufficient basis for understanding of the subsequent sections; for additional material and motivation the reader is referred to standard textbooks in database systems [15, 31].

6.2.1 Relation Schemes and Relations

It is imperative to recognize the distinction between the logical description and the physical contents of a *data object* (or an *entity*). For example, a person named J. Anderson can be represented by a character string "J. Anderson" with a description NAME. The latter is called an *attribute* and the former an *attribute value*. Each attribute A has a *domain* DOM(A), which is the set of all possible attribute values for A.

We are interested in databases that are finite in size and have a finite number of attributes. The set of all attributes will be denoted by U. When values of different attributes are mentioned together, they represent an association among these attribute values. For example, the fact that J. Anderson was born on February 15, 1922, is most conveniently represented by a pair (J. Anderson, 2-15-1922) with the description (NAME, DATE-OF-BIRTH). In general, if X is a collection of attri-

NAME	DATE-OF-BIRTH	JOB
J.Anderson	2-15-1922	congressman
J. Carter	10-1-1924	farmer
J. Carter	10-1-1924	governor
J. Carter	10-1-1924	president
R. Reagan	2-6-1911	actor
R. Reagan	2-6-1911	governor

Figure 6.1 An example of a relation scheme and a relation. We shall call the relation CAND (NAME, DATE-OF-BIRTH, JOB).

butes, that is, $X \subseteq U$, an *X-value* is an array of values, one for each attribute in X. That is, it is a mapping that assigns to each attribute A in X a value from the domain DOM(A). For example, (J. Anderson, 2-15-1922, congressman) is an X-value where X is (NAME, DATE-OF-BIRTH, JOB). An X-value $r(X)$ is also called a *tuple* of scheme X. If the scheme X is understood, then $r(X)$ is abbreviated to r.

A set R of X-values is referred to as a *relation* of scheme X. Again, we use $R(X)$ to capture both the logical construct X and the name of the set R, and we abbreviate it to just R if there is no need to indicate its scheme. The set X is called a *relation scheme*. Informally, we can view a relation as a two-dimensional table with rows corresponding to tuples and columns to attributes. As an example, a relation scheme called CAND, for candidates, and an instance of CAND are given in Figure 6.1.

Except for "real-life" examples, we shall use the beginning letter $A, B, C, \ldots$ for single attributes and the corresponding lower-case letters $a, b, c, \ldots$ for attribute values. The ending letters $\ldots, X, Y, Z$ will be used for relation schemes. We often do not distinguish between the attribute A and the relation scheme $\{A\}$ that contains only one attribute. We also use XY to mean the union of X and Y.

Thus, mathematically, a relation scheme is a set of attributes, or equivalently a subset of U, and a relation is a set of tuples of the same scheme. If we assume that values in all domains are of simple data types, such as integers, reals, strings, and so on, and are not sets themselves, then each X-value looks "flat" and each relation is said to be in *first normal form* (*1NF*) [12]. Throughout this chapter, a *database* is always assumed to be a set of 1NF relations. We will not be concerned with specific data types.

6.2.2 Relational Operations: Projection and Join

Let X and Y be two relation schemes such that $Y \subseteq X$. Let $r(X)$ be a tuple and $R(X)$ be a relation. We use $r[Y]$ to denote the Y-value obtained from $r(X)$. Likewise, $R[Y]$ is the set of tuples $\{r[Y]|r \text{ is in } R(X)\}$. The relation $R[Y]$ is called the *projection* of $R(X)$ onto Y. Thus, the projection $R[Y]$ causes columns corresponding to $X - Y$ to be removed. Since a relation is always a set, identical rows will also be consolidated.

Another important operation is the *natural join* or *join* for short. Let X and Y be two schemes, and $R(X)$ and $S(Y)$ two relations. The *join* of R and S, denoted by $R \bowtie S$, is the set of tuples $\{t(XY)|t[X]$ is in R and $t[Y]$ is in $S\}$. If X and Y are disjoint, then $R(X) \bowtie S(Y)$ is the cartesian product of the two relations.

Since the join operation is both commutative and associative, the definition can be extended to more than two relations. The join of $R_i(X_i)$, $i = 1, 2, \ldots, n$, written

$$R_1(X_1) \bowtie R_2(X_2) \bowtie \cdots \bowtie R_n(X_n) \quad \text{or} \quad \bowtie_{i=1}^{n} R_i(X_i)$$

is the set $\{t(X_1 X_2 \ldots X_n)|t[X_i]$ is in R_i for $i = 1, 2, \ldots, n\}$.

The projection operation reduces the number of attributes in a relation and the join operation "pastes" together attributes in two or more relations. In other words, projection decomposes and join composes relations. Naturally, the interplay of these two operations has been investigated. For instance, in Figure 6.1, CAND[NAME, DATE-OF-BIRTH] $\bowtie$ CAND[NAME, JOB] = CAND. However, CAND[NAME, JOB] $\bowtie$ CAND[DATE-OF-BIRTH, JOB] properly contains CAND. For example, the tuple (J. Carter, 2-6-1911, governor) is in the former but not the latter.

This situation has been formalized in [2]. Let $P = \{X_1, X_2, \ldots, X_n\}$ be a set of relation schemes, and let $R(X)$ be a relation such that $X = X_1 X_2 \ldots X_n$. The function δ_P that maps a relation $R(X)$ into its projections $\{R[X_i]|i = 1, 2, \ldots, n\}$ is called a *projection map*. On the other hand, the function $\bowtie$ that maps a set of relations $\{R_i(X_i)|i = 1, 2, \ldots, n\}$ to their join $\bowtie_{i=1}^{n} R_i(X_i)$ is called a *join map*.

The composition of the two functions $\bowtie \cdot \delta_P$ is called a *projection-join map*. A projection-join map first decomposes a relation into its projections and then joins them back into one. If this process $\bowtie \cdot \delta_P$ returns exactly the original relation, then the projection map δ_P is called a *lossless-join decomposition* of R [2]. It is interesting to note that every tuple in R is always in $\bowtie \cdot \delta_P(R)$. That is, we have

Proposition 1. $\bowtie \cdot \delta_P(R(X)) \supseteq R(X)$.

When the projection-join map produces more tuples than the original relation R, the added tuples obscure the exact information in R. Since we lose information in this sense, the join map is called a *lossy* join. In an earlier example, if we decompose the relation of CAND into CAND[NAME, JOB] and CAND[DATE-OF-BIRTH, JOB] and later join the two projections, we will obtain the tuple (J. Carter, 2-6-1911, governor). Since we take CAND as the true representation of facts in the database, this projection-join map yields meaningless information; i.e., associating Reagan's birthdate with Carter. This simple example explains why it is crucial to understand the meaning of a join. Lossy joins often have unexpected or unintended implications. We should specify a lossy join only when its meaning is clearly understood.

A class S of relations $R_1(X_1), R_2(X_2), \ldots, R_n(X_n)$ is said to satisfy the *universal relation assumption* if every relation in S is a projection of $\bowtie(S)$. That is, $\delta_P \cdot \bowtie(S) = S$. Hence, every relation can be recovered from the *universal* relation $\bowtie(S)$.

6.2.3 Constraints: Functional and Multivalued Dependencies

Before we design a database, we need to have a fairly good understanding of the enterprise that is to be represented by the database. An enterprise consists of entities, which are to be represented by the attributes in the relational model, and the interentity relationships, which will be represented by the relations. Domains of a relational database confine its attribute values and tuples. A relation is simply a subset of the cross-product of its corresponding domains.

Additionally, the enterprise we want to model often imposes constraints and thus further confines the possible tuple values. Many forms of constraints have been studied, and two of them are frequently mentioned in the literature: functional dependency and multivalued dependency. The process of relational database design can be viewed as the task of transforming a set of attributes, their values, and the constraints about them into a collection of relations.

We may require one value of an attribute to determine uniquely another value in another attribute. For instance, the fact that a person has exactly one birthdate can be modeled by the constraint "NAME uniquely determines DATE-OF-BIRTH." This motivates the introduction of functional dependencies [11, 12]. A *functional dependency* (*FD*) is a statement $f: X \rightarrow Y$, which is read X (functionally) *determines* Y, where X and Y are relation schemes. We say that *f holds* in a relation $R(Z)$ (or *R satisfies f*) if Z contains XY and for any pair of tuples r and t in R,

$$r[X] = t[X] \quad \text{implies} \quad r[Y] = t[Y]$$

Therefore $X \rightarrow Y$ is a constraint that requires any two tuples to agree on their Y-values whenever they agree on the X-values. It does not say anything about the attribute values for $Z - XY$.

In terms of Figure 6.1, NAME $\rightarrow$ DATE-OF-BIRTH holds in the relation CAND, NAME $\rightarrow$ JOB does not, and DATE-OF-BIRTH $\rightarrow$ NAME holds in CAND accidentally. This last FD may not hold when new tuples are added to CAND. Conceivably, when an FD is specified as a constraint of a database, it is meant to be a constraint for relation schemes and should be observed by all relations of these schemes at all times, not just by a particular relation at a particular time.

It should be emphasized that functional dependencies are statements about the uniqueness of certain attribute values, instead of what the attribute values are. For example if NAME $\rightarrow$ DATE-OF-BIRTH holds in both CAND(NAME, DATE-OF-BIRTH, JOB) and EMP(NAME, DATE-OF-BIRTH, SALARY), we cannot deduce that J. Anderson has the same DATE-OF-BIRTH in EMP as in CAND, even if J. Anderson is a valid NAME value in EMP. However, if we add the universal relation assumption, EMP and CAND must agree on (NAME, DATE-OF-BIRTH), since they both are projections of the universal relation. This is equivalent to saying that there can be at most one FD from X to Y for any pair of schemes X and Y.

Certain FDs are *trivial* because they automatically hold in any relation. For example, $X \to Y$ for $Y \subseteq X$ automatically holds in any relation whose scheme contains X. We call an FD $X \to Y$ *nontrivial* if $Y - X$ is nonempty.

Multivalued dependencies are weaker constraints than functional ones. A *multivalued dependency* (*MD*) is a statement m: $X \to \to Y$, which is read X *multidetermines* Y, where X and Y are subsets of U. We say that m *holds* in a relation $R(U)$ (or R satisfies m) if for $Z = U - X - Y$, whenever the tuples xy_1z_1 and xy_2z_2 are in R, so are the tuples xy_1z_2 and xy_2z_1. (We use x for an X-value, y_1 and y_2 for Y-values, and z_1 and z_2 for Z-values.) That is, if we fix an X-value, the corresponding Y-values in R are independent of the corresponding Z-values in R. In Figure 6.1, NAME $\to \to$ JOB holds in CAND. In Figure 6.2, we have added a new column WORK_LOCATION to CAND. The MD NAME $\to \to$ JOB no longer holds in this relation. This is because (J. Carter, 10-1-1924, farmer, Georgia) and (J. Carter, 10-1-1924, president, D.C.) are in this relation, but the tuple (J. Carter, 10-1-1924, farmer, D.C.) is not. Therefore, MDs are sensitive to the context U *in which* they are defined. In contrast, FDs are not sensitive to the context.

The meaning of an MD $X \to \to Y$ in the context of U can be understood as follows. Consider three separate sets of attributes X, Y, and $Z = U - XY$. Given an X-value, its associated Y-values, which can be more than one, and its associated Z-values, which again can be more than one, are independent. In other words, any of these Y-values and any of these Z-values can appear in a tuple in the universal relation. A join operation has the same flavor. When we join a relation with attributes XY with another one with attributes XZ, any Y-value will appear together with any Z-value in the join, provided that they are associated with the same X-value.

The most general case in our framework is to assume that a database has a set of constraints and that each MD constraint has its own context. MDs with a context that are not necessarily U are referred to as *embedded* MDs. Unfortunately, we do not completely understand the properties of embedded MDs. The special case that we understand comfortably is when all MDs have the same context U. In the rest of the chapter we shall consider only this case.

An MD $X \to \to Y$ with $XY = U$ automatically holds in any relation $R(U)$ and is considered *trivial*. If an FD $X \to Y$ holds in $R(Z)$, then the statement $X \to \to Y$

NAME	DATE-OF-BIRTH	JOB	WORK_LOCATION
J. Anderson	2-15-1922	congressman	D.C.
J. Carter	10-1-1924	farmer	Georgia
J. Carter	10-1-1924	governor	Georgia
J. Carter	10-1-1924	president	D.C.
R. Reagan	2-6-1911	actor	California
R. Reagan	2-6-1911	governor	California

Figure 6.2 NAME $\to \to$ JOB does not hold in this relation.

in the context of Z holds also in $R(Z)$. For this reason, we say that every FD is also an MD. It is not difficult to see that not every MD is an FD.

The concept of MD is important because it completely characterizes lossless-join decomposition of a relation into two of its projections.

Proposition 2.   The MD $X \to \to Y$ holds in $R(U)$ if and only if $R[XY] \bowtie R[X(U - Y)]$ is R.

Proof. See [17, 34, 36].

Since NAME $\to \to$ JOB holds in CAND,

CAND[NAME, DATE-OF-BIRTH] $\bowtie$ CAND[NAME, JOB] $=$ CAND.

6.2.4 Inference Rules for FDs and MDs

Given a dependency g, we say that a set H of dependencies *implies* g if for every relation $R(U)$ in which dependencies of H hold, so does g. For example, two FDs EMPLOYEE-NO $\to$ NAME and NAME $\to$ DATE-OF-BIRTH imply the FD EMPLOYEE-NO $\to$ DATE-OF-BIRTH. Therefore, it is impossible to construct a relation of scheme U in which dependencies of H hold and dependencies implied by H do not.

Inference rules are a set of rules by which new dependencies implied by a given set of dependencies can be derived. We say that a set of inference rules is *complete* for a type of dependency if for each set H of dependencies of this type, the set of dependencies of the same type that are implied by H can be derived from H by these inference rules.

Complete sets of inference rules for FDs and MDs have been identified by various authors [1, 6, 26]. Out of several equivalent sets of inference rules, we shall adopt the following rules for their simplicity, especially in contrasting the FD and MD cases.

(A) These are inference rules for FDs:

F1 (Reflexivity)   If $X \supseteq Y$, then $X \to Y$.

F2 (Augmentation)   If $X \to Y$ and $W \supseteq Z$, then $XW \to YZ$.

F3 (Transitivity)   If $X \to Y$ and $Y \to Z$, then $X \to Z$.

(B) These are inference rules for MDs:

M1 (Complementation)   If $X \to \to Y$, then $X \to \to U - X - Y$.

M2 (Augmentation)   If $X \to \to Y$ and $W \supseteq Z$, then $XW \to \to YZ$.

M3 (Transitivity)   If $X \to \to Y$ and $Y \to \to Z$, then $X \to \to Z - Y$.

TABLE 6.1   ADDITIONAL INFERENCE RULES FOR FDS AND MDS

Type	Label	Name	Rule
FD	F4	Pseudotransitivity	If $X \to Y$ and $YW \to Z$, then $XW \to Z$.
FD	F5	Union	If $X \to Y$ and $X \to Z$, then $X \to YZ$.
FD	F6	Decomposition	If $X \to YZ$, then $X \to Y$ and $X \to Z$.
MD	M4	Pseudotransitivity	If $X \to\to Y$ and $YW \to\to Z$, then $XW \to\to Z - YW$.
MD	M5	Union	If $X \to\to Y$ and $X \to\to Z$, then $X \to\to YZ$.
MD	M6	Decomposition	If $X \to\to Y$ and $X \to\to Z$, then $X \to\to Y \cap Z$, $X \to\to Y - Z$, and $X \to\to Z - Y$.
MD	M7	Reflexivity	If $X \subseteq Y$, then $X \to\to Y$.
MD	M8		If $X \to\to Y$ and $Z \to\to W$ and $Z \cap Y = \varnothing$, then $X \to\to YW$.
FD, MD	X3		If $X \to\to Y$ and $W \to Z$, where $W \cap Y = \varnothing$ and $Z \subseteq Y$, then $X \to Z$.

(C) These are mixed inference rules for FDs and MDs:

   X1 (FD-MD)   If $X \to Y$, then $X \to\to Y$.

   X2 (Mixed Transitivity)   If $X \to\to Y$ and $Y \to Z$, then $X \to Z - Y$.

The rules in (A) are complete for FDs [1, 6], those in (B) are complete for MDs [6, 26], and (A), (B), and (C) combined are complete for mixed sets of FDs and MDs [6, 38].

For a set H of dependencies, the inference rules above can be used to derive all dependencies implied by H. We shall use H^+, referred to as the *closure* of H, to denote the set of all dependencies that are derivable from H using a complete set of inference rules. Since a closure is often too large to work with, we look for a small enough representative of the closure. If a set H' has the same closure as H, it is called a *cover* of H; and it is a *nonredundant* cover if no proper subset of it is a cover of H. H is always its own cover, although it may not be its own nonredundant cover.

Table 6.1 gives some other known inference rules, which prove to be quite useful in relational database design.

Rules F5 and F6 imply that every FD $X \to A_1 A_2 \ldots A_n$ can be replaced by an equivalent set of FDs $X \to A_1$, $X \to A_2$, ..., $X \to A_n$. We say that an FD is *simple* if it has only one attribute on the right side and is nontrivial.[1]

---

[1] The theory of FDs and MDs allows for dependencies whose left sides or right sides are empty sets. When its right side is empty, the dependency must be trivial. If $\phi \to X$ or $\phi \to\to X$ holds in a relation $R(U)$, $R(U)$ is the cartesian product of $R[X]$ and $R[U\text{-}X]$. That is, they are two independent relations (or two "separate" databases). Thus, we will not consider empty sets in dependencies in our context.

Given any relation scheme X and a set H of dependencies, we can derive from H a maximal set such that X functionally determines each attribute A in the set. We shall denote this set by $fd_H(X)$, or simply $fd(X)$ if there is no confusion. Algorithm 1 computes $fd_H(X)$ where H is a set of simple FDs.

Algorithm 1 [7].

Input. $X \subseteq U$, and a set H of simple FDs.

Output. $fd_H(X)$.

Procedure.

Step 1. (Apply Rule F1.) SET $\leftarrow X$.

Step 2. (Apply Rules F2 and F3.)

While (there exists a $Y \to A$ in H such that $A \notin$ SET and $Y \subseteq$ SET),

do:

$$\text{SET} \leftarrow \text{SET} \cup \{A\}.$$

Step 3. Output SET.

Example 1

The database contains information about students (St), their majors (Mj) and years (Yr); and about instructors (In), their ranks (Rk) and salaries (Sa). It also keeps track of classes (Cl) and exam scores (Ex) for each student in a class. The database must satisfy the following FDs:

$$\text{St} \to \text{Mj} \tag{1}$$

$$\text{St} \to \text{Yr} \tag{2}$$

$$\text{In} \to \text{Rk} \tag{3}$$

$$\text{In} \to \text{Sa} \tag{4}$$

$$\text{Cl} \to \text{In} \tag{5}$$

$$\text{Cl, St} \to \text{Ex} \tag{6}$$

To compute $fd(\text{Cl, St})$, Algorithm 1 first puts Cl and St into SET in Step 1. Because of (5) and (6), Ex and In are added. Also, Mj and Yr are added as a result of (1) and (2). Then, Rk and Sa are added because of (3) and (4). Thus $fd(\text{Cl, St})$ contains all attributes.

M1, M5, and M6 imply that MDs are closed under boolean operations (on the right sides of MDs that share the same left side). Hence, given $X \subseteq U$ and a set H

of dependencies, we can derive a set $\{Y_1, Y_2, \ldots, Y_k\}$ such that

(1) $Y_1, Y_2, \ldots, Y_k$ is pairwise disjoint,
(2) $Y_1 Y_2 \ldots Y_k$ is $U - X$, and
(3) for any $X \to\to Z$ in H^+, $Z - X$ is the union of some Y_i's.

The set $Y_1, Y_2, \ldots, Y_k$ will be denoted by $md_H(X)$, or simply $md(X)$, and is often referred to as the *dependency basis* of X with respect to H. An MD $X \to\to Y$ is said to be *simple* if Y is in the dependency basis of X.

From (1), (2), and (3), we see that the dependency basis of X is the finest partition of attributes in the sense that any set Z that "depends" on X is a simple combination of attributes in the dependency basis. So, elements in the dependency basis are "atomic." We are interested in dependency basis precisely because of this atomicity.

Algorithm 2 computes the dependency basis of a given set of attributes.

Algorithm 2 [3].

Input. $X \subseteq U$, and a set H of simple FDs and arbitrary MDs.

Output. $md_H(X)$.

Procedure.

Step 1. (Apply Rule X1.) For each FD $Y \to A$, replace it by $Y \to\to A$.
Step 2. (Apply Rules M1 and M2.)

$$\text{SET} \leftarrow \{Z - X, U - Z - X | Y \to\to Z \text{ is in } H \text{ and } X \supseteq Y\}.$$

Step 3. (Apply Rule M6.)

While (there is a pair Y and Z in SET such that $Y \cap Z \neq \varnothing$), do:

replace Y and Z by $Y \cap Z, Y - Z$, and $Z - Y$ (in the latter two cases, only if they are nonempty).

Step 4. (Apply Rules M8 and M1.)

While (there is $Z \to\to W$ in H and Y in SET such that $Y \cap Z = \varnothing$,

$Y \cap W \neq \varnothing$, and $Y - W \neq \varnothing$), do:

replace Y by $Y \cap W$ and $Y - W$.

Step 5. Output SET.

Example 2

Assume that we have attributes St, Mj, Yr, In, Rk, Sa, Cl, and Ex as in Example 1. We also have sections (Se) in each class and textbooks (Tx) for each class. Each section meets on certain days (Dy) in certain rooms (Rm). We have a *new* set of constraints:

$$Cl, Se \rightarrow In \tag{1}$$

$$Cl, Se, Dy \rightarrow Rm \tag{2}$$

$$St \rightarrow Mj \tag{3}$$

$$St \rightarrow Yr \tag{4}$$

$$In \rightarrow Rk \tag{5}$$

$$In \rightarrow Sa \tag{6}$$

$$Cl, Se \rightarrow \rightarrow St, Mj, Yr, Ex \tag{7}$$

$$Cl, Se \rightarrow \rightarrow In, Rk, Sa \tag{8}$$

$$Cl \rightarrow \rightarrow Tx \tag{9}$$

$$Cl, Se, St \rightarrow \rightarrow Ex \tag{10}$$

Algorithm 2 computes md(Cl, Se) as follows. Step 1 will convert all FDs into MDs by rule X1. Step 2 will place the following sets in SET:

$$\{In\}, \{Rk, Sa, St, Mj, Yr, Ex, Tx, Dy, Rm\}$$

$$\{St, Mj, Yr, Ex\}, \{In, Rk, Sa, Tx, Dy, Rm\}$$

$$\{In, Rk, Sa\}, \{St, Mj, Yr, Ex, Tx, Dy, Rm\}$$

$$\{Tx\}, \{In, Rk, Sa, St, Mj, Yr, Ex, Dy, Rm\}$$

Step 3 performs all possible subtractions and intersections among elements in SET to produce

$$\{In\}, \{Rk, Sa\}, \{St, Mj, Yr, Ex\}, \{Tx\}, \{Dy, Rm\}$$

Finally in Step 4, the set $\{Rk, Sa\}$ and the MD In $\rightarrow \rightarrow$ Rk satisfy the conditions that $\{Rk, Sa\}$ and $\{In\}$ are disjoint, $\{Rk, Sa\}$ intersects $\{Rk\}$, and $\{Rk, Sa\} - \{Sa\}$ is nonempty. So we replace $\{Rk, Sa\}$ by $\{Rk\}$ and $\{Sa\}$. The dependency basis md_H(Cl, Se) is

$$\{In\}, \{Rk\}, \{Sa\}, \{St, Mj, Yr, Ex\}, \{Tx\}, \{Dy, Rm\}$$

We now present an algorithm that computes $fd_H(X)$ for a mixed set H of FDs and MDs.

Algorithm 3 [3].

Input. $X \subseteq U$, and a set H of simple FDs and arbitrary MDs.

Output. $fd_H(X)$.

Procedure.

Step 1. (Separate FDs from MDs.) $H1 \leftarrow$ FDs in H.

Step 2. (Apply Algorithm 1.) SET $\leftarrow fd_{H1}(X)$.

Step 3. (Apply Algorithm 2.) Compute $md_H(X)$.

Step 4. (Apply Rule X3.)

For each singleton A in $md_H(X)$ such that $Y \to A$ is in $H1$ for some Y do:

$$\text{SET} \leftarrow \text{SET} \cup \{A\}.$$

Step 5. Output SET.

Example 3

We use the database in Example 2 to compute $fd(\text{Cl}, \text{Se})$. Algorithm 1 will produce $\{\text{In}, \text{Rk}, \text{Sa}\}$ as the initial contents of $fd(\text{Cl}, \text{Se})$. Algorithm 2 will yield

$$\{\text{In}\}, \{\text{Rk}\}, \{\text{Sa}\}, \{\text{St}, \text{Mj}, \text{Yr}, \text{Ex}\}, \{\text{Tx}\}, \{\text{Dy}, \text{Rm}\}$$

in the dependency basis $md(\text{Cl}, \text{Se})$. The only singleton in $md(\text{Cl}, \text{Se}) - fd(\text{Cl}, \text{Se})$ is $\{\text{Tx}\}$. Since no FD exists with Tx on the right side, Step 4 cannot put Tx into $fd(\text{Cl}, \text{Se})$. Thus, $fd(\text{Cl}, \text{Se})$ is $\{\text{In}, \text{Rk}, \text{Sa}\}$.

Incidentally, the inference rules we used in Algorithms 1, 2, and 3 are complete for their corresponding types of dependencies. We note also that these three algorithms are presented in their simplest forms with no attempt to minimize their computational complexities. Improvements of these algorithms have been reported [4, 21, 30].

With Algorithms 1, 2, and 3, it is easy to determine whether a dependency is implied by H. For example, we can compute $fd_H(X)$; and $X \to Y$ is implied by H if and only if $fd_H(X)$ contains Y. Likewise, we can compute $md_H(X)$; and $X \to\to Y$ is implied by H if and only if Y is the union of some members of $md_H(X)$. These two problems have been referred to as the *membership* problems [5].

Another relevant problem is to find a nonredundant cover for a given set H of dependencies. Since a particular dependency g is redundant if and only if it is implied by $H-\{g\}$, the membership test can be used to check, one by one, whether each dependency g in H can be removed or not.

Finally, crucial to the understanding of database design algorithms is the concept of *projectivity* and *inverse projectivity*. Suppose $W \supseteq Z \supseteq XY$. We know that if $X \to Y$ holds in $R[Z]$ then $X \to Y$ holds in $R(W)$ and vice versa. We say that FDs enjoy both projectivity and inverse projectivity.

This is not the case for MDs. It can be shown that if $X \to\to Y$ holds in $R(U)$ and $U \supseteq U' \supseteq X$, then $X \to\to Y \cap U'$ holds in $R[U']$. The examples in Figures 6.1 and 6.2 prove that $X \to\to Y$ can hold in $R[U']$ but not in $R(U)$. Thus, MDs enjoy projectivity but not inverse projectivity. This is why MDs have to be defined within a context, whereas FDs can be context-free.

6.2.5 Extended Relational Model and Existence Dependencies

Since the advent of the relational model in 1970, its concept has gradually evolved into a data model of simple syntactic units with enriched semantic capabilities.

In the "first-generation" relational model, a database was viewed as a family of relations, and semantic connections between relations were left implicit. This "flat" view of databases tends to encourage the database user to associate relations incorrectly or to interpret these associations differently from the original intent of the database designer. The information needed for maintaining interrelational consistency during database updates was left out of the database schema and the schema design process.

Efforts have been expended to enhance our capability to capture more of the meaning of data. (See Chapter 3.) Although it may be an oversimplification, it is fair to say that the improvement over the first-generation relational model is in the explicit interrelational semantics. In his modern relational model RM/T, Codd proposes to include the concepts of "entity," "property," and "association." Each entity *type*, such as employee, project, and assignment, is represented by a one-attribute relation, called an *E-relation*, for entity-relation, and the attribute values in this relation are unique system-assigned identifiers of the entities, called *surrogates* [14].

The semantic connection between two relations is based on the concept of *existence dependency* (*ED*) [10]. An ED is a statement in the form of $Y[\theta]X$, where θ can be $\subseteq$ or $=$. Two relations $S(Y)$ and $T(X)$ *satisfy* the ED $Y[\theta]X$ if $X \subseteq Y$ and $S[X]\theta T(X)$. For example, if ASSIGNMENT(EMPLOYEE, PROJECT) is a relationship between employees and the projects they are assigned to, and EMP(EMPLOYEE) is a one-column table of all employees, then we would expect ASSIGNMENT[EMPLOYEE] to be a subset of EMP. That is, an employee assigned to a project must appear in the employee master file. Thus, ASSIGNMENT and EMP satisfy the ED (EMPLOYEE, PROJECT)[$\subseteq$]EMPLOYEE.

EDs are phrased as insertion and deletion rules in RM/T. Existence dependency is manifested in at least three cases in RM/T: single-valued properties of an entity, multivalued properties of an entity, and associations of entities.

Suppose that an entity type has certain single-valued properties, such as DATE-OF-BIRTH of PERSON, or NAME of PERSON, represented by a *P-relation* (for property-relation). Then, the connection between the E-relation and the P-relation is governed by the following rule, taken directly from [14]:

ED1 (Property Integrity).   A tuple t may not appear in a P-relation unless the corresponding E-relation asserts the existence of the entity that t describes. In other words, the surrogate primary key component of t must occur in the corresponding E-relation.

If $R(X)$ is a P-relation describing the E-relation T with an attribute A, then the rule ED1 states that R and T must satisfy the interrelational constraint $R[A] \subseteq T(A)$—i.e., the ED $X[\subseteq]A$.

Example 4

> We have an E-relation PERSON and its P-relation with attributes {PERSON, NAME, DATE-OF-BIRTH}. The contents of these relations are given in Figure 6.3. According to ED1, if we delete PERSON β, then the tuple (β, J. Carter, 10-1-1924) must also be deleted.

Each entity may have some multivalued properties, such as JOB_HISTORY of EMPLOYEE. (Beware: MDs do not exactly model multivalued properties; the subtle difference is due to the fact that an MD must have an explicit context. For example, JOB is a multivalued property of NAME in the relation in Figure 6.2, but it is not true that NAME $\to \to$ JOB in that relation.)

A multivalued property of an entity is itself considered an entity, called a *characteristic entity*. Each characteristic entity type is again represented by an E-relation; however, this E-relation exists to describe tuples in another E-relation. The relation between a characteristic entity and the entity it describes is recorded in a P-relation, which gives the properties of the characteristic entities.

Example 5

> The information in Figure 6.2 can be represented by the relations in Figure 6.4. PERSON is described in Figure 6.3.

Insertion and deletion of characteristic entities must satisfy another rule.

ED2 (Characteristic Integrity). A characteristic entity cannot exist in the database unless the entity it describes most immediately is also in the database.

When R is the E-relation of a characteristic entity type named A, S the E-relation of the entity type B that R describes, and $T(A, B)$ the P-relation tying together R and S, then ED2 states that R, S, and T must satisfy the interrelational constraints $T[A] = R(A)$ and $T[B] \subseteq S(B)$—i.e., the EDs $(A, B)[=]A$ and $(A, B)[\subseteq]B$.

PERSON		PERSON	NAME	DATE-OF-BIRTH
α		α	J. Anderson	2-15-1922
β		β	J. Carter	10-1-1924
γ		γ	R. Reagan	2-6-1911

An E-relation   A P-relation

Figure 6.3 Single-valued properties of the entity type PERSON can be represented by a P-relation.

Associations of several entities are also treated as instances of a type of entity, called an *associative entity type*. Each associative entity type is represented by an E-relation and zero or more P-relations.

Example 6

We intend to represent the association MEMBER_OF, which shows the PARTY that a PERSON belongs to. (PERSON is described in Figure 6.3.) Figure 6.5 gives the PARTY relation, its P-relation, and the association.

Since we are not equipped to consider null values, we shall adopt an insertion and deletion rule that will force the deletion of an association when an entity participating in it is deleted.

ED3 (Association Integrity). An associative entity cannot exist in the database unless all entities participating in the association also exist in the database.

We can state ED3 equivalently as follows: If $R(A)$ is the E-relation of an associative entity type, $S(B)$ the E-relation of an entity type participating in R, and $T(A, B, \ldots)$ the P-relation tying together the participating entity types, then $T[A] = R(A)$ and $T[B] \subseteq S(B)$.

POSITION
δ
ε
λ
μ
θ
ψ

An E-relation of a
characteristic entity

POSITION	JOB	WORK_LOCATION
δ	congressman	D.C.
ε	farmer	Georgia
λ	governor	Georgia
μ	president	D.C.
θ	actor	California
ψ	governor	California

A P-relation describing
entity POSITION

POSITION	PERSON
δ	α
ε	β
λ	β
μ	β
θ	γ
ψ	γ

A P-relation

Figure 6.4   Multivalued properties are given as characteristic entity types.

PARTY
ζ
ξ

An E-relation

PARTY	PARTY_NAME
ζ	Democratic
ξ	Republican

A P-relation
describing PARTY

MEMBER_OF
π
ρ
ω

An E-relation of an
associative entity

MEMBER_OF	PERSON	PARTY
π	α	ζ
ρ	β	ζ
ω	γ	ξ

A P-relation
describing MEMBER_OF

Figure 6.5 Associative entities relate other entities to form higher-level semantic units.

Therefore, deletion of PERSON α in Figure 6.5 will trigger the automatic deletion of tuples about the associative entity π—namely the tuple (π, α, ζ) in (MEMBER_OF, PERSON, PARTY) and the tuple π in MEMBER_OF.

It now becomes clear that one of the database design objectives is to make the interrelational semantics explicit. Within our framework, this can be done by listing all the EDs.

6.3 THE DATABASE DESIGN PROCESS

Database design should not be considered a fully automated process; at least, the state of the art of database technology has not reached such a stage. We can envision relational database design as comprising the following activities:

1. Gather pertinent information about the enterprise that the database will model.
2. Identify domains, attributes, and constraints.
3. Identify relation schemes.

The actual process may involve a great deal of human activity, especially on the part of the database designer, making use of database design aids and iterating through steps 1, 2, and 3 until satisfactory results are obtained.

We will concentrate on the algorithmic processes that convert a set of attributes and constraints into relation schemes. Relational database design algorithms can be viewed as a set of design tools to be used as part of the total cycle of database design.

We first present a formal framework for the algorithmic part of relational database design. We then give several and sometimes conflicting design objectives. Specific design algorithms are given in the next section.

6.3.1 A Formal Framework

A relational database is a pair of finite sets $\langle \mathbf{R}, H \rangle$, where $\mathbf{R}$ is a set $\{ R_1(X_1), R_2(X_2), \dots \}$ of relations and H is a set $\{ C_1, C_2, \dots \}$ of constraints. The types of constraints that we are concerned with will be FDs, MDs, and EDs. We shall also fix a set U of attributes that is the superset of all relation schemes; that is, U is our set of "alphabets."

Now consider $\mathbf{S}_1$ and $\mathbf{S}_2$ as two families of relational databases. A database *translation* procedure from $\mathbf{S}_1$ to $\mathbf{S}_2$ is a function f that maps each database in $\mathbf{S}_1$ to one in $\mathbf{S}_2$. Since a database consists of two parts, relations and constraints, the function f can be viewed as having two components f_r and f_c such that $f(\langle \mathbf{R}, H \rangle) = \langle f_r(\langle \mathbf{R}, H \rangle), f_c(\langle \mathbf{R}, H \rangle) \rangle$ for any $\langle \mathbf{R}, H \rangle$ in $\mathbf{S}_1$. We shall use the subscript r to denote the translation of relations and the subscript c for the translation of constraints.

Therefore, a database design algorithm is formally a translation procedure. Under the universal relation assumption, the input to the design algorithms is thus a *universal* relational database $\langle R(U), H \rangle$ whose first component is simply a relation of scheme U.

For the algorithms presented in this chapter, it is helpful to identify several families of relational databases. A family of databases will be denoted by a boldface $\mathbf{S}$ with two subscripts. The first subscript is either a 1 for the universal relational databases or a $+$ for relational databases with one or more relations. The second subscript is F, M, E, or any combination of them, to indicate that the types of constraints in the databases are FDs, MDs, EDs, or any mixture of them, respectively. Thus, universal relational databases with only FDs will be denoted by $\mathbf{S}_{1,F}$ and relational databases with both EDs and MDs by $\mathbf{S}_{+,ME}$.

Let $\mathbf{S}_1$ be one of $\mathbf{S}_{1,F}, \mathbf{S}_{1,M}$, and $\mathbf{S}_{1,FM}$. All design algorithms considered here can be viewed as examples of a translation procedure f that takes a universal relational database $\langle R, H_1 \rangle$ in $\mathbf{S}_1$, finds a set P of relation schemes, and returns $\langle \delta_P(R), H_2 \rangle$ as the end result. In other words, the subprocedure f_r is always a projection map.

We have so far avoided the interpretation of the ordered pair $\langle \{ R_1, R_2, \dots, R_n \}, H \rangle$. Obviously, we want the constraints in H to be satisfied by the relations. In the special case that H contains MDs, we assume that all MDs are constraints for the relation $\bowtie (R_1, R_2, \dots, R_n)$ and must hold in this relation. For FDs, inverse projectivity and projectivity imply the following result.

Proposition 3. Let $R(U)$ be a universal relation, P be a set of relation schemes $\{ X_i | X_i \subseteq U \}$ whose union is U, and H be a set of FDs. For each FD $f: X \to Y$ in H, let P_f be the subset $\{ X_j | X_j$ contains $XY \}$ of P. Suppose that P_f is not empty for every f in H. Then, for every f in H, f holds in $\bowtie \cdot \delta_P(R)$ if and only if it holds in the relations in $\delta_{P_f}(R)$.

Proof. Let R' be the relation $\bowtie \cdot \delta_P(R)$. By Proposition 1, $R' \supseteq R$. Also, $R'[X_i] \subseteq R[X_i]$; hence, $R'[X_i] = R[X_i]$. If f holds in some $R[X_i]$, then f must hold in $R'[X_i]$ and hence in R'. Conversely, if f holds in R' and X_i is in P_f, then f holds in $R'[X_i]$, which is $R[X_i]$.

Thus, if a database design algorithm takes $\langle R, H_1 \rangle$ as input and produces $\langle \delta_P(R), H_2 \rangle$, we can verify that $\bowtie \cdot \delta_P(R)$ satisfies the constraints in H_2 by checking whether every FD f in H_2 holds in $\delta_{P_f}(R)$. That is, no FD needs to be verified against the join of two or more relations in $\delta_P(R)$. Technically, we say that there is no *interrelational join constraint*.

Using this translation from $\langle R, H_1 \rangle$ to $\langle \delta_P(R), H_2 \rangle$, we can illustrate several design questions. For example, does the translation preserve information in R? By Proposition 1, every tuple in R is in $\bowtie \cdot \delta_P(R)$. But if $\bowtie \cdot \delta_P(R)$ introduces tuples not in R, then we have a lossy join.

Does the translation preserve the constraints in H_1? We can routinely return all data dependencies in H_1 as H_2 during the translation, but then this strategy may cause some dependencies to become interrelational join constraints, which presumably are more expensive to enforce. Hence, the pertinent question is whether the translation can preserve dependencies without making some dependencies interrelational join constraints. Also, do we have redundant relations in $\delta_P(R)$? Perhaps a proper subset of P may be sufficient to preserve information in R.

Are relations in $\delta_P(R)$ normalized? Which normal form [12, 17]? And finally, to which family of databases does the output of the design algorithm belong? Is it a first-generation relational database? Does it have explicit interrelational semantics?

We shall now elaborate on these points and develop a set of design principles.

6.3.2 Design Principles

Given the framework presented earlier, the algorithmic phase of database design can be viewed conveniently as a database translation process. More specifically, each existing relational database design algorithm can be modeled by a translation procedure f which maps a universal relational database $\langle R(U), H_1 \rangle$ in the family $\mathbf{S}_1$ (which can be one of $\mathbf{S}_{1,F}, \mathbf{S}_{1,M}$, and $\mathbf{S}_{1,FM}$) to $\langle \delta_P(R), H_2 \rangle$, for some collection P of relation schemes, in some family $\mathbf{S}_2$ of relational databases.

The characteristics of a design algorithm can be presented as formal properties of the translation procedure f. We now look into several of these properties.

Property 1: Content-Preserving. A design algorithm f is *content-preserving* if the original relation R can be reconstructed from the relations in $\delta_P(R)$. In other words, we must have $\bowtie \cdot \delta_P(R) = R$.

Property 2: Dependency-Preserving.   The algorithm f is *dependency-preserving* if the original dependencies in H_1 can be reconstructed from H_2. In other words, there must exist a translation g from $\mathbf{S}_2$ to $\mathbf{S}_1$ such that $g_c(\langle \delta_P(R), H_2 \rangle)$ is a cover of H_1. When H_1 and H_2 are dependencies of the same type, f is dependency-preserving when H_1 and H_2 have the same closure.

Property 3: Free of Interrelational Join Constraints.   Let P be a class of relation schemes and H_2 a set of FDs and MDs. We say that the database $\langle \delta_P(R(U)), H_2 \rangle$ has *interrelational join constraints* if there exists an FD $X \to Y$ or an MD $X \to \to Y$ in H_2 such that XY is not contained in any relation scheme of P. When an interrelational join constraint $X \to Y$ or $X \to \to Y$ is present, it *often* (not always) requires that several relations in $\delta_P(R)$ be joined together to check whether the constraint holds in $\Delta \cdot \delta_P(R)$. Since the join operation is usually expensive to compute, interrelational join constraints are costly to enforce.

Note that all MDs are assumed to have U as the context; hence, finding out whether an MD $X \to \to Y$ holds in $\Delta \cdot \delta_P(R)$ appears to require the join operation on the entire collection of relations in $\delta_P(R)$, which would certainly be expensive. However, in some cases we do not need to compute the join map, or any join operations at all. We shall come back to this point later.

Existence dependencies mentioned earlier are another form of interrelational constraints; they can be considered interrelational *projection* constraints. Whether $R[X] \subseteq S(X)$ (or $R[X] = S(X)$) holds or not can easily be checked by inexpensive projection operations.

Property 4: Minimally Content-Preserving.   When f translates $\langle R, H_1 \rangle$ into $\langle \delta_P(R), H_2 \rangle$, f is *minimally content-preserving* if P does not contain any proper subset P' such that $\Delta \cdot \delta_P(R) = R$. Hence, no relation in $\delta_P(R)$ is redundant for recovering the contents originally in R.

Property 5: Minimally Dependency-Preserving.   When f is dependency-preserving, all dependencies in H_1^+ can be recovered from H_2. We say that f is *minimally dependency-preserving* if H_1^+ cannot be computed from any proper subset of H_2 (by way of the function g_c).

Therefore, Properties 4 and 5 address the issue of redundancy. We now move on to consider the issue of normalization.

Historically, normal forms were introduced to correct certain update (insert, delete, or change) anomalies. The story of the discovery of new strains of anomalies parallels that of definitions of new normal forms. One peculiar historical fact is that these anomalies, which anticipated their corresponding normal forms, were always illustrated by examples and never formally defined. Therefore, we do not know exactly what kinds of anomalies are removed by the normalization processes. As a consequence, researchers accept various normal forms as the de facto standards of the relational design process. Several authors have recognized this problem and have provided partial answers [8, 20]. A thorough understanding of anomalies is still desired.

Suppose that we are given a set H of FDs. A subset X of a relation scheme W is said to be a *key* of W if $X \to W$ is in H^+, and for no proper subset X' of X is $X' \to W$ in H^+. Thus, a key X can be viewed as the constraint $X \to W$ that any relation $R(W)$ must satisfy. A subset of W is a *superkey* of W if it contains a key of W. In Example 1, (Cl, St) is a key of (St, Mj, Yr, In, Rk, Sa, Cl, Ex), and there is no other key.

A relation scheme may have several keys. An attribute A in W is called a *key attribute* if it appears in one of the keys of W; otherwise, it is a *non-key* attribute. Thus, Mj, Yr, Rk, Sa, In, and Ex are all non-key attributes in Example 1.

An attribute A is *fully determined* by X if $X \to A$ is in H^+ and there exists no proper subset X' of X such that $X' \to A$ is in H^+. A relation scheme W is in *second normal form* (2NF) if each of its non-key attributes is fully determined by every key of W.

Example 7

> We use the database in Example 1. Consider the relation schemes $X = \{Cl, St, Mj, Yr\}$ and $Y = \{Cl, In, Rk, Sa\}$. In X, $\{Cl, St\}$ is the only key; and in Y, $\{Cl\}$ is the only key. Y is in 2NF because In, Rk, and Sa are all fully determined by Cl. X is not in 2NF because Mj and Yr are not fully determined by the key $\{Cl, St\}$.

The simple FD $X \to A$ is said to be *elementary* if A is fully determined by X [38].

Property 6: (3NF).   A relation scheme W is in 3NF with respect to a set H of FDs if for every elementary FD $X \to A$ in H^+ such that $XA \subseteq W$, either

(a) X is a key of W, or
(b) A is a key attribute of W.

The procedure f that translates $\langle R, H_1 \rangle$ into $\langle \delta_P(R), H_2 \rangle$ is said to produce a *3NF database* if every relation scheme in P is in 3NF with respect to H_1.

Example 8

> In Example 6, $Y = \{Cl, In, Rk, Sa\}$ is in 2NF. However, the elementary FD In $\to$ Rk has the property that In is not a key of Y (for In does not determine Cl) and Rk is not a key attribute. Thus, Y is not in 3NF. In a relation $R(Y)$, we observe the following problems:
>
> 1. *Change anomalies*: If the instructor Smith teaches three classes, then the information about Smith (i.e., Rk, Sa) will be repeated three times in R. In making any change to Smith's Sa or Rk we will have to make sure that all three tuples are changed at the same time. Failure to do so would introduce inconsistency.
> 2. *Insertion anomalies*: We cannot add an instructor unless the instructor also teaches at least one class.

3. *Deletion anomalies*: The result of deleting classes depends on how many classes an instructor teaches. Deleting the last (i.e., only) class that an instructor teaches causes the unintended removal of information about this instructor.

All these problems go away if we decompose Y into $\{Cl, In\}$ and $\{In, Rk, Sa\}$.

Boyce and Codd introduce an improvement over 3NF, known as *Boyce-Codd normal form* (*BCNF*) [13].

Property 7: (BCNF).   A relation scheme W is in BCNF with respect to a set H of FDs if for every elementary FD $X \rightarrow A$ in H^+ such that $XA \subseteq W$,

(a) X is a key of W.

The procedure f is said to produce a *BCNF database* if every relation scheme in P is in BCNF with respect to H_1.

Properties 6 and 7 have been stated to show the similarity between the definitions of 3NF and BCNF [38]. It is now easy to see that a BCNF database is a 3NF database.

Example 9

The database contains information about instructors (In), classes (Cl), and students (St). We also assume that each class is taught by one instructor and each instructor teaches only one class. Thus, we have the FDs

$$Cl \rightarrow In$$

$$In \rightarrow Cl$$

Consider the relation scheme $X = \{Cl, In, St\}$. There are two keys, $\{Cl, St\}$ and $\{In, St\}$. Since every attribute is a key attribute, X is in 3NF. For the elementary FD $Cl \rightarrow In$, Cl is not a key for X. Thus, X is not in BCNF. Anomalies similar to those in Example 8 can be found.

When MDs are taken into consideration, another advanced normal form, *fourth normal form* (*4NF*) can be defined [17].

Property 8: (4NF).   A relation scheme W is in 4NF with respect to a set H of FDs and MDs if for any nontrivial MD $X \rightarrow \rightarrow Y$ in H^+ such that $XY \subseteq W$,

(a) X is a superkey of W with respect to FDs in H.

The procedure f produces a *4NF database* if every relation scheme in P is in 4NF with respect to H_1.

Again, each 4NF database is a BCNF database [17].

Example 10

Using the database in Example 2, we can determine that the only key in $X = \{Cl, St, Tx\}$ is X itself. X is in BCNF since no elementary FD $Y \rightarrow A$ exists with $YA \subseteq X$. However, X is not in 4NF, because $Cl \rightarrow \rightarrow Tx$ is a nontrivial MD and Cl is not a superkey of X. Again, change anomalies are present because several textbooks may be used by one class and these textbooks will have to be repeated for each student in the class. Insertion anomalies are also present, because no textbooks can be recorded for a class until at least one student enrolls in the class. Deletion anomalies can be similarly stated.

The eight properties given above are among the objectives that design algorithms strive for. Each single property is reasonable in its own right but usually is inadequate as the sole objective of the design algorithm. However, some combinations of these properties may not be realizable. For example, we might want to design an algorithm that is minimally content-preserving, minimally dependency-preserving, and free of interrelational join constraints and that produces 4NF databases. Unfortunately, this is not possible.

Proposition 4.[4]   There exists no translation procedure from $S_{1,F}$ to $S_{+,F}$ which produces BCNF databases and is both dependency-preserving and free of interrelational join constraints.

Proof. We need give only one database in $S_{1,F}$ that cannot be mapped by any dependency-preserving translation procedure into a BCNF database without introducing interrelational join constraints.

Let $R(ABC)$ be any relation that satisfies FDs in $H = \{AB \rightarrow C, C \rightarrow A\}$. Clearly, $\langle R, H \rangle$ is a database in $S_{1,F}$. Also, ABC is not in BCNF with respect to H because $C \rightarrow A$ is elementary but C is not a key of ABC.

Now let f be any dependency-preserving procedure from $S_{1,F}$ to $S_{+,F}$, which maps $\langle R, H \rangle$ to $\langle R', H' \rangle$. Since H and H' must have the same closure, we can conclude that $AB \rightarrow C$ must be in H' by brute-force enumeration of redundant covers of H. Thus, either R' contains a relation with scheme ABC and so is not in BCNF, or $AB \rightarrow C$ becomes an interrelational join constraint.

Corollary.   There exists no translation procedure from $S_{1,FM}$ to $S_{+,FM}$ that produces 4NF databases and is both dependency-preserving and free of interrelational join constraints.

6.4 DATABASE DESIGN ALGORITHMS

We now examine in detail five classes of relational database design algorithms.

6.4.1 A 3NF Synthesis Algorithm

Bernstein proposed a scheme synthesis algorithm that takes a set of FDs and produces 3NF relation schemes.

Algorithm 4

Input. A database $\langle R(U), H \rangle$ in $\mathbf{S}_{1, F}$, where H is a set of simple FDs.

Output. A 3NF database $\langle \delta_P(R), H' \rangle$.

Procedure.

Step 1. (Find a cover. See Algorithm 1 and its discussion.)

Find a nonredundant cover G of H that consists of elementary FDs only. Also, save G in H'.

Step 2. (Partition.)

Partition G into groups such that all FDs with the same left side are in one group.

Step 3. (Merge equivalent keys.)
>   3.1 $J \leftarrow \varnothing$.
>   3.2   For each pair of groups G_i and G_j, with left sides X and Y respectively, do:

$$\text{if } X \rightarrow Y \text{ and } Y \rightarrow X \text{ are in } G^+, \text{ then}$$
$$\{$$
$$J \leftarrow J \cup \{X \rightarrow Y, Y \rightarrow X\};$$
$$G_i \leftarrow G_i - \{X \rightarrow A | A \in Y\};$$
$$G_j \leftarrow G_j - \{Y \rightarrow B | B \in X\};$$
$$\text{merge } G_i \text{ and } G_j;$$
$$\}.$$

Step 4. (Find a cover again.)

Find a smallest subset G' of G such that

$$(G' \cup J)^+ = (G \cup J)^+.$$

Return each FD in J to the appropriate group of G' according to its left side.

Step 5. (Construct relation schemes and FDs.)
>   5.1 $P \leftarrow \phi$.
>   5.2   For each group G_i', do:

$$\{$$
$$P \leftarrow P \cup \{X_i\}, \text{ where } X_i \text{ is the set}$$
$$\text{of all attributes appearing in } G_i';$$
$$\}.$$

Step 6. (Output.) Return $\langle \delta_P(R), H' \rangle$.

The relation-scheme synthesis (Steps 1 through 5) of Algorithm 4 can be implemented to run with complexity $O(|H|^2)$, where $|H|$ denotes the size of any reasonable representation of FDs in H, such as pairs of integers and integer matrices.

Since H' is a nonredundant cover of H, the algorithm is minimally dependency-preserving. By Step 5, no interrelational join constraint is possible. That the algorithm produces 3NF databases is proved in [4].

Example 11

Again our database contains information about St, In, Cl, and Ex, as in Example 1. In addition, we also keep track of hours (Hr) and rooms (Rm) for each class. The FDs are listed below.

Cl → In	(one instructor per class)	(1)
Cl, St → Ex	(one score per student per class)	(2)
Hr, Rm → Cl	(no classes share rooms at same time)	(3)
Hr, St → Rm	(a student can be in only one room at one time)	(4)
Hr, In → Rm	(likewise, for an instructor)	(5)
Hr, St → Cl	(a student can be in only one class at one time)	(6)
Hr, In → Cl	(likewise, for an instructor)	(7)
Hr, Cl → Rm	(a class can take only one room at one time)	(8)

There are redundant FDs. For example, (1) and (5) imply (8); (3) and (5) imply (7); (3) and (4) imply (6); (6) and (8) imply (4). Assume that Algorithm 4 will produce a cover G that consists of $\{1, 2, 3, 5, 6\}$ in Step 1. Since no two FDs share the same left side, each will appear in one group in Step 2. In Step 3 we observe that the left side of (3) and the left side of (5) are equivalent keys; that is, Hr, Rm → Hr, In and Hr, In → Hr, Rm. Thus, we merge (3) and (5) into one group.

Step 4 does not remove any FD in G in this example. In Step 5 we construct the following relation schemes:

{Cl, In}	Key: Cl
{Cl, St, Ex}	Key: Cl, St
{Hr, Rm, Cl, In}	Keys: Hr, Rm; Hr, In; Hr, Cl
{Hr, St, Cl}	Key: Hr, St.

The scheme {Hr, Rm, Cl, In} is in 3NF because Hr, Rm, Cl, and In are all key attributes. However, it is not in BCNF because Cl → In and Cl is not a key.

This example shows that Algorithm 4 is not minimally content-preserving. (In fact, in general Algorithm 4 may not be content-preserving.) Beeri and Bernstein proposed to keep the redundant relation scheme {Cl, In} on the ground that many database management systems have the capability to maintain keys but not FDs; i.e., keys can be explicitly specified in their data-definition languages, but not FDs [4]. If we were to remove $\{Cl, In\}$, the FD $Cl \rightarrow In$ could not be enforced through the key mechanism.

Example 12

Assume that we add a new FD to the database in Example 11.

$$In \rightarrow Cl \qquad \text{(an instructor teaches only one class)} \qquad (9)$$

Then, (8) and (9) imply (5). Applying Algorithm 4, we first compute a nonredundant cover G; say it consists of $\{1, 2, 3, 6, 8, 9\}$. Step 3 will put (1) and (9) together, and (3) and (8) together. Finally, we will produce the set of relation schemes

$\{Cl, In\}$	Keys: Cl; In
$\{Cl, St, Ex\}$	Keys: Cl, St
$\{Hr, Rm, Cl\}$	Keys: Hr, Rm; Hr, Cl
$\{Hr, St, Cl\}$	Keys: Hr, St

All schemes are in BCNF. No relation schemes can be removed while preserving contents, even though the first three contain all the attributes.

Biskup, Dayal, and Bernstein further observe that if P in Step 5 is augmented by a key X of the universal scheme U, then Algorithm 4 is also content-preserving [9]. In Example 11, the key (Hr, St) of the universal scheme already appears in the scheme (Hr, St, Cl). Thus, the set of relation schemes in Example 11 is content-preserving. The same is true for Example 12.

6.4.2 A BCNF Decomposition Algorithm

Beeri and Bernstein have strongly argued that Algorithm 4 probably cannot be extended to the synthesis of BCNF databases without losing its time complexity [4]. Their argument is based on several observations: It is not always possible to produce BCNF databases without introducing interrelational join constraints, as we indicated in Proposition 4. It is computationally very difficult to determine whether a given set of relation schemes is in BCNF with respect to a given set of FDs. It is also very difficult to determine, for a given database in $S_{1, F}$, whether there exists a dependency-preserving translation procedure that will map the given database into a BCNF database.

Nevertheless, it is quite easy to produce BCNF databases from $S_{1, F}$, if we can accept high computational complexity and interrelational join constraints. A procedure based on decomposition is given in Algorithm 5.

Algorithm 5

Input. A database $\langle R(U), H_1 \rangle$ in $S_{1, F}$.

Output. A BCNF database $\langle \delta_P(R), H_2 \rangle$.

Procedure.

Step 1. Find a nonredundant cover H_2 of H_1.

Step 2. $P \leftarrow \{U\}$.

Step 3. If there is a U_1 in P such that for some elementary FD $X \rightarrow A$ in H_2^+, $U_1 \supseteq XA$, and X is not a key or U_1 (that is, U_1 is not in BCNF with respect to H_2), then

{
remove U_1 from P;
add XA and $U_1 - \{A\}$ to P;
}.

Step 4. Repeat Step 3 until all relation schemes in P are in BCNF with respect to H_2.

Step 5. Output $\langle \delta_P(R), H_2 \rangle$.

Since each FD is also an MD by the inference rule X1 and Proposition 2, Step 3 uses only lossless decomposition. Thus, Algorithm 5 produces BCNF databases and is content-preserving. It is also dependency-preserving, but there may be interrelational join constraints.

Example 13

We use the database in Example 11 to illustrate Algorithm 5. Suppose that we start with a nonredundant cover $\{1, 2, 3, 5, 6\}$, as in Example 11. The initial scheme is $U = \{Cl, In, St, Ex, Hr, Rm\}$. The only key is $\{Hr, St\}$. Thus U can be decomposed according to (1) to produce $P = \{\{Cl, In\}, \{Cl, St, Ex, Hr, Rm,\}\}$. Since $\{Cl, In\}$ is already in BCNF, we will proceed with the second scheme, which has $\{Hr, St\}$ as the only key. Suppose that we decompose it according to (2); then $P = \{\{Cl, In\}, \{Cl, St, Ex\}, \{Cl, St, Hr, Rm\}\}$. Again, $\{Cl, St, Ex\}$ is already in BCNF.

The scheme $\{Cl, St, Hr, Rm\}$ has several elementary FDs in it: (3), (4), (6), and (8). We have the following possible combinations:

$\{Hr, Rm, Cl\}$,	$\{Hr, Rm, St\}$	according to (3)
$\{Hr, St, Rm\}$,	$\{Hr, St, Cl\}$	according to (4)
$\{Hr, St, Cl\}$,	$\{Hr, St, Rm\}$	according to (6)
$\{Hr, Cl, Rm\}$,	$\{Hr, Cl, St\}$	according to (8)

The second and third lines are identical. Thus, we may obtain one of the following three sets of schemes:

$$\{\{Cl, In\}, \{Cl, St, Ex\}, \{Hr, Rm, Cl\}, \{Hr, Rm, St\}\} \qquad (A)$$

$$\{\{Cl, In\}, \{Cl, St, Ex\}, \{Hr, St, Rm\}, \{Hr, St, Cl\}\} \qquad (B)$$

$$\{\{Cl, In\}, \{Cl, St, Ex\}, \{Hr, Cl, Rm\}, \{Hr, Cl, St\}\} \qquad (C)$$

In case (A), (5) becomes an interrelational join constraint because the schemes in (A) can only enforce $\{1, 2, 3, 4, 8\}$ through keys and they do not imply (5). Likewise, (3) and

(5) become interrelational join constraints for (B); and (5) is the interrelational join constraint in (C). Also, (C) is the same set of schemes as produced by Algorithm 4 for Example 12 even though a different set of FDs was used there.

6.4.3 A 4NF Decomposition Algorithm

The BCNF decomposition algorithm can be extended to FDs and MDs to produce 4NF databases. For the sake of simplicity, we shall first consider only MDs.

Suppose we are given a set H of MDs. We can reasonably assume that every MD $X \rightarrow \rightarrow Y$ in H is simple; that is, Y is in the dependency basis of X with respect to H.

We say that a relation scheme U_1 is *decomposable* with respect to an MD $X \rightarrow \rightarrow Y$ if $U_1 \supseteq X$, $U_1 \cap Y \neq \varnothing$, and $U_1 - XY \neq \varnothing$. In the context where no FDs are present, a relation scheme is not in 4NF with respect to H if and only if it is decomposable with respect to a nontrivial MD in H^+.

A cover H_1 of H is said to be a *4NF cover* if the following condition is satisfied: For any relation scheme U_1, U_1 is not decomposable with respect to any nontrivial MD in H^+ if and only if U_1 is not decomposable with respect to any MD in H_1. A nonredundant 4NF cover is a 4NF cover of which no proper subset is also a 4NF cover. Thus, to check that a relation scheme is in 4NF, we need only verify it against a minimal 4NF cover.

Unfortunately, we do not know of any efficient way to compute a nonredundant 4NF cover. We only know that a nonredundant cover may not be a 4NF cover. We also have the following necessary condition.

Proposition 5.   Let H be a nonredundant cover and H_1 be a 4NF cover of H. If V is a left side in $H_1 - H$, then V must contain the left side of some MD in H and V is itself nondecomposable with respect to MDs in H [23].

Thus, an exponential-time algorithm can be constructed to compute a nonredundant 4NF cover for H.

We are now ready to present a 4NF decomposition algorithm. Algorithm 6 was first proposed in [23] as an improved version of Fagin's 4NF decomposition approach [17, 18, 23].

Algorithm 6

Input. A database $\langle R(U), H_1 \rangle$ in $S_{1,M}$, where H is a set of simple MDs.

Output. A 4NF database $\langle \delta_P(R), H_2 \rangle$.

Procedure.

Step 1.   Find a nonredundant 4NF cover H_2 of H_1.

Step 2. $P \leftarrow \{U\}$.

Step 3.   Partition MDs in H_2 into groups such that all MDs with the same left side are in one group. Label the groups $G_1, G_2, \ldots, G_k$ so that $LS(G_i) \subseteq$

$LS(G_j)$ implies $1 \le i \le j \le k$, where $LS(G_i)$ denotes the left side of MDs in G_i.

Step 4.   For $i = 1$ until k do:

              while (there is some U_1 in P such that U_1 is

              decomposable with respect to some MD $X_i \to\to W$ in G_i),

do:

                 {

                 remove U_1 from P;

                 add $U_1 \cap X_iW$ and $U_1 - W$ to P;

                 }.

Step 5.   Output $\langle \delta_P(R), H_2 \rangle$.

Algorithm 6 can be transformed into translating databases in $\mathbf{S}_{1, FM}$ to 4NF databases. (FDs need not be simple.) The changes involve the computation of a nonredundant 4NF cover for a mixed set of FDs and MDs. In the subsequent steps, FDs can be treated as MDs.

Algorithm 6 is dependency- and content-preserving and produces 4NF databases. In fact, it is also minimally content-preserving [23]. By Proposition 4, this algorithm may produce databases with interrelational join constraints.

Example 14

We use Example 2 to illustrate Algorithm 6. The set U consists of Cl, Se, St, Mj, Yr, Ex, In, Rk, Sa, Tx, Dy, and Rm. The MDs can be replaced by the following cover:

$$\text{Cl} \to\to \text{Tx} \tag{1}$$

$$\text{St} \to \text{Mj}, \text{Yr} \tag{2}$$

$$\text{In} \to \text{Rk}, \text{Sa} \tag{3}$$

$$\text{Cl}, \text{Se} \to\to \text{In} \tag{4}$$

$$\text{Cl}, \text{Se} \to\to \text{Dy}, \text{Rm} \tag{5}$$

These MDs form a nonredundant 4NF cover; thus, they can be used directly for decomposition. The process of repeated decomposition can be represented by a *decomposition tree*. Each node of the tree corresponds to one dependency (FD or MD). We shall attach the dependency, and the relation scheme to be decomposed, to the node as its label. The leaves of a decomposition tree are always labeled by relation schemes only.

Suppose we start to decompose U according to (1). At the end of the decomposition, the tree becomes

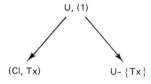

The leaf labeled (Cl, Tx) is already in 4NF; thus, it requires no further decomposition. But $U - \{Tx\}$ is not in 4NF, since St $\rightarrow$ (Mj, Yr) is a nontrivial MD and St is not a key of $U - \{Tx\}$. Hence, Step 4 of Algorithm 6 will continue to decompose $U - \{Tx\}$ with respect to (2). At the end of that step, we have

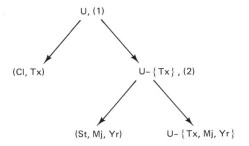

Likewise, we can continue decomposition along the rightmost leaf. After (1), (2), (3), (4), and (5) are used, we have the decomposition tree shown in Figure 6.6. A different set of relation schemes may be obtained if we start with a different 4NF cover or use a different decomposition sequence. For example, if (4) is used ahead of (3) in the decomposition sequence, rank and salary information will appear with classes and sections—a very unnatural relation scheme.

Decomposition trees are a concise way to represent the process of decomposition. For the sake of brevity we will refine the labels used in decomposition trees: each node will be labeled only by the left side of the corresponding dependency. This is because the relation scheme to be decomposed is always the union of the leaves of the subtree rooted at this node. The exact dependency used in the decomposition can also be inferred from the immediate successors of the node. Since

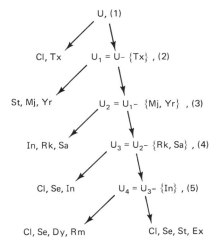

Figure 6.6   A decomposition tree.

MDs are simple, decomposition with respect to a group of MDs sharing the same left side can be represented by a single node with several successors, instead of just two, in the decomposition tree. The new version of the decomposition tree in Figure 6.6 is given in Figure 6.7.

Decomposition trees keep track of which dependencies are being used in the decomposition process. If an MD is used in the process, its left side will appear as an internal node of the decomposition tree. Unfortunately, it is not always possible to construct a decomposition sequence in which all MDs are used. This is because decomposition according to one MD may divide the attributes in the left side of another MD and thus eliminate it from the subsequent decompositions. MDs not used in the decomposition process become interrelational join constraints.

For this reason, we now turn to a restricted class of relational databases in $S_{1, M}$, in which these conflicting MDs are ruled out. We say that two left sides X and Y are *conflict-free* if their dependency bases $md_H(X)$ and $md_H(Y)$ satisfy the following condition: For some $i \geq 0, j \geq 0$, and $k \geq 0$, and for possibly empty Z_a and Z_b,

$$md_H(X) = \{V_1, V_2, \ldots, V_k, X_1, X_2, \ldots, X_i, (Z_a Y_1 Y_2 \ldots Y_j)\}$$

$$md_H(Y) = \{V_1, V_2, \ldots, V_k, Y_1, Y_2, \ldots, Y_j, (Z_b X_1 X_2 \ldots X_i)\}$$

and

$$\{V_1, V_2, \ldots, V_k\} \subseteq md_H(X \cap Y), Z_a X = Z_b Y$$

In this definition, we assume $\text{DEP}(\varnothing) = \varnothing$. If the left sides in a set H of MDs are pairwise conflict-free, we say that H is conflict-free. We use $S_{1, CM}$ to denote the relational databases $\langle R(U), H \rangle$ where H is conflict-free.

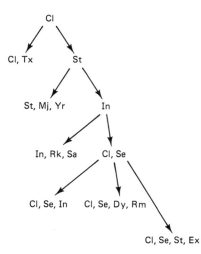

Figure 6.7 A concise version of the decomposition tree in Figure 6.6.

Example 15

We again consider the dependencies in Example 2. All FDs are treated as MDs (by rule X1). The two left sides In and {Cl, Se} are in conflict. This is because $md(\text{Cl, Se})$ is

$$\{\text{In}\}, \{\text{Rk}\}, \{\text{Sa}\}, \{\text{St, Mj, Yr, Ex}\}, \{\text{Tx}\}, \{\text{Dy, Rm}\}$$

and $md(\text{In})$ is

$$\{\text{Rk}\}, \{\text{Sa}\}, \{\text{Cl, Se, St, Mj, Yr, Ex, Tx, Dy, Rm}\}$$

but {Rk} and {Sa} are not in $md(\{\text{In}\} \cap \{\text{Cl, Se}\})$.

Example 16 [23]

Let U be {Cl, Dy, St, Mj, Ex, Tu, Hr, Of} and H be as follows:

$$\text{Cl} \to\to \text{Dy} \tag{1}$$

$$\text{St} \to\to \text{Mj} \tag{2}$$

$$\text{Tu} \to\to \text{Of} \tag{3}$$

$$\text{Cl, St} \to\to \text{Ex} \tag{4}$$

$$\text{Cl, Tu} \to\to \text{Hr} \tag{5}$$

The database consists of three types of entities: Cl (classes), St (students), and Tu (tutors). A class meets on certain days (Dy). A student has majors (Mj) and a tutor has offices (Of). A student has a set of exam scores (Ex) for a given class. A tutor has a schedule of office hours (Hr) for a given class. According to (1) and M1, the complementation rule, each student in a class is assigned a set of tutors. Hence, it is inconsistent with the constraints of H to infer that every student in a class can visit any tutor in the class.

We have the dependency bases for all left sides as follows.

$$md(\text{Cl}) = \{\text{Dy}\}, \{\text{St, Mj, Ex, Tu, Of, Hr}\}$$

$$md(\text{St}) = \{\text{Mj}\}, \{\text{Cl, Dy, Ex, Tu, Of, Hr}\}$$

$$md(\text{Tu}) = \{\text{Of}\}, \{\text{Cl, Dy, St, Mj, Ex, Hr}\}$$

$$md(\text{Cl, St}) = \{\text{Ex}\}, \{\text{Dy}\}, \{\text{Mj}\}, \{\text{Tu, Of, Hr}\}$$

$$md(\text{Cl, Tu}) = \{\text{Hr}\}, \{\text{Dy}\}, \{\text{Of}\}, \{\text{St, Mj, Ex}\}$$

We can easily check that each pair of left sides is conflict-free.

Proposition 6.   If H is a set of conflict-free MDs and is its own nonredundant cover, then H is also a nonredundant 4NF cover (of H).

Proof. We assume to the contrary that H is not a 4NF cover and that an MD with left side V must be added. That is, for some relation scheme U_1, U_1 is not decomposable with respect to any MD in H and yet U_1 is decomposable with respect to an MD in H^+, say, $V \to\to S$. Without loss of generality, we can assume that $\mathbf{S}$ is in $md_H(V)$.

By Proposition 5, V must properly contain the left side of an MD, say X_1, and VS must be contained by $X_1 Y_1$ for some Y_1 in $md_H(X_1)$.

Assume that V properly contains $X_1, X_2, \ldots, X_i$, where X_m's$(1 \leq m \leq i)$ are left sides in H, and VS is contained in $X_m Y_m (1 \leq m \leq i)$, where Y_m is in the dependency basis $md_H(X_m)$. It is easy to show that S is properly contained in $T = (Y_1 - V) \cap (Y_2 - V) \cap \cdots \cap (Y_i - V)$. This implies that if we use Algorithm 2 to compute $md_H(V)$, rules M1, M2, and M6 are not adequate to obtain S (Steps 1 and 2).

Therefore, there must exist another MD $Z \rightarrow \rightarrow W$ in H such that $Z - V \neq \varnothing$, $T \cap Z = \varnothing$, $T \cap W \neq \varnothing$, and $T - W \neq \varnothing$. But this is not possible: Since Z and X_m $(1 \leq m \leq i)$ are conflict-free, Z must be contained in $X_m Y_m$ $(1 \leq m \leq i)$. Thus, $Z \subseteq (X_1 Y_1 \cap X_2 Y_2 \cap \cdots \cap X_i Y_i) = VT$, which violates the conditions that $Z - V \neq \varnothing$ and $T \cap Z = \varnothing$. This concludes the proof that H must be a 4NF cover.

Proposition 6 illustrates another reason to study conflict-free databases. Since nonredundant covers of a set of MDs can be easily computed, Algorithm 6 can be used to decompose conflict-free databases in $\mathbf{S}_{1,CM}$, without incurring an exponential time complexity in Step 1. In fact, Algorithm 6 can be implemented to run in $O(|H|^2 \cdot |U|^2)$ for $\mathbf{S}_{1,CM}$, where $|U|$ is the number of attributes in U and $|H|$ is the size of any reasonable representation of H [23].

Conflict-free databases have another interesting property: as long as the decomposition is according to one of the orders satisfying the constraint in Step 3 of Algorithm 6, the relation schemes produced are the same [24]. This is not true in the general class $\mathbf{S}_{1,M}$.

6.4.4 An Algorithm That Preserves Interrelational Semantics

When a relational database is conflict-free, we can utilize a decomposition tree to construct EDs.

Algorithm 7

Input. A database $\langle R(U), H_1 \rangle$ in $\mathbf{S}_{1,CM}$, where H_1 consists of simple MDs.

Output. A database $\langle \delta_P(U), H_2 \rangle$, where H_2 is a set of EDs.

Procedure.

Step 1. Find a nonredundant cover H of H_1.

Step 2. Apply Algorithm 6 to decompose $R(U)$ with respect to H. Let DT be the corresponding decomposition tree.

Step 3. $P \leftarrow \{\text{labels of nodes in DT}\}$.

Step 4. $H_2 \leftarrow \varnothing$.

Step 5. For each arc $\langle X, Y \rangle$ in DT do:

$\{$

Find a node Z in the subtree rooted at Y such that Z contains X, and no nodes in between X and Y contain X and are contained by Z; $H_2 \leftarrow H_2 \cup \{Z[=]X\}$;

$\}$.

Step 6. Output $\langle \delta_P(R), H_2 \rangle$.

The set of EDs can be represented by a graph. We use an arc between X and Y, where X contains Y, to represent an ED $X[=]Y$. The graph so constructed is called a *relation hierarchy* [23]. The relation hierarchy produced by Algorithm 7 is always connected and acyclic.

The ordering in Step 3 of Algorithm 6 and the fact that H_1 is conflict-free guarantee the existence of a node Z satisfying the condition put forth in Step 5 of Algorithm 7. In general, several such nodes may exist in a decomposition tree.

Example 17

Let U and H be the sets given in Example 16. H is a nonredundant 4NF covering of itself. We shall apply Algorithm 6 to normalize U. According to the ordering (1)(2)(3)(4)(5), Algorithm 6 produces the decomposition tree in Figure 6.8. Applying Algorithm 7, we may produce the relation hierarchy shown in Figure 6.9.

We note that there is no direct path from Cl to (Cl, Tu). In fact, $R[\text{Cl}, \text{Tu}] \bowtie R[\text{Cl}, \text{St}]$ may not be $R[\text{Cl}, \text{Tu}, \text{St}]$ for any $R(U)$ in which H holds. If we were to include an arc from Cl to (Cl, Tu) along with other arcs directed out of Cl, it might mislead the user into forming the lossy join $R[\text{Cl}, \text{Tu}] \bowtie R[\text{Cl}, \text{St}]$. Note that the existence dependency $(\text{Cl}, \text{Tu})[=]\text{Cl}$ is redundant; it can be derived from the path between the two nodes.

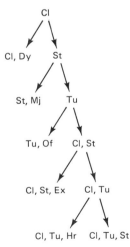

Figure 6.8 Decomposition tree for Example 17.

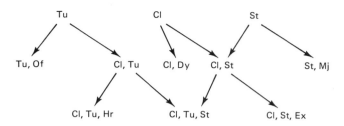

Figure 6.9 A relation hierarchy for Example 17.

The relation hierarchy in Figure 6.9 illustrates two important points. First, EDs serve to make interrelational semantics explicit, but implied EDs, such as $(Cl, Tu)[=]Cl$, sometimes mislead the user into forming lossy joins. Navigation by EDs (or by relation hierarchies) may cause semantic errors. Second, the present treatment of dependencies leaves us no choice but to exclude null values. We cannot derive EDs of the form $Y[\subseteq]X$. Therefore, information about a student who takes no courses cannot be recorded in the database. Preliminary treatments of null values have been reported [22, 24, 25, 32, 33, 37].

Algorithm 7 is content-preserving but not minimally so, because all internal nodes in the decomposition tree correspond to redundant contents. However, these internal nodes will not be redundant if we allow null values and a weaker form of EDs, such as $Y[\subseteq]X$. All relation schemes in a relation hierarchy are in 4NF.

Another interesting property of Algorithm 7 is that it is minimally dependency-preserving. Minimality comes from the fact that the output relation hierarchy is acyclic. The claim that it is dependency-preserving was proved in [24]. Essentially, we can reconstruct MDs from the relation hierarchy as follows. For each node X in the graph, its removal produces disconnected components of the graph. For each component, we can construct an MD $X \to \to Y - X$, where Y is the set of attributes appearing in the component.

6.4.5 Mixed Decomposition Algorithm

Extending the notion of elementary FDs to MDs, Zaniolo proposed two criteria for preserving dependencies. We shall come to these two criteria after stating a few definitions.

Suppose $m: X \to \to Y$ and $n: Z \to \to W$ are two MDs, each of which has disjoint left and right sides. We say that $m \leq n$ if $X \subseteq Z$ and $Y \subseteq W$. When both m and n are simple and $m \leq n$, then $Y = W$. Note that $\leq$ is a partial order.

Given a set H of MDs, we use H_d to denote the set $\{m: X \to \to Y | X \cap Y = \varnothing, m$ is in $H^+\}$. The minimal elements of H_d with respect to the partial order $\leq$ are called *elementary* MDs. If m is elementary and there is another elementary *MD* in H_d sharing the same left side, then m is *multiple elementary*.

A multiple elementary MD is a nontrivial elementary MD, but the converse is not true. For example, $\{AB \to \to C, A \to \to D\}$ with $U = \{A, B, C, D\}$ contains a nontrivial elementary MD $AB \to \to C$ that is not multiple elementary. Likewise, every multiple elementary MD must be simple, but the converse is not true. For example, $\{ A \to \to B, AC \to \to B \}$ with $U = \{ A, B, C \}$ contains two simple MDs, but $AC \to \to B$ is not even elementary. A careful study of elementary and multiple elementary MDs can be found in [39].

Suppose that V is a relation scheme and H a set of elementary FDs and multiple elementary MDs. The basic step in decomposition is to replace V and H by a pair of schemes V_1 and V_2 and their corresponding sets H_1 and H_2 of dependencies derived from H. In order to preserve contents, this decomposition step is always performed with respect to an MD in H. On the other hand, preserving dependencies is a lot more difficult.

How are H_1 and H_2 derived? We first consider only the FDs in H. By inverse projectivity, FDs that hold in V_1 or V_2 continue to hold in V. Thus, it is sufficient to require that FDs in H_1 and H_2 form a cover of FDs in H. (This may not be necessary. For example, MDs in H_1 and H_2 may interact with their FDs to imply new FDs.) The first criterion suggested by Zaniolo and Melkanoff is

$$F_i = \{ f \colon W \to A | f \text{ is in } F \text{ and } WA \subseteq V_i \} \qquad i = 1, 2$$

and

$$F \subseteq (F_1 \cup F_2)^+ \qquad\qquad\qquad \text{(I)}$$

where F, F_1, and F_2 are FDs in H, H_1, and H_2, respectively. For MDs, we have the following observation.

Proposition 7. [39]   Let $X \to \to Y$, with $X \cap Y = \varnothing$, be an MD that holds in $R(U)$. Let $m \colon Z \to \to W$, with $Z \cap W = \varnothing$, be a statement such that $W \cap XY = \varnothing$ and $ZW \subseteq U - Y$. Then m holds in $R(U - Y)$ if and only if it holds in $R(U)$.

Proof. If m holds in $R(U)$, it also holds in $R(U - Y)$ by projectivity of MDs. Conversely, if m holds in $R(U - Y)$, then we have

$$
\begin{aligned}
R(U) &= R(U - Y) \bowtie R(XY) & (X \to \to Y \text{ in } R(U))\\
&= (R(ZW) \bowtie R(U - Y - W)) \bowtie R(XY) & (Z \to \to W \text{ in } R(U - Y))\\
&= R(ZW) \bowtie (R(U - Y - W) \bowtie R(XY)) & \text{(associativity of join)}\\
&= R(ZW) \bowtie R(U - W) & \text{(projectivity of MD)}
\end{aligned}
$$

Thus $Z \to \to W$ also holds in $R(U)$.

Suppose that V is decomposed with respect to $X \to \to Y$ in H; that is, $V_1 = XY$ and $V_2 = V - Y$. Let M_1 denote the set of multiple elementary MDs $Z \to \to W$ in H such that $ZW \subseteq V_1$ and $W \cap V_2 = \varnothing$. Likewise, M_2 is $\{ m \colon Z \to \to W | m$ is in H, $ZW \subseteq V_2$, $W \cap V_1 = \varnothing \}$. Recall that F is the set of FDs in H. The second criterion suggested by Zaniolo and Melkanoff is

$$M \subseteq (M_1 \cup M_2 \cup F)^+ \tag{II}$$

where M is the set of MDs in H.

Zaniolo and Melkanoff proposed to use (I) and (II) as the two criteria for choosing an MD for decomposition. In general, when a relation scheme V and a set H of dependencies are considered for decomposition, we look for one MD in H, say $X \rightarrow \rightarrow Y$, and see if the corresponding sets of dependencies F_1, M_1, F_2, M_2 will satisfy conditions (I) and (II). If so, $X \rightarrow \rightarrow Y$ will be used to decompose V. If no such MD exists, then V will not be decomposed.

Algorithm 8.

Input. A data base $\langle R(U), H_1 \rangle$ in $\mathbf{S}_{1, FM}$ where H is a set of FDs and MDs.

Output. $\langle \delta_P(R), H_2 \rangle$.

Procedure.

Step 1. Let F and M denote elementary FDs and multiple elementary MDs in H_1^+, respectively.

Step 2. $G \leftarrow \varnothing; J \leftarrow M; K \leftarrow \varnothing; P \leftarrow \varnothing$.

Step 3. Call *decomp*(U, F, M).

Step 4. Apply Algorithm 4 to obtain $\langle \delta_{P_0}(R), H_0 \rangle$ with $R[U_0]$ and G as input, where U_0 is the set of attributes that appear in G.

Step 5. $H_2 \leftarrow H_0 \cup J \cup K; P \leftarrow P \cup P_0$.

Step 6. Output $\langle \delta_P(R(U)), H_2 \rangle$.

Function *decomp*(V, F, M):

        / $*$ V is a relation scheme.

        F is a set of elementary FDs.

        M is a set of elementary MDs. $*$ /

        / $*$ G, J, K, and P are global variables. $*$ /

Step 1. For each $f: W \rightarrow A$ in F do:

    If $WA = V$ then $G \leftarrow G \cup \{f\}$.

Step 2. Consider M to be a set of MDs in the context of V. Remove from M all MDs which are not multiple elementary and add them into K.

Step 3. If M is empty, then

$$P \leftarrow P \cup \{V\}$$

    else

        {

For each MD $X \rightarrow\rightarrow Y$ in M, do:
$$
\begin{aligned}
&\{ \\
&V_1 \leftarrow XY;\ V_2 \leftarrow V - Y; \\
&F_1 \leftarrow \{ f\colon W \rightarrow A | f \text{ is in } F, WA \subseteq V_1 \}; \\
&F_2 \leftarrow \{ f\colon W \rightarrow A | f \text{ is in } F, WA \subseteq V_2 \}; \\
&M_1 \leftarrow \{ m\colon Z \rightarrow\rightarrow W | m \text{ is in } M, ZW \subseteq V_1, W \cap V_2 = \varnothing \}; \\
&M_2 \leftarrow \{ m\colon Z \rightarrow\rightarrow W | m \text{ is in } M, ZW \subseteq V_2, W \cap V_1 = \varnothing \}; \\
&\text{if } (F \subseteq (F_1 \cup F_2)^{+} \text{ and } M \subseteq (M_1 \cup M_2 \cup F^{+})) \text{ then} \\
&\qquad \{ \\
&\qquad J \leftarrow J - (M - M_1 - M_2); \\
&\qquad decomp(V_1, F_1, M_1); \\
&\qquad decomp(V_2, F_2, M_2); \\
&\qquad \}; \\
&\}; \\
&\}.
\end{aligned}
$$

In Step 3 of the function *decomp*, a candidate $X \rightarrow\rightarrow Y$ is chosen for decomposition. It then computes F_1, F_2, M_1, and M_2 and checks that $F \subseteq (F_1 \cup F_2)^{+}$ and $M \subseteq (M_1 \cup M_2 \cup F)^{+}$. If these two conditions are satisfied, then $X \rightarrow\rightarrow Y$ is actually used to decompose V; otherwise, another candidate is chosen. It is possible that all MDs will fail the two conditions.

Example 18

Let U contain A, B, C, D, E, and F. Let M be the following MDs:

$$A \rightarrow\rightarrow B \tag{1}$$

$$A \rightarrow\rightarrow CD \tag{2}$$

$$A \rightarrow\rightarrow EF \tag{3}$$

$$CE \rightarrow\rightarrow AB \tag{4}$$

$$CE \rightarrow\rightarrow D \tag{5}$$

$$CE \rightarrow\rightarrow F \tag{6}$$

We also assume that there are no FDs.

Initially, we call $decomp(U, \varnothing, M)$. Suppose we start with $A \rightarrow\rightarrow B$. Step 3 will produce

$$V_1 = AB, \qquad V_2 = ACDEF$$
$$M_1 = \{1\}$$

and

$$M_2 = \{2, 3, 5, 6\}$$

Since $(M_1 \cup M_2)^{+} = M^{+}$, this is a successful decomposition. Therefore, we call $decomp(ACDEF, \varnothing, M_2)$.

If we were to begin with $A \to\to CD$, it would break M_2 into two sets $\{2\}$ and $\{3\}$, from which M_2 could not be recovered. The same would be true if $A \to\to EF$, $CD \to\to D$, or $CE \to\to F$ were chosen for decomposition. Thus, Algorithm 8 will leave $ACDEF$ undecomposed.

Clearly, Algorithm 8 may stop with a relation not in 4NF. In other words, when freedom from interrelational join constraints and normalization to 4NF cannot be achieved simultaneously, the algorithm favors the former objective. An interesting question to ask is: What property should the input set of MDs have in order to attain both objectives in using Algorithm 8? Zaniolo and the author have found that conflict-freeness is exactly this property. We omit the proof of the next proposition because it is tedious and is not essential to the understanding of this chapter.

Proposition 8.   Let M be a nonredundant cover of a set of MDs defined on U. All relation schemes produced by $decomp(U, \varnothing, M)$ are in 4NF if and only if M is conflict-free.

However, when FDs are present, the dependency-preserving conditions may dictate the choices of MDs used in the decomposition. The following example shows that MDs which are not conflict-free may still be used to produce a 4NF database.

Example 19

We apply Algorithm 8 to the database in Example 14. Recall that U consists of Cl, Se, St, Mj, Yr, Ex, In, Rk, Sa, Tx, Dy, Rm. Also, the following dependencies are given.

$$\text{Cl} \to\to \text{Tx} \tag{1}$$

$$\text{St} \to \text{Mj} \tag{2a}$$

$$\text{St} \to \text{Yr} \tag{2b}$$

$$\text{In} \to \text{Rk} \tag{3a}$$

$$\text{In} \to \text{Sa} \tag{3b}$$

$$\text{Cl, Se} \to \text{In} \tag{4}$$

$$\text{Cl, Se} \to\to \text{Dy, Rm} \tag{5}$$

$$\text{Cl, Se} \to\to \text{St, Mj, Ex, Yr} \tag{6}$$

$$\text{Cl, Se} \to\to \text{In, Rk, Sa} \tag{7}$$

$$\text{Cl, Se} \to\to \text{Tx} \tag{8}$$

$$\text{Cl, Se, Dy} \to \text{Rm} \tag{9}$$

$$\text{Cl, Se, St} \to\to \text{Ex} \tag{10}$$

In Step 1 of Algorithm 8, F will contain $\{2a, 2b, 3a, 3b, 4, 9\}$. F will also contain the following FDs:

$$Cl, Se \rightarrow Rk \tag{11}$$

$$Cl, Se \rightarrow Sa \tag{12}$$

During the consideration of elementary MDs, these FDs will be treated as MDs according to the inference rule X1. By the complementation rule (M1), we will have the following multiple elementary MDs:

$$Cl \rightarrow \rightarrow U - \{Cl, Tx\} \tag{13}$$

$$St \rightarrow \rightarrow U - \{St, Mj, Yr\} \tag{14}$$

$$In \rightarrow \rightarrow U - \{In, Rk, Sa\} \tag{15}$$

The MD (7) is not elementary, because of (4). The MD (8) is not elementary either, because of (1). The MD (9) is elementary, but not multiple elementary. The same is true for the MD (10). Thus, we have

$$F = \{2a, 2b, 3a, 3b, 4, 9, 11, 12\}$$

$$M = \{1, 2a, 2b, 3a, 4, 5, 6, 11, 12, 13, 14, 15\}$$

We are ready to call *decomp* (U, F, M). In Step 3 of *decomp* we will assume that (4) is considered first as a candidate for decomposing U. This leads to $V_1 = \{Cl, Se, In\}$ and $V_2 = U - \{In\}$. Also, F_1 is $\{4\}$ and F_2 is $\{2a, 2b, 9\}$. M_1 and M_2 are $\{4\}$ and $\{1, 2a, 2b, 5, 6, 11, 12\}$, respectively. It is clear that $(F_1 \cup F_2)^+$ is not F^+. Hence, this candidate should be rejected. The same reasoning can be applied to reject (11) and (12).

Suppose that we try (5). Then, $V_1 = \{Cl, Se, Dy, Rm\}$ and $V_2 = U - \{Dy, Rm\}$. Also,

$$F_1 = \{9\}$$
$$F_2 = \{2a, 2b, 3a, 3b, 4, 11, 12\}$$
$$M_1 = \{5\}$$

and

$$M_2 = \{1, 2a, 2b, 3a, 3b, 4, 6, 11, 12\}$$

Since $F_1 \cup F_2 = F$ and $(M_1 \cup M_2 \cup F)^+ = M^+$, this is a good candidate for decomposition. Thus, we proceed to call *decomp* (V_1, F_1, M_1) and *decomp* (V_2, F_2, M_2). The execution of the former leaves FD (9) in the set G and $\{Cl, Se, Dy, Rm\}$ in P. The rest of the procedure is presented in the tree in Figure 6.10. In each node, we show the input $\langle V, F, M \rangle$ and either an MD used to decompose V or the result of a call to *decomp* in terms of G and P. At the end, we have

$$G = \{9, 2a, 2b, 3a, 3b, 4\}$$

and

$$P = \{V_1, V_3, V_7, V_9, V_{10}, V_{11}, V_{13}, V_{14}\}$$

as shown in node n_{14}.

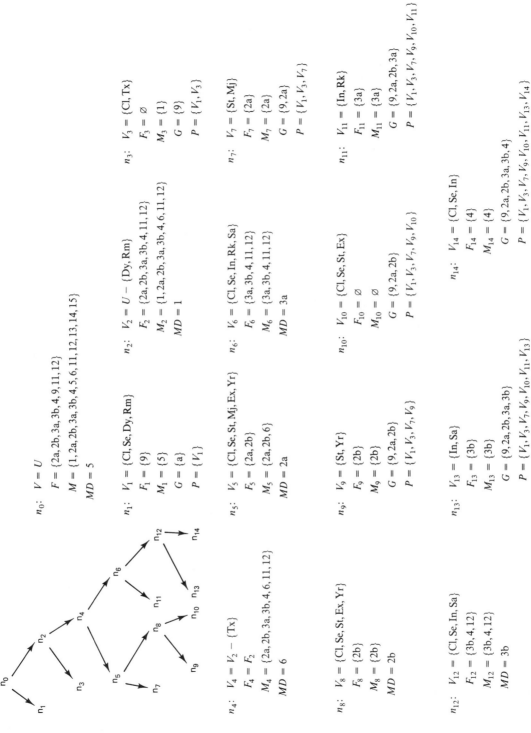

n_0: $V = U$
$F = \{2a, 2b, 3a, 3b, 4, 9, 11, 12\}$
$M = \{1, 2a, 2b, 3a, 3b, 4, 5, 6, 11, 12, 13, 14, 15\}$
$MD = 5$

n_1: $V_1 = \{Cl, Se, Dy, Rm\}$
$F_1 = \{9\}$
$M_1 = \{5\}$
$G = \{a\}$
$P = \{V_1\}$

n_2: $V_2 = U - \{Dy, Rm\}$
$F_2 = \{2a, 2b, 3a, 3b, 4, 11, 12\}$
$M_2 = \{1, 2a, 2b, 3a, 3b, 4, 6, 11, 12\}$
$MD = 1$

n_3: $V_3 = \{Cl, Tx\}$
$F_3 = \varnothing$
$M_3 = \{1\}$
$G = \{9\}$
$P = \{V_1, V_3\}$

n_4: $V_4 = V_2 - \{Tx\}$
$F_4 = F_2$
$M_4 = \{2a, 2b, 3a, 3b, 4, 6, 11, 12\}$
$MD = 6$

n_5: $V_5 = \{Cl, Se, St, Mj, Ex, Yr\}$
$F_5 = \{2a, 2b\}$
$M_5 = \{2a, 2b, 6\}$
$MD = 2a$

n_6: $V_6 = \{Cl, Se, In, Rk, Sa\}$
$F_6 = \{3a, 3b, 4, 11, 12\}$
$M_6 = \{3a, 3b, 4, 11, 12\}$
$MD = 3a$

n_7: $V_7 = \{St, Mj\}$
$F_7 = \{2a\}$
$M_7 = \{2a\}$
$G = \{9, 2a\}$
$P = \{V_1, V_3, V_7\}$

n_8: $V_8 = \{Cl, Se, St, Ex, Yr\}$
$F_8 = \{2b\}$
$M_8 = \{2b\}$
$MD = 2b$

n_9: $V_9 = \{St, Yr\}$
$F_9 = \{2b\}$
$M_9 = \{2b\}$
$G = \{9, 2a, 2b\}$
$P = \{V_1, V_3, V_7, V_9\}$

n_{10}: $V_{10} = \{Cl, Se, St, Ex\}$
$F_{10} = \varnothing$
$M_{10} = \varnothing$
$G = \{9, 2a, 2b\}$
$P = \{V_1, V_3, V_7, V_9, V_{10}\}$

n_{11}: $V_{11} = \{In, Rk\}$
$F_{11} = \{3a\}$
$M_{11} = \{3a\}$
$G = \{9, 2a, 2b, 3a\}$
$P = \{V_1, V_3, V_7, V_9, V_{10}, V_{11}\}$

n_{12}: $V_{12} = \{Cl, Se, In, Sa\}$
$F_{12} = \{3b, 4, 12\}$
$M_{12} = \{3b, 4, 12\}$
$MD = 3b$

n_{13}: $V_{13} = \{In, Sa\}$
$F_{13} = \{3b\}$
$M_{13} = \{3b\}$
$G = \{9, 2a, 2b, 3a, 3b\}$
$P = \{V_1, V_3, V_7, V_9, V_{10}, V_{11}, V_{13}\}$

n_{14}: $V_{14} = \{Cl, Se, In\}$
$F_{14} = \{4\}$
$M_{14} = \{4\}$
$G = \{9, 2a, 2b, 3a, 3b, 4\}$
$P = \{V_1, V_3, V_7, V_9, V_{10}, V_{11}, V_{13}, V_{14}\}$

Figure 6.10 The execution of *decomp* for Example 19.

The FDs in G are used as an input to Algorithm 4 to produce additional relation schemes in Step 4. The result is

$$P_0 = \{\, \{Cl, Se, In\}, \{St, Mj, Yr\}, \{In, Rk, Sa\}, \{Cl, Se, Dy, Rm\} \,\}$$

If we remove the redundant schemes V_7, V_9, V_{11}, and V_{13}, we have the following relation schemes:

$$\{Cl, Se, Dy, Rm\}$$

$$\{Cl, Tx\}$$

$$\{St, Mj, Yr\}$$

$$\{Cl, Se, St, Ex\}$$

$$\{In, Rk, Sa\}$$

$$\{Cl, Se, In\}$$

which are identical to the schemes obtained in Example 14. Also, in Step 5, we have $H_2 = \{1, 2a, 2b, 3a, 3b, 4, 5, 6, 9\}$. Compared to the MDs in Example 14, H_2 contains a redundant MD, (6). The MD (6) is also an interrelational join constraint. However, Proposition 7 implies that MDs of these types can be replaced by EDs as in Algorithm 7.

TABLE 6.2 **Summary of Major Relational Database Design Algorithms**

	Algorithm				
	4	5	6	7	8
Scope	3NF synthesis	BCNF decomposition	4NF decomposition	Schema graph synthesis	Mixed decomposition
Input	$\mathbf{S}_{1,F}$	$\mathbf{S}_{1,F}$	$\mathbf{S}_{1,FM}$	$\mathbf{S}_{1,CM}$	$\mathbf{S}_{1,FM}$
Output	$\mathbf{S}_{+,F}$	$\mathbf{S}_{+,F}$	$\mathbf{S}_{+,FM}$	$\mathbf{S}_{+,E}$	$\mathbf{S}_{+,FM}$
Content-preserving	Yes [9]	Yes	Yes	Yes	Yes
Dependency-preserving	Yes	Yes	Yes	Yes	Yes
Interrelational join constraint	No	Yes	Yes	No	Yes
Minimally content preserving	No	No	Yes	No (Yes, if null values are allowed)	No
Minimally dependency-preserving	Yes	Yes	Yes	Yes	No
Normal form	3NF	BCNF	4NF	4NF	3NF
Time complexity	$O(|H|^2)$	Exponential	Exponential	$O(|H|^2 \cdot |U|^2)$	Exponential
References	[4, 7, 9]	[18, 31]	[18, 23]	[23, 24]	[39]

6.5 SUMMARY

Each database design algorithm considered in this chapter offers some unique features, and no single algorithm stands out as the best. We summarize these features in Table 6.2.

REFERENCES

1. Armstrong, W.W., "Dependency Structures of Data Base Relationships," *Proc. IFIP 74*, pp. 580–583. New York: North-Holland, 1974.
2. Aho, A.V., C. Beeri, and J.D. Ullman, "The Theory of Joins in Relational Databases," *ACM Trans. on Database Systems*, Vol. 4, No. 3 (Sept. 1979), pp. 297–314.
3. Beeri, C., "On the Membership Problem for Multivalued Dependencies in Relational Databases," TR-229, Department of Electrical Engineering and Computer Science, Princeton University, Princeton, N.J., Sept. 1977, to appear, *ACM Trans. on Database Systems*.
4. Beeri, C., and P.A. Bernstein, "Computational Problems Related to the Design of Normal Form Relational Schemas," *ACM Trans. on Database Systems*, Vol. 4, No. 1 (March 1979), pp. 30–59.
5. Beeri, C., P.A. Bernstein, and N. Goodman, "A Sophisticate's Introduction to Database Normalization Theory," *Proc. 4th Int'l. Conf. on Very Large Data Bases*, Berlin, Sept. 1978, pp. 113–124.
6. Beeri, C., R. Fagin, and J.H. Howard, "A Complete Axiomatization for Functional and Multivalued Dependencies in Database Relations," *Proc. ACM-SIGMOD Int'l. Conf. on Management of Data*, Toronto, August 1977, pp. 47–61.
7. Bernstein, P.A., "Synthesizing Third Normal Form Relations from Functional Dependencies," *ACM Trans. on Database Systems*, Vol. 1, No. 4 (Dec. 1976), pp. 277–298.
8. Bernstein, P.A., and N. Goodman, "What Does Boyce-Codd Normal Form Do?" *Proc. 6th Int'l Conf. on Very Large Data Bases*, Montreal, October 1980, pp. 245–259.
9. Biskup, J., U. Dayal and P.A. Bernstein, "Synthesizing Independent Database Schemas," *Proc. ACM-SIGMOD Int'l Conf. on Management of Data*, Boston, May 1979, pp. 143–151.
10. Chen, P.P.-S., "The Entity-Relationship Model—Towards a Unified View of Data," *ACM Trans. on Database Systems*, Vol. 1, No. 1 (March 1976), pp. 9–36.
11. Codd, E.F., "A Relational Model for Large Shared Data Bases," *CACM*, Vol. 13, No. 6 (June 1970), pp. 377–387.
12. Codd, E.F., "Further Normalization of the Data Base Relational Model," in *Data Base Systems*, ed. R. Rustin, pp. 33–64, Englewood Cliffs, N.J.: Prentice-Hall, 1972.
13. Codd, E.F., "Recent Investigations in Relational Database Systems," *Information Processing 74*, pp. 1017–1021. New York: North-Holland, 1974.
14. Codd, E.F., "Extending the Database Relational Model to Capture More Meaning," *ACM Trans. Database Systems*, Vol. 4, No. 4 (December 1979), pp. 397–434.

15. Date, C.J., *An Introduction to Database Systems*, 2d ed. Reading, Mass.: Addison-Wesley, 1977.

16. Delobel, C., "Normalization and Hierarchical Dependencies in the Relational Data Model," *ACM Trans. on Database Systems*, Vol. 3, No. 3 (Sept. 1978), pp. 201–222.

17. Fagin, R., "Multivalued Dependencies and a New Normal Form for Relational Databases," *ACM Trans. on Database Systems*, Vol. 2, No. 3 (Sept. 1977), pp. 262–278.

18. Fagin, R., "The Decomposition Versus the Synthetic Approach to Relational Database Design," *Proc. 3rd Int'l. Conf. on Very Large Data Bases*, Tokyo, Oct. 1977, pp. 441–446.

19. Fagin, R., "Normal Forms and Relational Database Operators," *Proc. ACM-SIGMOD Int'l. Conf. on Management of Data*, Boston, May 1979, pp. 153–160.

20. Fagin, R., "A Normal Form for Relational Databases That Is Based on Domains and Keys," IBM Research Report 2305, San Jose, Calif., 1979.

21. Hagihara, K., M. Ito, K. Taniguchi, and T. Kasami, "Decision Problems for Multivalued Dependencies in Relational Databases," *SIAM J. Comp.*, Vol. 8, No. 2 (May 1979), pp. 247–264.

22. Lien, Y.E., "Multivalued Dependencies with Null Values in Relational Data Bases," *Proc. 5th Int'l Conf. on Very Large Data Bases*, Rio de Janeiro, October 1979, pp. 61–66.

23. Lien, Y.E., "Hierarchical Schemata for Relational Databases," *ACM Trans. on Database Systems*, Vol. 6, No. 1 (March 1981), pp. 48–69

24. Lien, Y.E., "On the Equivalence of Database Models," *Journal of ACM*, Vol. 29, No. 2 (April 1982), pp. 333–362.

25. Lipski, W. Jr., "On Semantic Issues Connected wth Incomplete Information Databases," *ACM Trans. on Database Systems*, Vol. 4, No. 3 (September 1979), pp. 262–296.

26. Mendelzon, A.O., "On Axiomatizing Multivalued Dependencies in Relational Databases," *Journal of ACM*, Vol. 26, No. 1 (January 1979), pp. 37–44.

27. Nicolas, J.M., "Mutual Dependencies and Some Results on Undecomposable Relations," *Proc. 4th Int'l. Conf. on Very Large Data Bases*, Berlin, September 1978, pp. 360–367.

28. Rissanen, J., "Theory of Relations for Databases-A Tutorial Survey," *Mathematical Foundations of Computer Science*, Lecture Notes in Computer Science 64, pp. 537–551. New York: Springer-Verlag, 1978.

29. Sadri, F., and J.D. Ullman, "A Complete Axiomatization for a Large Class of Dependencies in Relational Databases," *Proc. ACM 12th Symp. on the Theory of Computing*, Los Angeles, April 1980, pp. 117–121.

30. Sagiv, Y., "An Algorithm for Inferring Multivalued Dependencies with an Application to Propositional Logic," *Journal of ACM*, Vol. 27, No. 2 (April 1980), pp. 250–262.

31. Ullman, J.D., *Principles of Database Systems*. Potomac, Md.: Computer Science Press, 1980.

32. Vassiliou, Y., "Null Values in Data Base Management: A Denotational Semantics Approach," *Proc. ACM-SIGMOD Int'l Conf. on Management of Data*, Boston, May 1979, pp. 162–169.

33. Vassiliou, Y., "Functional Dependencies and Incomplete Information," *Proc. 6th Int'l Conf. on Very Large Data Bases*, Montreal, October 1980, pp. 260–269.

34. Yang, J.N., "A Query Language and Data Base Management for Relational Model," Ph.D. dissertation, University of California, Berkeley, September 1974.

35. Yannakakis, M., and C.H. Papadimitriou, "Algebraic Dependencies," *Proc. IEEE Foundations of Computer Science Conf.*, 1980, pp. 328–332.

36. Zaniolo, C., "Analysis and Design of Relational Schemata for Database Systems," Tech. Rep. UCLA-ENG-7769, Department of Computer Science, UCLA, July 1976.

37. Zaniolo, C., "Relational Views in Data Base Systems: Support for Queries," *Proc. IEEE Computer Society Computer Software and Applications Conference*, Chicago, November 1977, pp. 267–275.

38. Zaniolo, C., "A New Normal Form for the Design of Relational Database Schemas," *ACM Trans. on Database Systems*, Vol. 7, No. 3 (September 1982), pp. 489–499.

39. Zaniolo, C., and M.A. Melkanoff, "On the Design of Relational Database Schemas," *ACM Trans. on Database Systems*, Vol. 6, No. 1 (March 1981), pp. 1–47.

7

Computer-Assisted Hierarchical Database Design

George U. Hubbard
IBM Corporation
Dallas, Texas

7.1 INTRODUCTION

Database design by manual techniques has traditionally been a long and tedious process that can be characterized as more an art than a science. And the cost of poor design can be enormous. In addition to the usual design concerns of performance, integrity, security, and so on, other concerns are the length of time required to get a new database and its applications into productive use, and the sometimes prohibitive cost of restructuring an existing database (or its application) once poor design has been recognized.

Computer assistance can be applied to the logical design process, and, when used with appropriate human interfaces, it can help the designer produce a logical design more quickly and with the expectation of better quality.

In this chapter the concepts of computer-assisted logical database design will be reviewed and applied to the design of DL/I hierarchical structures. The basic concepts will be summarized, and then the balance of the chapter will elaborate on these concepts, illustrating by applying them to the design of a database for the order entry example. The salient benefits of the process in editing and in deriving a logical schema will be demonstrated. In conclusion, desirable roles of a data dictionary in the design process will be discussed.

The concepts of computer-assisted database design in general and of database design aid (DBDA) in particular have been presented in the literature [4, 5, 7]; the reader may refer to these articles for further detail.

7.2 COMPUTER-ASSISTED DESIGN

In order to appreciate the potential of applying computer assistance to the logical design process, we should ask ourselves what improvements are desirable in current design procedures. Some of these desired improvements are the following:

> More thorough predesign analysis of the data requirements.
>
> Closer communication between the database designers and the application specialists.
>
> The ability to discover errors, inconsistencies, and omissions earlier in the design process.
>
> The ability to process changed requirements without redoing the entire design.
>
> The ability to evaluate the impact of new or changed requirements on an existing design.
>
> The ability to relieve the designer of much of the labor and tedium of design and to provide more complete information for human decision making.

These are precisely the benefits to be derived from computer-assisted logical design.

7.3 PRELIMINARY CONCEPTS

The design process to be described is based on associations (one-way) between data elements rather than on the more familiar notion of mappings (two-way). Therefore, before launching into a description of the process, we will review associations briefly. Also, the rules of hierarchical DL/I databases that are pertinent to the logical design process will be reviewed.

7.3.1 Mappings and Associations

The concept of mappings is well known to database designers. The one-to-many ($1:M$) mapping between data elements A and B means that a given value of A can identify many values of B, but each value of B identifies one and only one value of A. The mapping between department and employees is an example. The many-to-many ($M:M$) mapping implies that a given value of either element identifies many values of the other. The mapping between parts and suppliers is a frequently used illustration. The $1:M$ mapping normally constitutes the parent-child relationship in hierarchical structures. The $M:M$ mapping, as implemented in DL/I structures, usually applies to the physical parent and logical parent of a logical relationship. Mappings describe two-way relationships between pairs of related elements.

In the process to be described it is desirable to express data relationships in terms of one-way association types rather than two-way mappings. For example, to one user who requires that the values of one data element be used to identify values of another data element in some manner, the nature of the inverse relationship may be irrelevant, and an arbitrary choice may conflict with the more firm requirements of one or more other users. It is when the data requirements for the several applications that will use the database are brought together into a composite model, and specified associations can be related with their inverse associations (that may have been specified by someone else), that the familiar mapping terminology becomes appropriate.

Further, associations (as will be seen) are used to define key-to-attribute relationships, and in most cases, relationships are not specified from attributes back to their keys. Therefore, the design procedures to be presented are based on data relationships specified in terms of association types rather than in terms of mappings.

Three types of associations are defined as follows:

Type 1 (functional).
Type M (complex).
Type C (conditional).

7.3.2 Type 1 (Functional) Association

A given occurrence of the "from" element identifies one and only one occurrence of the "to" element. The identification is unique (single-valued, atomic), and it represents a functional dependency. One example in Figure 7.1 is EMPLOYEE-NO to SOCIAL-SECURITY-NO. Another example is EMPLOYEE-NO to DEPT-NO. An employee has only one social security number and belongs to only one department. Nothing is said about the nature of the relationship in the inverse direction. This association type is frequently called a *simple association*. It is analogous to the functional dependency, with the universal relation assumption, defined in Chapter 6.

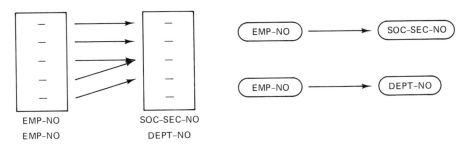

Figure 7.1   Type 1 (functional) association.

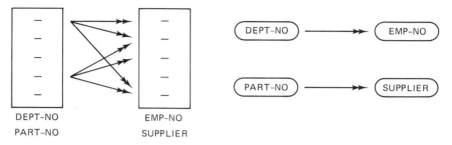

Figure 7.2   Type M (complex) association.

7.3.3 Type M (Complex) Association

A given occurrence of the "from" element identifies any number (0, 1, or more than 1) of occurrences of the "to" element. The identification is not necessarily unique, and it represents a multivalued determination. It is analogous to the multivalued dependency defined in Chapter 6. In Figure 7.2, an example is DEPT-NO to EMPLOYEE-NO. Another example is PART-NO to SUPPLIER. A given department may have many employees, and a given part may be furnished by many suppliers. Again, nothing is said about the nature of the inverse association.

7.3.4 Type C (Conditional) Association

For a given occurrence of the "from" element, a corresponding occurrence of the "to" element may or may not exist, but if it does exist, there is only one. The identification, if made, is unique. An example of EMPLOYEE-NO to TERMINA-TION-DATE is shown in Figure 7.3. Another example is HOSPITAL-BED to PATIENT. An employee may or may not have a termination date, but if he has one, he has only one. A hospital bed may or may not have a patient assigned to it, but if there is a patient, hopefully, there is only one. It will be explained later that in some contexts a type C association is treated as a type 1 and in other contexts as a type M.

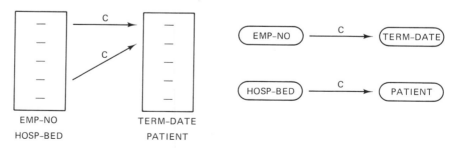

Figure 7.3   Type C (conditional) association.

7.4 CHARACTERISTICS OF DL / I DATABASES

Computer-assisted design procedures must be tailored to the type of database being designed. The procedures to be presented in this chapter apply to hierarchical DL/I databases as featured in IBM's Information Management System (IMS); therefore, before we launch into the computer-assisted design techniques, a brief review of the rules for DL/I structures is in order. With slight adaptations, these same procedures can also be used to assist in designing relational and CODASYL databases.

DL/I databases are basically hierarchical, although they frequently consist of separate trees connected by logical relations to form restricted networks. Within a hierarchical tree, each node (segment type) other than the root has one and only one higher-level (parent) node. At the top of a tree is a single node called the *root segment*. In this context we speak of a physical child having a physical parent.

Under certain conditions, trees can be connected by associating a node (logical child) in one tree to a node (logical parent) in another tree. This logical relation is similar to, but more restrictive than, the networking concept of CODASYL data structures. Logical relations can also be implemented within a single tree by relating a child to certain nodes (including its physical parent). All entries to the DL/I database are made through a root segment or via a secondary index, which is a device to permit entry at a selected lower-level segment. The IMS database management system works in such a way that regardless of whether segments are accessed by descending down the tree or by following a logical relation to another tree, the segments to be accessed appear to the application programmer to be hierarchically related in a single pseudotree (logical database) of which the first segment accessed is the root.

In doing the logical design for DL/I databases, the following rules are pertinent:

Each segment (other than the root, which has no parents) must have one and only one physical parent.

A nonroot segment may also have one logical parent.

Each parent may have any number of child segment types.

A parent segment may have any number (including 0 or 1) occurrences of a child segment type.

A hierarchical tree can have no more than 15 levels and no more than 255 segment types.

For a given segment type, each segment occurrence is identified by a unique sequence field (key) or by its relative position (first, second, etc.) under its parent.

Within a keyed segment, the values of the nonsequence fields (attributes) are considered to be uniquely identified by the sequence field (key).

A logical child cannot have a logical child.

Any field (key or attribute) in a segment may serve as the source field of a secondary index, but the target (first segment accessed) cannot be lower in the hierarchical path than the segment containing the source field.

7.5 DL/I LOGICAL DESIGN

Based on the structuring rules given above, techniques for computer-assisted logical design have been developed. The starting point for the process to be described assumes that the applications are sufficiently designed so that their data requirements are initially established. As will be shown, the design process, which is iterative, can help the designer in editing and making final determination of the data requirements.

Application program design and the initial determination of the data elements required by each application function, while vital to the overall design process, are beyond the scope of this chapter, although it is believed that the technique presented herein could be extended to assist with application design.

After having identified the data elements required by each application that will use the database, the designers must specify which elements are used to identify which other elements and the nature of such associations. For each pair of elements so related, the designer (or end user) determines if the identification is unique or nonunique. He or she then assigns a Type 1, M, or C association to that element pair. Based on the data elements, their names, and the association types defined between them by the designers (or by the end users), the computer-assisted procedures can perform many editing and diagnostic operations and can derive DL/I hierarchical structures.

The process to be described assumes that certain structuring can be deduced automatically from the data requirements while other structuring decisions should merely be "suggested" to the designer for his review and implementation decisions. Some helpful information to assist the designer with such decisions is also provided.

The design process is iterative. The first logical schema to be derived after diagnostics are resolved is called the *canonical logical schema*, and it is derived according to the criteria presented in the next section. Additional iterations of the process may be used by the designer to *refine* the design according to performance criteria provided by the process and also according to the designer's own judgment and expertise.

7.5.1 Deriving the Logical Schema

The data requirements (data-element pairs and the associations defined between them) can be structured into a canonical logical design according to the following criteria.

1. *Remove transitivity*: In tracing the paths of Type 1 associations to determine keys, attributes, and child-parent relationships, tests are made for transitivity,

and it is removed wherever it occurs. The designer is always notified of transitive relationships that are removed, and he or she has the option of specifying their inclusion in subsequent iterations. Removing transitive relations is a very important step with possible far-reaching consequences, and it is discussed more fully in a separate section below.

2. *Identify keys*: Any element that identifies another element with a Type 1 association is a unique identifier and is therefore classed as a key. A key defines a DL/I segment.

3. *Identify attributes*: Elements identified by a Type 1 or C association from a key but which do not in turn identify other elements with a Type 1 association are called *attributes* and are clustered into the segment(s) of their key(s) as nonsequence fields. The attribute identified by a Type C association represents a field that may or may not occur in the segment. Redundant data (attributes appearing in two or more segments) can be identified at this point and suitable diagnostics printed to alert the designers.

4. *Determine segments*: Each key automatically defines a DL/I segment. There are no segments without a unique sequence field in this process. Should the designer want to define a non-keyed segment, a dummy element to represent a relative positioning of the segment occurrences must be introduced. Note that a segment need not have attributes. An element can define a key-only segment if it merely identifies another key with a Type 1 association.

5. *Calculate performance weights*: Given sufficient information about the expected frequency of use of the application functions and the expected number of accesses to the data elements, performance weights can be calculated to give an estimate of the relative use of the paths of the derived hierarchies. These weights are helpful to the designer in making performance judgments about the logical design. They can also be helpful in deriving the logical schema (see the next step). The method of calculating performance weights is described below, following the section on removing transitivity.

6. *Derive physical child-parent relationships*: Type 1 associations between keys are used to deduce child-parent (not parent-child) relationships between segments. By following a path of Type 1 associations, we derive the hierarchical tree in a bottom-up fashion. Type M or C associations in the downward direction that are inverses to the Type 1 associations merely confirm the parent-child relationships already deduced. When a child has two or more parents, the physical parent can be the one in the path having the highest performance weight.

7. *Derive logical-relation candidates*: "Candidates" for logical relations are suggested by the following criteria:

   (a) A segment has two or more possible parents as defined by the Type 1 associations.

   (b) An M : M or M : C mapping exists between two keys.

   (c) A lone Type M or Type C association exists between two keys.

Such candidates should be reported to the designer who will make the final structuring decision.

8. *Derive secondary-index candidates*: "Candidates" for secondary indexes are suggested by the following criteria:

   (a) An element serving as the desired entry point for an application function is not the key of the root segment in the derived structure.

   (b) A Type M association exists from an attribute to a key in the same or in a higher-level segment.

Such candidates should be reported to the designer who will make the final structuring decision.

The foregoing are the fundamentals on which the design techniques are based. In an actual design many subtleties, inconsistencies, and intermediate decision points may be encountered, and frequent human-machine interfaces at appropriate points are essential to the success of the process. A detailed presentation of the process is beyond the scope of this chapter, but with the foundation thus far established, the example to be presented should give a good general understanding of computer-assisted database design as applied to DL/I structures. The process is described in more detail in [5, 7].

7.5.2 Identifying and Removing Transitivity

A Type 1 association between two data elements is said to be *nonessential* (or *transitive*) if there is at least one other path of Type 1 associations leading from the source element to the target element. Presumably, the transitive association can be removed without destroying the capability of traversing from the source to the target element. Figure 7.4 illustrates the transitivity property. By removing the association from *A* to *C*, one can still traverse from *A* to *C* via the intermediate element *B*. Detailed algorithms for this redundancy removal, such as the third-normal-form synthesis algorithm, are presented in Chapter 6.

Transitivity among Type M associations is more elusive, but it does not concern us in these procedures because it is the Type 1 associations (functional dependencies) that are being analyzed to determine the physical relationships between data elements (i.e., keys, attributes, and physical parent-child relationships). The Type M associations are analyzed only to determine candidates for logical relations and secondary indexes.

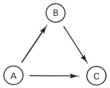

Figure 7.4 Concept of transitivity.

The purpose of removing transitivity is to eliminate potential redundancies and also to eliminate potential update anomalies, as explained by Codd [2], Date [3], and others. But removal of transitivity can also produce undesirable design results in DL/I structures. Although access can still be made from A to C by going from A to B and then from B to C (Figure 7.4), the following questions become pertinent to the designer:

> Can the application stand the performance degradation of extra accesses to reach the target element?
>
> Will the desired occurrence (value) of the target element be obtained by taking a different route?
>
> Will there be a loss of information, such as detail or summary information, when taking a different route?
>
> Is it really a transitive situation, or does it merely appear to be so because of imprecise naming conventions?

Serious consideration must be given to transitivity by both the designers and the end users. Computer-assisted procedures make a major contribution by identifying *all* transitive situations (according to the data requirements as specified), so that none are overlooked by the designers.

7.5.3 Performance Weights

Performance weights are dimensionless weights to be used in a comparative sense. For example, if the performance weight for Path A is ten times larger than that for Path B, then Path A can be considered to be ten times more important than Path B from a performance standpoint. Note that we are not saying, necessarily, that Path A is traversed ten times more often than Path B. The calculated number of traversals can be weighted by other factors, such as processing option, on-line usage, and so on.

The basic inputs for performance-weight calculations are the setup period and frequency of processing for each application function (local view), along with the expected frequency of use of the association paths to be traversed within each function, the processing option for each access, and the relative weighting of batch vs. online work. The method of calculation is given in [5, 7]. As a simplified example, consider two abstract local views.

Assume Local View 1 to be an online transaction invoked an average of 100 times a day. It involves elements A, B, C, and D related as shown in Figure 7.5. The entry point is A. For each access to A there will be an average of two accesses to B, for each access to B there will be an average of five accesses to C, and for each access to C there will be an average of three accesses to D. Assume that all accesses are reads. Assume further that online response is four times more critical than batch response, thus making the online factor 4.

$$A \xrightarrow{\text{(2)}} B \xrightarrow{\text{(5)}} C \xrightarrow{\text{(3)}} D \qquad \textbf{Figure 7.5}$$

Assume Local View 2 to be a batch transaction invoked twice a month. It involves elements A, B, C, and E related as shown in Figure 7.6. The entry point is A. For each access to A there will be one access to B, for each access to B there will be ten inserts of C, and for each C there will be one E. Assume further that all accesses to A and B are reads. Assume also, for this example, that one insert will require as many physical IOs as ten reads. Finally, assume 22 working days in a month, so that the daily accesses in Local View 1 can be compared to the semimonthly accesses in Local View 2.

For each local view, performance weights can be calculated as follows:

$$\text{P.F.} = \text{RFU} \times \left(\frac{\text{setup}}{\text{factor}}\right) \times \left(\frac{\text{processing option}}{\text{factor}}\right) \times \left(\frac{\text{online}}{\text{factor}}\right)$$

where RFU (resultant frequency of use) represents the total number of traversals of a path in the local view.

For Local View 1, the following values have been given:

RFU $(A \rightarrow B) = 2$	Setup factor $\quad = 100 \times 22 = 2200$
RFU $(B \rightarrow C) = 2 \times 5 = 10$	Processing options $= 1$ (reads only)
RFU $(C \rightarrow D) = 2 \times 5 \times 3 = 30$	Online factor $\quad = 4$

For Local View 2, the following values have been given:

RFU $(A \rightarrow B) = 1$	Setup factor $\quad = 2 \times 1 = 2$
RFU $(B \rightarrow C) = 1 \times 10 = 10$	Processing options $= 1$ (reads)
RFU $(C \rightarrow E) = 1 \times 10 \times 1 = 10$	$\quad = 10$ (inserts)
	Online factor $\quad = 1$

For each association, the final performance weight is obtained by summing the performance-weight contributions from each local view.

$$
\begin{array}{llll}
 & \overbrace{\begin{pmatrix}\text{From Local}\\\text{View 1}\end{pmatrix}} & \overbrace{\begin{pmatrix}\text{From Local}\\\text{View 2}\end{pmatrix}} & \\
\text{P.F.}\,(A \rightarrow B) = & 2 \times 2200 \times 1 \times 4 & + \quad 1 \times 2 \times 1 \times 1 & = \;17{,}602 \\
\text{P.F.}\,(B \rightarrow C) = & 10 \times 2200 \times 1 \times 4 & + 10 \times 2 \times 10 \times 1 & = \;88{,}200 \\
\text{P.F.}\,(C \rightarrow D) = & 30 \times 2200 \times 1 \times 4 & & = 264{,}000 \\
\text{P.F.}\,(C \rightarrow E) = & & 10 \times 2 \times 1 \times 1 & = \qquad 20
\end{array}
$$

$$A \xrightarrow{\text{(1)}} B \xrightarrow{\text{(10)}} C \xrightarrow{\text{(1)}} E \qquad \textbf{Figure 7.6}$$

7.6 PREDESIGN DATA-REQUIREMENTS ANALYSIS

7.6.1 Gathering the Data Requirements

In determining the data requirements of the application functions, the designers must be cognizant of the different perspectives from which data may be viewed. Specifically, they must understand the notions of the conceptual view, the external view, and the internal view which are illustrated in Figure 7.7. As described in the ANSI-SPARC report [11], these three views are summarized below. The ANSI-SPARC framework is treated in Chapter 2.

It is also helpful to recognize that in the database community there are three realms in which an enterprise, or the real world in general, can be perceived (Figure 7.8). There is the enterprise (1) as it actually is (reality), (2) as it is perceived by humans (descriptive representation), and (3) as it is described by symbols (data). The conceptual, external, and internal views from which the database is designed are based on this third realm, and it is vital that they be derived in such a way that the enterprise is accurately characterized.

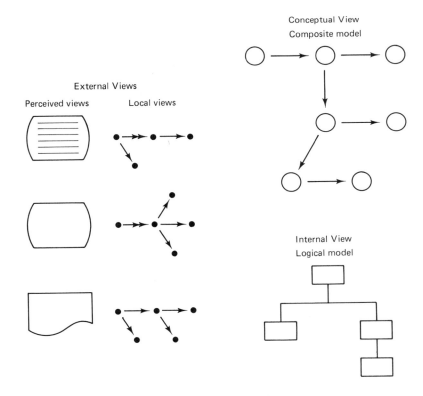

Figure 7.7   Views of data.

The *external* view of the data represents the data requirements of a given application function (or program) as viewed externally from its reports, screens, transactions, and so on. Thus, there is an external view for each function. Within an application area the various external views usually overlap to some extent but are rarely identical.

Along with external views, we introduce the notion of *local* views. There is a local view for each application function, and the local view describes what the database must contain in order that the external view for its function may be materialized. For example, an external view may contain net pay and gross pay, whereas the local view may contain gross pay and deductions from which the application can calculate net pay. Or the external view may contain age, while birth date would be preferable in the local view. Using the external views as starting points, it is the local views that the designers must specify for the design procedures. The local views are analogous to the program specification block (PSB) in DL/I systems.

As it is

As it is
perceived by
humans

As it is
described by
symbols

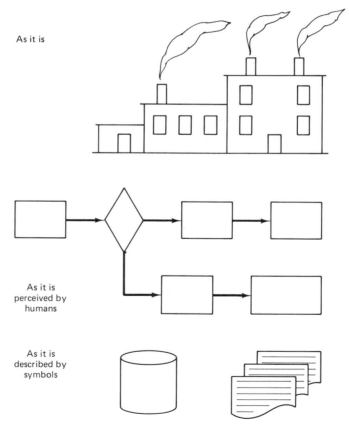

Figure 7.8   Representations of reality.

The *conceptual* view is more of an abstract notion representing the entire set of data requirements specified by the external and local views. In its broadest sense, the conceptual view can be construed to represent the total information requirements of the enterprise being modeled. This can include nonstored data for manual procedures as well as data to be included in the database. There is only one conceptual view for the enterprise being modeled, and it is non-structural with regard to networks, hierarchies, or relations.

The *internal* view of the data represents the integrated database itself. Theoretically, the internal view is a subset of the conceptual view. Practically, the internal view is derived from the composite of the local views. The internal view is roughly analogous to the database description (DBD) in DL/I systems. In logical design it is represented by a logical schema showing the data organized into the structures of a given database management system. In physical design, a physical schema shows how these structures are implemented onto the physical storage devices.

7.6.2 Starting Points

There are three general approaches for specifying data requirements for a design study. One approach begins by identifying the entities and their attributes and then determining the relationships between the entities [1]. In this context, entities are considered to be anything about which data is to be recorded, including objects, ideas, actions, roles, and so on. A second approach is to specify individual data elements, as identified from the inputs, outputs, and other functional requirements of the applications, and to specify the relationships between pairs of associated elements [4, 5, 7]. From this approach, the notion of entities can be derived. A third approach is again to identify the individual elements, to do a statistical analysis of their usage patterns to determine which ones are used together most frequently, and to group them into records, segments, or tuples accordingly. This latter technique, while catering to high-performance retrievals, can group elements together that have no real relationship with one another and may be subject to the update anomalies we avoid through normalization. The technique described herein can be applied to either the first or second of these approaches.

7.6.3 Editing and Diagnostics

While this chapter will emphasize deriving the logical schema from the composite model, we must also stress the importance of editing the user's data requirements and also the structuring diagnostics that can be produced.

Computer assistance aids the designer by its ability to accept data requirements from different applications and from different sources within the enterprise, then to combine and edit these requirements and produce useful lists that help identify inconsistencies in the naming conventions and usage of the data elements. This aspect of computer assistance is often underemphasized, but many designers have found it to be a valuable assist in formulating consistent and complete data requirements. In addition to uncovering inconsistencies between various user groups, some users report that this technique has been helpful in uncovering inconsistencies within a single user group.

The diagnostics produced by the structuring process can be much more meaningful if the designer does *not* submit the entire set of data requirements all at once to the process. Rather, the requirements for two or three high-volume transactions should be processed iteratively until their diagnostics are resolved and a reasonable design is obtained. Then the requirements of a few additional functions should be added and the entire process repeated again. In this manner the conflicts and alternatives created by the new and lesser functions can be more easily identified and dealt with. As conflicts and alternatives are detected, the designers are supplied with specific questions to be resolved and their dialogs with the end users can be more meaningful and productive.

Computer assistance also helps the designer by its ability to add new or changed data requirements to previously stored requirements, thus allowing the designer to (1) hold the existing design fixed and identify any conflicts caused by the new requirements, (2) allow the existing design to vary in order to accommodate the new requirements with consistency, or (3) obtain desired design results by imposing constraints between these two extremes.

Again, the editing and diagnostic reports serve to enhance communication between the designers and the end users.

7.6.4 Content of Local Views

The content of the local views required by computer-assisted techniques is defined below. Of the items to be specified, some are required for logical structuring, while others are optional. The amount of design information provided by the computer-assisted process is increased as more optional items are specified.

The following items are required for any use of the design procedures:

> Name of the local view.
>
> Names of the data elements.
>
> Association types (showing the element pairs being related).

With this information, the algorithms can perform most of their editing and can derive a canonical logical schema consisting of segment contents and physical parent-child relationships. However, the resulting logical schema may contain unresolved alternatives that could have been resolved automatically, had more input information been available.

If performance-oriented information is also provided, performance weights can be calculated which give an indication of the frequency of use and type of use of each of the paths in the derived hierarchies. This type of information can be quite useful in determining (1) the left-to-right ordering of the segment types, (2) the final contents of the segments, (3) the choices of physical and logical parentage, or (4) other performance-related design alternatives.

In order to obtain performance weights, the following frequency-of-use information is also required, as previously explained.

Frequency of use and setup period of the function represented by the local view.

Estimated accessing frequencies and processing options of the data elements in the local view.

The information in these items can be used in calculating performance weights from which several performance-related decisions can be made.

Additional information, helpful in physical design, can also be obtained by including the following additional items in the input:

Expected number of occurrences of each data element—To be used in estimating database size and identifying potentially long twin chains.

Finally, the data-requirements editing can be enriched if the following additional information is available:

Data-element characteristics (e.g., length, type, format)—To be used for calculating segment sizes and for editing the use of the same data names from different local views.

Data-element sources—To indicate that there is a source, either as input data or as the result of a calculation, for all data used by a local view.

7.7 LOGICAL DESIGN CASE STUDY

The initial data requirements of the order entry application are depicted by the ten local views of Figures 7.9 to 7.18. Figure 7.9 shows a required report (external view) and a schematic of the data requirements (local view) derived from it by the designer in consultation with the end users. For brevity, Figures 7.10 through 7.18 merely show the schematics (local views) of the remaining data requirements. The numbers in parentheses indicate the expected number of accesses to the target element, when different from 1, for each access to the source element.

The reader should assume that the requirements have been prepared by different people in different departments of the enterprise. In such situations, there are usually some inconsistencies in the naming, meanings, and relationships of the data elements that are used by more than one function. In this example, the inconsistencies have been exaggerated in order to more fully demonstrate the help that can be provided by the editing processes.

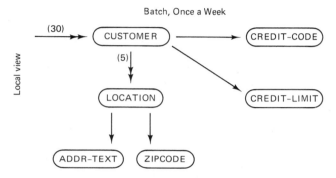

Figure 7.9   Local view 1.

7.7.1 Editing Reports

After combining the local views and editing them for errors, omissions, and inconsistencies, the editing results can be reported in a variety of reports. Among those that can be produced are where-used lists showing the descriptions and characteristics of each element and the local views in which it is used and also showing each associated pair of elements and the local views where they are used.

As the ten local views of the order entry example are processed, certain of the editing reports are especially revealing in identifying editing problems. For purposes

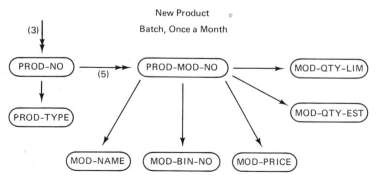

Figure 7.10   Local view 2.

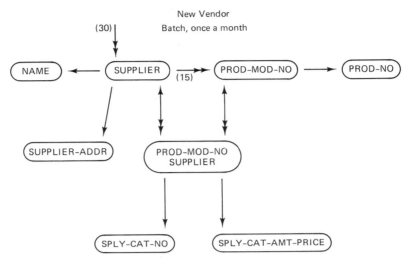

Figure 7.11   Local view 3.

of this chapter, the following three editing reports and their use will be illustrated:

Keyword-in-context (KWIC) list.

Attribute-analysis report.

Inconsistent-associations report.

Keyword-in-context (KWIC) list.   The KWIC list is an alphabetic listing of each qualifier of each data name arranged to show the context in which all instances of names and qualifiers are used. Such a list is very helpful in aiding the designer in finding synonyms and homonyms and names that are insufficiently qualified for their meanings to be clear. Extracts from the KWIC list that would be produced for the order entry example are presented in Figure 7.19.

In this example we see that ADDR is used in three contexts, and in the third case it is not clear whether ADDR-TEXT refers to customer, to vendor, or to something else. Further, in the first instance, should ADDR also be ADDR-TEXT? MOD-NAME and ZIPCODE appear also to be inconsistently qualified and could represent different meanings. SPLY and VEND give rise to other questions. These seem to be used synonymously for the same entity. It is evident that naming standards have not been consistently used. With specific questions such as these, the designer can work more meaningfully with the end user for resolution.

Attribute-analysis report.   This report gives a list of attributes identified by more than one key. It is derived by listing each attribute that is identified with a Type 1 or C association from more than one key. Such a list may indicate naming-standard problems in which two or more names are used for the same data

Order Entry
Online, 100 times a day

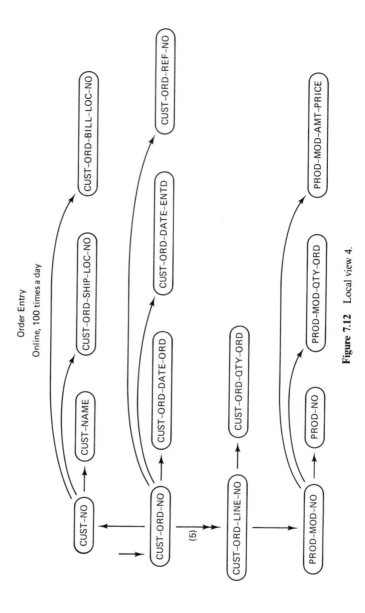

Figure 7.12 Local view 4.

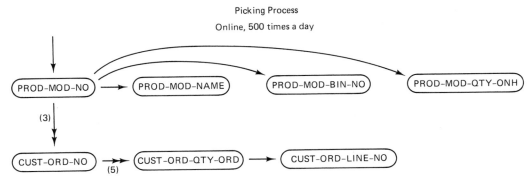

Figure 7.13   Local view 5.

element (key), or it may indicate truly redundant data in which two or more distinct keys are referencing the same attribute. In either case, the designer needs to know of all such situations. From the order entry example, two entries from the Attributes Analysis Report are presented graphically in Figure 7.20.

On the left we see that SUPPLIER and VEND-NO have both been used to identify NAME. It is likely that these are two synonyms for the same identifier. Also, NAME should be qualified according to standards, for there may eventually be several types of names. On the right, CUST-LOC-ADDR-TEXT is identified by two

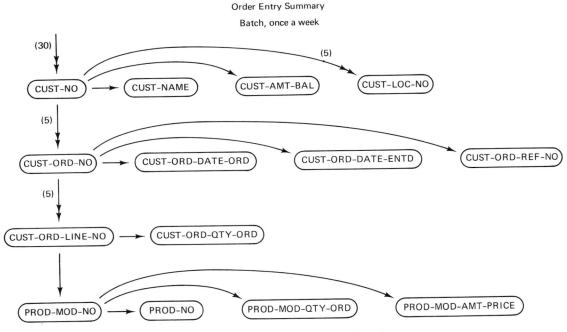

Figure 7.14   Local view 6.

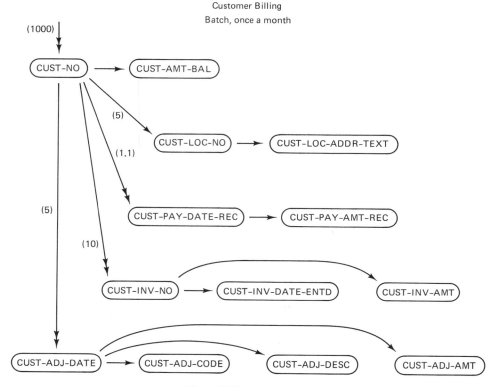

Figure 7.15   Local view 7.

keys. We will assume that the designer and the end users have agreed that this is legitimate, and that CUST-LOC-ADDR-TEXT will indeed be redundant data in two different segments. With a report such as this, redundant data is not overlooked; the designers are aware of all such situations.

Inconsistent-associations report.   This is a list of data-element pairs related by more than one association type in the same direction. This situation occurs when one analyst assumes a functional dependency from a key to a given attribute while another analyst expects a multivalued dependency from the same key to the same attribute (or to a different attribute that happens to carry the same name). It is likely that the different association types were specified for different applications by different user groups, but sometimes they are the result of confusion of analysts within the same application area.

In the order entry example, two associations have been specified inconsistently. In one case they are Type M, and in the other case they are Type 1. Again, the designer and end users have specific things to resolve. Must the designer accommodate both viewpoints in the model? If not, which is more appropriate? In addition,

Order History

Batch, once a month

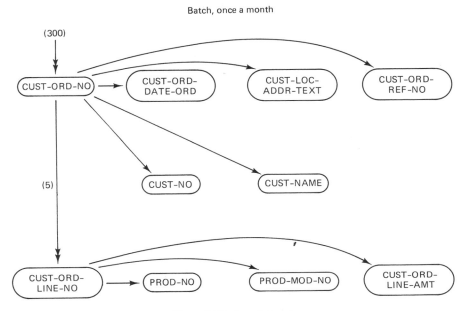

Figure 7.16   Local view 8.

the application programmers must know whether CUST-LOC-NO, for example, will be uniquely identified as an attribute in the CUST-NO segment or whether they will have to search for it as children of CUST-NO.

7.7.2 The Editing Process

Much research is currently underway to include the semantic meaning of data names and relationships (see Chapter 3) in the editing process, and much work still needs to be done. Yet, several types of editing lists are currently available to provide rich indications of possible problems, and they serve usefully in stimulating dialogs between designers and end users by suggesting specific questions about data names and usage. Three such lists have been illustrated above.

Customer Mailing

Online, 100 times a day

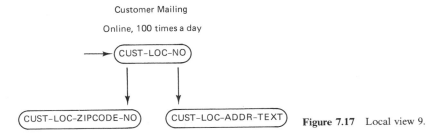

Figure 7.17   Local view 9.

Vendor Inquiry

Online, 50 times a day

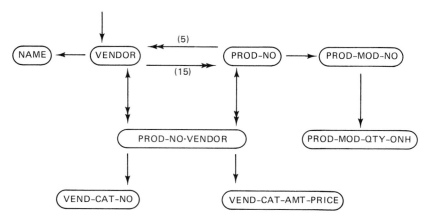

Figure 7.18   Local view 10.

SUPPLIER-	ADDR
CUST-LOC-	ADDR-TEXT
	ADDR-TEXT
SPLY-	CAT-AMT-PRICE
VEND-	CAT-AMT-PRICE
SPLY-	CAT-NO
VEND-	CAT-NO
	MOD-NAME
PROD-	MOD-NAME
	ZIPCODE
CUST-LOC-	ZIPCODE-NO

Figure 7.19   Keyword-in-context.

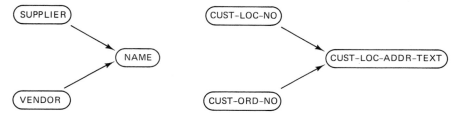

Figure 7.20   Attribute analysis.

FROM	TO	TYPE	LOCAL VIEW
CUST-NO	CUST-LOC-NO	M	ORDER ENTRY SUMMARY
		1	CUSTOMER BILLING
PROD-NO	PROD-MOD-NO	M	NEW PRODUCT
		1	VENDOR INQUIRY

Figure 7.21   Inconsistent associations.

Editing is an iterative process which may require several iterations of automated processing and designer–end-user dialogs. Assuming these iterative dialogs have occurred for the order entry example and that the designers and the end users are agreed upon changes to be made, it is determined that five of the local views must be revised to obtain the consistency needed in naming standards and in usage of the data. The editing changes to be made are summarized below.

The general CUSTOMER and the more specific CUST-NO and CUST-NAME are used synonymously. The specific terminology is to be used.
Erroneous Local View: 1.   Identifying Report: KWIC.

Variations of VENDOR and SUPPLIER have been used synonymously and with no distinction between the identification number and name of the sellers of the products. VEND-NO and VEND-NAME are to be used.
Erroneous Local Views: 3, 10.   Identifying Reports: KWIC, Attr. Anal.

Inconsistent levels of qualifications have been used in several instances on names of the same data item, e.g., MOD-NAME and PROD-MOD-NAME. The more detailed qualifications are to be used.
Erroneous Local View: 2.   Identifying Report: KWIC.

Two sets of inconsistent associations are detected. The associations from CUST-NO to CUST-LOC-NO and from PROD-NO to PROD-MOD-NO are to be made Type M consistently.
Erroneous Local Views: 7, 10.   Identifying Report: Incon. Assns.

Redundant data, CUST-LOC-ADDR-TEXT is detected and accepted.
Erroneous Local Views: 7, 8.   Identifying Report: Attr. Anal.

The detection of homonyms, while not illustrated in this example, is also an important problem which these reports can help identify. For example, in set of petroleum applications, is a well a "hole in the ground" or a "hole in the ground with black liquid issuing from it"? It makes a difference to exploration and production departments. Early detection of homonyms is frequently provided by the KWIC and Inconsistent Associations reports.

For this example, the five revised local views, 1, 2, 3, 7, and 10, are shown in Figures 7.22 through 7.26.

From these revised local views along with the five unchanged local views, we can now produce the resulting composite model from which the logical design will proceed.

New Customer Report

Batch, once a week

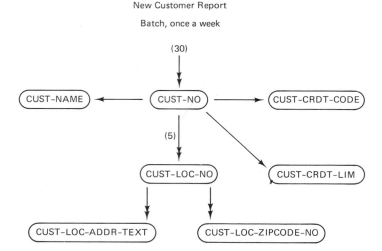

Figure 7.22   Local view 1 (revised).

7.7.3 The Composite Model

The composite model resulting from combining the ten edited local views is too large to be illustrated here in its fullness. Hence, a reduced version showing only those data elements classified as keys is shown in Figure 7.27. It is derived as the logical sum of the individual local views. Lone Type M associations between keys are automatically transformed into M : 1 mappings although the designers should review them as possible candidates for logical relations. Numbers to the left of the association arrows are the performance weights in the upward direction.

New Product

Batch, once a month

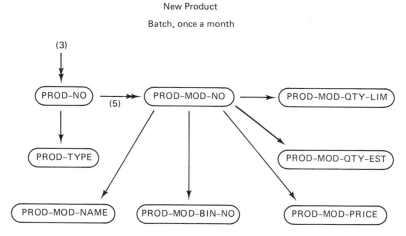

Figure 7.23   Local view 2 (revised).

New Vendor

Batch, once a month

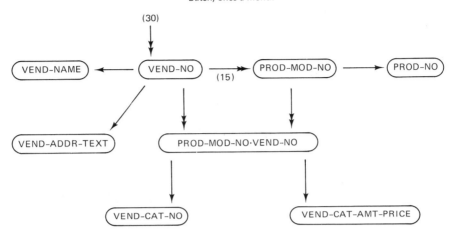

Figure 7.24 Local view 3 (revised).

Customer Billing

Batch, once a month

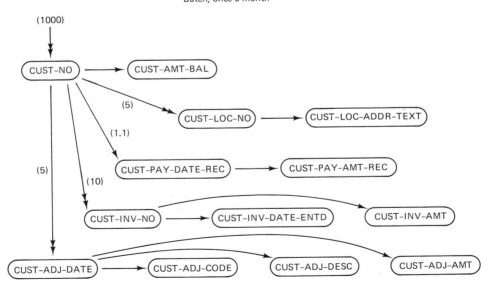

Figure 7.25 Local view 7 (revised).

Vendor Inquiry

Online, 50 times a day

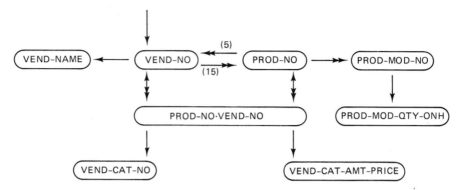

Figure 7.26   Local view 10 (revised).

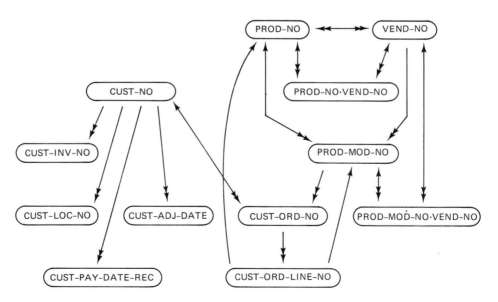

Figure 7.27   Composite model.

The reader should keep in mind that there are attributes for each of the keys, although the attributes are not illustrated here. Each illustrated data element, as a key, represents an entity and may be represented by a DL/I segment in the resulting logical schema.

7.7.4 Deriving the Logical Schema

From the composite model, a logical schema is derived according to the rules previously outlined in Section 7.5.1. This also implies iterative use of the automated procedures, continuing until all diagnostics are resolved. At that point a canonical logical design has been obtained.

Many diagnostics can be obtained, most of which are enumerated in [5, 7]. Basically they are reports of inconsistencies, omissions, and alternatives that the designers should review and resolve. DL/I show-stoppers such as loops, too many segment types, too many levels in the hierarchy, logical children of logical children, and so on can also be reported. Some of the more important general diagnostics are illustrated in the sections that follow.

The remainder of this example is devoted to the concept that, after the canonical logical schema is derived by the automated procedures, there is still much design work to be done, and that these automated procedures also provide much information helpful to the *human* designer for the refinement process.

7.7.5 Design and Diagnostic Reports

The canonical logical schema that will be derived from the composite model of Figure 7.27 is depicted by the parent-child graph of Figure 7.28, the suggested-segments report of Figure 7.29, and the candidates for secondary indexes of Figure 7.30. Diagnostic information that is pertinent to the example at hand is presented in the transitive-association report of Figure 7.31 and the complex-associations report of Figure 7.32. The use of all this information will be indicated in the discussion of the refinement process.

Parent-child graph.   The parent-child graph, which can include candidates for logical relations, is a pictorial representation of the logical schema. It is obtained by considering each key element as a segment and by tracing the Type 1 associations between keys after removal of transitivity. A Type 1 association from key Y to key X defines a physical parent-child relationship with X as the parent and Y as the child. Candidate logical relations can be indicated whenever a child has more than one parent. In such cases, the largest performance weight from parent to child determines the physical parent. If there are more than two possible parents for a child (a violation of IMS rules), appropriate diagnostics will be provided. In addition, loops cannot be graphed in a hierarchical structure. If X, Y, and Z are keys connected by Type 1 associations from Z to Y to X to Z, the segments represented by these keys will not appear, and dependent segments may be unconnected to the upper portions of the tree. Again, appropriate diagnostics will be provided.

In the parent-child graph of Figure 7.28 the boxes represent segments organized hierarchically into physical databases. The names inside the boxes are the names of the keys. Segment names are not yet determined. The dotted lines represent possible logical relations from logical child to destination (logical) parent. The numbers are the performance weights that have been calculated. The number to the left of a path is the performance weight downward from parent to child, and the number to the right of a path is the performance weight upward from child to parent.

Suggested-segments report.   The suggested-segments report (Figure 7.29) gives the contents and some characteristics of the segments suggested by the logical schema. For each key it shows the attributes that are related to the key by Type 1 or Type C associations. These are the attributes that could be mapped into each key's segment. The supporting information is intended to help the designer determine if the segments should be accepted as shown or if some should be split or combined in some way. A few reasons for splitting a segment are excessive length, mixture of frequently and infrequently used fields (PERF WEIGHT), mixture of read-only and update fields (PROC OPT), or mixture of fields from different local views. Segments may sometimes be combined to reduce the number of accesses by eliminating a level from the hierarchy (parent-child graph) or by combining segments used by the same local views.

Candidates for secondary indexes.   This report shows suggested entries into the logical schema, at points other than the root segments, to support one or more local views. Any key that is an entry point for a local view but is not a key of a root segment in the resulting hierarchies is listed as a candidate. Also, if a local view

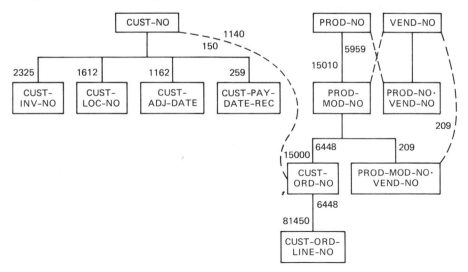

Figure 7.28 Parent-child graph.

KEY	ATTRIBUTE	PERF WEIGHT	LENGTH	PROC OPT	LOCAL VIEWS
CUST-ADJ-DATE			6		
	CUST-ADJ-AMT	1162	6	R	7
	CUST-ADJ-CODE	1162	1	R	7
	CUST-ADJ-DESC	1162	30	R	7
CUST-INV-NO			8		
	CUST-INV-AMT	2325	4	I	7
	CUST-INV-DATE-ENTD	2325	6	I	7
CUST-LOC-NO			4		
	CUST-LOC-ADDR-TEXT	2462	20	G	1, 7, 9
	CUST-LOC-ZIPCODE-NO	1300	5	G	1, 9
CUST-NO			6		
	CUST-NAME	1000	15	G	1, 4, 6
	CUST-ORD-BILL-LOC-NO	1000	4	G	4
	CUST-ORD-SHIP-LOC-NO	1000	4	G	4
	CUST-AMT-BAL	263	6	R	6, 7
	CUST-CRDT-CODE	60	1	R	1
	CUST-CRDT-LIM	60	6	R	1
CUST-ORD-LINE-NO			3		4, 5, 6
	CUST-ORD-QTY-ORD	80750	5	I	4, 5, 6
	CUST-ORD-LINE-AMT	698	6	I	8
CUST-ORD-NO			8		
	CUST-ORD-DATE-ORD	1290	6	I	4, 6, 8
	CUST-ORD-REF-NO	1290	6	I	4, 6
	CUST-ORD-DATE-ENTD	1150	6	I	4, 6
	CUST-LOC-ADDR-TEXT	140	20	I	8
CUST-PAY-DATE-REC			6		
	CUST-PAY-AMT-REC	256	6		7
PROD-MOD-NO			8		
	PROD-MOD-QTY-ONH	20750	4	R	5, 6, 10
	PROD-MOD-AMT-PRICE	5750	6	R	4, 6
	PROD-MOD-BIN-NO	5007	4	G	2, 5
	PROD-MQD-NAME	5007	10	G	2, 5
	PROD-MOD-QTY-ORD	5000	4	R	4
	PROD-MOD-PRICE	7	6	R	2
	PROD-MOD-QTY-EST	7	4	R	2
	PROD-MOD-QTY-LIM	7	4	R	2
PROD-NO			6		
	PROD-TYPE	1	3	G	2
VEND-NO			6		
	VEND-NAME	1014	15	G	3, 10
	VEND-ADDR-TEXT	14	20	G	3
PROD-MOD-NO *			0		
VEND-NO	VEND-CAT-AMT-PRICE	209	6	R	3
	VEND-CAT-NO	209	8	G	3
PROD-NO * VEND-NO			0		
	VEND-CAT-AMT-PRICE	15000	6	R	10
	VEND-CAT-NO	15000	8	G	10

Figure 7.29 Suggested segments.

requires a multivalued dependency (Type M) from an attribute back to its key or to some other key higher in the hierarchy, such attributes are also listed. An example of this second criterion is: Give me a list of part numbers for all parts costing less than $5.00. Whether or not secondary indexes should be implemented at these suggested points is a designer decision that will be based largely on expected frequency of use and on update requirements.

From the order entry example three candidates for secondary indexing are listed in Figure 7.30. All are keys and entry points of local views but are not roots in the resulting hierarchies.

Transitive-associations report.   The transitive-associations report lists the transitive associations that have been identified and removed from the model. It also lists the path(s) to be followed in lieu of the removed associations. With this report the designer can judge whether each transitive association should remain excluded from the model or whether it should be reinserted for accessing efficiency or for integrity. Or it may be that apparent transitivity exists because of imprecise naming of data elements. The designer can make these evaluations with confidence that there are no undiscovered transitivities. A programming procedure for detecting transitive associations is given in [4]. The reader may also want to review Algorithm 4 in Chapter 6 of this volume. Four transitive associations are detected in the order entry example and are illustrated in Figure 7.31.

Complex-associations report.   The complex-associations report presents situations that may require logical relations for implementation. All M : M and M : C mappings and all lone Type M associations between keys are listed. To avoid redundancy in DL/I databases, these mappings may be implemented by logical relations. The report also shows if a third element is present to define the intersection (logical child) of the logical relation. In addition, this report can show other candidates for logical relations such as multiple parents of a common child. It can also give warnings, such as flagging intersection segments that could be implemented as logical children of logical children, a violation of DL/I rules. Diagnostics of this type can be very useful to the designer when evaluating candidates for logical relations. The kind of information presented in this report is depicted pictorially in Figure 7.32.

For the order entry example, there is only one M : M mapping to report, along with three cases of unrelated multiple parents of common children. The M : M mapping relates PROD-NO and VEND-NO with PROD-NO∗VEND-NO as an intersection, and with PROD-MOD-NO also as an intersection. Whether or not to combine these intersections depends on several factors, such as which local views use

CUST-LOC-NO

CUST-ORD-NO

PROD-MOD-NO

Figure 7.30 Candidates for secondary indexes.

CUST-ORD-LINE-NO → PROD-MOD-NO   A.W. = 6448

    CUST-ORD-LINE-NO
      CUST-ORD-NO
        PROD-MOD-NO

CUST-ORD-LINE-NO → PROD-NO   A.W. = 698

    CUST-ORD-LINE-NO
      CUST-ORD-NO
        PROD-MOD-NO
          PROD-NO

CUST-ORD-NO → CUST-NAME   A.W. = 140

    CUST-ORD-NO
      CUST-NO
        CUST-NAME

PROD-MOD-NO * VEND-NO → VEND-NO   A.W. = 0

    PROD-MOD-NO * VEND-NO
      PROD-MOD-NO
        VEND-NO

Figure 7.31   Transitive associations.

them, whether or not they have common attributes, the destination values required, frequency of use, and size.

7.7.6 Refining the Logical Schema

The refinement concept emphasizes the true role of computer-assisted design procedures. The procedures do not perform a logical design per se. Rather they serve as a computational tool which organizes the data requirements into a canonical logical schema and which performs documentation, diagnostics, and quality-control checks of the designer's refinements. In the refinement phase, the human designer does the real logical design with the assistance of such a tool. This overall process is depicted in Figure 7.33.

The concept of refinement by the designer is indicated by two examples. Suppose, for example, that the schema of Figure 7.34(a) has been produced, and that C is a candidate for secondary indexing because C is a root key of some of the local views but not the root of the resulting structure. If most entries into the database are

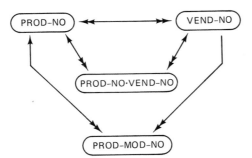

Figure 7.32   Complex associations.

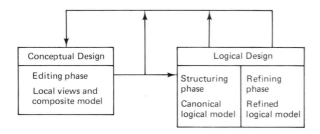

Figure 7.33 The refinement concept.

through the root segment, *A*, then the design may be efficient as it stands. But if most entries are through *C*, then a performance improvement may be gained by making *C* and its children a separate database and logically relating *A* and *C* [Figure 7.34(b)].

As another example of refinement for performance reasons, the designer may choose to add some redundancy to the database in order to reduce the number of required accesses. For example, by placing a replicated value of a data element into a second segment, perhaps the accesses for a high-volume transaction can be limited to one segment rather than to two or more. The performance gain must be evaluated against the redundancy and update anomalies that may be created.

For the order entry example, a complete exposition of refinements and their rationale is impossible without our knowing more about the application than has been specified thus far. However, for illustrative purposes, three refinements suggested by the design and diagnostic reports will be explored.

One change to the canonical logical schema is suggested by noticing in the attributes analysis report (Figure 7.20) and in the suggested-segments report (Figure 7.29) that the intersection segments, PROD-MOD-NO * VEND-NO and PROD-NO * VEND-NO, have exactly the same attribute fields redundantly. In addition, the designer observes in the complex-association report (Figure 7.32, not fully illustrated) the possibility of implementing PROD-MOD-NO * VEND-NO as a logical child of PROD-MOD-NO which Figure 7.28 shows to be a possible logical child of VEND-NO. Thus the designer feels that the database would be much cleaner and just as complete if one of these intersections could be eliminated entirely. But further investigation is in order. PROD-NO * VEND-NO is a direct intersection of PROD-

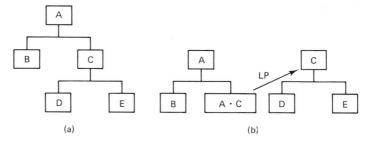

Figure 7.34 Example of a performance refinement.

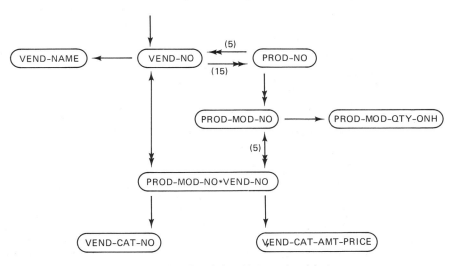

Figure 7.35   Local view 10 (second revision).

NO and VEND-NO. Referring back to the parent-child graph (Figure 7.28) and to the appropriate local view(s) (Figure 7.24), it becomes apparent that PROD-MOD-NO * VEND-NO, while a direct intersection of PROD-MOD-NO and VEND-NO, is also an indirect intersection of PROD-NO and VEND-NO. From the names used, it appears that one of these intersections was misdesigned in its local view(s). Conversations with the end user confirm what the designer now suspects, that the intersection attributes, VEND-CAT-NO and VEND-CAT-AMT-PRICE, are functionally related to PROD-MOD-NO and VEND-NO, and that trying to relate them directly to PROD-NO and VEND-NO will result in the loss of information about the catalog numbers and prices of the individual models produced by each vendor. As a result, the segment keyed by PROD-NO * VEND-NO is removed from the database, the end users are so advised, and the designer is careful to implement PROD-MOD-NO * VEND-NO as a physical child of PROD-MOD-NO. Local View 10 is revised again as shown in Figure 7.35, and a subsequent iteration of the automated procedures will document the new logical schema and will determine if any necessary paths have been removed and if any additional diagnostics have been generated.

Another refinement is suggested by reviewing the suggested-segments report (Figure 7.29). The designer may wish to consider splitting the CUST-NO segments and the PROD-MOD-NO segments. In the PROD-MOD-NO segment, for example, performance weights show that three elements, PROD-MOD-PRICE, PROD-MOD-QTY, and PROD-MOD-QTY-LIM, are very rarely used in relation to the other elements in the segment, and they are used only in Local View 2. By removing these elements and placing them into a new segment, we can block the remaining frequently used elements more tightly, and thus they may require fewer physical I/Os when being accessed. Two other elements used by Local View 2, PROD-MOD-BIN-NO and PROD-MOD-NAME, are also used by Local View 5, but they probably are not subject to frequent change. Therefore, they can be replicated into the two segments without undue updating anomalies. The resulting segments will have the contents shown in Figure 7.36.

By a similar rationale, the designer could also choose to split the CUST-NO segment. But this is a root segment, the differences in the performance weights among its fields are not so great as in the PROD-MOD-NO segment, and the larger fields are used in most accesses to the segment. Therefore, the designer chooses not to alter the CUST-NO segment.

Transitive associations can be left out or they can be reinserted into the database by means of logical relations or by controlled creation of redundant data. The transitive associations CUST-ORD-LINE-NO → PROD-MOD-NO and CUST-ORD-LINE-NO → PROD-NO will be used with moderate frequency as indicated by the performance weights shown in Figure 7.28. If they are not reinserted, two and three accesses will be required to go from CUST-ORD-LINE-NO to PROD-MOD-NO and to PROD-NO, respectively. We would like to avoid these extra accesses. One solution comes from noting in Local Views 4 and 6 that when coming from CUST-ORD-LINE-NO to PROD-MOD-NO, PROD-MOD-QTY-ORD and PROD-MOD-AMT-PRICE are also wanted. Assuming that these values are not subject to change once an order is entered, the above transitivity can be avoided and retrieve performance can be improved by redundantly including PROD-NO, PROD-MOD-NO, PROD-MOD-QTY-ORD, and PROD-MOD-AMT-PRICE in the CUST-ORD-LINE-NO segment.

The transitive associations, CUST-ORD-NO → CUST-NAME and PROD-MOD-NO-VEND-NO → VEND-NO, will not need additional attention because logical relations are already suggested that will enable the target elements to be obtained in one access.

The reader should keep in mind that the refinements illustrated above are merely representative of the type of thinking the designer should do after obtaining the canonical logical schema and of the help provided for that thinking process. There are, as has been indicated, many other factors that the designer should consider before finalizing the design.

After refinements have been determined, an additional iteration through the automated procedures is recommended as a quality-control check to verify that all

PROD-MOD-NO (1)   PROD-MOD-NO (2)

PROD-MOD-QTY-ONH   PROD-MOD-BIN-NO
PROD-MOD-AMT-PRICE   PROD-MOD-NAME
PROD-MOD-BIN-NO   PROD-MOD-PRICE
PROD-MOD-NAME   PROD-MOD-QTY-EST   **Figure 7.36** Divided PROD-MOD-NO
PROD-MOD-QTY-ORD   PROD-MOD-QTY-LIM   segment.

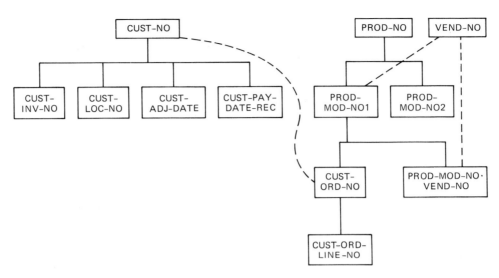

Figure 7.37 Final parent-child graph.

necessary paths are still present and to determine if any new diagnostics will be reported. Having the data requirements in machine-readable form makes additional iterations trivial in terms of additional labor. But assuming, for the sake of example, that the analysis outlined above is sufficient and complete, the new parent-child graph shown in Figure 7.37 documents the final results of the computer-assisted logical design of the order entry example. The corresponding revised suggested-segments report is not shown.

7.8 USING A DICTIONARY IN DATABASE DESIGN

A dictionary system is normally regarded as a mechanism for storing definitive and descriptive information about the content and organization of the database. A dictionary will contain the names of the data elements, textual definitions of their meanings, and descriptions of their characteristics (length, format, and so on). Alternate names (synonyms) for the same data are maintained and controlled. Information regarding ownership, security, and update control of the data is also maintained. In addition, dictionaries contain where-used information relating data to programs and to program owners so that those affected can be identified whenever changes to the database are proposed.

Dictionaries may also contain descriptions of the structure of the database. With regard to IMS, they contain descriptions showing the relationships of data elements to segments, segments to physical databases, and physical databases to logical databases. In this respect, they contain sufficient information for generating physical and logical database definitions (DBDs) and program specification blocks (PSBs).

A dictionary system and a computer-assisted database design process, closely integrated, have much to offer one another. They both deal with descriptions and characteristics of data elements and with the logical structures obtained from these elements and their relationships. A dictionary can provide input to the design process, and the design process can store its results into a dictionary.

The desirable interfaces between a dictionary and a database design process fall into three categories:

Initial data entry and editing.

Logical schema structuring.

Physical schema structuring.

7.8.1 Initial Data Entry and Editing

Data entry. The data-requirements information needed by computer-assisted database design procedures is almost a complete (proper) subset of the information normally stored in current commercial dictionary systems. If, in a dictionary, the unstructured data elements can be related to their local views and if the association types between related pairs of unstructured data elements can be included along with the relative frequencies of use of these associations, then the dictionary descriptions can serve as input to the automated design procedures.

Potentially speaking, duplicate entry of essentially the same information into a dictionary system and also into an automated design procedure can and should be avoided. The duplication becomes especially critical when dealing with large databases of hundreds or even thousands of elements. The suggestion is that entry of information about raw data elements be made to the dictionary system, and that an interface exist to allow the design procedures to access this information in named aggregations (local views).

Editing.   Initial data entry is rarely clean in the sense that names, usage, and characteristics of the data elements may not yet be standardized across local views. Synonyms, homonyms, and inconsistent characteristics of the same data usually result when data requirements are gathered from different sources. The editing phases of the conceptual design process, and the reports produced therein, can serve as an input filtering function for the dictionary. When the iterative editing phases are completed, obsolete information (e.g., nonstandard names) can be removed from the dictionary, such that the information remaining permanently is clean and consistent. Synonyms that the designers desire to retain can be maintained in a controlled manner, with reasons for their retention being included in their textual descriptions.

7.8.2 Logical Schema Structuring

Initial design.   The logical structuring procedure should be able to extract filtered, unstructured data-element information in named aggregates (local views) from the dictionary such that the composite model and the derived logical schemas can be generated in the normal manner. After diagnostics have been resolved and refinements made, the results of the logical design can be stored into the dictionary.

Storing the results of a logical design.   Once the computer-assisted design process is completed and a suitable logical design has been obtained, the results of that design can be stored into the dictionary. Assuming the unstructured data elements are already described in the dictionary, the relationships defining segments, databases, logical relations, and secondary indexes are now stored. Naming of the segments and the resulting databases, while not a part of the design procedures that have been described, can be performed prior to dictionary storage by means of special structure specification commands. Final designer decisions regarding logical relations and secondary indexes can be communicated to the design procedures in the same manner. Thus the dictionary can become a repository for the candidate logical designs awaiting physical design and evaluation.

An additional desirable feature is the ability to delete from the dictionary the descriptions of earlier candidate logical designs.

Adding new requirements to existing designs.   When processing new functions or adding new data to an existing database, the design process should be able to extract from the dictionary a description of the existing design along with the filtered, unstructured data-element information for that which is new. A set of constraints must also be imposed on the freedom of the structuring process to restructure the existing design. On the one hand, no restructuring should be permitted. The database already exists and is in productive use, and the designer merely wants to know how well the new requirements are supported by the existing database and where conflicts may exist. On the other hand, the enterprise may not yet be locked into the existing design, and the designer wants to allow full freedom of restructuring for best overall results.

Additional constraint levels between these two extremes may also be desirable. For example, the designer may want to constrain the hierarchical relationships while allowing segment contents to vary. The reasoning is that variations of segment content may have a relatively minor impact on existing programs, since they usually require only a macro update and a recompilation, whereas changes to the hierarchical relationships can require a redesign of program logic. Also the designer may want the ability to constrain certain local views from change while allowing other local views to be modified.

7.8.3 Physical Model Structuring

Computer assistance for determining the physical design options (e.g., device type, access method, block sizes, data set groups, pointer options) can be designed to place these choices appropriately into the dictionary in order that test DBDs can be generated for the physical design procedures. These test DBDs from the dictionary,

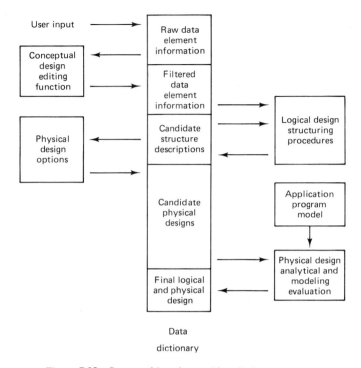

Figure 7.38 Suggested interfaces with a dictionary system.

along with source code for the application model, can serve as input for physical design procedures. After the designer has selected the final logical and physical design, he should be able to communicate that decision to the dictionary and delete (optionally) the previous candidate designs.

7.9 SUMMARY

Computer-assisted logical design is intended to assist the designer in obtaining a good design in minimum time. Proper use of its concepts can contribute greatly toward obtaining these goals. When used as intended, computer-assisted logical design can assist the database designer in the following ways:

Improve the design quality:
Force a more thorough analysis of the application specifications.
Reveal errors, inconsistencies, omissions, in the data requirements.
Remove nonessential (transitive) associations.
Identify redundancies.
Identify structural design alternatives.

Analyze performance consequences.

Provide convenient extensibility studies.

Shorten the design cycle:

Reduce the number of design iterations.

Reduce the time for each iteration.

Document the results.

With this assistance the human designer can make the necessary design decisions more intelligently and usually more quickly.

REFERENCES

1. Chen, P.S., "The Entity-Relationship Model: Towards a Unified View of Data," *ACM Transactions on Database Systems*, March 1976.
2. Codd, E.F., "A Relational Model for Data for Large Shared Data Banks," *Communications of the ACM*, Vol. 13 (June 1970), pp. 377–387.
3. Date, C.J., *An Introduction to Database Systems*. Reading, Mass.: Addison-Wesley Publishing Co., 1977.
4. Hubbard, G.U., "A Technique for Automated Logical Database Design," *Proceedings of the New York University Symposium on Database Design*, New York University, 1978.
5. IBM Corporation, *Data Base Design Aid* (Version 2): *Designer's Guide*, Publication No. GH20-1627, 1977.
6. Martin, James, *Principles of Data-Base Management*. Englewood Cliffs, N.J.: Prentice-Hall, Inc., 1976.
7. Raver, N., and G.U. Hubbard, "Automated Logical File Design," *IBM Systems Journal*, Vol. 16, No. 3 (1977), pp. 287–312.
8. Smith, J.M., and D.C.P. Smith, "Principles of Database Design," *Proceedings of the New York University Symposium on Database Design*, New York University, 1978.
9. Smith, J.M., and D.C.P. Smith, "Database Abstractions: Aggregation and Generalization," *ACM Transactions on Database Systems*, June 1977.
10. Wang, C.P., and H.H. Wedekind, "Segment Synthesis in Logical Data Base Design," *IBM Journal of Research and Development*, Vol. 19, No. 1 (Jan. 1975), pp. 71–77.
11. Yormark, B., *The ANSI/SPARC/SGDBMS Architecture, The ANSI/SPARC DBMS Model*. New York: North-Holland, 1977.
12. Hubbard, G.U., *Computer-Assisted Data Base Design*. New York, N.Y.: Van Nostrand-Reinhold, 1981.

8

Network Database Design Methods

Alan R. Hevner and S. Bing Yao
University of Maryland
College Park, Maryland

8.1 INTRODUCTION

The network data model is widely used as the data structure base of many popular database management systems. IDMS [10], IDS/II [19], DMS 1100 [24], and TOTAL [7] are among systems that use network structures for conceptual modeling. The network model (described more fully in Chapter 3) provides a flexible and general approach for the representation of relationships among entities. Many-to-many relationships, as well as one-to-many relationships, can be naturally represented as a network. Bachman diagrams [1] provide a convenient way of viewing network structures, as in Figure 8.1.

The network data model is the basis of the database management system specifications published by the CODASYL Data Base Task Group (DBTG) [8, 9]. The language and system specifications in these reports define an approach for describing information in a network data model and then mapping this data representation to physical storage structures.

This chapter presents design algorithms for network databases based upon the information requirements of an application environment. The design problem can be viewed as having three distinct phases [23, 30]:

1. Requirements analysis and description of information.
2. Conceptual data structure (or schema) design.
3. Physical storage structure and access-path design.

It is popular to term the first two phases the *logical design* of the database and the

(a) One-to-one relationship
CUSTNUM: CUSTNAME

(b) One-to-many relationships
CUSTOMER: ORDER

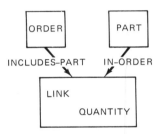

(c) Many-to-many relationships
ORDER: PART

Figure 8.1 Network structures.

third phase the *physical design*.

In this chapter logical design methods for network schemas will be studied in detail. In particular, techniques for mapping information descriptions into DBTG-type data structures will be presented. Several of the methods described will include aspects of physical design [6]; however, such design questions will not be emphasized here.

There are two basic approaches for the logical design of a database. The first, or *subjective*, approach involves a detailed requirements-analysis phase in which the designer uses structured methods of gathering information on user requirements. The designer then draws upon common sense, previous design experience, and knowledge of user applications to develop a conceptual schema. In accepting one design, the designer rejects numerous alternative, legal designs. The subjective design approach does not attempt to compare alternative designs in a quantitative manner in order to select an "optimal" design. Practitioners of this approach point out that many important properties of a schema design are unquantifiable—for example, flexibility, ease of use, security, and integrity. The selection of the best design remains, in some sense, an art. Design methods that use this approach include [11, 22].

The *objective* approach uses quantitative methods to select good schema designs. The application environment is described as a well-defined set of input parameters to an optimization method. The method determines the feasibility and cost of alternative designs in order to select a proper design. An advantage of this approach is that optimization programs can be implemented on a computer and the design process can be partially automated.

Several tested network schema design methods based on the objective approach will be presented here. Section 8.2 describes two techniques for constructing effective, feasible network schemas, starting from a description of the data needs in the system. These methods are heuristic in that no claim of optimal schema design is made. Section 8.3 presents a method that starts with data in third-normal-form relations. A procedure forms the relations into a network structure that preserves the advantages of the normal form while minimizing data redundancy.

Section 8.4 describes a mathematical programming model that derives an optimal implementation of a DBTG network schema based upon the information requirements and constraints in the system. The implementation is based upon selecting among the different techniques of representing record types and set types as physical data structures. Section 8.5 concludes the paper with a discussion of how to integrate these various design methods into an automated design tool.

We will use a common database design example to illustrate the design methods discussed in the chapter. (The example application environment is similar to the one used in [12].) For expository purposes, the example database is rather simple. However, its use will clarify the processing involved in deriving a network schema. Table 8.1 contains a description of the entities, relationships, and data items

TABLE 8.1 EXAMPLE DATABASE

Entities:

CUSTOMER
ORDER
PART
DELIVERY
DATE

Relationships:

CUSTOMER : ORDER	One-to-many
ORDER : PART	Many-to-many
DELIVERY : ORDER	One-to-many
DATE : DELIVERY	One-to-many

Data Items:

CUSTNUM	PARTNUM
CUSTNAME	PARTNAME
CUSTADDR	DELIVNUM
CUSTPHONE	DATE
ORDNUM	QUANTITY

in the example database. A common set of database queries will be introduced in Section 8.2 to represent user applications on the database.

8.2 HEURISTIC SCHEMA DESIGN METHODS

Common to all design methods is the initial requirements analysis. This step seeks to identify each application on the database and, for each, analyzes the requirements regarding the content and use of the database. Requirements analysis should provide an accurate representation of the user applications and a complete specification of the required database. A methodology for requirements analysis must include techniques for data collection, a well-defined specification of the data, and a structured format or language for the data requirements (see Chapters 1 and 4).

The output of the requirements-analysis step is used to develop an effective, feasible conceptual schema for the database. In this section we present two network schema design methods. The object-class method [5] highlights the data content of the queries used on the database. The query-assertion method [16] emphasizes the process structure of the queries. Both methods require a complete knowledge of all queries that will be applied to the database.

8.2.1 The Object-Class Method

The required entities in the database are defined as *base object classes*. A set of base object classes constitutes an *information object class* when there exists a user query to access data from that set. In Table 8.2 the five base object classes are listed for the example database. The grouping of data items into base object classes is done as the initial step of this methodology. This grouping is performed by the designer from knowledge of the application environment. Note that the designer has placed QUANTITY in both classes ORDER and PART, since different applications will access QUANTITY as grouped in both ways. The number of records in each class is its *cardinality value*.

TABLE 8.2   OBJECT CLASSES

Base Object Class	Data Items	Cardinality
CUSTOMER	CUSTNUM, CUSTNAME, CUSTADDR, CUSTPHONE	500
ORDER	ORDNUM, QUANTITY	2250
PART	PARTNUM, PARTNAME, QUANTITY	250
DELIVERY	DELIVNUM	150
DATE	DATE	60

Information object classes are represented by the set of base object classes accessed in a query. The query "Retrieve the address and phone number of a specific customer" defines the information object class $B_1 = \{\text{CUSTOMER}\}$. The query "Retrieve all order numbers for a specific customer" defines the information object class $B_2 = \{\text{CUSTOMER, ORDER}\}$.

A *constituent* relation is defined among information object classes such that B_i $(<)$ B_j if and only if the set of base object classes in B_j is a strict subset of the base object classes in B_i. In other words B_i constitutes a finer division of data in the schema. In the above two queries B_2 $(<)$ B_1 since information about an order of a customer, $\{\text{CUSTOMER, ORDER}\}$, is considered a refinement of information about a customer, $\{\text{CUSTOMER}\}$. Note that constituent relations have the transitive property: B_k $(<)$ B_i and B_i $(<)$ B_j implies that B_k $(<)$ B_j.

User queries and updates are defined by the information object class that each affects, the sort order of the base object classes in the query access path, and the frequency of occurrence. Response-time requirements and update-time requirements are given as modeling constraints. Certain information properties are not quantified in the model. However, qualitative statements are made about such properties as security, availability, flexibility, and ease of use of the schema design. These statements serve as guidance constraints in the schema design.

The design of network schemas is guided by the requirement to support all specified queries and updates. An objective of the design is to accept ad hoc queries by allowing for retrieval of any combination of base object classes. Once a feasible schema is found, then the schema is refined to meet performance requirements.

The object-class design method finds an initial feasible schema by explicitly introducing a network access path for every known query. A query defines an information object class B_i that consists of two parts B_i^1 and B_i^2 such that $B_i = B_i^1 \cup B_i^2$ and $B_i^1 \cap B_i^2 = \varnothing$. The query requires unique access to all base object classes in B_i^1. Base objects in B_i^2 are associated with specific base objects in B_i^1. For example, consider the query, "What orders are being delivered on delivery D23?" The information object class is $B_i = \{\text{DELIVERY, ORDER}\}$. Since unique access is to delivery D23, we have $B_i^1 = \{\text{DELIVERY}\}$ and $B_i^2 = \{\text{ORDER}\}$. The access path for the query would be a direct access to the delivery record type and a set type with DELIVERY as owner and ORDER as member.

We will use the following six queries as the functional basis for a network schema design.

Query 1: Retrieve CUSTNUM, CUSTNAME, and ORDNUM for all orders delivered on 1 July.

$$B_1 = \{\text{DATE, DELIVERY, ORDER, CUSTOMER}\}$$

$$B_1^1 = \{\text{DATE}\}$$

$$B_1^2 = \{\text{DELIVERY, ORDER, CUSTOMER}\}$$

Query 2: Retrieve CUSTNUM for customers who have ordered part P12 in quantities over 100.

$$B_2 = \{\text{PART, ORDER, CUSTOMER}\}$$

$$B_2^1 = \{\text{PART}\}$$

$$B_2^2 = \{\text{ORDER, CUSTOMER}\}$$

Query 3: Retrieve PARTNUM, PARTNAME, and QUANTITY of all parts on delivery D30.

$$B_3 = \{\text{DELIVERY, ORDER, PART}\}$$

$$B_3^1 = \{\text{DELIVERY}\}$$

$$B_3^2 = \{\text{ORDER, PART}\}$$

Query 4: Retrieve CUSTNUM, CUSTNAME, CUSTPHONE, and all ORDNUM for customers in Washington, D.C.

$$B_4 = \{\text{CUSTOMER, ORDER}\}$$

$$B_4^1 = \{\text{CUSTOMER}\}$$

$$B_4^2 = \{\text{ORDER}\}$$

Query 5: Retrieve the DATE on which customer C50 will receive an order containing part P69.

$$B_5 = \{\text{CUSTOMER, PART, ORDER, DELIVERY, DATE}\}$$

$$B_5^1 = \{\text{CUSTOMER, PART}\}$$

$$B_5^2 = \{\text{ORDER, DELIVERY, DATE}\}$$

Query 6: List all PARTNUM, PARTNAME, and QUANTITY on order 0721.

$$B_6 = \{\text{ORDER, PART}\}$$

$$B_6^1 = \{\text{ORDER}\}$$

$$B_6^2 = \{\text{PART}\}$$

The following design steps will generate an initial feasible schema alternative, given the base object classes and information object classes for a database.

1. Define all information object classes, B_i. To provide for unanticipated operations, include an information object class consisting of all base object classes. (Note that B_5 above is such a class.)
2. For all B_i, where $B_i^2 = \varnothing$, make B_i a record type. Provide direct access via a system set to this record type.
3. Find object classes B_i^1 whose objects (*owner*) uniquely identify a set of objects (*member*) of the information object class B_i. Note that the constituent relation

B_i $(<)$ B_i^1 holds by definition. Define a record type identified by the base object classes in B_i^1 and indicate it as directly accessible. Define another record type by the base object classes in B_i.

4. Establish a set type from each owner record type in step 3 to its member record type. Define each member record type as sequentially accessible.

5. For queries where $B_i^1 = \varnothing$, define the information object class B_i as a record type with SYSTEM as the owner. Define the member record type as sequentially accessible.

Using these techniques, the schema in Figure 8.2 is constructed based upon the information object classes B_1 to B_6. Observe that the schema is oriented toward rapid response for queries, since a separate access path exists for each query. The costs of providing this rapid response are a large number of record types and set types and considerable redundant data in the record types. The object-class method uses a series of schema refinement steps which lead to a more efficient treelike schema. These refinement procedures are summarized in Figure 8.3. The use of these refinements results in the schema in Figure 8.4. This figure includes cardinality estimates of each record type (marked inside the box) and the expansion ratio of

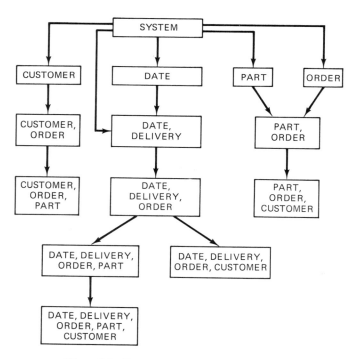

Figure 8.2 Response-oriented network schema.

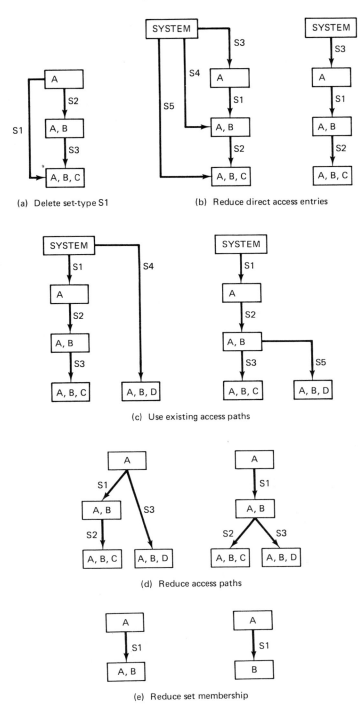

(a) Delete set-type S1

(b) Reduce direct access entries

(c) Use existing access paths

(d) Reduce access paths

(e) Reduce set membership

Figure 8.3   Schema refinement.

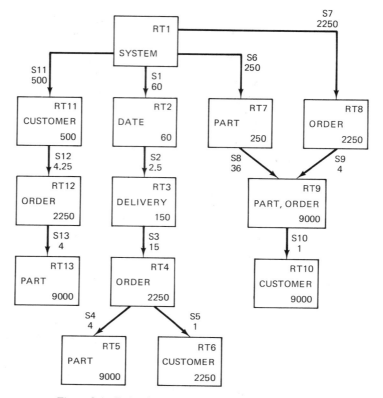

Figure 8.4 Refined response-oriented network schema.

each set type (marked on the arcs), where 1 owner record is related to x member records.

Thus, the object-class design method requires as input a set of base object classes and a set of information object classes as defined by the system application queries. Explicit access paths for each query are constructed and the overall network schema is built by integrating the access paths. The schema can be refined by eliminating redundant set types and redundant data in record types. The output is a feasible network schema that is oriented to reducing query response time.

Different heuristic search techniques can be used during the integration of the query access paths. For example, an update-oriented schema can be designed to avoid the redundant storage of information. The initial response-oriented schema is first constructed. The designer then strips away all the record types and set types except those along the main branch of the schema (record types RT1 to RT6 and set types S1 to S5 in Figure 8.4). An effort is made to use this schema to answer all the required queries. For each query the following techniques are considered [5].

1. Queries with base object classes in the *same* sort order as the main branch, but with one or more levels omitted, can be answered effectively by adding new set types linking the involved levels. The cost of implementing these set types must be considered in the decision on whether to add new set types or use the existing set types along the main branch.

2. Queries that require access in an order *not* corresponding to the main branch can be supported by including dummy record types. The new record types serve as owners in set types that link back into the main branch. Any number of the dummy record types may be added to reduce the costs of answering the queries through the main branch.

This procedure produces the schema in Figure 8.5. The schema contains fewer record types (9 versus 13) and requires less storage than the response-oriented alternative. With further modifications a designer can tune the logical schema to satisfy many different performance objectives. The guiding constraint is that all queries and the corresponding information object classes must be supported on the schema.

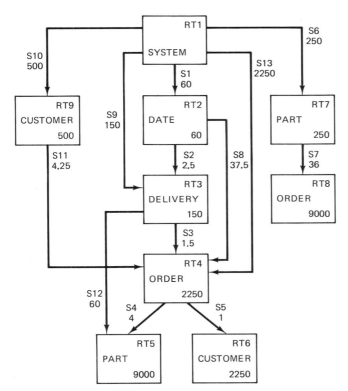

Figure 8.5 Refined update-oriented network schema.

8.2.2 Query-Assertion Method

This method of network schema design analyzes the procedural structure of each query applied to the database. The query analysis captures the grouping of data items into record types in addition to defining set types between record types. By analyzing a set of queries on a database, an overall network schema can be constructed by integrating and reconciling the grouping assertions and relationship assertions found. An example of this design method uses the HI-IQ (hierarchical interactive query) language developed by Gerritsen [16]. The following discussion uses HI-IQ to illustrate the query-assertion design method.

In this method, queries are individually identified and statistics, such as query frequency, priority, and expected number of records accessed, are gathered. The query statistics are stored for later input to a physical database design module, as described in Section 8.4.

Each query is decomposed into a set of assertions that must hold in the eventual network schema for the query to be supported. The relationship of data items in the query can be one-to-one, one-to-many, or many-to-many (Figure 8.1). As in the DBTG network model, the many-to-many relationship is represented by using a linking record type and two set types; this is termed a *confluent hierarchy*. As each query is analyzed, three types of assertions are generated:

ABOVE(A, B): Record type A is hierarchically above record type B in the query.

INORABOVE(I, A, B): Data item I is contained in record type A or in a record type above A, unless record types A and B form a confluent hierarchy, in which case data item I is contained in or above the linking record type of the confluent hierarchy.

CALCPORT(I): Data item I is used in a predicate equality clause (e.g., PARTNUM = P69) and may be selected as a hash key in the implementation of the record type.

The result of this query analysis is a list of assertions that must be satisfied in the database schema. Once all queries have been decomposed, the design process inputs the complete assertion list and generates a logical schema design in two steps: (1) designing relationships among record types (set types), (2) designing the record contents (record types). The following assertions are generated during this processing:

CONFLUENCY(A, B): Records A and B form a confluent hierarchy.

HIERARCHYGROUP(A, B, S): Record A is the owner and record B is a member of set S.

CONTAINS(A, I): Record A contains item I.

RING(A, B): Structure contains at least one ring containing records A and B.

Designing set types involves five steps:

1. Detect Confluencies: If ABOVE(A, B) and ABOVE(B, A) exist, then add assertion CONFLUENCY (A, B) and delete the ABOVE assertions.

2. Eliminate Redundant ABOVE: If ABOVE(A, B), ABOVE(A, C), and ABOVE(B, C) exist, eliminate ABOVE(A, C) because of transitivity.

3. Construct Confluent Hierarchies: If CONFLUENCY(A, B), ABOVE(A, C), and ABOVE(B, C) exist, the confluent hierarchy is established by the ABOVE assertions with C as the linking record type. Delete CONFLUENCY(A, B). If no linking record exists for CONFLUENCY(A, B), construct record type D and assert ABOVE(A, D) and ABOVE(B, D). Delete CONFLUENCY(A, B). Alter all INORABOVE(I, A, B) assertions to INORABOVE(I, C, –) or IN-ORABOVE(I, D, –).

4. Detect Rings: If ABOVE(A, B), ABOVE(B, C), and ABOVE(C, A) exist, assert RING(A, B, C) and signal a possible error. Since ring structures cannot be modeled directly in a network structure, the designer must analyze the data requirements that led to the RING assertion.

5. Generate Direct Hierarchies: Transform all ABOVE(A, B) assertions to HIERARCHYGROUP(A, B, SYMnn) assertions, where SYMnn ($00 \leq nn \leq 99$) is the name of the set type.

Designing record contents involves three steps:

1. Eliminate Redundant Assertions: INORABOVE(I, A, –) is redundant if IN-ORABOVE(I, B, –) exists and B = A or B is above A.

2. Find Common Owners: If more than one INORABOVE assertion exists for I, then find a record type X that connects all substructures in which I occurs. If no such X is found, generate a new record type X and assert INORABOVE(I, X, –). Delete all other INORABOVE assertions on I.

3. Create CONTAINS: Transform all INORABOVE(I, A) to CONTAINS(A, I) assertions.

The query-assertion design method is illustrated with the example database. The decomposition of Query 1 into assertions will be described in detail; then we simply list the assertions after the remaining queries.

Query 1: Retrieve CUSTNUM, CUSTNAME, and ORDNUM for all orders delivered on 1 July.

Since (DATE = 1 July) is an equality predicate that can be used as an access path in the query, DATE is asserted as a possible hash key.

CALCPORT(DATE)

ABOVE assertions are generated by hierarchical (one-to-many) access paths between record types in the query. In this query one date determines many deliveries, one delivery determines many orders, and one delivery determines many customers. Thus:

```
ABOVE(DATE, DELIVERY)
ABOVE(DELIVERY, ORDER)
ABOVE(DELIVERY, CUSTOMER)
```

The INORABOVE assertions identify data items and their positions in the access path.

```
INORABOVE(CUSTNUM, CUSTOMER, –)
INORABOVE(CUSTNAME, CUSTOMER, –)
INORABOVE(ORDNUM, ORDER, CUSTOMER)
```

Query 2: Retrieve CUSTNUM for customers who have ordered part P12 in quantities over 100.

The query assertions are:

```
CALCPORT(PARTNUM)

ABOVE(PART, ORDER)
ABOVE(CUSTOMER, ORDER)

INORABOVE(PARTNUM, PART, –)
INORABOVE(QUANTITY, PART, ORDER)
```

Query 3: Retrieve PARTNUM, PARTNAME, and QUANTITY of all parts on delivery D30.

The query assertions are:

```
CALCPORT(DELIVNUM)

ABOVE(DELIVERY, ORDER)
ABOVE(ORDER, PART)

INORABOVE(PARTNUM, PART, –)
INORABOVE(PARTNAME, PART, –)
INORABOVE(QUANTITY, PART, ORDER)
INORABOVE(DELIVNUM, DELIVERY, –)
```

Query 4: Retrieve CUSTNUM, CUSTNAME, CUSTPHONE, and all ORDNUM for customers in Washington, D.C.

The query assertions are:

CALCPORT(CUSTADDR)

ABOVE(CUSTOMER, ORDER)

INORABOVE(CUSTNUM, CUSTOMER, –)
INORABOVE(CUSTNAME, CUSTOMER, –)
INORABOVE(CUSTPHONE, CUSTOMER, –)
INORABOVE(CUSTADDR, CUSTOMER, –)
INORABOVE(ORDNUM, ORDER, –)

Query 5: Retrieve the DATE on which customer C50 will receive an order containing part P69.

The query assertions are:

CALCPORT(PARTNUM)
CALCPORT(CUSTNUM)

ABOVE(CUSTOMER, ORDER)
ABOVE(PART, ORDER)
ABOVE(DELIVERY, ORDER)
ABOVE(DATE, DELIVERY)

INORABOVE(CUSTNUM, CUSTOMER, –)
INORABOVE(PARTNUM, PART, –)
INORABOVE(DATE, DATE, –)

Query 6: List all PARTNUM, PARTNAME, and QUANTITY on order 0721.

The query assertions are:

CALCPORT(ORDNUM)

ABOVE(ORDER, PART)

INORABOVE(PARTNUM, PART, –)
INORABOVE(PARTNAME, PART, –)
INORABOVE(QUANTITY, ORDER, PART)

The assertions are combined, with duplicate assertions eliminated, in a single list. The assertion list is processed by the design method discussed above. Figure 8.6

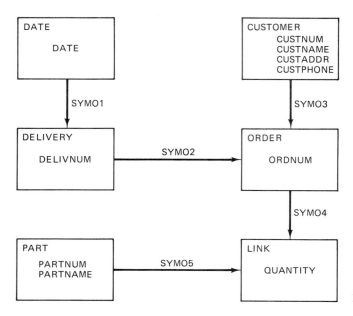

Figure 8.6 Network schema.

contains the network schema created by these methods. The ORDER-PART confluency is detected from the assertions ABOVE(PART, ORDER) and ABOVE(ORDER, PART). Since no record type exists as a base of this confluency, the record type LINK is generated and ABOVE(PART, LINK) and ABOVE(ORDER, LINK) are included in the assertion list. Since QUANTITY is INORABOVE both PART and ORDER, the new assertion INORABOVE(QUANTITY, LINK, –) is added. The assertion ABOVE(DELIVERY, CUSTOMER) is transitive via ABOVE(DELIVERY, ORDER) and ABOVE(ORDER, CUSTOMER) and is deleted. All remaining ABOVE assertions result in set types in the network schema.

The INORABOVE assertions in the resulting list include only one assertion for each data item. No new record types need to be generated as a common owner of some data item. Thus the grouping of data items into record types is straightforward. The remaining CALCPORT assertions are used to aid the designer in the selection of record-type hash keys in the schema implementation.

The resulting schema is a legal network structure that is guaranteed to support the input queries. This design method, as implemented in HI-IQ queries, is limited by the fact that multiple relationships between record types are not distinguished. Also, if unanticipated queries are entered into this database schema, their access paths may not be supported. By adding assertions based on the new queries, this method can reprocess the expanded assertion list to generate a new schema.

8.2.3 *Comparison of the Design Methods*

The two design methods presented in this section produce feasible DBTG network schemas. Both employ a functional approach by using the user queries on the database to guide the design of the schema. The design methods are heuristic in that they do not make any claims for the resulting schema except that it is feasible and that it supports the processing of the defined user queries.

As input, both methods require a set of base record types (base object classes) in the database along with the set of user queries. New record types may be added during the schema design. The query-assertion method also inputs the names of data items in order to group them in record types. The object class method does not deal with the attributes of base object classes (i.e., INORABOVE-type assertions are not considered).

The design procedures in both methods are similar. The ABOVE query assertion corresponds directly to the constituent-relation concept. In the object class method a set type is defined by dividing an information object class B_i into two mutually exclusive parts B_i^1 and B_i^2; B_i^1 contains the base objects to which the query requires unique access. The constituent relation $B_i (<) B_i^1$ holds with B_i^1 as the owner record type and B_i as the member record type of the defined set type. In the query-assertion method, we say that record type B_i^1 is ABOVE record-type B_i. (Note that the schema refinement process in the object class method eventually reduces the number of base object classes in each record type to one.) Therefore, while a single query can produce a number of ABOVE assertions in the assertion method, it can generate only one set type in the object-class method.

The handling of many to many relationships, or confluences, is similar in both methods. The assertions ABOVE(PART, ORDER) and ABOVE(ORDER, PART) produce a confluent hierarchy with a LINK record type. In the same manner the constituent relations {PART, ORDER} (<) {PART} and {PART, ORDER} (<) {ORDER} would lead to two set types with {PART, ORDER} as the member record type; one with {PART} as the owner record type and the other with {ORDER} as the owner record type.

The principal difference between the two design models is the large number of possible record types and set types produced initially by the object-class method (e.g., Figure 8.2). Different arrangements of the same set of base object classes may produce different record types because of different access paths in the queries that produced them. The designer is presented with an extreme, response-oriented schema with explicit access paths for all queries. The designer then uses refinement techniques to reduce the size and complexity of the schema. During this refinement the schema can be tuned to correspond to different performance objects (e.g., update-oriented schemas). Thus, the object-class method provides a more flexible tuning capability; however, the designer must play a significant role in the tuning.

The query-assertion method, on the other hand, is more straightforward and can be completely automated. More detail on grouping data items into record types is included. Only by adding or deleting query assertions can the designer influence the schema design. Thus, the tuning capability is limited. The network schema design, beyond guaranteeing the support of all defined queries, does not consider performance questions. These questions are deferred until the physical design phase.

8.3 NETWORK DESIGN USING NORMALIZED RELATIONS

Many widely used database design methods represent data in *normalized* relational forms. As discussed in Chapter 7, placing data items into third-normal-form (3NF) relations eliminates anomalies in the insertion, deletion, and modification of data values. Techniques that build 3NF relations based upon the functional dependencies among data items in the database are well understood [27, 28].

In this section we present a method for transforming a set of 3NF relations, $R_1, \ldots, R_m$, into a DBTG-type network schema. A complete knowledge of the functional dependencies among relation attributes is also required input.

For our example database, the following set of functional dependencies are assumed to be valid and complete.

$$
\begin{array}{ll}
\text{CUSTNUM} & \rightarrow \text{CUSTNAME} \\
\text{CUSTNUM} & \rightarrow \text{CUSTADDR} \\
\text{CUSTNUM} & \rightarrow \text{CUSTPHONE} \\
\text{PARTNUM} & \rightarrow \text{PARTNAME} \\
\text{ORDNUM} & \rightarrow \text{CUSTNUM} \\
\text{ORDNUM} & \rightarrow \text{DELIVNUM} \\
\text{DELIVNUM} & \rightarrow \text{DATE} \\
\text{ORDNUM, PARTNUM} & \rightarrow \text{QUANTITY}
\end{array}
$$

Based on these dependencies, a set of 3NF relations are formed. Methods for the construction of 3NF relations are discussed in Chapter 7.

```
DATE(DATE)
DELIVERY(DELIVNUM, DATE)
ORDER(ORDNUM, CUSTNUM, DELIVNUM)
CUSTOMER(CUSTNUM, CUSTNAME, CUSTADDR, CUSTPHONE)
ORDER-PART(ORDNUM, PARTNUM, QUANTITY)
PART(PARTNUM, PARTNAME)
```

The first task of the design method is to recognize the *common attribute groups* that may exist in the relational description. This is done simply by forming an m-by-n "belongs-to" matrix over all relations $R_1, \ldots, R_m$ and all attributes $A_1, \ldots, A_n$. Any attribute having more than one mark in its column is a *common* attribute and is placed in a set C. If common attributes always appear together in relations, they are termed a *common attribute group*. These groups, which may be composed of only one attribute, are placed in a set G. The "belongs-to" matrix for the example database is:

	CUST NUM	CUST NAME	CUST ADDR	CUST PHONE	PART NUM	PART NAME	ORD NUM	QUANTITY	DELIV NUM	DATE
DATE	0	0	0	0	0	0	0	0	0	1
DELIVERY	0	0	0	0	0	0	0	0	1	1
ORDER	1	0	0	0	0	0	1	0	1	0
CUSTOMER	1	1	1	1	0	0	0	0	0	0
ORDER-PART	0	0	0	0	1	0	1	1	0	0
PART	0	0	0	0	1	1	0	0	0	0

The set of common attributes is

$$C = \{\text{CUSTNUM, ORDNUM, PARTNUM, DELIVNUM, DATE}\}$$

The set of common attribute groups is identical to C:

$$G = \{\text{CUSTNUM, ORDNUM, PARTNUM, DELIVNUM, DATE}\}$$

The network schema is formed by the operations of *splitting* groups of attributes into separate record types and *merging* the record types into a consistent network schema [14]. When a split occurs, a valid set type is formed between the separate record types. These two operations are defined below.

8.3.1 The Split(S, N) Operation

S and N are groups of attributes from a relation where S is contained in N. The SPLIT operation separates S from $S' = N - S$ and places them into separate record types. The proper set type is constructed between the record types based upon the functional dependency rules given here.

1. If $S \rightarrow S'$ (i.e., the set of attributes in S functionally determines the set of attributes in S') and $S' \nrightarrow S$, then a set type is formed with owner S' and member S. The relationship is one-to-many from S' to S.
2. If $S' \rightarrow S$ and $S \nrightarrow S'$, then a set type is formed with owner S and member S'. The relationship is one-to-many from S to S'.
3. If $S \rightarrow S'$ and $S' \rightarrow S$, then a set type is formed with either S' or S as owner and the other as member. The relationship is one-to-one between S and S'.
4. If $S \nrightarrow S'$ and $S' \nrightarrow S$, then an intersection record type is created, and two set types are formed—one with owner S and the other with owner S'. Both have the intersection record type as member. The relationship is many-to-many between S and S'.

Before the split, the set of attributes in N may be an owner or member record type in a previously existing set type. Let M be the member record type in the new set type generated by the SPLIT operation. The former set types in which N was the owner are converted to M-owner set types. The former set types in which N was the member are converted to M-member set types.

8.3.2 The Merge(S, N₁, N₂) Operation

S is a set of attributes and N_1 and N_2 are existing network structures. S is contained in both structures. All occurrences of S in N_1 are merged with all occurrences of S in N_2, without duplicating any values. The existing set types in which S is an owner or member are also merged into the resulting network structure. A simple MERGE example is given in Figure 8.7.

Using the SPLIT and MERGE operations, the following algorithm designs a network schema. Let A_{R_i} denote the set of attributes in R_i. Let N be the set of attributes that represents the current state of the network structure that is being constructed.

8.3.3 Algorithm

Begin
1. Set N to empty. For each relation R_i, $i=1,\ldots,m$, perform steps 2 through 5.
2. Let G_i be the set of all common attribute groups in G whose attributes are in A_{R_i}. Order the groups in G_i so that groups containing candidate keys are at the end.
3. Select the first group X in G_i. If A_{R_i} is equivalent to common attribute group X, then either add X to the network as a separate record type (i.e., $N \leftarrow N \cup X$) or, if the group is already in the network, then MERGE(X, A_{R_i}, N).
4. If X is a proper subset of A_{R_i}, then SPLIT(X, A_{R_i}). As above, if X is not already in the network, add it ($N \leftarrow N \cup X$), else MERGE(X, A_{R_i}, N).
5. Delete X from G_i and A_{R_i}. If G_i is not empty, go to step 3. If G_i is empty and A_{R_i} is not, then add A_{R_i} to N ($N \leftarrow N \cup A_{R_i}$).

End.

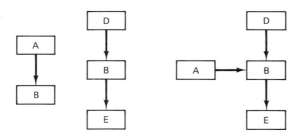

(a) Before   (b) After   **Figure 8.7** A simple MERGE example.

When the algorithm completes, a network structure is formed. Each common attribute group is a record type. Ungrouped attributes in a relation form a record type. The maximum number of record types is thus $|G| + m$, where $|G|$ is the number of common attribute groups in G and m is the number of relations in the database.

We now follow the formation of the network schema for our example database. The network N is initially empty. Each relation is processed separately and its record types are merged into the schema N. The order of considering the input relations is irrelevant; the resulting network schema would be the same regardless of order. The steps of the schema formation are shown in Figure 8.8.

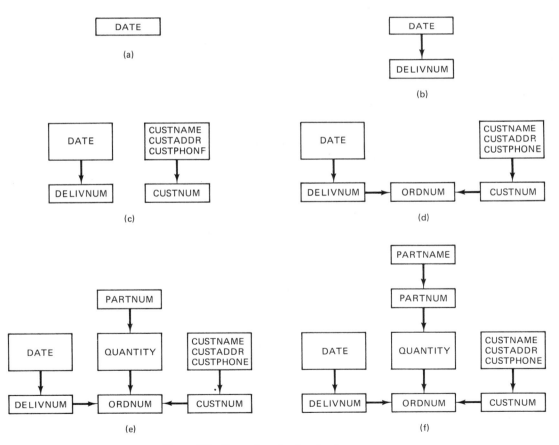

Figure 8.8 Formation of network schema.

DATE

$$A_{R_1} = \{DATE\}$$

The only common attribute group is $G_1 = \{DATE\}$. Since $X = A_{R_1}$, X is added to N. The result is Figure 8.8(a).

DELIVERY

$$A_{R_2} = \{DELIVNUM, DATE\}$$

$$G_2 = \{(DATE), (DELIVNUM)\}$$

Set $X = (DATE)$ and SPLIT(X, A_{R_2}). Since DATE is already in N, MERGE(X, A_{R_2}, N).

Set $X = (DELIVNUM)$. Since DELIVNUM is already in N because of the previous MERGE, perform a trivial MERGE(X, A_{R_2}, N). The result is Figure 8.8(b).

CUSTOMER

$$A_{R_3} = \{CUSTNUM, CUSTNAME, CUSTADDR, CUSTPHONE\}$$

$$G_3 = \{CUSTNUM\}$$

Set $X = (CUSTNUM)$ and SPLIT(X, A_{R_3}). Since CUSTNUM is not in N, add record types $\{CUSTNUM\}$ and $\{CUSTNAME, CUSTADDR, CUSTPHONE\}$ to N. The result is Figure 8.8(c).

ORDER

$$A_{R_4} = \{ORDNUM, CUSTNUM, DELIVNUM\}$$

$$G_4 = \{(CUSTNUM), (DELIVNUM), (ORDNUM)\}$$

Set $X = (CUSTNUM)$ and SPLIT(X, A_{R_4}). Since CUSTNUM is already in N, MERGE(X, A_{R_4}, N).

Set $X = (DELIVNUM)$ and do the same procedure; SPLIT(X, A_{R_4}) and MERGE(X, A_{R_4}, N).

Set $X = (ORDNUM)$. Since ORDNUM is already in N, only a trivial MERGE is performed. The result is Figure 8.8(d).

ORDER-PART

$$A_{R_5} = \{ORDNUM, PARTNUM, QUANTITY\}$$

$$G_5 = \{(ORDNUM), (PARTNUM)\}$$

Set $X = (ORDNUM)$ and SPLIT(X, A_{R_5}). Since ORDNUM is in N, MERGE(X, A_{R_5}, N).

Set $X = (PARTNUM)$ and SPLIT(X, A_{R_5}). Since PARTNUM is not in N, add record types $\{PARTNUM\}$ and $\{QUANTITY\}$ to N. The result is Figure 8.8(e).

PART

$$A_{R_6} = \{\text{PARTNUM, PARTNAME}\}$$

$$G_6 = \{\text{PARTNUM}\}$$

Set $X = (\text{PARTNUM})$ and $\text{SPLIT}(X, A_{R_6})$. Since PARTNUM is in N, $\text{MERGE}(X, A_{R_6}, N)$. The final schema result is Figure 8.8(f).

It is shown in [14] that the above design method will generate a network schema that minimizes the number of appearances of attributes in the network. Also, given that the number of attribute appearances is minimized, the number of record types is minimized. It can be readily seen that if the algorithm starts with 3NF relations, the network generated will maintain the properties of third normality. In other words, the schema record types do not display insertion, deletion, and update anomalies.

As an improvement to the above design method, we can reduce the number of record types and set types in the schema at the expense of some data redundancy. After the network schema is produced, a final processing step is added to the algorithm.

6. Find all set types in which each attribute in the owner record type is functionally dependent upon the set of attributes that constitute the member record type. Combine the two record types into one record type and eliminate the set type.

The example network schema after processing this step is given in Figure 8.9. Note that the dependent attributes may require additional storage for redundant values. For example, a PARTNAME, say BOLT, now must be repeated with each of its corresponding PARTNUMs. Thus, the property of minimal number of attribute appearances no longer holds. However, the advantages of fewer set-type linkages

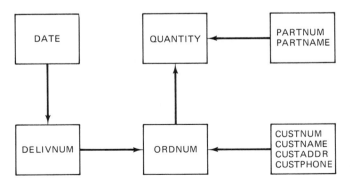

Figure 8.9   Improved network schema.

and a more natural record structure are often more beneficial. The properties of third normality are also maintained.

8.4 OPTIMIZATION MODELS FOR NETWORK SCHEMA IMPLEMENTATION

Network schema optimization can be done using a variety of mathematical models [3, 14, 15, 20, 21]. Models have been constructed with varying input specifications and optimization cost objectives. We divide these models into two categories—those that do and do not require a fully constructed DBTG network schema as input.

For the models that require a schema [14, 15], one of the design methods described in Sections 8.2 and 8.3 is first executed in order to derive an effective schema. A primary advantage of this model category is that the logical network design remains independent of the physical implementation of that design. The principal decision variable in these models is the selection of an implementation alternative for each set type in the schema. The possible implementations are based on the physical structuring capabilities in the database system. There are three broad classes of implementations for a set type $S_k(A, B)$, where A is the owner record type and B is the member record type.

1. *Duplication*: Duplicate copies of B (or A) related to a given A (or B) record are stored in A (or B) as repeating groups. The duplication of data is done for access efficiency.
2. *Aggregation*: Again, B (or A) records are stored with the related A (or B) records as repeating groups. In aggregation, however, the records are not duplicated, and all set types that involve A or B must be defined over this aggregated record type.
3. *Chaining*: A and B are stored separately as distinct record types. Set types are implemented through various chaining methods or pointer arrays. Many implementations are possible, depending upon the combination of next, prior, owner, and other pointer associations in the set type.

Notice that the use of duplication or aggregation in set type implementation may cause record types to become unnormalized (i.e., not in 3NF). Thus, the properties stated in Section 8.3 for a schema of 3NF record types will no longer hold. The grouping of record types, however, allows greater access efficiency. This efficiency is important if the set type is used extensively for retrieval in the database. The update, insertion, and deletion anomalies caused by this grouping must be recognized and handled correctly by either the user or the underlying database system.

The second category of mathematical models does not require a predesigned schema [3, 20, 21]. These models require four types of input; data items, associations among data items, user queries, and system storage constraints. The model decision variable is the selection of an implementation for each association between data items. As before, the classes of possible implementations for associations are duplication, aggregation, and chaining (i.e., forming set types). Note that the grouping of data items into record types is done by selecting the aggregation implementation for the association between the primary key and its dependent attributes. The associations between keys become set types if some form of chaining is chosen as the implementation alternative.

We now present the formulation of an optimization model for network schema design [20]. This model is embedded in the interactive design system IDBD as described in [12]. The model is an example of the second category. A model of the first category (e.g., [14]) is similar, with record types in place of data items and set types in place of associations. We will accompany the model with input data from our example database.

8.4.1 Model Input

The input variables to the optimization model are listed below.

Data items

$$\text{NAME}(DI_i) = \text{name of data item.}$$

$$\text{SIZE}(DI_i) = \text{size of data item in characters.}$$

$$\text{CARD}(DI_i) = \text{cardinality of data item.}$$

The input data items for the example are:

DATA ITEM	SIZE	CARDINALITY
DATE	6	60
DELIVNUM	5	150
ORDNUM	6	2250
PARTNUM	8	250
PARTNAME	10	250
QUANTITY	8	9000
CUSTNUM	5	500
CUSTNAME	30	500
CUSTADDR	30	500
CUSTPHONE	10	500

Associations

$\text{ASNAME}(R_k) = \text{name of association.}$

$\text{COMP1}(R_k) \quad = DI_i \text{—origin of association.}$

$\text{COMP2}(R_k) \quad = DI_j \text{—destination of association.}$

$\text{DCARD}(R_k) \quad = \text{number of ordered pairs.}$

$\text{DMINR1}(R_k) = \text{minimum number of } DI_i \text{ values related to one } DI_j \text{ value.}$

DMAXR1(R_k) = maximum number of DI_i values related to one DI_j value.

DMINR2(R_k) = minimum number of DI_j values related to one DI_i value.

DMAXR2(R_k) = maximum number of DI_j values related to one DI_i value.

The input data items for the example are:

ASNAME	COMP1	COMP2	DCARD	DMINR1	DMAXR1	DMINR2	DMAXR2
DAT-DELIV	DATE	DELIVNUM	150	1	1	1	20
DELIV-ORD	DELIVNUM	ORDNUM	2250	1	1	1	40
CUST-ORD	CUSTNUM	ORDNUM	2250	1	1	0	40
C-CNAME	CUSTNUM	CUSTNAME	500	1	1	1	1
C-CADDR	CUSTNUM	CUSTADDR	500	1	1	1	1
C-CPHONE	CUSTNUM	CUSTPHONE	500	1	1	1	1
ORD-PART	ORDNUM	PARTNUM	9000	1	25	0	200
O-P-AMNT	ORD-PART	QUANTITY	9000	1	1	1	1
P-PNAME	PARTNUM	PARTNAME	250	1	1	1	1

Note that the association ORD-PART is considered as a data item in its association with QUANTITY.

User applications.   Queries and updates are described as a group of data-manipulation operations. Each application is given a frequency value for the number of times it is executed per unit time. The following operations are used to describe the procedural processing of database queries.

FIND UNIQ A: Find a specified value of the data item A.

FIND SEQ A: Find all A values.

GET ALL B: Retrieve all B values under the current owner value.

GET B: Retrieve one B value under the current owner value.

GET * B: Retrieve * B value under the current owner value, where * represents one of {FIRST, NEXT, LAST, PREV, ASCENDING, DESCENDING}.

Other data-manipulation operations for insert, delete, and modification exist in the model, but they are not used in this example.

As an illustration, Query 1, "Retrieve CUSTNUM, CUSTNAME, and ORDNUM for all orders delivered on 1 July," is input into the model as:

```
RUN-UNIT custinf QUERY EXECUTED 5 TIMES
FIND UNIQ DATE
    GET ALL DELIVNUM
        GET ALL ORDNUM
            GET CUSTNUM
            GET CUSTNAME
```

The remaining example queries are entered into the model in similar format. The following frequency-of-execution values are entered into the model:

Query	Frequency (per unit time)
1	5
2	10
3	10
4	10
5	15
6	15

Storage and record sizes

MAXRCD = maximum allowable record size in characters.

MAXSTR = maximum allowable storage in characters.

PNTR   = pointer size.

CNTR   = counter size.

For this example, the input values of these variables are:

$$\text{MAXRCD} = 200, \quad \text{MAXSTR} = 100{,}000{,}000$$
$$\text{PNTR} = 10, \quad \text{CNTR} = 5$$

8.4.2 The Optimization Algorithm

The model provides a set of 21 possible implementations for each association between data items. The duplication and aggregation implementations form data items into record types, while the chaining implementations form set types between record types.

Two costs are calculated for each feasible network schema implementation. A *storage cost* is defined as the amount of storage required to implement each association. An *access cost* is defined by estimating the cost of each data-manipulation operation times the frequency of the operation's occurrence. The cost of each operation is based on the implementation of access path used. Costs are defined in terms of records retrieved along the access path.

The optimization problem is described as follows:

Let X_j = the implementation chosen for association j,

$C_j(X_j)$ = the total access cost for association j,

$S_j(X_j)$ = the storage cost for association j,

NUMB   = total number of associations to be implemented,

MAXSTR   = maximum allowable storage space.

The network design problem may be formulated as a nonlinear integer programming problem:

Minimize: $\displaystyle\sum_{j=1}^{\text{NUMB}} C_j(X_j)$

subject to constraints:

1. $\displaystyle\sum_{j=1}^{\text{NUMB}} S_j(X_j) \le \text{MAXSTR}.$

2. Based on the type of association j; either one-to-one, one-to-many, or many-to-many; the selected implementation is feasible.

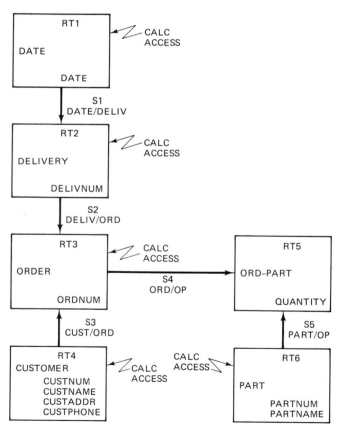

Access cost = 5645 record accesses
Storage cost = 28619550 bytes

Figure 8.10 Minimum cost network schema.

3. X_j is an integer representing a feasible implementation alternative.

4. The selection of implementations for two or more associations should not result in invalid DBMS-dependent structures.

5. Implementation of associations should not make a record type larger than MAXRCD.

This design model has been implemented using a branch-and-bound algorithm guaranteed to find the minimal-cost network schema [12, 20]. By executing this program with the example input data, we derive the network schema in Figure 8.10.

The program compared the access and storage cost of 4032 feasible DBTG network schema implementations. Several implementations provided an identical minimum access cost of 5645 record accesses. The minimum storage cost from among these implementations was achieved by the schema in Figure 8.10. Record types CUSTOMER and PART are formed by aggregating the included data items. All the schema set types are implemented by chaining the records in the member record type with next and owner pointers. Direct access (CALC access) is provided to all record types except the ORD-PART record type.

8.5 AUTOMATING THE DATABASE DESIGN PROCESS

A goal of database design research is to develop automated tools to assist in performing all three phases of design: requirements analysis, logical design, and physical design. Owing to their size and complexity, these problems require computer support. A fully automatic system, however, may not adequately capture all the design requirements that users desire in a system. Features not adapted to quantitative description (e.g., security, ease of use, integrity) are likely not to be considered in the automatic derivation of a system design. A computer-aided approach that allows human interaction in the design decision processes appears most desirable.

The functional network design methods surveyed in this chapter are all amenable to computer implementation. No completely automated design tool exists, however, that integrates all the design phases. The remarks that follow summarize the current state-of-the-art in automatic network design tools and suggest approaches for integration of the tools into a complete design system.

Automatic approaches to requirements analysis [18, 25] provide the designer with structured methods of describing data objects, relationships among objects, transactions on the system, and system constraints and dynamics. This information is stored and managed by the computer. It is contingent upon the designer, however, to insure that the input information is both accurate and complete. Data-name inconsistencies should be reconciled here. On the other hand, redundant relationships and access paths among data objects should be retained and reconciled later in the design process. The output of requirements analysis is a formal description of the information requirements. These descriptions provide input to the logical and physical design tools.

The logical network design methods described in Sections 8.2 and 8.3 input information descriptions and requirements to produce a feasible DBTG schema. The object-class method designs a schema determined by base object classes and information object classes. The procedures to produce an initial response-time oriented schema and the subsequent refinements to that schema can be automated. Additional modifications to the schema can produce update-oriented designs.

The query-assertion method has been implemented in the automatic design tool DESIGNER [17]. A list of data names and HI-IQ queries are the input to DESIGNER. The program analyzes the query assertions and constructs record types and set types in a DBTG schema.

Several automated methods exist to construct 3NF relations from initial information requirements [4, 29]. Once data is represented as 3NF relations, the translation to a DBTG schema can be accomplished by the procedure described in Section 8.3. This design method automatically produces feasible network schemas and guarantees that they satisfy the properties of normalized record types and minimal data redundancy.

Automated physical design tools construct an optimal implementation of a schema design and evaluate the cost of the total database design. Physical design models differ in their input requirements. Certain models require as input a network schema in terms of record types and set types; other models require only data items and the associations between them. These models generate a network schema as part of the optimization processing. Optimization models can be automated as mathematical programs using branch-and-bound techniques or dynamic programming techniques. The final database design, along with its estimated costs, is presented as output to the designer. The designer, through an interface to the design system, can suggest alternative logical or physical designs. The physical design tool will evaluate the alternative's cost and supply the cost figures to the designer. The designer can iterate over the design process until a satisfactory database design is found.

When the database has been implemented, performance monitoring can provide the actual costs for the selected design. Changes in user and system requirements can also be analyzed. With this new information, certain phases of the design procedure can be repeated in order to find improved logical and physical designs.

Current network design systems that are computer-aided include DESIGNER DBD-DSS (Data Base Design-Decision Support Systems) [15, 17]; the Logical Database Optimizer [3, 20, 21]; and the Interactive Data Base Designer (IDBD) [12]. These systems allow significant designer interaction in all phases of design. The eventual goal of automating the complete database design process will not be realized without significant breakthroughs in information modeling [26]. While questions of physical database design have been studied extensively [2], more research is needed in the areas of requirements analysis and logical database design. There is a need to develop methods of representing information that capture a complete and accurate picture of the database and its application environment and that are adaptable to computer implementation. This requires that design factors be represented in quantifiable terms that can be part of a mathematical program. As we have seen, no effective techniques for quantifying factors such as reliability, user friendliness, or data integrity exist. Therefore, no totally objective design approach for automation has been developed in the present state-of-the-art. A human designer's skill in adapting network structures to the information requirements of an application environment remains crucial for a successful database design.

REFERENCES

1. Bachman, D., "Data Structure Diagrams," *Data Base*, Vol. 1, No. 2 (1969).

2. Batory, D., ed., "Directions in Physical Database Research," *Database Engineering*, Vol. 5, No. 1 (March 1982).

3. Berelian, E., and K. Irani, "Evaluation and Optimization of Database Design in a Paging Environment," *Proceedings Third VLDB Conference*, Tokyo, 1977.

4. Bernstein, P., "Synthesizing Third Normal Form Relations from Functional Dependencies," *ACM Transactions on Database Systems*, Vol. 1, No. 4 (1976).

5. Bubenko, J., S. Berild, E. Lindencrona-Ohlin, and S. Nachmens, "From Information Requirements to DBTG-Data Structures," *Proceedings of Conference on Data: Abstraction, Definition and Structure*, Salt Lake City, 1976.

6. Chen, P., and S.B. Yao, "Design and Performance Tools for Data Base Systems," *Proceedings Third VLDB Conference*, Tokyo, 1977.

7. Cincom Systems Inc., *TOTAL/8 Data Base Administration User Manual*, Cincinnati, 1978.

8. CODASYL, "Data Base Task Group Report." New York: Association of Computing Machinery, 1971.

9. CODASYL, "Data Description Language Committee," *DDLC Journal of Development*, Canada, 1978.

10. Cullinane Corporation, *IDMS Utilities*, Release 5.0, Boston, 1978.

11. Curtice, R., and P. Jones, "Key Steps in the Logical Design of Data Bases," *Proceedings NYU Symposium on Database Design*, New York, 1978.

12. Dahl, R., J. Bubenko, and SYSLAB, "IDBD—An Interactive Design Tool for CODASYL-DBTG-Type Data Bases," *Proceedings Eighth VLDB Conference*, Mexico City, 1982.

13. Date, C., *An Introduction to Database Systems*. Reading, Mass.: Addison-Wesley Publishing Co., 1981.

14. De, P., W. Haseman, and C. Kriebel, "Toward an Optimal Design of a Network Database from Relational Descriptions," *Operations Research*, Vol. 26, No. 5 (1978).

15. Gambino, T., and R. Gerritsen, "A Database Design Decision Support System," *Proceedings Third VLDB Conference*, Tokyo, 1977.

16. Gerritsen, R., "A Preliminary System for the Design of DBTG Data Structures," *Communications of the ACM*, Vol. 18, No. 10 (October 1975).

17. Gerritsen, R., "Tools for the Automation of Database Design," *Proceedings NYU Symposium on Database Design*, New York, 1978.

18. Hammer, M., W. Howe, V. Kruskal, and I. Wladawsky, "A Very High Level Programming Language for Data Processing Applications," *Communications of the ACM*, Vol. 20, No. 11 (November 1977).

19. Honeywell Information Systems, *Data Management IV*, Data Base Administration Reference Manual, 1978.

20. Irani, K., S. Purkayastha, and T. Teorey, "A Designer for DBMS-Processable Logical Database Structures," *Proceedings Fifth VLDB Conference*, Rio de Janiero, 1979.

21. Mitoma, M., and Irani, K., "Automatic Data Base Schema Design and Optimization," *Proceedings First VLDB Conference*, Framingham Mass., 1975.

22. Palmer, I., "Practicalities in Applying a Formal Methodology to Data Analysis," *Proceedings NYU Symposium on Database Design*, New York, 1978.

23. Senko, M., E. Altman, M. Astrahan, and P. Fehder, "Data Structures and Accessing in Data-Base Systems," *IBM Systems Journal*, Vol. 12, No. 1 (1973).

24. Sperry Univac, *Data Management System (DMS 1100) Level 8R2: Schema Definition and Data Manipulation Language*, 1980.

25. Teichroew, D., and E. Hershey, "PSL/PSA: A Computer-Aided Technique for Structured Documentation and Analysis of Information Processing Systems," *IEEE Transactions on Software Engineering*, Vol. SE-3, No. 1 (January 1977).

26. Teorey, T., and J. Fry, "The Logical Record Access Approach to Database Design," *ACM Computing Surveys*, Vol. 12, No. 2 (June 1980).

27. Ullman, J.D., *Principles of Database Systems*. Computer Science Press, 1980.

28. Vetter, M., and R.N. Maddison, *Database Design Methodology*. Englewood Cliffs, N.J.: Prentice-Hall, Inc., 1981.

29. Wang, D., and H. Wedekind, "Segment Synthesis in Logical Data Base Design," *IBM Journal of Research and Development*, January 1975.

30. Yao, S.B., S. Navathe, and J. Weldon, "An Integrated Approach to Logical Database Design," *Proceedings NYU Symposium on Database Design*, New York, 1978.

9

An Interactive System for Database Design and Integration

S. Bing Yao
University of Maryland, College Park, Maryland

V. Waddle
IBM
T. J. Watson Research Center, Yorktown, Heights, N.Y.

B. C. Housel
IBM Corporation, Research Triangle Park, North Carolina

9.1 INTRODUCTION

The process of database design can be divided into several distinct phases [24]. It begins by specifying the design requirements of the database (requirement analysis). Next, users enter their "local view" of the logical database and describe how they will use the database (view modeling). The local views are then integrated to form a global description of the database (view integration). The global description is then mapped into a structure which is compatible with the data model supported by the DBMS (view restructuring). Finally, this structure is analyzed and mapped into storage structures the DBMS supports (schema analysis and mapping). These design phases can be classified into two types: logical and physical database design. Logical database design consists of the steps of view modeling through view restructuring. Schema generation is normally referred to as physical design.

Typical techniques for database design rely heavily on the designer's skill and experience—an approach that is neither efficient nor effective. The large size of realistic design problems makes the design decisions time-consuming and error-prone. An interactive design aid can help by storing many design parameters and performing simple preprocessing before a design decision must be made.

This chapter describes an interactive database design system which aids in all phases of database design. It accepts and stores definitions of local views and processing requirements. Next, it provides an interactive integration process. It suggests design changes in the local views while filtering out changes which obviously should not be made, thus making the human designer more productive. The size of the search space is controlled by adjustable parameters which limit the number of alternatives at each decision point. A multilevel design evaluation provides the necessary performance estimated at various design stages.

The design system is based on a model which enables a user to describe a local view. Such a model is referred to as a *semantic* or *conceptual model*. This model should be simple and be invariant to design decisions, such as the grouping of data items into records. The model should be sufficiently general to represent most of the views and constraints. It must also facilitate the development of tools to assist in the design process and in making design decisions.

Processing information is needed in the design process in order to insure the correctness and efficiency of the design. Approaches based solely upon semantic information [2, 6, 9, 12, 14, 17, 21, 22, and 23] are unable to estimate the processing requirements of a design. Further, they may produce a design which is grossly inefficient.

We will describe a functional data model (FDM) and a transaction specification language (TASL) developed to be used by an interactive database design system. A preliminary description of FDM and TASL was reported in [11]. The generality of FDM and TASL was demonstrated by comparing them with existing semantic models. We also extend FDM and TASL and show how they are used in the database design system.

9.2 METHODOLOGY

As we have seen, previous approaches to logical database design suffer both from solving only a portion of the problem (optimizing either information structure or processing efficiency) and from unrealistic assumptions (e.g., the "uniqueness assumption"[1]) or extensive bookkeeping for information structure, incomplete models for processing, and the like. Our approach is to develop a comprehensive design aid incorporating both semantic and processing information. This allows us to achieve a better solution to the design problem and to make a trade-off in the design between

---

[1] The "uniqueness assumption" states that between any two entities there is at most one functional dependency. (See [28] for a more extensive discussion.)

processing costs and semantic information. The result will be more reasonable and realistic without having to satisfy the constraints of a certain "normal form."

The design aid will function as an assistant to the designer, with the designer retaining control over the design process. It will aid the designer by suggesting some changes, screening out others which obviously should not be made, and automating bookkeeping tasks (e.g., estimation of the processing costs of a design). It also will give the designer the option of using automatic design algorithms. This permits a quick generation of a design for evaluation by the users.

There are three major steps in our methodology. First, the user's local views are stated in FDM and TASL. Next, these local views are integrated to form one or more global views, which are reviewed by the designer and users. During view integration, redundant functions and data nodes are eliminated. Heuristics are developed so that redundancy elimination is based on both syntactic and semantic information derived from the design requirement. For example, heuristics are used to identify those functions which are not redundant (although they appear to be redundant syntactically). The designer must approve the elimination of every function. This task is, therefore, simplified, because the designer's attention is focused on fewer functions which have a higher probability of being truly redundant. In this way, we avoid the "universal relation" assumption without requiring either an excessive amount of user input or a completely manual design.

In addition to shielding the designer from unnecessary detail during view integration, the design aid also performs extensive bookkeeping. For example, processing specifications (TASL) are modified automatically by the design system to reflect changes made on the data model (FDM) during the integration process. The design aid also permits the integration process to produce several global models along with estimated performance indications. This allows the designer to present the users with several alternatives, as there may be no single correct design.

Schema generation is the last step in our design methodology. In this step the global model produced from the integration phase is used to generate possible schemas, which are evaluated for their storage and access costs. Data items are now incorporated into records, and some of the constraints of the DBMS's data model are introduced. Some performance features such as indices and linking (which are not in data models) are introduced. The schema generated is not required to be in a normal form, allowing processing costs to be traded off against update costs. Criteria such as flexibility, "naturalness," and the like are imposed by the designer's guidance of the schema generation process. Again, the design aid allows for the generation of multiple schemas.

9.3 THE FUNCTIONAL DATA MODEL

The *functional data model* (*FDM*) consists of sets and functions between sets. In the FDM schemas, *sets* are represented by labeled *nodes*; the terms nodes and sets are used interchangeably. Entity nodes are drawn as rectangles and represent sets of values in a database. A *function* is defined on a pair of nodes. The names of nodes and functions are unique within a local view.

FDMs have two levels of abstraction, corresponding to the two node types. Entity nodes and functions between them model reality. Data nodes and functions between them model the data and relationships that are to be implemented in a DBMS. Functions between entity nodes and data nodes represent the relationships between reality and the model of reality realized in the DBMS.

In this section we will define the FDM's constructs and illustrate them with examples. First we show the data level of modeling. Next we show how relationships between entities and their data items are modeled. Finally, we illustrate the modeling of entity-to-entity relationships.

9.3.1 Data-to-Data Relationships

9.3.1.1 Node Structure

Nodes in the FDM can be classified as either simple or tuple, as shown in Figure 9.1. *Simple nodes* represent sets of "atomic" data elements. They have a *name* and certain attributes such as *data type* (*character*, *integer*, or *real*) and *length* (in *bytes*).

Tuple nodes are used to represent nonfunctional (i.e., many-to-many) relationships among nodes (including other tuple nodes). Tuple nodes contain sets of tuples of atomic data elements. In Figure 9.3 the SUP_TO node represents a ternary many-to-many relationship between the PROJ, PNO, and SNO nodes. The white (hollow) arrows on F4, F5, and F6 indicate that these nodes are the components of SUP_TO. Additionally, each component of a tuple node has a name, data type, and length.

It may be noted that the introduction of tuple nodes results in data redundancy. The concept of a tuple node has several advantages that enhance the model. First, the need for "pointers" is eliminated. This simplifies the transaction (processing) specification. Second, the generation of schemas for relational systems is simplified. That is, the data elements of a tuple node can be mapped immediately to the primary key of a relation. More generally, the tuple nodes provide a basis for evolving from an FDM schema to DBMS schema consisting of record types,

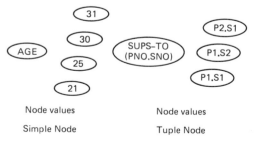

Node values   Node values

Simple Node   Tuple Node   **Figure 9.1** Simple node and tuple node.

relations, or segments (as in IMS). Of course, in mapping to CODASYL schema, a tuple node may result in a "link" record type with no data redundancy.

9.3.1.2 Functional Relationships

Three types of functions are defined:

1. *Many-one function*: a single-valued mapping from one node to another (Figure 9.2(a)).

2. *One-one mapping*: one-to-one function from one node to another (Figure 9.2(b)).

3. *Identity function*: a one-to-one function between identical values in distinct nodes whose values are drawn from the same value set (Figure 9.2(c)). This type of function indicates that the nodes have values in common.

The *domain* and *range* are defined as in mathematics. For one-to-one and identity functions, one node is arbitrarily selected as the domain.

$F: A \rightarrow B$ denotes a many-one function from the domain node A to the range node B; $F: A \leftrightarrow B$ denotes a one-one function; and $F: A \Leftrightarrow B$ indicates an identity function. If we wish to discuss a function from A to B without giving its type, we denote it by $F: A \Rightarrow B$. Note that $F: A \leftrightarrow B$ and $F: B \leftrightarrow A$ are equivalent, as are $F: A \Leftrightarrow B$ and $F: B \Leftrightarrow A$.

A graphic notation is used to further define the functions in FDM. In Figure 9.3 a white dot on the domain end of a function's arc indicates a partial function. A black dot indicates a total function. Similarly, a white dot on the range end of a function's arc indicates a function which is into, and a black dot an onto function. For example, in Figure 9.3, not all parts are supplied to projects, nor do all projects use parts. Similarly, not all projects have a time limit. It is convenient to explicitly define the subset of a domain or range that is involved with a function.

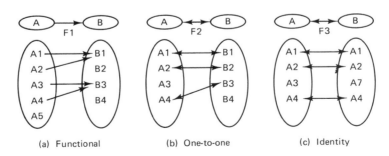

(a) Functional   (b) One-to-one   (c) Identity

Figure 9.2 Dependency types.

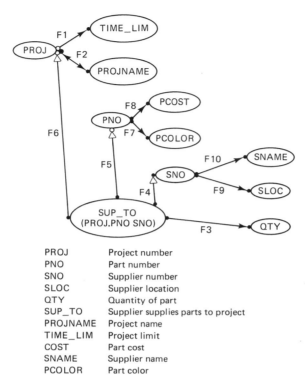

PROJ	Project number
PNO	Part number
SNO	Supplier number
SLOC	Supplier location
QTY	Quantity of part
SUP_TO	Supplier supplies parts to project
PROJNAME	Project name
TIME_LIM	Project limit
COST	Part cost
SNAME	Supplier name
PCOLOR	Part color

Figure 9.3 An example FDM.

Let *node function* indicate the values of *node* which are in the range or domain of *function*. For example, PROJ.F1 is the set of all projects (numbers) that have a time limit, and PROJ.F6 is the set of all projects (numbers) that use some parts.

9.3.1.3 Assertions

No data model can provide a complete data description, and FDM is no exception. For example, there could be ambiguity if there were more than one white dot on the same node. In Figure 9.3, we cannot determine if projects with time limits use parts (i.e., what is the relationship between the domain of function F1 and the range of F6?). This problem is solved by using additional assertions. In Figure 9.4, for example, PROJ.F1 ∩ PROF.F6 = ∅ indicates that projects with time limits don't use parts. The assertion PROF.F1 = PROJ.F6 would indicate that parts are used only by projects with time limits. While these assertions do not describe all possible relationships, they will be sufficient for our purpose.

1) EXP1 ⊂ EXP2

2) EXP1 ⊆ EXP2

3) EXP1 = EXP2

4) I(EXP1.EXP2) = (EXP1 ∩ EXP1 ≠ ∅ &
   EXP1 ⊄ EXP2 & EXP2 ⊄ EXP1)

5) EXP1 ∩ EXP2 = ∅

6) EXP1 ? EXP2 (RELATIONSHIP UNKNOWN)

Figure 9.4 Possible relationships between a pair of domain or range sets.

9.3.2 Entity-to-Data Relationships

In this section we will show how the identification and attributes of entities are modeled. Sets of entities are represented by rectangular entity nodes. For example, the node PEOPLE (Figure 9.5) represents the set of people employed by a company. (See Example 1 below.) The identifier of an entity is represented by a data node which has an identity function to the entity node. The attributes of an entity are represented by data nodes which are connected to the entity node through nonidentity functions.

Example 1

> The model of Figure 9.5 shows employees working in a company. The only entity represented is PEOPLE. The data nodes SS (social security number) and ENO (employee number) represent identifiers of people (as shown by the dependencies I1 and I2). The nodes OFFICE, NAME, and SAL are the attributes of people.
>
> OFFICE could have been modeled as another entity but here was modeled as an attribute of an employee. Note also that OFFICE could have been modeled as an identifier of PEOPLE, since it has a one-to-one relationship with PEOPLE.

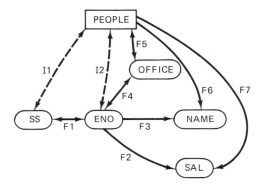

Figure 9.5 Entity-to-data relationship.

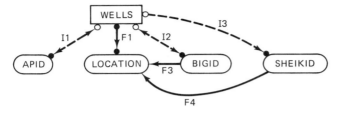

Assertions:

WELLS.I1 overlaps WELLS.F1
WELLS.I2 overlaps WELLS.F1
WELLS.I3 overlaps WELLS.F1

Figure 9.6   Multiplier indentifiers.

Entity nodes enable us to model how an entity is identified in the database. This is sometimes referred to as "signification" [29]. Many models assume there is a straightforward relationship between entities and their identifiers. This may not be the case. An entity may or may not have a unique identifier. In even more complex cases, more than one type of identifier can be defined for an entity set. The following example, due to [30], contains several similar cases.

Example 2

Figure 9.6 shows oil wells and their identifiers. Oil companies assign their own identifiers to their oil wells. Thus, Big Oil Co. has its own identifier for its wells (BIGID), as does Sheik Oil Co. (SHEIKID). In addition, some, but not all, wells have an identifier assigned by the American Petroleum Institute. Thus, no single kind of identifier represents all the entities in WELLS.

9.3.3 Entity-to-Entity Relationships

This level of the model is used to model reality. The constructs from the previous sections are used, but additional refinements are necessary to model some additional situations here.

The first problem occurs in modeling a many-to-many relationship between entities. Such a relationship can be modeled either as an entity or simply as a relationship. If the relationship is an entity, it is drawn as an entity node (rectangle) with component functions to the related entity nodes. If it is modeled as a relationship, it is drawn as a data node with appropriate component functions. For example, Figure 9.7 shows the alternatives for a parts-suppliers relationship. Figure 9.7(a) shows an inventory item (INV-Q) modeled as a relationship between PARTS and SUPPLIERS entities. Figure 9.7(b) shows the same relationship modeled as an entity. Note the connections between entity nodes and the corresponding data items.

A problem unique to the entity level is the "composed" relationship (i.e., one kind of entity can be composed of a set of another kind of entity [31]). This relationship is shown by an additional arrow on a function arc. For example, a FAMILY is composed of a set of PEOPLE (Figure 9.8). Further, a person can be a

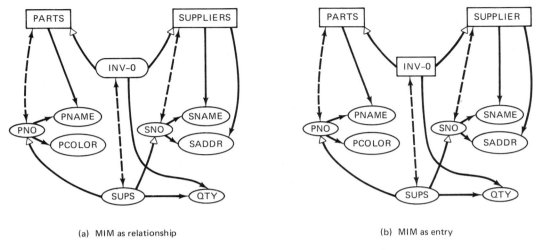

(a) MIM as relationship   (b) MIM as entry

Figure 9.7   Alternate ways of modeling a relationship.

member of several families (e.g., as a child in one and a parent in another). The many-to-many relationship is shown by the tuple node MEMBER-OF. The additional arrow on the arc to FAMILY shows that each family is composed of several people.

Another issue concerning entities is whether they have types. Some recent models [29, 32, 33] have entities classified into types. Entities are typeless in FDM. Entity types are not necessary for the analysis we perform, and their omission simplifies the model.

Further, a number of complications [30] occur when entity types are included in the model. Among these are:

1. "...no obvious criteria for when a characteristic of an object should be treated as a type, a role, or a relationship with another object."

2. A mechanism is needed to handle interrelationships among types and for allowing multiple types within a role.

3. The type of an object could change.

Figure 9.8   Composed entity relationship.

The second problem is the most serious, since some models [29, 32] attempt to have entity types remain disjoint. As a result, such models are unable to represent certain cases.

Example 3

Figure 9.9 shows a model of corporations (COMP), their products (PRODS), employees (ENO), and their customers (CUST). The identifiers for both corporations and customers are formed by concatenating their name and address. Companies make products, which are then bought by customers. We see that the entities PEOPLE and CORP can also be elements of the entity node LEGAL-PERSON. Employees are people, companies are corporations, and customers are legal persons, since a product could be purchased by either a company or a person.

This example cannot be handled very well by a model which gives entities disjoint types. If disjoint types are required, PEOPLE and CORP entities must have the

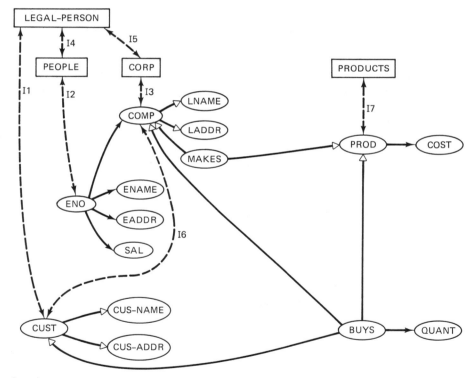

Assertions:

LEGAL-PERSON.I4 overlaps LEGAL-PERSON.I1
LEGAL-PERSON.I5 overlaps LEGAL-PERSON.I1

A overlaps B ≡ A ⊄ B & B ⊄ A & A ∩ B ≠ ∅

Figure 9.9   Example to show that entities cannot have disjoint types.

same type. If not, then LEGAL-PERSON violates the requirement that entities have a single type and that the types are disjoint. It is unnatural to give people the same type as corporations.

The final situation is that relationships between entities imply relationships on data and vice versa. Thus, a relationship between two entities implies that the same relationship exists between their identifiers. This is illustrated in the example above by the fact that a person could be both an employee and a customer (LEGAL-PERSON.I4 overlaps LEGAL-PERSON.I1). In order to represent this information, we may add a one-to-one function between ENO and CUST. An alternate way is to create a tuple node with ENAME and EADDT as components. The tuple node then has an identity function to CUST. This latter method is more consistent with the representation of companies and customers (COMP and CUST) as tuple nodes composed of a name and address.

In general, the data-to-data relationships represent a "slice" of the reality presented in entity-to-entity relationships. Thus, some relationships on the entity level may not be modeled directly on the data level, although relationships on the data level are easily included on the entity level.

9.4 TRANSACTION SPECIFICATION LANGUAGE

The processing requirements of a database system are specified using a *transaction specification language* (*TASL*). The TASL language is the specification facility in the database design system and provides a number of useful functions as described below:

1. *Model parameter specification*: In addition to providing a means for describing the FDM schema, TASL provides a natural and easy way to define such parameters as frequency of transaction execution, number of instances of sets and functions, and so on.

2. *Dynamic information specification*: Control constructs and operations are used to capture access patterns and query and update activity. This can be used in later phases to define record types and useful clusterings. The TASL constructs model database access but omit application details that are irrelevant to database design.

3. *Effects of schema restructuring*: As will be shown, schema restructuring operations are automatically reflected in the process model (given by TASL) as well as the data model. This provides useful information regarding code complexity with respect to different designs.

4. *Design simulations*: Having a process model enables us to simulate the effect of database transactions. Thus, TASL transactions can be executed with a simulator and the database activity measured for a given design.

5. *Transaction skeletons*: When a design is chosen, the TASL transactions serve as a high-level specification for application developers.

The language contains a set of operations to model data retrieval and manipulation in the functional data model. Since the only information-carrying objects in the FDM are nodes and functions, they are the basic elements for data access. Navigation in FDM is represented by an access path of functions.

Only three operations are needed to traverse the model. The ENTRY operation retrieves an initial set of values from a node, thus indicating the starting point of the access path. The ITEM operation traverses in the direction of a function arc (arrow). The SET operation traverses in the reverse direction of a function and is, therefore, multivalued. A more precise definition of these operations is given below.

Let F denote a many-to-one function $F: A \rightarrow B$ and $P(x)$ denote a predicate on the value x. Consider the two subsets, $A' \subset A$ and $B' \subset B$.

1. ENTRY(A) WHERE P
   returns $\{a$ in $A|P(a)\}$
2. ITEM(F, A') WHERE P
   returns $\{b$ in $B|$ for some a in A', $F(a)=b$ and $P(a)\}$
3. SET(F, B') WHERE P
   returns $\{a$ in $A|$ for some b in B', $F(a)=b$ and $P(a)\}$

The WHERE condition is optional. If it is omitted, the default WHERE TRUE is assumed.

We define a few other useful operations.

1. INTERSECT(A, B)$=A \cap B = \{x|x$ in A and x in $B\}$.
2. UNION(A, B)$=A \cup B = \{x|x$ in A or x in $B\}$
3. MINUS(A, B)$=A - B = \{x|x$ in A and not $(x$ in $B)\}$.

The following example illustrates the use of these operations to represent data manipulation.

Example 4

Refer to the example in Figure 9.3. Parts which are red and cost more than $.50 are retrieved by:

```
INTERSECT (SET(F8, ENTRY(PCOST) WHERE PCOST=.50),
SET(F7,ENTRY(PCOLOR) WHERE PCOLOR='RED'));
```

First, values of PCOST greater than $.50 are retrieved. Part numbers associated with these costs are then retrieved by traversing F8. Similarly, the value 'RED' is retrieved, and red parts are retrieved by traversing F7. The two sets of part numbers are then intersected.

In order to represent more complex data manipulation, TASL provides several types of statements:

1. The assignment statement assigns a value or set of values to a variable.
2. The FOR-WHILE construct is a loop similar to the PL/I loop construct.
3. The IF-THEN-ELSE is a conditional construct.
4. The READ/WRITE statements are used to input/output values or sets of values.
5. The COMPUTE statement expresses the fact that some computation has taken place. The syntax is:

> COMPUTE *result list* USING (*function name*) *argument list*;
> where *function name* gives a descriptive name to the computation.

6. Data-manipulation statements. Several data-manipulation operations on the functional data model are defined in [11]. For example, CREATE and DELETE add and remove values from nodes; LINK and UNLINK connect and disconnect the values in nodes with instances of functions. These operations are not relevant to the techniques in this paper and will not be described further. TASL also provides a mechanism to indicate performance information about a transaction to the design tool. The probability of the condition of an IF statement is an example of such information. The example below illustrates some of these data-manipulation statements in the TASL.

Example 5

Again, refer to Figure 9.3. An application that lists all projects and their suppliers is represented in the following TASL statements.

```
APPLICATION LIST_PROJ_AND_SUPS 10 / YEAR:
DESCRIPTION LIST PROJECTS AND THEIR SUPPLIERS:

PROJECTS: SUBSET OF PROJ;
SNOS:SUBSET OF SNO;
S: ELEMENT OF SNO;
P: ELEMENT OF PROJ;

PROJECTS := ENTRY(PROJ);
FOR P IN PROJECTS DO
     WRITE(P);
     SNOS := ITEM(F4,SET(F6,P));
     FOR S IN SNOS DO
         WRITE(S);
     ENDFOR;
ENDFOR;
```

The first two lines give the name and descriptive information about the application. The next three lines declare objects which will be used in the application. PROJECTS and SNOS contain PROJECT and SNO values, respectively. S and P are declared as variables for SNO and PROF nodes, in the local view.

The application begins by retrieving all project numbers using the ENTRY operation. Each time through the loop, P takes on a project number, and the related supplier numbers are retrieved into SNOS. The inner loop then outputs the supplier numbers for that project.

9.5 OPERATIONS ON THE MODEL

In this section we define operations to restructure the functional data model during the view-integration process. The view-integration process combines local views into a single global view. This has two motivations: (1) a single global model is easier to understand and implement than many local views; (2) redundant data in several local views may cause storage waste and data inconsistency.

Two types of redundancy can occur in the FDM: (1) Several nodes represent the same set of values. In this case we combine the redundant nodes into a single node using the MERGE operation. (2) Several functions represent the same relationship. Here, all but one of the functions must be removed from the model using the REMOVE operation.

Since TASL defines processing specifications on FDM, the MERGE and REMOVE operations must also make changes in the TASL representation corresponding to the changes in FDM. Otherwise, the processing specifications become invalid. The MERGE and REMOVE operations preserve the information in FDM in the sense that any transaction or query on the original FDM structure has an equivalent representation in the restructured model. To restructure TASL specifications, the MERGE operation modifies the ENTRY operation and the REMOVE operation modifies the ITEM and SET operations. We now define these operations as follows:

1. REMOVE(F;F1,..., Fn). The redundant function F is removed from the model, and traversals on F are replaced by traversals on $F_1, \ldots, F_n$. We say F: $B \Rightarrow C$ is *redundant* on F_1: $A \Rightarrow A_1$; ...; F_n: $A_{n-1} \Rightarrow A_n$; if $B.F \subset A.F_1$ and, for all a in $B.F$, $F(a) = F_n(\ldots F_2(F_1(a))\ldots)$.

We note that redundancy of a function can only be verified by examining the data semantics. The redundancies must be verified by users during database design. In the next section we will provide heuristics that assist users in determining redundant functions.

The TASL processing specifications are restructured as follows: let I1: $B \Leftrightarrow A_0$ and I2: $C \Leftrightarrow A_n$ denote $B.F \subset A_0.F_1$ and $C.F \subset A_n.F_n$, respectively. Every occurrence of

$$\text{"SET}(F, argument)\text{ WHERE P"}$$

in TASL is replaced by the new expression[2]

$$\text{ITEM}(I1, \text{SET}(F1, \ldots, \text{SET}(Fn, \text{ITEM}(I2, argument)))\ldots)) \text{ WHERE P}$$

Similarly,

$$\text{ITEM}(F, argument) \text{ WHERE P}$$

is replaced by

$$\text{ITEM}(I2, \text{ITEM}(Fn, \ldots, \text{ITEM}(F1, \text{ITEM}(I1, argument)))\ldots)) \text{ WHERE P}$$

2. MERGE(A,B;C). Merge nodes A and B to form node $C = A \cup B$. For all functions F such that $F: X \Rightarrow A$ or $F: A \Rightarrow X$ for some node S, the dependencies are restructured to $F: X \Rightarrow C$ or $F: C \Rightarrow X$. Similar restructuring operations are performed for B. All functions between A and B must be identity functions. The merge operation results in the elimination of all functions between A and B.

These changes in the model are not necessarily sufficient to guarantee that the same processing can be performed before and after the merge. Suppose we merge A and B and that $A \subset B$. After the merge, there may be no equivalent expression to "ENTRY(A)".

In order to remedy this problem, the MERGE operation creates a *separation node* whose values are used to separate the values in a merged node. The node created by the merge is a *combined node*. The creation of a separation node is required unless an assertion exists stating that $A = B$. Let SAB denote the separation node created by MERGE(A,B;C) where $A \subset B$. The MERGE operation also creates a dependency $S: C \rightarrow SAB$.

The TASL specification is restructured so that every occurrence of "ENTRY(A) WHERE P" is replaced by "SET(S,ENTRY(SAB) WHERE SAB='A') WHERE P", where 'A' is in SAB.

Example 6

Figure 9.10 gives an FDM model about three kinds of pets: dogs, cats, and turtles. Cats and turtles are considered HOUSE-PETS. The separation node SEP1 separates HOUSE-PETS into two sets, one containing only cats, the other containing only turtles. PETS contains cats, dogs, and turtles; CANINES contains only dogs. The use of separation nodes is illustrated by merging CANINES and HOUSE-PETS into PETS.

---

[2] If B and A_0 are the same node, then "ITEM(I1,...)" is omitted in the restructured TASL expression. Similarly, if C and A_n are the same node, "ITEM(I2,...)" is omitted.

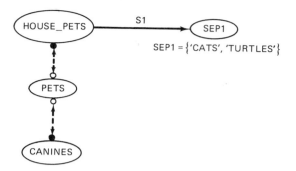

Figure 9.10   SEP1 as a separation node.

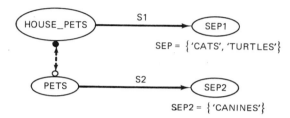

Figure 9.11   Merge of CANINES with PETS creating SEP2 as a separation node.

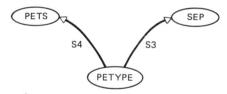

SEP = {'CATS', 'TURTLES', 'CANINES', 'HOUSE_PETS'}   **Figure 9.12**   Merge of separation nodes.

First, CANINES are merged into pets, as shown in Figure 9.11. This creates separation node SEP2. "ENTRY(CANINES)" is replaced by "SET(S2, ENTRY(SEP2) WHERE SEP2='CANINES')".

Next, the PETS and HOUSE-PETS nodes are merged as shown in Figure 9.12. The node SEP=SEP1 ∪ SEP2 ∪ {'HOUSE-PETS'}. The relationship between SEP and PETS is now many-to-many, because the values related to 'CATS' and 'TUR-TLES' are subsets of those related to HOUSE-PETS and is represented by the tuple node PETYPE. The operation "SET(S2, ENTRY(SEP2) WHERE SEP2='CANINES')" becomes "ITEM(S4, SET(S3, ENTRY(SEP)) WHERE SEP='CANINES')".

As shown in the example above, sometimes the nodes merged already have separation nodes. The existing separation nodes may have to be modified. There are two cases:

1. One node has a separation node—add appropriate value(s).
2. Both nodes have separation nodes—combine separation nodes and add appropriate values.

As separation values are added, "ENTRY" operations on that node are replaced by an expression which retrieves the name of the component node from the separation node and traverses to the combined node. Also, the relationship between the combined node and its separation node may change from many-to-one to many-to-many as a result of these manipulations. If this happens, a tuple node is created between the two nodes. TASL traversals between the nodes are changed to reflect this.

Figure 9.13 illustrates these manipulations and the changes made by the third step of PROCEDURE MERGE. Suppose the nodes being merged have no separation node (starting case 1). If the nodes represent the same set of values, a single node results with no separation node created (resulting case 1). If either node is a subset of the other, then MERGE produces resulting case 2. The separation node contains a value which is used to retrieve the node which was a subset. If the nodes have a nonempty intersection but neither is a subset of the other, the result (resulting case 3) is a separation node with a many-to-many relationship with its combined node. The separation node contains two values, one for each node which was merged. Similar considerations hold for the other starting cases.

Let us summarize the above discussion:

Procedure MERGE:

1. Remove any $F\colon A \Leftrightarrow B$, and replace any "ITEM(F,EXPRESSION)" by "EXPRESSION".
2. Create node $C = A \cup B$, and all $F\colon X \Rightarrow A$ ($F\colon A \Rightarrow X$) are replaced by $F\colon X \Rightarrow C$ ($F\colon C \Rightarrow X$), and similarly for B.
3. Case 1. $A = B$:
    Replace "ENTRY(A) WHERE *expression*" and "ENTRY(B) WHERE *expression*" by

    "ENTRY(C) WHERE *expression*."

If necessary, combine separation nodes, but no values are added to the separation node.

Case 2. $A \subseteq B$:
    Replace "ENTRY(B) WHERE *expression*" by

    "ENTRY(C) WHERE *expression*."

Add separation value for A.

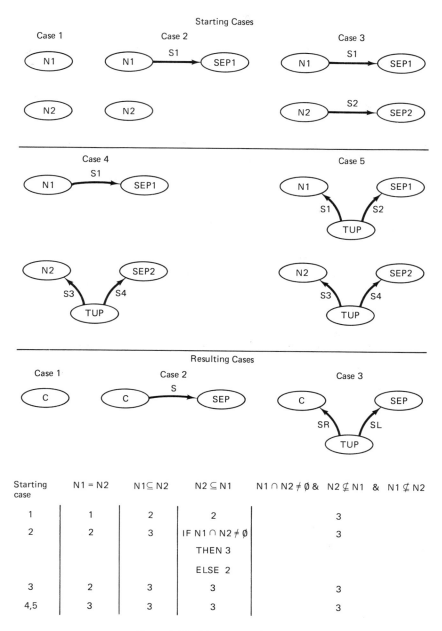

Figure 9.13 Merge operation cases.

Starting case	N1 = N2	N1⊆ N2	N2 ⊆ N1	N1 ∩ N2 ≠ ∅ & N2 ⊄ N1 & N1 ⊄ N2
1	1	2	2	3
2	2	3	IF N1 ∩ N2 ≠ ∅ THEN 3 ELSE 2	3
3	2	3	3	3
4,5	3	3	3	3

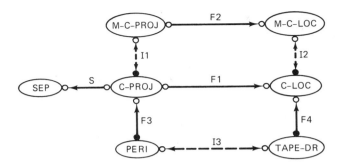

Figure 9.14 An FDM for the computer projects example.

Item	Significance
M-C-PROJ	Mini-computer project
M-C-LOC	Mini-computer project location
C-PROJ	Computer project
SEP	Separation node for C-PROJ
PERI	Peripheral manufacturer supplying peripherals for computer projects
TAPE-DR	Tape-drive manufacturer (located in city given in C-LOC through F4, and supplying computer projects in that city)
CONSTRAINT:	Peripheral manufacturers must be located in the same city as the projects they supply

Case 3. $A \cap B = 0$ and $A \not\subseteq B$ and $B \not\subseteq A$:

Add separation value for A.

Add separation value for B.

Example 7

Suppose we wish to simplify the model in Figure 9.14 by removing redundant functions and merging nodes which have nonempty intersections. Since minicomputer projects are a subset of computer projects, F2 is redundant with F1. Thus, we can retrieve the location of a minicomputer project by traversing I1, F1, and then I2. Similarly, traversing F4 is equivalent to traversing I3, F3, and F1. F2 and F4 are removed by

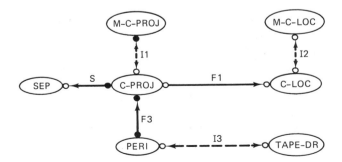

Figure 9.15 Redundant functions are removed.

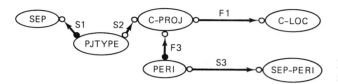

Figure 9.16 Resulting FDM after the merge operation.

REMOVE(F2;F1) and REMOVE(F4;F3,F1), which produce Figure 9.15. (The identity functions I1, I2, and I3 are filled in by the system.) A specification which performed "SET(F2,...)" now performs "ITEM(I1, SET(F1, ITEM(I2,...)))."

M-C-PROJ and M-C-LOC are now isolated from other nodes. Merging them with other nodes simplifies the model as well as retrievals which traverse I1 and I2. Similarly, we merge TAPE-DR with PERI. MERGE(M-C-PROJ, C-PROJ; C-PROJ), MERGE(M-C-LOC, C-LOC; C-LOC), and MERGE(TAPE-DR, PERI; PERI) result in Figure 9.16.

MERGE(M-C-PROJ, C-PROJ; C-PROJ) causes a value to be added to SEP (say 'M-C-PROJ'), so an expression equivalent to "ENTRY('M-C-PROJ')" can be performed after the merge. The merge changed the relationship between SEP and C-PROJ to many-to-many. The tuple node PJTYPE was created to represent this relationship. The separation node SEP-PERI was created to allow an expression equivalent to "ENTRY(TAPE-DR)" to be performed. No separation node was created when M-C-LOC was merged with C-LOC, since M-C-LOC = C-LOC. Finally, note that our example retrieval "ITEM(I1, SET(F1, ITEM(I2,...)))" is simplified to "SET(F1,...)" by these merges.

9.6 MODEL INTEGRATION

The main problems in the integration process are to connect the local views into a global view using identity functions, and to determine and remove redundant functions. Entities are used to guide global view creation. Heuristics are used to direct the designer's attention to functions that may be redundant.

In this section we give heuristics to filter out from consideration dependencies which are not redundant. These are illustrated with an example. We then give an integration algorithm using these heuristics and demonstrate it on a sample problem.

In developing heuristics that aid in identifying redundant functions, it is essential to estimate the relative size of node.function in database design. Let %node function = |node.function|node|*100 denote the percentage of a node contained in the domain or range of a function. Thus, %PROJ.F1 = 60 indicates that the set PROJ.F1 contains 60 percent of the values in the PROJ node.

A value in the range of a many-to-one function is related to one or more values in the domain. We refer to this number as the *fanout* of the function with respect to that value. Let *function*.MIN denote the minimum permitted fanout for *function*, and *function*.MAX denote the maximum fanout. If there is no upper limit, then *function*.MAX = ∞. In Figure 9.3, F6.MAX = 1000 and F6.MIN = 10 indicates that projects which use parts have at least 10 inventory items and at most 1000.

Four types of heuristics are developed that use information about: (1) how the domains and ranges of composition functions overlap; (2) the fanout limits of functions; (3) the average fanouts of functions; (4) the type of functions involved.

Let A, B, C, and subscripted A's denote nodes, and F denote a function. The composition of G_1: $A_0 \rightarrow A_1$; ..., G_n: $A_{n-1} \rightarrow A_n$ is denoted by $(G_n)^+ \equiv G_n \circ G_{n-1} \circ \cdots \circ G_1$. An arbitrary G_i in this composition is referred to by $G_i \in (G_n)^+$. In describing our heuristics, we will define them in terms of the functions F: $B \Rightarrow C$ and $(G_n)^+$: $A_0 \Rightarrow A_n$. We now present the four types of heuristics.

1. *Subset information heuristics*:

   (a) *Subset information test on range and domain*: If F is redundant with $(G_n)^+$, then $B \cdot F \subseteq A_0 \cdot (G_n)^+$ and $C \cdot F \subseteq A_n \cdot (G_n)^+$, by definition. If either $B \cdot F \not\subseteq A_0 \cdot (G_n)^+$ or $C \cdot F \not\subseteq A_n \cdot (G_n)^+$, then, from the assertions, the F is not redundant with $(G_n)^+$ because there is part of F's domain or range which is not part of $(G_n)^+$'s.

   (b) *Equality test on range and domain*: If $B \cdot F = A_0 \cdot (G_n)^+$ and F is redundant on $(G_n)^+$, then we must have $C \cdot F = A_n \cdot (G_n)^+$. This is because if two functions are the same and have the same domain, then they must have the same range as well. Thus, $C \cdot F \neq A_n \cdot (G_n)^+$ implies that F is not redundant on $(G_n)^+$.

   (c) *Nonempty intersection*: If there exists $G_i, G_{i+1} \in (G_n)^+$ such that $A_i \cdot G_i \cap A_i \cdot G_{i+1} = \varnothing$, then $(G_n)^+$ has an empty range.

2. *Fanout limit heuristics*: Each FDM function has associated with it the maximum fanout permitted. If F is redundant with $(G_n)^+$, then it must be that

$$F \cdot \text{MAX} \leq \prod_{i=1}^{n} g_i \cdot \text{MAX} \qquad (\text{assume that } k * \text{INF} = \text{INF})$$

If not, then the fanout limits of F are outside those of $(G_n)^+$, and F is not redundant on $(G_n)^+$. Thus, if the condition fails to hold, then F is not redundant with $(G_n)^+$.

3. *Average fanout information*: Suppose we make the "uniform assumption" that (a) a function has a *uniform fanout*, i.e., each value in the range is related to about the same number of values in the domain, and (b) $A_i \cdot G_{i+1}$ contains the same percentage of $A_i \cdot G_i$ as its percentage of the node. Under these assumptions, F is redundant if and only if

$$\frac{|B| * \%B \cdot F}{|C| * \%C \cdot F} \geq \frac{|A_0| * \%A_0 \cdot G_1}{|A_1| * \%A_1 \cdot G_1} * \%A_1 \cdot G_1 * \frac{|A_1| * \%A_1 \cdot G_1}{|A_2| * \%A_2 \cdot G_2} * \cdots$$

$$* A_{n-1} \cdot G_n * \frac{|A_{n-1}| * \%A_{n-1} \cdot G_{n-1}}{|A_n| * \%A_n \cdot G_n}$$

that is,

$$\frac{|B| * \%B \cdot F}{|C| * \%C \cdot F} \geq \frac{|A_0| * \%A_0 \cdot G_1}{|A_n| * \%A_n \cdot G_n} * \prod_{i=1}^{n-1} (\%A_i \cdot G_{i+1})$$

Also,

$$\frac{|B| * \%B \cdot F}{|C| * \%C \cdot F} \leq \frac{|A_0| * \%A_0 \cdot G_1}{|A_n| * \%A_n \cdot G_n}$$

Otherwise, F is not redundant.

4. *Type of functions involved*: Suppose F is a many-one function; then, if F is redundant with $(G_n)^+$, at least one $G_i \in (G_n)^+$ must be a many-one function.

Example 8

The model of Figure 9.17 shows graduate students, professors, and their offices. The function F gives a graduate student's office. F_2 gives a professor's office. Graduate students who have passed their qualifying examination have a major professor, who is given by F_1. As can be seen in the figure, there are 60 students, 15 professors, and 30 offices. The node sizes and the %node together are used to determine the average fanout in Figure 9.17.

If the "universal relation" (uniqueness) assumption held, the function F would be redundant, and F would give the office of the student's major professor. However, this is not the case in the example. We will apply our heuristics to this model to determine if F is redundant.

Subset test: F fails the subset test, since F contains values in both its range and domain which are not contained in the composition of F_2 and F_1. (Neither GRAD.F $\subseteq$ GRAD.F1 or OFFICE.F $\subseteq$ OFFICE.F2 holds.)

Fanout limit test: F fails the fanout limit test, since the maximum fanout for the composition of F_1 and F_2 is $3 = 3 * 1$. The maximum fanout for F is 4, which is larger than the fanout of $F_1 \cdot F_2$. Therefore F fails the fanout limits test.

Uniform fanout test: F also fails the uniform fanout test. Under the uniformity assumption, the composition of F_1 and F_2 has a fanout of $2 * 1 = 2$. F has a fanout of 4, and fails this test.

The integration algorithm can be summarized as follows:

Algorithm INTEGRATE:

1. Merge identical entity nodes from different views. (This is done by their names. Recall that entity-node names are unique globally.)
2. (Connect identifiers for entity nodes.) For each entity node (say A), ask designer how to connect identifiers for A from different views. (They are connected with either one-to-one or identity function.)
3. (Connect attributes of each entity node.) For each entity node (say A), ask how to connect the attribute nodes of A from different views. (Recall that attributes of an entity are data nodes connected to an entity node with a nonidentity function.)

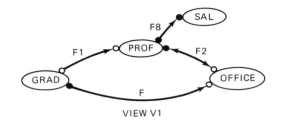

VIEW V1

Node	Inode1	Definition
GRAD	60	Graduate student's name
PROF	15	Professor's name
OFFICE	30	Office numbers
SAL	10	Professor's salaries

Functions	Definition
F	Graduate student's office
F1	Graduate student's major professor
F2	Professor's office
F8	Professor's salary

Function Information

Function	Max fanout	Avg.	% domain node	% range node
F	4	4	100	50
F1	3	2	33	67
F2	1	1	100	50
F8	INF	1.5	100	100

Subset information:

$GRAD.F1 \subseteq GRAD.F$
$PROF.F1 \subseteq PROF.F2$
$OFFICE.F2 \cap OFFICE.F = \emptyset$

Figure 9.17   Local view, V1.

4. Ask how to connect nodes which are not attributes of an entity but are connected to an entity identifier node through a single dependency.

5. (Merge nodes with same values.) For all nodes (say A), if there exists a node B such that $A = B$ and there are no nonidentity functions between A and B, then MERGE(A,B;A).

6. (Merge nodes which are subsets of other nodes.) For all nodes (say A), if there exists a node B such that $A \subset B$ and there are no nonidentity functions between A and B, then MERGE(A,B;B).

7. (Remove redundant functions.) For each nonidentity function F, if F is redundant, heuristics then ask designer if F is redundant and to REMOVE if necessary.

Example 9

The first four steps in the integration process connect the local views to form a global view. These steps connect the views V1, V2, and V3 (Figures 9.17, 9.18 and 9.19) to form the model of Figure 9.20. First, the entity nodes for PEOPLE are merged from the various views, as well as the OFFICE nodes.

Next, the identifier nodes for entities are connected. The system asks for the relationship between V1: GRAD and V2: STU and is given the assertion V1: GRAD = V2: STU. (The names of nodes and functions are prefixed with their view names to insure they have unique names.) The identity function X3 is created from this assertion. Since the nodes are equal, the function involves all of both nodes; i.e., %V1: GRAD.X3 = %V2: STU.X3 = 100.

We also have the assertion that V3: M-PROF ⊂ V1: PROF, which creates the identity function X2. Since V3: M-PROF.X2 ⊂ V1: PROF, we have %V3: M-PROF.X2 = 100. However, only part of V1: PROF is involved in X2, and the system enters 60 percent for %V1: PROF.X2. The succeeding connection steps (2 through 4) result in the model of Figure 9.20.

Figures 9.21 through 9.23 for convenience, note that the dots have been omitted for the remainder of the process depict how the remainder of the integration process is carried out. Note that Figure 9.17 shows that V1: GRAD is the same as V2: STU, as

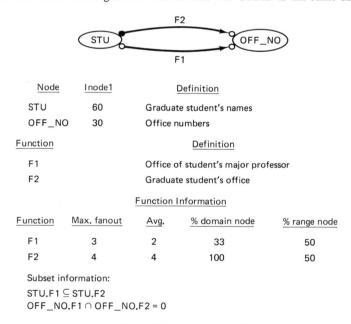

Node	Inode1	Definition
STU	60	Graduate student's names
OFF_NO	30	Office numbers

Function	Definition
F1	Office of student's major professor
F2	Graduate student's office

Function Information

Function	Max. fanout	Avg.	% domain node	% range node
F1	3	2	33	50
F2	4	4	100	50

Subset information:
STU.F1 ⊆ STU.F2
OFF_NO.F1 ∩ OFF_NO.F2 = 0

Figure 9.18 Local view, V2.

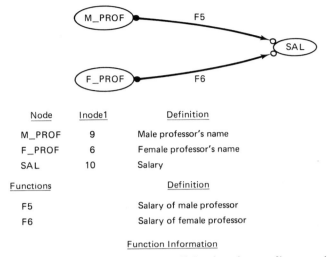

Node	Inode1	Definition
M_PROF	9	Male professor's name
F_PROF	6	Female professor's name
SAL	10	Salary

Functions	Definition
F5	Salary of male professor
F6	Salary of female professor

Function Information

Function	Max. fanout	Avg.	% domain node	% range node
F5	INF	1.5	100	60
F6	INF	1	100	60

Subset information:

SAL.F5 $\cap$ SAL.F6 $\neq$ 0 and SAL.F5 $\subseteq$ SAL.F6 and SAL.F6 $\subseteq$ SAL.F5

Figure 9.19   Local view, V3.

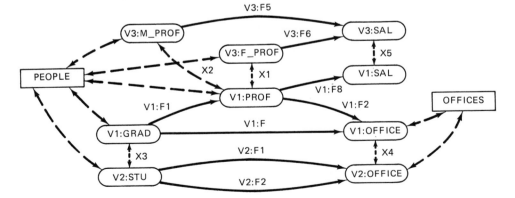

Figure 9.20   Global view integrated from the local views V1, V2 and V3.

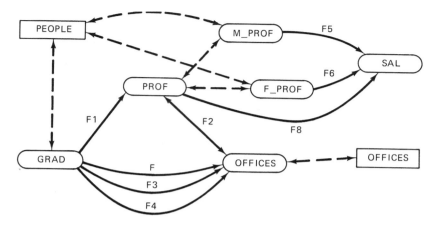

Figure 9.21 The modified global view after merging identity nodes.

are V1: OFFICE and V2: OFF-NO. Also, V3: M-PROF and V3: F-PROF are both subsets of V1: PROF. Step 5 merges the nodes representing the same sets of values. This results in Figure 9.21, in which nodes and functions have been renamed. V1: GRAD and V2: STU are merged to form the node GRAD. The OFFICE node is the result of merging V1: OFFICE and V2: OFF-NO.

Next, nodes which are subsets of other nodes are merged. Nodes M-PROF and F-PROF in Figure 9.21 are subsets of PROF. Merging them into PROF results in Figure 9.23. The separation node SEX is created as a result of this merge. SEX contains the values 'M' and 'F' to separate values of M-PROF and F-PROF. Applications which performed "ENTRY(M-PROF)" now perform "SET(F7, ENTRY(SEX) WHERE SEX = 'M')."

The final step in this example is to REMOVE redundant functions. The functions F5 and F6 pass all heuristics for redundancy on F8, and the designer confirms

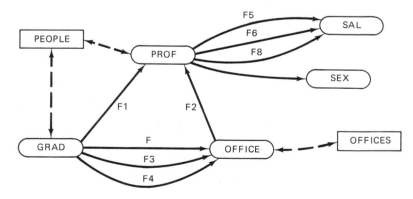

Figure 9.22 The M-PROF and F-PROF nodes are merged.

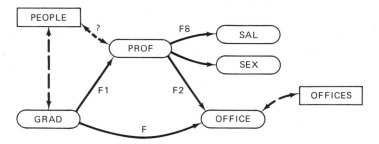

Figure 9.23   The final integrated global view.

that the design tool should REMOVE them. The system then tests F3 for redundancy on F, F4, and on the composition of F1 and F2. F1 is found to be redundant on the composition of F1 and F2, and the designer tells the tool to remove F3. Similarly, F4 is eventually removed as redundant on F. The result is the model of Figure 9.23.

9.7 DESIGN EVALUATION

Once a global model of the database has been created, the next design stage is the generation of a schema incorporating the constraints of the data model used by the DBMS. Many schemas are generally possible for a given design problem. They must be evaluated in order to select a "good" one. There are a number of criteria for evaluating a schema—"naturalness," flexibility, and performance (storage and access costs), and others. Here we will focus on performance evaluation, since many of the other criteria are difficult to quantify. Further, they can be imposed by the designer guiding the design process.

Any evaluation of a design's performance must introduce some notions normally associated with physical design (e.g., index selection). While data independence requires separate facilities for specifying logical views (seen by application programs) and physical views (seen by access methods), good performance requires that the derivation of the physical views (i.e., indexes, links, etc.) take into account the actions of the applications programs on the logical views. Thus, logical and physical design are interdependent.

The information contained in FDM is not sufficient for design evaluation, since the efficiency of an application depends on available access paths. Section 9.7.1 describes some simple extensions to the FDM which permit the designer to input high-level access-path information. The goal is not to provide a detailed performance estimate, but to provide a relative measure to allow a rough comparison between alternative schemas. Section 9.7.2 defines the concept of a "logical access" and gives an example comparing two alternative schemas.

9.7.1 Access-Path Specifications

In this section we use $F: A(x) \rightarrow B(y)$, where x and y may be "P" or "T" to denote a function. $A(P)$ and $A(T)$ indicate that F is *partial* or *total*, respectively. $B(P)$ and $B(T)$ denote that F is *into* or *onto*, respectively. This notation corresponds to the use of solid and hollow dots on the functional arrows in the graphical notation.

Hierarchical sequential access.   Each function defines equivalence classes on its domain and an ordering. So for a given parent (range value), all the children (associated domain occurrences) can be accessed in a given sequential order.

Ordered sequential access.   Often, an application program must process a set sequentially in a given order (e.g., FIFO, LIFO, by value). This is specified by a special singular set SYS and functions of the form: $F: D(T) \rightarrow$ SYS, ⟨ordering criteria⟩. Since SYS contains only one element, and since the domain is total, order is defined on the domain D. For example, to specify that PNO in Figure 9.24 is in ascending order, we would specify: S1: PNO(T) → SYS, ORDERED BY (PNO ASC); The set SYS is diagrammed as a small, solid triangle (Figure 9.25(a)).

Direct access by value.   Direct access by value requires the introduction of *indexed set*. Indexed sets are shown in the schema diagram by triangle nodes (Figure 9.25(b)). There must also be an accompanying *index function* of the form:

(a) $F(X): \text{PNO}(T) \rightarrow \text{PNO}X(T)$ or
(b) $F(X): \text{PNO}(T) \Leftrightarrow \text{PNO}X(T)$

The parenthesized X denotes that F is an index function. In case (a) F denotes a secondary index, since an index entry could point to many PNO values. Case (b) represents a primary index.

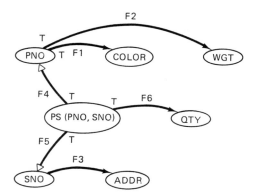

Figure 9.24   A simple FDM schema.

E1:PNO, T1 – SYS

(a) Ordered sequential access

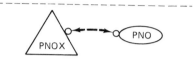

(b) Index sequential direct access

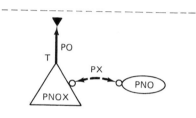

(c) Index sequential access

Figure 9.25 Access path extensions.

Index sequential access. This type of access is shown by a composite of ordered sequential access and direct access by value (Figure 9.25(c)). PNOX is the index set for PNO. The function PO indicates that PNOX can be accessed in ascending order. The PNO set is accessed through the function PX. PNOX can also be entered directly by value; then sequential access proceeds by the ordering defined by PO.

9.7.2 Quantitative Measurements

We define a unit of measure called a *logical access* (*LAC*) for use during the early design stages. An LAC occurs whenever a new member of an FDM set is accessed (stored or retrieved). This happens whenever a traversal is made from one set to another or from one member to the next within a given set. For simplicity, we assume the cost of all LACs is the same regardless of the set being accessed. These costs could be weighted for different access paths in a more refined evaluation. The access costs for a design can be stated as:

$$TC = SUM(\mathit{freq}(Q_i) * C(Q_i)) \qquad \text{for all } Q_i$$

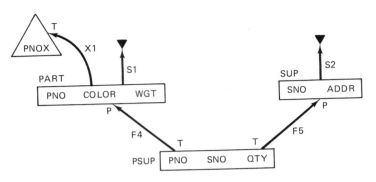

Figure 9.26   Design 1.

where TC is total cost, Q_i is the ith transaction, $freq(Q_i)$ is the execution frequency of Q_i, and $C(Q_i)$ is the cost of executing transaction Q_i one time (in number of LACs). The $C(Q_i)$ is a function of the access patterns for Q_i, and of the quantitative data about the FDM schema such as set cardinalities. To be more specific, the following notation is introduced:

SCARD(S): Cardinality of set S (i.e., no. of instances)

AVGDPR(F): Average number of domain values per range value for function F.

PFRAC(F): If the range of F is labeled "P", then PFRAC(F) is the fraction of the range covered by the function; otherwise, PFRAC(F)=1.0.

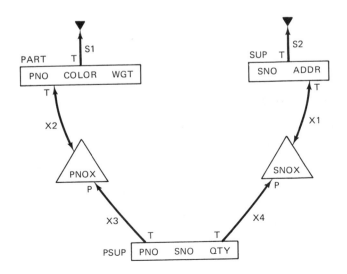

Figure 9.27   Design 2.

Process Restructuring for Design 2

QUERY Q1:

```
FOR P IN SET(S1,SYS) DO
    P1 = ITEM(X2,P);
    FOR S IN SET(X3,P1) DO
        WRITE(P.PNO,S.SNO,S.QTY);
    ENDFOR;
ENDFOR;
```

QUERY Q2:

```
PARTNO = ENTRY(PNOX WHERE PNOX = value);
FOR P1 IN SET(X3,PARTNO) DO
    S1 = ITEM(X4,P1);
    S2 = SET(X1,S1);
    WRITE(P1.PNO,P1.QTY,S2.ADDR);
ENDFOR;
```

QUERY Q3:

```
FOR S IN SET(S2,SYS) DO
    S1 = ITEM(X1,S);
    WRITE(S.SNO,S.ADDR);
    FOR PS1 IN SET(X4,S1) DO
        IF PS1.QTY 100 THEN(0.75)
            P1 = ITEM(X3,PS1);
            P2 = SET(X2,P1);
            WRITE(P2.PNO,P2.COLOR,PS1.QTY);
        ENDIF;
    ENDFOR;
ENDFOR;
```

Figure 9.29 Restructure of processes for design 2.

Restructured Process Specification for Design 1

QUERY Q1:

```
FOR P IN SET(S1,SYS) DO
    FOR S IN SET(F4,P) DO
        WRITE (P.PNO,S.SNO,S.QTY);
    ENDFOR;
ENDFOR;
```

QUERY Q2:

```
PARTNO = ENTRY(PNOX WHERE PNOX = value);
P1 = SET(X1,PARTNO);
FOR P2 IN SET(F4,P1) DO
    SUP1 = ITEM(F5,P1);
    WRITE(PARTNO,P2.SNO,P2.QTY,SUP1.ADDR);
ENDFOR;
```

QUERY Q3:

```
FOR S IN SET(S2,SYS) DO
    WRITE(S.SNO,S.ADDR);
    FOR P IN SET(F5,S) DO
        IF P.QTY 100 THEN(0.75)
            P1 = ITEM(F4,P);
            WRITE(P.PNO,P.QTY,P1.COLOR);
        ENDIF;
    ENDFOR;
ENDFOR;
```

Figure 9.28 Restructure of processes for design 1.

To illustrate the concepts of access-path specification and design evaluation, two designs derived from Figure 9.24 are given in Figures 9.26 and 9.27. The corresponding process descriptions are given in Figures 9.28 and 9.29 and are evaluated for access efficiency. Note that the original ENTRY statements have been changed to use the available access paths. The original TASL specifications are access-path independent. Also, note that the proposed designs are still given abstractly in terms of functional dependencies. An interpretation could be given for either a relational or DBTG (network) type data management system.

TABLE 9.1   DATA FOR EVALUATION EXAMPLE

freq(Q1) = 2; freq(Q2) = 800; freq(Q3) = 5;

Set Data

Schema	NAME	SCARD
FDM	PNO	10000
	SNO	100
	PS	630,000
Design 1	PNOX	10000
	PART	10000
	SUP	100
	PSUP	630,000
Design 2	PART	10000
	SUP	100
	PSUP	630,000
	PNOX	10000
	SNOX	100

Function Data

Schema	NAME	FANOUT	PFRAC
FDM	F4	63	0.70
	F5	6300	0.90
Design 1	S1	10000	1.0
	S2	100	1.0
	X1	1	1.0
	F4	6300	0.90
	F5	63	0.70
Design 2	S1	10000	1.0
	S2	100	1.0
	X1	1	1.0
	X2	1	1.0
	X3	6300	0.90
	X4	63	0.70

TABLE 9.2   COMPUTATION OF DESIGN ACCESS COSTS

		COST COMPUTATION (Design 1)		
QRY	* ACCESS *	COMPUTATION	*	COST(LACs)
Q1	PART VIA S1	SCARD(PART)		10000
	PSUP VIA F4	SCARD(PART) * FANOUT(F4)		$63(10**6)$
			C(Q1) =	$63.01(10**6)$
Q2	DIRECT ACC TO PNOX			1
	PART VIA X1			1
	PSUP VIA F4	FANOUT(F4)		6300
			C(Q2) =	6302
Q3	SUP VIA S2	SCARD(SUP)		100
	PSUP VIA F5	SCARD(SUP) * FANOUT(F5)		6300
	PART VIA F4	(0.75) * SCARD(SUP) * FANOUT(F5)		4725
			C(Q3) =	11125

$TC = 2*C(Q1) + 800*C(Q2) + 5*C(Q3) = 131.1(10**6)$

		COST COMPUTATION (Design 2)		
Q1	PART VIA S1	SCARD(PART)		10000
	PNOX VIA X2	SCARD(PART)		10000
	PSUP VIA X3	SCARD(PART) * FANOUT(X3)		$63(10**6)$
			C(Q1) =	$63.02(10**6)$
Q2	DIRECT ACC TO PNOX			1
	PSUP VIA X3	FANOUT(X3)		6300
	SNOX VIA X4	FANOUT(X3)		6300
	PSUP VIA X1	FANOUT(X3)		6300
			C(Q2) =	18900
Q3	SUP VIA S2	SCARD(SUP)		100
	SNOX VIA X1	SCARD(SUP)		100
	PSUP VIA X4	SCARD(SUP) * FANOUT(X4)		6300
	PNOX VIA X3	(0.75) * SCARD(SUP) * FANOUT(X4)		4725
	PART VIA F4	(0.75) * SCARD(SUP) * FANOUT(X4)		4725
			C(Q3) =	15950

$TC2 = 2*C(Q1) + 800*C(Q2) + 5*C(Q3) = 141.2(10**6)$

COMPARISON: (TC2 − TC1)*100/TC1 = 7% (design 1 better)

We can now evaluate the two designs. Table 9.1 gives the quantitative information for original and derived schemas. Table 9.2 details the cost computations for the two designs. Because of the simplicity of the example, the result reflects intuition. Thus, design 2 evaluates as 7 percent less efficient than design 1, owing to the overhead of the index processing. This facility enables the designer to easily evaluate a design with different usage profiles (as defined in Table 9.1). For example, if $freq(Q_i) = 1$ and $freq(Q_3) = 500$, design 2 computes to be 17 percent worse than design 1.

9.8 SUMMARY

An effective logical database design tool must consider both semantic and processing information. To reduce the magnitude of the design task, we should be able to specify the processing and semantics of local views and then integrate these views to form a global model of the database. A database design tool must be able to manipulate both semantic and processing information during the design process.

In this chapter we have presented a semantic model based on functions (the functional data model) and a language (transaction specification language) to specify processing on the model. Functions reflect constraints on data and are invariant with respect to the grouping of data items into records. TASL specifications are based on functions and are also invariant.

REFERENCES

1. Abrial, J.R., "Data Semantics," in J.W. Klimbie and K.L. Koffman, eds., *Data Base Management*. 1974.

2. Bernstein, P.A., "Synthesizing Third Normal Form Relations from Functional Dependencies," *ACM TODS*, Vol. 1, No. 4, pp. 277–298.

3. Bracchi, G., P. Paolini, and G. Pelagatti, "Binary Logical Associations in Data Modeling," in G.M. Nijssen, ed., *Modeling in Data Base Management*. 1976.

4. Bubenko, J.A., et al., "From Information Requirements to DBTG Structures," *Proc. Conference on Data: Abstraction, Definition, and Structure, 1976*.

5. Buneman, P., and R.E. Frankel, "FQL—A Functional Query Language," *ACM-SIGMOD Conference 1979*, pp. 52–58.

6. Chen, P., "The Entity-Relationship Model: Towards a Unified View of Data," *ACM TODS*, Vol. 1 (1976), pp. 9–36.

7. Codd, E.F., "A Relational Model of Data for Large Shared Data Banks," *CACM*, Vol. 13, pp. 377–387.

8. Codd, E.F., "Further Normalization of the Data Base Relational Model," in R. Rustin, ed., *Data Base Systems*. 1972.

9. Fagin, R., "The Decomposition versus the Synthetic Approach to Relational Database Design," *Proc. Third VLDB Conference, 1977*, pp. 441–446.

10. Gerritsen, F., "A Preliminary System for the Design of DBTG Data Structures," *CACM*, Vol. 18, No. 10, pp. 551–557.

11. Housel, B.C., B.E. Waddle, and S.B. Yao, "The Functional Dependency Model for Logical Database Design," *Proc. Fifth VLDB Conference, 1979*.

12. Hubbard, G., and N. Raver, "Automating Logical File Design," *Proc. First VLDB Conference, 1975*, pp. 227–283.

13. Kahn, B.K., "A Method for Describing Information Required by the Database Design Process," *Proc. ACM-SIGMOD Conf., 1976*, pp. 53–64.

14. Mijares, I., and F. Peebles, "A Methodology for the Design of Logical Database Structures," in G.M. Nijssen, ed., *Modeling in Data Base Management Systems*. 1976.

15. Mitoma, M.F., and K.B. Irani, "Automated Schema Design and Optimization," *Proc. First VLDB Conference, 1975*, pp. 286–321.

16. Novak, D.O., and J.P. Fry, "The State of The Art of Logical Database Design," *Proc. Fifth Texas Conf. on Computing Systems, 1976*.

17. Raver, N., and G. Hubbard, "Automatic Logical Data Base Design: Concepts and Applications," *IBM Systems Journal*, No. 3, 1977, pp. 287–312.

18. Senko, M.E., "DIAM 11: The Binary Infological Level and its Database Language—FORAL," *Proc. Conf. on Data: Abstraction, Definition, and Structure, 1976*.

19. Shipman, D.W., "The Functional Data Model and the Data Language DAPLEX," *ACM-SIGMOD Conf., 1979* (to appear in *ACM TODS*).

20. Sibley, E.H., and L. Kerschberg, "Data Architecture and Data Model Considerations," *Proc. National Computer Conf., 1977*, pp. 85–96.

21. Smith, J.M., and D.C.P. Smith, "Data Base Abstractions: Aggregation and Generalization," *ACM TODS*, Vol. 2, No. 2, pp. 105–133.

22. Vetter, C.M., "Data Base Design by Applied Data Synthesis," *Proc. Third VLDB Conference, 1977*, pp. 428–440.

23. Wang, C.P., and H.H. Wedekind, "An Approach for Segment Synthesis in Logical Data Base Design," *IBM Journal of Research and Development*, Vol. 19, No. 1, pp. 71–77.

24. Yao, S.B., S.B. Navathe, and J.L. Weldon, "An Integrated Approach to Logical Database Design," *Proc. NYU Symposium on Database Design, 1978*, pp. 1–14.

25. Beeri, C., and P.A. Bernstein, "Computational Problems Related to the Design of Third Normal Form Relational Schemas," *ACM TODS*, Vol. 1, No. 4, pp. 30–59.

26. Palmer, I.R., "Practicalities in Applying a Formal Methodology to Data Analysis," *Proc. NYU Symposium on Database Design, 1978*, pp. 67–84.

27. Waddle, V., and S.B. Yao, "Database Design by Example," *Database Systems Research Center Tech. Report*, University of Maryland, 1981, submitted for publication.

28. Yao, S.B., V.E. Waddle, and B.C. Housel, "View Modeling and Integration Using the Functional Data Model, *IEEE Transactions on Software Engineering*, Vol. 8, No. 6, pp. 544–553.

29. Falkenburg, E., "Significations: The Key to Unify Data Base Management," *Information Systems*, Vol. 2, No. 1.

30. Kent, W., "Limitations on Record Based Information Models," *ACM TODS*, Vol. 4, No. 1, pp. 107–131.

31. Hammer, M., and D. Malleod, "The Semantic Data Model: A Modeling Mechanism for Data Base Applications," *Proc. SIGMOD Conf.*, 1978.

32. Ceri, S., G. Pelagatti, and G. Bracchi, "A Structural Methodology for Designing Static and Dynamic Aspects of Data Base Applications," Rapporto NT. N. 79-10, Lab. Calc., Inst. di Elettrotecnica Poli, di Milano 1980.

33. Bubenko, J.A., "Information Modeling in the Context of System Development," Tech. Report S-41296, Goteborg, Sweden, Dec. 79.

10

Schema Implementation and Restructuring

Shamkant B. Navathe*
University of Florida
Gainesville, Florida

10.1 INTRODUCTION

This chapter discusses the major issues of schema implementation and restructuring in the context of database design. First we would like to point out the relative position of this phase with respect to the entire span of database design.

Figure 10.1 shows the various models of information/data that exist in going from a universe of discourse drawn from the real world to a database which is populated with data stored on a physical machine-readable medium and is made available to the users.

The *enterprise model* comprises data expressed in terms of objects, things, events, policies, concepts, and so on, which refer to an overall enterprise. It also incorporates at a broad level the attributes and relationships among these objects. As an example, let us consider the university as an enterprise and suppose that the universe of discourse for a given context includes the instructors, the students, the physical facilities, including buildings and equipment, the courses, and so on. In this case, the enterprise schema would include all the above objects plus relevant associations—for example:

A student enrolls in a course;

A course is taught by an instructor in a certain room;

Each piece of equipment has a fixed maintenance schedule;

Instructors teach labs, which are special classes meeting in rooms designated as labs.

*The author wishes to acknowledge the initial contribution of Robert W. Taylor, Britton-Lee, in formulating the structure of this chapter.

The above are a few of the possible relationships about which there may be a need to store data in the database. The enterprise model sometimes includes the type of processing to which the corresponding data is subjected. The process-modeling techniques described in Chapter 4 are generally *not* used to model the high-level description of an enterprise. The enterprise model should contain relatively static or invariant data which characterizes the enterprise in terms of its relevant aspects for a particular database.

   The *application-requirement models* shown in Figure 10.1 capture the dynamics of the enterprisewide information by developing requirement specifications of individual applications. In the case of the above example of a university, the application-requirement models may refer to applications such as registration, generation of class rosters, faculty office assignments, classroom assignments, and preparation of inventories of equipment by buildings, departments, or rooms. In a top-down design methodology using successive refinements of specification, the applications will be described in successively detailed levels that were discussed in Chapter 4.

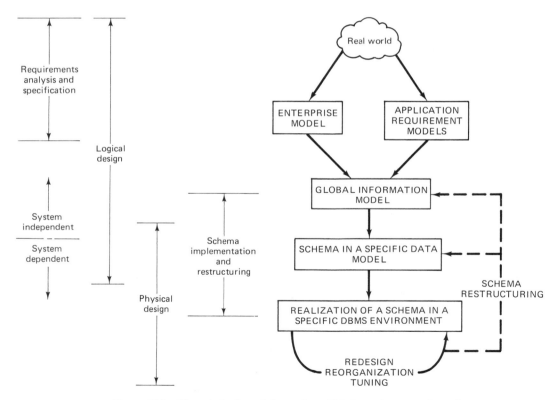

Figure 10.1   Characterization of the real world information at various phases of design.

The term *global information model* refers to an output of the integration process which integrates the enterprise model with the individual application models. A global information model should typically be described by using a semantic model (see Chapter 3) or a data-abstraction model as a tool to capture the structure and semantics of relevant information as perceived by the entire user population as a whole. One such model has been presented by Su and Lo [31]. Approaches to the "view integration" of multiple users and the underlying problems have been described by some researchers (e.g., Navathe and Gadgil [22], Wiederhold and El-Masri [35]). Their results show that the integration process should remain an interactive one with a constant feedback to the users (or their representatives). More often than not, integration gives rise to a modification of the application-requirement models. In its ideal form, the global information model idea is rather utopian. Organizations where user groups place widely varying demands on the data and, in fact, want to see their "own (not necessarily compatible) versions" of a database may have to settle for more than one global model.

We do not want to propagate the idea that coming up with a global information model is a prerequisite for good database design or that it is the only recommended procedure. More and more organizations are distributing the control of their data into the hands of local user groups. For them, the view-integration activity proceeds first at the local level and then, depending on the need, a global information model may or may not be constructed. It has not been shown conclusively that a global information model is a must for distributed data magangement. In our opinion, the phrase "conceptual schema" in the ANSI/SPARC proposal [1] or as used by Nijssen [25] corresponds most closely to our "global information model" concept than any other term used in Figure 10.1. Some authors (e.g., Steel [30]) consider what we call the enterprise model to be the conceptual schema.

Having clarified the above terms, we can now embark on defining the scope of the present chapter. As shown in Figure 10.1, we are dealing with the phase of design which starts off with the global information model and ends with the realization of the schema in a specific DBMS environment, i.e., defines the DDL, the integrity constraints, the privacy and security constraints, and the processing of the database in that DBMS. For simplicity we shall refer to this phase as the *schema implementation* (*SI*) phase. It is obvious that the following overlaps exist:

1. The SI phase overlaps with the process of view integration, which is responsible for generating the global information model.
2. The SI phase overlaps with the physical mapping of a DBMS schema into the corresponding files and/or storage structures in the DBMS.

It is difficult to draw well-defined boundaries between physical and logical database design and further between SI and logical design or between SI and physical design. In this chapter we will not attempt to define these boundaries. Instead, we will attempt to clarify the issues that are crucial in considering and dealing with these overlaps.

Furthermore, a database is continually subjected to performance degradation due to use and changing user requirements. We assume that the DBA monitors a database and keeps tabs on these factors. At certain intervals the database would be subjected to tuning: changes in processing programs, in physical structures, in logical data relationships, or in mapping with respect to the device space. Sometimes the tuning operation may be so widespread that the database may need to be redesigned or the schema may need to be modified. Such modifications to the schema will be addressed by the term *schema restructuring*. Use of schema restructuring during database design/redesign will also be discussed in greater detail in the present chapter.

10.2 THE IMPORTANCE OF SCHEMA IMPLEMENTATION AND RESTRUCTURING

It is worthwhile to point out the importance of schema implementation and restructuring relative to the other phases of database design:

1. With the assumption that a database management system is to be employed to manage the data resource in an organization, it is imperative that
   (a) the relevant data for all users in an organization be modeled into a schema and the actual data values be mapped into occurrences of that schema in the given DBMS environment;
   (b) the relevant data be made available for applications or for processing in general;
   (c) the data in DBMS truly reflect the data needs of user groups and for the organization.

   These reasons necessitate the mapping of the global information model into a schema based on a widely accepted data model such as the hierarchical, network, or relational model. The schema is further implemented in a system supporting that model.

   One obvious trend in schema implementation and restructuring is to develop tools as an aid to users and/or designers. An aid is not meant to accomplish the desired mapping optimally and automatically, but to lead a user through and guide him or her in making the right design decisions.

2. When current database management systems are used, the schema restructuring problem is unavoidable. If DBMS software truly had full logical independence, the problem would not arise; the DBA could monitor the logical database structure and keep modifying it so as to reflect the most up-to-date user view of data. So long as no new data or no new relationships were added, the application programs could still be processed. However, currently available

software systems are far from being logically independent or self-organizing. The redesign and restructuring problems are here to stay. They may be alleviated by the introduction of more logical independence in the form of system overhead as processing becomes cheaper and cheaper, but they cannot be removed entirely.

3. Finally, the schema restructuring/redesign problem being addressed is more general in nature. It encompasses not only the modification of a single database in the context of one DBMS, but also the transferring of a database from one hardware/software environment into a different one when the users' view of data may, in fact, be unchanged. In our discussion of schema restructuring, we shall consider it in either sense—i.e., due to a change in user needs or due to a change in the system environment.

Thus, schema implementation and restructuring is *necessary* in mapping a global information model into a new database structure, and it is *unavoidable* for almost all databases which undergo changes in user requirements and/or system environment.

10.3 WHAT IS INVOLVED IN SCHEMA IMPLEMENTATION

The basic function of schema implementation is to produce a series of statements in the target database management system's data-definition language. These statements implement the schema and reflect the structure and integrity constraints of the global information model while also taking into account the idiosyncrasies of the database management system. More precisely, we assume the following input:

1. A global information model including structure and processing requirements. The processing requirements may be input as application specifications in terms of a high-level language like TASL (see Chapters 4 and 9).
2. A statement of the integrity constraints that must be obeyed during all database transactions.
3. Volume and usage estimates or statistics of the various transactions.
4. Any environmental constraints, including especially any capacity and configuration limitations that the design must obey. If physical design of a schema is included in this phase, the rules of formulating DBMS processable schemas and subschemas must also be input.

From these inputs, the following outputs are derived:

1. A DBMS processable schema. By "schema" we mean a fully processable declaration of the logical and physical database structure together with system

support for all integrity constraints that can be supported by the system (the remaining constraints will presumably be enforced within the application programs).

2. A set of DBMS processable subschemas, together with the information about which subschemas should be used with which database transactions.

3. Guidance for usage of subschemas by application programs. For example, the system might produce a report of which access paths should be traversed in a network-oriented system or a statement of which relations should be joined, and on which columns, in a relational system. A more sophisticated system might even generate a subroutine to carry out the relevant function and place the subroutine in a library for later use by the application programmer.

4. For each application program, a statement of the integrity constraints which must be enforced within it. This could take the form of a report or, in a more sophisticated system, a series of subroutines to be called from the application program.

5. A trace of how real-world objects and entities are mapped into a global information model and further into a DBMS processable schema would prove very useful. It may be stored in a data dictionary environment.

6. In addition, a summary of the requirements, integrity constraints, and system constraints may be documented as an aid to the database administrator.

Thus, we are postulating an algorithm which is able to map a very general, DBMS-system-independent statement of a schema and to try various alternatives for embodying the essential features of the high-level schema into a DBMS processable form. It should be understood that very little is known about the ultimate capabilities of such an algorithm, and research into this question is in its very early stage. Still, this stage of database design is carried out by designers today, in that they map high-level requirements statements, written in a natural language mixed with various graphic and notational aids, to DBMS processable schemas.

It seems possible to formulate rules which distinguish a "good" schema from a "bad" one, and many of these rules could be checked by computers. A *design-assistance algorithm* which mimics the behavior of an experienced designer would be highly useful. Given below is a sampling of some qualitative and quantitative rules. Ultimately the viability of such a tool will depend, in the author's opinion, on the ability to formulate "rules of good practice" which are relatively independent of the problem domain that the database addresses. If this can be done, then a substantial computerization of this stage of the design process is not beyond possibility.

The rest of this section will discuss various "rules of thumb" which can be used to compare one schema design with another. These rules could be incorporated into the design system. The intent is not so much to obtain one overall measure of the merit of a schema as to examine various potential trouble spots and suggest alternatives.

10.3.1 Qualitative Measures of Schema Evaluation

Qualitative measures of schemas are those which are not easily reduced to numeric form and which have only an indirect effect on the more quantitative measures, such as size of the database and number of secondary storage accesses per query. Nonetheless, these measures can be an important component in schema evaluation, since they affect the usability of the schema (and subschemas) and also the long-range usage and evolution of the implemented schema. The point of considering them is to avoid major design blunders rather than to pick a completely perfect schema implementation. Experience has shown that the avoidance of gross errors in complex systems is of prime importance. Database design is so complex that it is hopeless to talk of *optimality* of a design; one must talk only of a design's *sufficiency*.

10.3.1.1 Understandability

Because schemas and subschemas are used by people, their understandability is of prime importance. Only if the schema can be understood can the implementation be checked for self-consistency and consistency with the global DBMS-independent schema.

We list below some rules of thumb which may be used to make schemas more understandable.

1. Hierarchical schemas:
   (a) A hierarchy should behave like a hierarchy.
   (b) Avoid cycles (if cycles can be created in such a DBMS).
   (c) Make relationships explicit.
   (d) Don't make a relationship serve two purposes.
   (e) Identify natural partitions and use them.
2. Network DBTG schemas:
   (a) Avoid cycles involving all automatic set types.
   (b) Don't use singular sets where a CALC or DIRECT location mode (if applicable) will serve the purpose.
   (c) Don't create link record types where the relationship being modeled is $1 : n$ rather than $m : n$.
   (d) Don't create overlapping record types.
   (e) Don't create multiple relationships among the same pair of record types unless each has a distinct meaning.
3. Relational schemas (not yet used very widely):
   (a) Avoid decomposition (normalization) unless there is enough justification for it in terms of heavy update frequency or the like.

(b) Avoid relations where the same domain occurs multiple times under different roles.

(c) Don't create predefined joins of relations unless application loads justify them.

10.3.1.2 Integrity and Security

A schema produced as an output of the schema implementation phase can be subjected to another qualitative test: to what degree are integrity and security built into it? Integrity depends upon the extent to which data value constraints, data interdependence, and semantic relations are specified as a part of the schema. A schema is considered "good" with respect to integrity if it can hold the integrity constraints under all types of database modifications.

Security is a criterion closely related to users. A schema is highly secure if it provides good protection against deliberate or unintentional disclosure of data, unauthorized access or modification, and unintended loss of data. A schema considered as having adequate security in one user environment may not be secure in another.

10.3.1.3 Evolvability

A schema is designed for a spectrum of users who belong to some organization engaged in a business, industrial, or scientific activity. Since organizations are dynamic and have to respond to changing trends in economy, technology, and business climate, the needs of people in terms of information continuously evolve. A schema must be designed so that there is ample scope for evolution; e.g., in a hierarchical structure, critical data elements which are liable to change rapidly should not be placed deep down in a hierarchy. Relationships which are transitory in nature should not be modeled as permanent sets in a network model environment. Evolvability is not something that enters into consideration at this late stage in the schema mapping. It should be of prime importance in the enterprise model and the global information model.

10.3.1.4 Completeness

This is another important qualitative measure which is impossible to quantify. It is customary to describe the "completeness" of a relational query language in the sense of an ability to describe and query expressible in the first-order predicate calculus. One could similarly define a formal measure for the completeness of a schema. "Completeness" implies that the target DBMS schema must completely account for all the structural and processing requirements of information collected during the early phase of design.

10.3.1.5 Correctness and Consistency

Correctness of programs is another topic currently under close scrutiny. Although correctness of a schema refers to a correct and true modeling of user requirements, it is to be distinguished from the concept of producing a correct result by means of an algorithm which is a basis for proving programs correct. How users use a given schema and whether their applications produce the desired results are concerns that fall outside the scope of database design. However, the implemented schema must be a correct representation of the user's original views and it should stand together as a consistent global model without internal conflicts, especially regarding integrity constraints. For example, the following is incorrect: An 'Employee-number' is a 5-digit unique ID for payroll purposes but the same name refers to the 9-digit social security number in another application dealing with insurance claims.

10.3.1.6 Adherence to Policies and Standards

The view-integration exercise which precedes the creation of the global information model has to deal with conflicting application requirements. At that stage, some policy decisions need to be made regarding the relative priority of applications, the relative merit of keeping certain data relationships, the setting up of authorization hierarchies for security purposes, and so on. These policies, as well as standards regarding naming, nature of output, type of interfaces for users, documentation, and the like, play a role in the final design of a schema. Qualitatively, a good schema should score high by maintaining the previous policy decisions and making new design decisions consistent with the policies and standards.

10.3.2 Quantitative Measures of Schema Evaluation

Physical design of a schema is viewed as an activity subsidiary to the schema implementation phase [15]. Under such an approach a physical design algorithm exists for the given target DBMS which may be invoked as needed with appropriate parameters to analyze various possible alternatives of implementing a certain schema feature. (For example, a set type would be analyzed for its implementations using pointer arrays, chains, linked lists with pointers to owner, etc.) The physical design problem is considered in great detail in the second volume of this book. Hence, we shall refrain from repeating the discussion of the performance measures applied to schemas regarding storage and time efficiencies.

It is possible to do a certain amount of analysis during the schema implementation phase which is independent of physical considerations. The most commonly used quantitative measure here is the estimation of total logical accesses required to support all application requirements. A *logical access unit* (*LAU*) must be defined for each type of target system being considered. For example, in a hierarchy, an access to a data object which is three levels below the root data object may be considered to be worth 3 LAUs. In a network, an access into a data object using indexing or hashing or database keys may be equivalent to 1 LAU, an access from a parent record to member record or vice versa would be 1 LAU, whereas accesses between member records such as NEXT or PRIOR may be a fraction of an LAU.

Analysis of this nature at the logical level tends to be too gross to be of much significance during the final implementation. In the above example of a network schema, the traversal of a pointer to process the owner and member record occurrences in a set occurrence is not always comparable. It really depends upon the clustering used, page boundaries or device boundaries involved, and the like. In relational schemas, logical accesses would be even more difficult to quantify, since the number of accesses performed in searching for a tuple satisfying several constraints on multiple domains is dependent on several factors: the order of processing, type of secondary access mechanism provided, mapping of the relation onto pages or extents, and so on.

A variation of the LAU is the measure of the total number of records accessed in order to meet a certain processing load. This gets around the problem of determining "how" each record access is carried out and, therefore, simplifies matters. But the net result again is that it cannot be very meaningful as a quantitative measure of the performance of a schema.

10.3.3 Steps of Schema Implementation

The activity we have been referring to as schema implementation typically proceeds in three steps:

1. Conversion of a global schema in a data model to a global schema for a particular DBMS.
2. Design of subschemas based on the above global schema in order to support the given applications.
3. The actual specification of application programs based on predefined requirements.

How much of step 3 should be included as a part of schema implementation is debatable. It is reasonable to expect, however, that since steps 2 and 3 are very tightly coupled, they proceed almost in parallel. Some work on high-level specification of application programs exists (e.g., Zloof and de Jong [36], Hebalkar [12]). With the trend toward more declarative and nonprocedural languages, it will become possible to give a specification of an application system in terms of a modular hierarchy and then to expand each module using the high-level specification language. Subschemas should serve as integral parts of the application system specification. As new applications are needed, steps 2 and 3 are repeated with the global schema as given. But, as we describe in the next section, new applications in many instances require one to go back to step 1 or even further.

10.4 SCHEMA RESTRUCTURING

Schema restructuring can be defined as the process of changing the structure of a database by modifying its schema. The purpose of schema restructuring is to meet new requirements for the schema in terms of either the information structure or its processing. Although the term connotes changes in data at the schema level, it is imperative that these changes also be accomplished at the instance level. Thus, whenever a particular schema modification has to be effected, in turn it calls for modifications to the instances of data in the original database. There are two different contexts under which schema restructuring may be applied:

1. Restructuring which is a part of initial schema design.
2. Restructuring which arises during redesign.

Since these two restructuring types are different enough, we have devoted separate subsections to them below. However, the commonality in the above two contexts is that each deals with a situation where the input consists of some given database structure (schema) in a particular model and corresponding data occurrences/values (instances). The output is typically a database schema in a *different* model with data instances which are in conformity with that target model, yet representing the same data as in the given original database. In each context there is also a need for some governing or controlling mechanism to guide the restructuring process.

10.4.1 Schema Restructuring for Initial Design

In reference to Figure 10.1, this type of restructuring comes into play during the mapping of the global information model (GIM) into a schema in a specific data model. The GIM may have been expressed in terms of any suitable model of data abstraction. Consider the example in Figure 10.2. In this example, the GIM recognizes entities Publisher, Book, and Author, all of which are "self-identified" (following the notation in Navathe and Schkolnick [24], a # sign next to the entity models this fact) in the sense of containing their own unique identifiers. "Publishes" and "Writes" are two associations among entities as shown with owners Publisher and Author respectively. Assuming that this GIM is to be modeled in the hierarchical data model (specifically as defined by the IMS constructs) Figure 10.2(b) shows three possible restructured versions of the same data. Alternately, Figure 10.2(c) shows the schemas in the network model of a system called TOTAL [3].

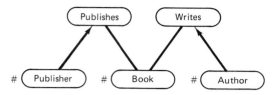

(a) A global information model expressed in terms of the Navathe and Schkolnick (1978) model

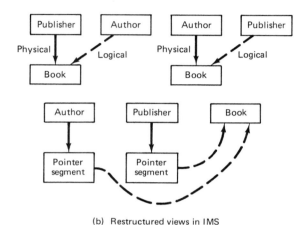

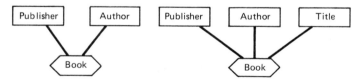

(b) Restructured views in IMS

(c) Restructured views in TOTAL

Figure 10.2 A simple example of schema restructuring for initial design.

In general, the schema restructuring process seen in the context of initial design has the following inputs:

1. The GIM expressed in terms of some semantic or data-abstraction model.

2. A description of the features or constraints of the data model in which the target schema must be expressed. Typically, existing DBMSs are implementations of the hierarchical network and relational models. However, owing to a lack of standardization of these models, each system uses its own version of the model including its own terminology. For example, System 2000 and IMS are both hierarchical; but repeating groups and key and non-key items exist only

in System 2000, whereas segments and physical versus logical parent-child relationships exist only in IMS. Different systems also support different data types. For example, System 2000 supports name, text, integer, decimal, date, and money as distinct data types.

The following types of features about a system's data model need to be supplied:

Number of relations in which a record (or a group or a data aggregate) may participate as a member. In a hierarchical system this number is 1 (with modifications to allow "logical relations" as in the case of IMS). In network systems this is some finite number based on the limitations of a specific implementation.

Maximum number of levels of hierarchy.

Maximum number of record types.

Maximum size of a record type.

Maximum number of elements per group.

Maximum number of relations in which a group can be an owner.

The above parameterization of a system's data model is not very easy to accomplish. The major problems are as follows:

1. There is a large overlap of the logical and the physical schema features in many systems. Consequently,
2. The logical design of a target schema becomes dependent on an evaluation of the physical alternatives available to realize it.

An example of problem 1 is the two types of files in TOTAL called Master files and Variable files. They correspond to the logical concept of a record type but have rigid connotations regarding the type of access available, order of processing, number of incident relationships possible with other record types, and so on. Obviously, some standard parameterized data cannot adequately model these features. If schema restructuring were to be automated so that a number of alternative structures could be generated, this would present a problem. Instead of having a set of parameters to describe individual systems, it would be necessary to have "hard-coded" information in terms of *procedures* that would process the various features in a system.

As an example of problem 2 above, consider the IMS schema alternatives in Figure 10.2(b). The third alternative shows "pointer segments" which are based on efficiency considerations—that is, avoiding duplication and multiple updates into the database. In Figure 10.1 these considerations belong to the next activity during design: schema realization. Several examples can be given where the schema restructuring and physical realization of a schema in storage are so tightly coupled that they can hardly be dealt with separately.

During the schema restructuring for initial design, the processing is governed by two overriding considerations:

1. The target alternative schemas must be equivalent to the GIM in terms of the information they represent.
2. Each target alternative schema must be able to support all the application requirements originally compiled in the requirements phase.

In summary, this type of schema restructuring must be able to map the GIM without a loss of information and without compromising processing requirements. The net result is alternative schemas in a target data model. An evaluation of these schemas is generally impossible without a reference to the physical design routines. The approaches that we discuss later under redesign can be applied to this process with minor modifications.

10.4.2 Schema Restructuring for Redesign

This type of schema restructuring can arise frequently after a database is in place. The causes leading to it may be one or more of the following:

1. Changing requirements of users. The changes may fall into the following categories:
   (a) Changes in corporate policy regarding the relative importance of the different parts of a database.
   (b) Growth of the organization leading to changes in the enterprise model and a diversification of applications.
   (c) Changes in the relative frequencies and priorities of application programs of transactions.
   (d) Changes in access patterns.
2. Changing environment of hardware/software. This would include moving to a new hardware/processor configuration, changing storage devices, changing the degree of centralization or distribution, and so on. As far as software is concerned, operating system, database management system, or user interface languages and facilities may change.

Such situations basically lead to a "static" schema restructuring. A static restructuring process is carried out in isolation as a one-shot process. It calls for restructuring the entire source database (or parts of a database) into a target database, during which process no user transactions are allowed. This is a part of an overall data-translation activity (see Birss and Fry [3]).

In a "dynamic" schema restructuring, on the other hand, after the desired result of restructuring is specified (or sometimes inferred), an immediate execution of the restructuring is required. With the advent of distributed databases, this type of restructuring will come into play whenever a user expects results in terms of a data model different from the one in which the data is actually stored.

In an extreme sense of the term, wherever a user query or a retrieval transaction requires existing data in a database to be transformed, rearranged, summarized, or presented in any form different from the original, it involves "dynamic" restructuring of the schema. In these situations a user's required schema is typically a very small subset of the original schema. In general, dynamic restructuring would rarely apply to an entire database; static restructuring, however, is just the opposite.

The rest of the discussion in this chapter will focus on schema restructuring for *redesign* which is *static in nature* and is *driven by a target schema* in some target data model. This implies the existence of a translation specification language to describe the source-to-target mapping.

In the following we list some issues as being relevant to a proper delineation of the schema restructuring activity:

1. *Schema-instance interaction*: Any modification in a schema construct affects instances of data. Schema restructuring operations are completely defined only when their effect on instances is fully specified and understood.

2. *Inclusion of logical access paths*: In any database a minimal set of access paths are implied by virtue of the data relationships specified in the schema. In addition, some access paths are provided for improving the efficiency. A schema restructuring specification must consider all logical access paths that are inherent in the schema definition as well as those explicitly defined. Secondary accessing on indexes and so on is *not* relevant to schema restructuring; that is,

   (a) preservation of secondary access paths, indexes, and the like is not guaranteed during schema restructuring. And similarly,

   (b) just a change in secondary indexes and the like is not considered schema restructuring.

3. *Information preservation and reversibility*: Schema restructuring must preserve information unless some is deliberately deleted. Information preservation in the database parlance is not as yet a well-defined or standardized term. It is important to know whether a certain schema restructuring is reversible and whether the original database can be recreated. In the next section we shall address schema restructuring as modifications to an existing schema and its corresponding instances with no information explicitly deleted or added. Such modifications are supposed to be reversible in that the source database can be built from the target database by a reverse restructuring specification.

10.5 APPROACHES TO SCHEMA RESTRUCTURING

We stated in Section 10.4 the exact nature of the schema restructuring which we propose to discuss in further detail. Two approaches have been advocated and implemented (see [6]). The first is an operational specification of schema-modification operations. The second is an access-path specifications approach, wherein a procedure is developed for accessing the source data and transforming it into the instances of a target schema.

The overall restructuring scenario is depicted in Figure 10.3. The source data is unloaded/read/traversed by accessing all instances of data at least once. This sequential stream of data instances is passed into the schema-definition language specification and converts these instances into instances of the target database schema. They are then written onto the target database. Variations of this approach have been implemented at the Universities of Pennsylvania and Michigan [27, 3] and at IBM [28, 29].

10.5.1 The Operational Specification Approach

This approach is exemplified by the work of Navathe and Fry [21]. A category of operations to restructure hierarchical databases into other hierarchical databases is developed. The data model used to describe restructuring models a database using the schema constructs listed and defined below.

> *Item.* An item (elementary item, atom) is the lowest generic level of data structure. Stored data in a database contains occurrences of different items. Most DBMSs offer a variety of item types (e.g., name, integer, text, date). For a given DBMS, the set of item types is fixed, in that no operators exist which can select components of an item.
>
> *Group.* A group is the result of a grouping operation which associates a name, a group type, and sometimes other attributes (e.g., an identifier or an access lock) with a previously defined set of items and groups. Some of these

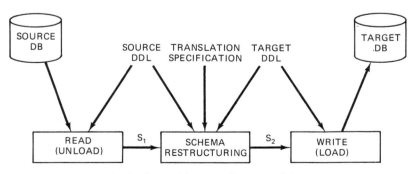

S_1, S_2: Sequential streams of instances of data

Figure 10.3   The process of static, target-schema-driven schema restructuring.

attributes, e.g., an access lock, would not be relevant to the schema-analysis procedure to be discussed. The items that are immediate constituents of a given group, i.e., not constituents of any other group which is a member of the given group, are called *principal items*. If all components of a group are principal items, the group is *simple*; otherwise it is *compound*.

Group relation. In general, an *n*-ary group relation is a set of ordered pairs of groups. A binary group relation is a single ordered pair (owner group, member group). It is written

$$R = (G_1, G_2)$$

As shown in Table 10.1, many DBMSs in wide use today provide a terminology which closely corresponds to the above constructs.

An instance of an item is a value from the allowable set of values for that item. An instance of a simple group is a collection of values, one for each of the principal items. An instance of a binary group relation is defined by one instance of the parent group and an instance of the dependent group which is related to it. An *assembly* of a dependent group is a collection of instances of that group which is related (via a binary group relation) to *the same* instance of the parent group [5].

In using the above terms to describe and analyze stored databases, we need to make a few simplifying assumptions. We restrict ourselves to simple groups. A compound group can be modeled by considering its constituent groups separately and establishing a group relation with each constituent. These assumptions lend much simplicity to the analysis procedure and are not particularly restrictive, since the overall aim of this exercise is to provide a restructuring user with an aid to understand and to delineate schema restructuring.

The basic schema-building operations are those of *naming* a schema construct, *combining* schema constructs of one type into a higher type, and *relating* schema categories (see Figure 10.4). To describe the effect of schema modifications in terms of instances, instance operations called group instance operations and group relation instance operations were defined. At the lowest level, these were further described in terms of data-value operations. Figure 10.5 shows a complete classification of the operations [18]. The schema operations are briefly described below:

Renaming is the process of establishing a correspondence between a source schema construct and a target schema construct. The renaming operation can be applied to some or all of the constructs in a source database schema. Moreover, since the source and the target schema constructs have unique names, the mapping specified in the renaming operation is a one-to-one mapping.

Compression of two or more groups $G_1, G_2, \ldots, G_i$ is defined, provided these groups belong to a continuous hierarchical path (with group relations serving as edges) in the database schema. (For example, in Figure 10.6, A-B, B-C, B-D, A-B-C, A-B-D, A-E, A-F, F-G, and A-F-G can be compressed, but not A-C

TABLE 10.1 EQUIVALENCE OF TERMS USED TO DESCRIBE DATA STRUCTURES IN DBMS's (Source: [14])

Term Systems →	IMS	System 2000	DBTG-based	TOTAL [4]
1. Item	Field	Data element	Data item	Data field
2. Group*	Segment type	Repeating group	(i) Data aggregate (ii) Record type	(i) Data element (ii) Data set
3. Group relation	Parent/child relationship	N	Set	Linkage path†
4. An occurrence of a database schema	Database record (physical, logical)	Logical entry	N	N

Note. N indicates no specific term defined in the system.

*DBTG and TOTAL use two levels for groups.

†An approximate equivalent.

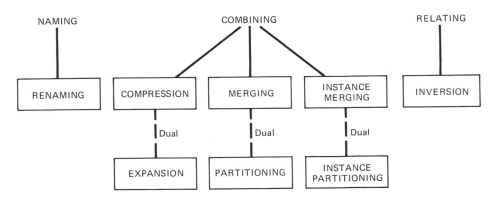

Figure 10.4   Schema operations.

nor A-B-F nor C-D nor D-G, etc.) Compression consists of creating a single group to replace the hierarchically related source groups $G_1, G_2, \ldots, G_i$.

Expansion is defined for any single group within the tree-structured database. It consists of creating one or more groups from the given group such that the newly created groups are hierarchically dependent upon each other and lie along a continuous hierarchical path. It is the dual of compression.

Merging is defined for two or more groups which have the same parent group. (Thus C-D, B-E-F, B-E, B-F, or E-F cannot be merged.) It consists of merging the instances from the source assemblies into the target assembly of a single group schema. Multiple source groups thus give rise to a single target group. The merging is normally controlled by a condition to match instances, and an item instance within an instance of the target group is assigned a value based on the source from which the instance is drawn.

Partitioning involves the participation of a single group. It consists of partitioning the assembly of the group under consideration and designating each partition as an assembly of a target group. A single source group thus gives rise to multiple target groups. The assignment of an instance to one or more partitions is governed by a set of criteria. This is the dual of assembly merging.

Instance merging is defined for two or more groups which have the same parent group. It consists of creating a new group in the target, each of which is generated by merging instances of multiple source groups which satisfy a given condition. In this type of restructuring, many source-group instances give rise to a single target-group instance, whereas in assembly merging a target-group instance originates from a single-group instance.

Instance splitting is a type of restructuring that involves the participation of a single group. It consists of splitting up every instance of the group schema and designating parts of it to make up the instances of two or more target-group schemas. The single source group thus gives rise to multiple target groups. This is the dual of instance merging.

Schema Modification Types	Level 1 — Schema Operation	Level 2 — Group Instance Operation	Level 2 — Relation Instance Operation	Level 3 — Item Value Operation(s)
Naming	Renaming	Association	Association	Copy
Grouping	Compression	Replication	Collapsing	Multiple copy
	Expansion	Factoring	Creation	1. Copy 2. Eliminate duplicate
	Merging	1. Enhancement 2. Union	Generalization	1. Conditional copy 2. Create null value 3. Merge values 4. Create value to differentiate between groups
	Partitioning	1. Conditional assignment 2. Reduction	Refinement	1. Conditional copy 2. Delete value to differentiate between groups
	Instance Merging	Union	Fusion	1. Conditional copy 2. Create null value 3. Merge values
	Instance Splitting	Projection	Refinement	Conditional copy
Relating	Inversion	1. Factoring 2. Replication 3. Item migration	Reversal	1. Copy 2. Eliminate duplicate 3. Multiple copy 4. Find concatenated identifier

Figure 10.5 A classification of restructuring of tree databases using the three levels of abstraction.

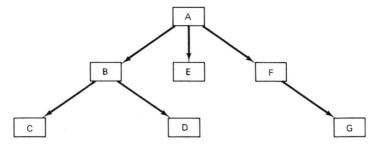

Figure 10.6   A hierarchically structured database schema.

Inversion is a type of restructuring that can be defined for a single group relation, for an indirect group relation, or for combinations of these along a continuous hierarchical path in the database schema. An *indirect group relation* is defined as a hierarchical relationship between two group schemas which lie along a continuous hierarchical path in the database schema, but which are not the parent and dependent of the same group relation. Thus, A-C, A-D, and A-G are the three pairs of group schema in Figure 10.6 which have an indirect group relation between them. Inversion consists of inverting the group relations (direct or indirect) so that the parent and dependent groups are interchanged and a hierarchy different from the source is created in the target.

The instance operations used under schema operations are defined as follows:

1. Under renaming: *Group association*: associating an instance of a source group with an instance of the target group. *Relation association*: associating an instance of the source-group relation with an instance of a target-group relation.

2. Under compression: *Group replication*: duplication of the parent-group instance for every instance of the member group in an instance of a group relation. *Relation collapsing*: a method of deleting a group relation by incorporating an instance of the dependent group into the instance of the parent group.

3. Under expansion: *Group factoring*: a process in which the instances of a group within one group-relation instance are compared, and identical item instances repeating in two or more group instances are factored out. *Subordinate group creation*: an operation implicit in the operation of group factoring. It concerns the relation of a subordinate group and assigning of appropriate instances to it with a one-to-one correspondence to the source group.

4. Under merging: *Group enhancement*: augmentation of a group instance by addition of one or more item instances. *Group union*: creation of a target-group instance by a union of the source-group instances which satisfy a matching

condition. For example,

$$\text{If} \qquad G_1 = \{\underline{I_1}, \underline{I_2}, I_3\} \quad \text{and} \quad G_2 = \{\underline{I_1}, \underline{I_2}, I_4\}$$

$$\text{then} \qquad G_1 \cup G_2 = \{\underline{I_1}, \underline{I_2}, I_3, I_4\}$$

Here, underlined items represent keys. *Relation generalization*: association of one or more individual group relations to create one target-group relation.

5. Under partitioning: *Group conditional assignment*: the conditional assignment of a group instance to one or more target groups based on a condition. *Relational refinement*: the dual of relation generalization. A given group relation R in the source can be refined into target-group relations $R_1, R_2, \ldots, R_i$ which have the same parent-group schema provided that $R_1 \Rightarrow R, R_2 \Rightarrow R, \ldots, R_i \Rightarrow R$.

6. Under instance merging: *Relation fusion*: the joining of two or more individual group relations having the same parent group. The fusion is conditional on the values of certain items within the group schemas. Thus group relations $R_1 = (G_1, G_2)$ and $R_2 = (G_1, G_3)$ may be fused so that the value of item I in G_2 is greater than the value of item J in G_3.

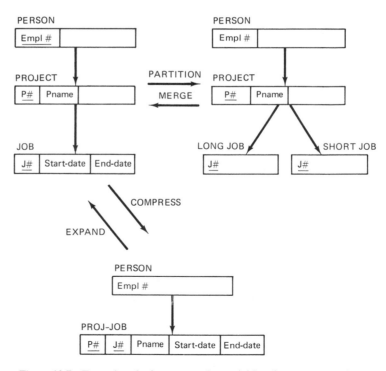

Figure 10.7 Examples of schema operations used in schema restructuring.

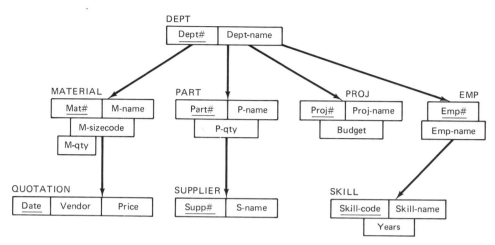

Source database

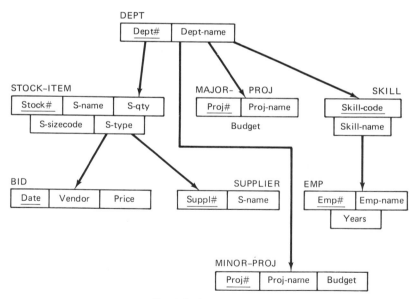

Target database

(a)

BEGIN;

    AMERGE (MATERIAL, PART) INTO STOCK-ITEM;

      EQUIVALENCE (M-name, P-name) = S-name;

      EQUIVALENCE (M-qty, P-qty) = S-qty;

      EQUIVALENCE (M-sizecode, NULL) = S-sizecode;

      NULL (S-sizecode) = 0;

    ENHANCE (S-type) = ('M', 'P');

    RENAME QUOTATION = BID;

END;

BEGIN;

    PARTITION PROJ INTO (MAJOR-PROJ, MINOR-PROJ);

      COND (MAJOR-PROJ) = Proj-name EQ 'PRIORITY' OR

        Proj-name NE 'LOW' OR Budget GT 100000;

      COND (MINOR-PROJ) = ELSE;

END;

BEGIN;

    INVERT (SKILL, EMP) INTO (EMP, SKILL);

    MIGRATE Years TO EMP;

END;

Figure 10.8 (a) Source and target databases in a hierarchical schema restructuring; (b) an RSL specification of above restructuring. (*Source*: [18]).

7. Under instance splitting: *Group projection*: the creation of two or more group instances from a single group instance so that the instance of the identifier in the source group is present in all the target-group instances. Furthermore, the instances of the remaining items from the source group are divided among the target-group instances.

8. Under inversion: *Relation reversal*: the interchange of the parent and dependent group's roles in the group relation.

Figure 10.7 shows an example with schemas of two databases, where schema operations of compression, expansion, merging, and partitioning are demonstrated.

Compression causes the groups PROJECT and JOB to be compressed into one group. Expansion is the reverse operation that Expands PROJ-JOB into PROJECT and JOB. Partitioning refers to the partitioning of JOB into LONG-JOB and SHORT-JOB based on a condition that deals with the START-DATE and END-DATE. Merging accomplishes a merging of the instances of these two groups under the same parent instance of PROJECT.

Navathe [18] developed a *restructuring specification language* (*RSL*) to specify schema restructuring using the above delineation. Figure 10.8 shows an example with an accompanying RSL specification. It uses the operation of merging on groups MATERIAL and PART to give the group STOCK-ITEM. The instance operation of group enhancement is used in the target group STOCK-ITEM, whereby item instance S-type in target has a value "M" or "P" depending upon whether the corresponding group instance was derived from the group MATERIAL or from PART. QUOTATION is renamed as BID in the target. Source group PROJ is partitioned into MAJOR-PROJ or MINOR-PROJ based on the condition described in the COND statement in the RSL. The group relation (EMP, SKILL) undergoes an inversion in this example.

10.5.1.1 Extensions of the Operational Specification Approach to Network-Structured Databases

The application of such operations to network structures has also been investigated [23]. The main difference stems from the fact that a hierarchical database has only hierarchical relations, whereas a network database has both hierarchical and non-hierarchical ones. This concept of hierarchical versus nonhierarchical group relations was defined based on the following [19]:

A group relation $R(A, B)$ is defined as a *hierarchical* (or identifying) *group relation* if in an instance of R consisting of an owner instance $\underline{A}_i$ of A and a collection $\underline{B}_{i_1}, \underline{B}_{i_2}, \ldots, \underline{B}_{i_m}$ of member instances of B, $\underline{A}_i$ provides external identification to the member instances. *External identification*, in turn, refers to the process of providing an external key toward unique identification of another group.

A group relation $R(A, B)$ is defined as a *nonhierarchical* (or nonidentifying) group relation if either:

1. B has a full internal identification of its own which is adequate to identify instances of B uniquely, or

2. When B is not internally fully identified, the internal identifier of A is *not* a part of the augmented identifier of B.

As a result of this distinction, in a network-structured database the schema operations defined for hierarchical structures are still candidates for application to a hierarchical path in the database consisting solely of hierarchical relations.

Consider the following example, where single arrows denote hierarchical and double arrows denote nonhierarchical relations. A # placed inside or next to a group indicates that the group is fully internally identified.

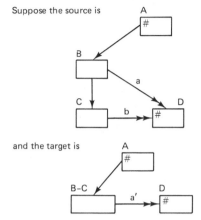

In the specification of the target schema the nonhierarchical relation a' is specified. A loss of information occurs here. If a' is derived from a, then the information contained in b is lost. If a' is derived from b, then the information contained in a is lost. There are two possible ways to remedy this problem. The first is to create group B in the target in addition to the B-C group (which is a compression of B and C) to render the following result:

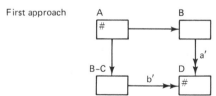

where a' is derived from a and b' is derived from b. The second way is to create the result:

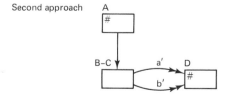

Hence both *a* and *b* are preserved.

In both approaches redundancy occurs. For the first approach the group *b* is duplicated and the hierarchical relations *A* to *B-C* and *A* to *B* represent the original group relation (A, B) redundantly. Here we can evaluate the trade-off by investigating the frequency of retrieval of *B* and *C* together as opposed to the frequency of retrieval of *B* only, and the degree of redundancy of *B*. For the second approach, since *B* is replicated for every subordinate occurrence of *C* and appears in the instance of group *B-C*, redundancy exists in the (B, D) association. Again, here we can evaluate the trade-off. An instance diagram of this example is shown below.

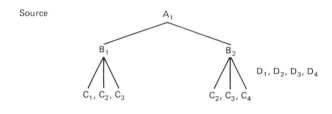

Source

A_1

B_1 B_2

C_1, C_2, C_3 C_2, C_3, C_4 D_1, D_2, D_3, D_4

Relationship instances

a: $\langle B_1, D_3 \rangle, \langle B_1, D_4 \rangle$
   $\langle B_2, D_1 \rangle$

b: $\langle C_2, D_1 \rangle$

Target instances:

(a) First approach

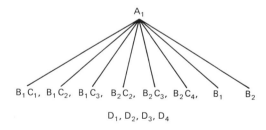

A_1

$B_1 C_1, \ B_1 C_2, \ B_1 C_3, \ B_2 C_2, \ B_2 C_3, \ B_2 C_4, \ B_1 \ \ B_2$

D_1, D_2, D_3, D_4

Relationship instances

b': $\langle B_1 C_2, D_1 \rangle, \langle B_2 C_2, D_1 \rangle$

a': $\langle B_1, D_3 \rangle, \langle B_1, D_4 \rangle, \langle B_2, D_1 \rangle$

(a) First approach

(b) Second approach

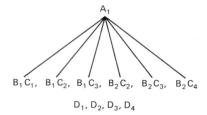

Relationship instances

b′: ⟨$B_1 C_2, D_1$⟩, ⟨$B_2 C_2, D_1$⟩

a′: ⟨$B_1 C_1, D_3$⟩, ⟨$B_1 C_2, D_3$⟩, ⟨$B_1 C_3, D_3$⟩,
    ⟨$B_1 C_1, D_4$⟩, ⟨$B_1 C_2, D_4$⟩, ⟨$B_1 C_3, D_4$⟩,
    ⟨$B_2 C_2, D_1$⟩, ⟨$B_2 C_3, D_1$⟩, ⟨$B_2 C_4, D_1$⟩

(b) Second approach

The example above adequately demonstrates the problems that arise when the same schema operations are extended from hierarchical to network structures. In general, every operation needs to be dealt with by considering:

1. The possible ways of handling a nonhierarchical relation when either its member or owner group has been split. This was demonstrated in the example above.

2. The possible ways of dealing with merging of nonhierarchical relations. Merging of assemblies, i.e., sets of member instances coming from different parent group instances has to be further generalized in case of many-to-many nonhierarchical group relations. For example, consider the instance merging of groups *C* and *CC* in the following example (assume that e, is the key field):

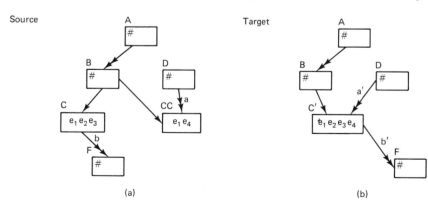

(a)   (b)

The merging may be conditioned on the value of items in C and CC. This may cause a loss of instances of nonhierarchical relations (C, F) and (D, CC) in which C and CC participate. One solution is to create group C'' by an instance merging based on the condition which is the complement of the condition in the merging to form C':

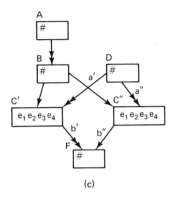

(c)

The relations (C'', F) and (D, C'') now account for the information that would otherwise have been lost. Because of the above difficulties, the operational specifications approach is not very advisable in the case of network-structured databases.

10.5.2 The Access-Path Specification Approach

This approach is exemplified by the work of Deppe and Swartwout [7, 32] in conjunction with the University of Michigan Data Translator. It is a procedural and navigational counterpart to the one discussed at length above, which is more declarative and somewhat nonprocedural. Each restructuring transformation is described in terms of a procedure of traversing a source database to obtain the information needed for the target, then creating the target data instances from it.

The access-path specification language (APSL) embodies a high-level specification of access paths. It is a block-structured language (see Figure 10.9) wherein there is one block per record type in the target database. Each target record statement gives the selection criteria as well as the accessing schema for retrieving the information needed to construct this record from the source database. Each target set statement (see Figure 10.9) refers to a set in which the target record type is a member. The access-path statement gives the source record types which need to be accessed in order to construct a target record instance. A new target item statement

TARGET RECORD STATEMENT
  TARGET SET STATEMENT
    ACCESS PATH STATEMENT
      NEW TARGET ITEM STATEMENT
      SOURCE RECORD STATEMENT
        ITEM QUALIFICATION STATEMENT
        ITEM ASSIGNMENT STATEMENT

       •
       •
    SOURCE RECORD STATEMENT

     •
     •
  ACCESS PATH STATEMENT

   •
   •
  TARGET SET STATEMENT

  •
  •
TARGET RECORD STATEMENT

 •   **Figure 10.9**   Structure of APSL specifica-
 •   tion. (*Source*: [8])

refers to a new item being created in the target receiving some constant value. The same record statements refer to the record types from the source database used in traversing it. The item qualification and assignment statements pick up items from the source database meeting certain conditions and assign those values to the proper target items.

    Let us look at an example that demonstrates the above approach (source: [8]). Figure 10.10(a) shows the source and target databases. Figure 10.10(b) is its APSL specification (simplified). It shows how implicit information in the source database can be made explicit in the target. This approach has been implemented at the University of Michigan Data Translation Project and was used on IDS databases.

10.5.3 An Evaluation of the Approaches to Schema Restructuring

We described above two basically different approaches to a specification of schema restructuring. Past experience with their implementation has shown that

1. The access-path specification approach is easier to implement. It allows for the development of a more efficient restructuring algorithm.
2. The access-path specification approach can be considered more general, since it can specify navigation of data through essentially any mode.

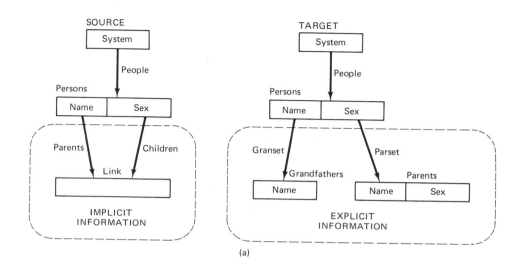

(a)

1. TARGET RECORD PERSONS
2.   ACCESS PATH PERSONS
3.   SOURCE RECORD PERSONS ACCESS VIA PEOPLE
4.   ACTUAL DATA IN ORDER
5. TARGET RECORD PARENTS
6.   ACCESS PATH PARENTS
7.   SOURCE RECORD PERSONS ID = KID ACCESS VIA PEOPLE
8.   NAME ASSIGN TO NAME⟨PARSET⟩
9.   SOURCE RECORD LINK ACCESS VIA PARENTS FROM ID = KID
10.   SOURCE RECORD PERSONS ID = PARENT ACCESS VIA CHILDREN
11.   ACTUAL DATA IN ORDER
12. TARGET RECORD GRANDFATHERS
13.   ACCESS PATH GRNDAD
14.   SOURCE RECORD PERSONS ID = GRNDAD ACCESS VIA PEOPLE
15.   SEX SELECT IF EQ 'MALE'
16.   NAME ASSIGN TO NAME
17.   SOURCE RECORD LINK ID = STEP 1 ACCESS VIA CHILDREN FROM ID = GRNDAD
18.   SOURCE RECORD PERSONS ID = PARENT ACCESS VIA PARENTS FROM ID = STEP 1
19.   SOURCE RECORD LINK ID = STEP 2 ACCESS VIA CHILDREN FROM ID = PARENT
20.   NAME⟨PARENTS⟩ASSIGN TO NAME⟨GRANDSET⟩

Figure 10.10   (a) Source and target database in a network schema restructuring; (b) an APSL specification of the above restructuring (based on an example in [8]).

3. From a user's standpoint the operational specification approach is probably simpler. It is less procedural and allows the user to concentrate on the database transformation rather than on the procedure for its traversal.

4. The operational specification approach has a decided advantage in case of hierarchical structures, since accessing specifications are easily circumvented in hierarchies. For network structures, the access path approach is better by the same token.

Some schema restructuring software has been built and is currently available. The highlights of its implementation are briefly summarized below.

10.6 DEVELOPMENT OF SCHEMA CONVERSION AIDS

The phases of schema implementation and schema restructuring were discussed above mainly in two contexts: first, the design and implementation of a database; second, the modification and redesign of an existing database. There has been hardly any major effort to develop software aids to address the issues of schema restructuring from a global information model into specific target DBMSs. Some database design aids have been developed. The Ph.D. dissertations of Gerritsen [10], Mitoma [16, 17], Berelian [2], and Purkayastha [14, 26] dealt with the design of DBTG structures. Bubenko and colleagues in Sweden [6] have also been involved in the development of DBTG design aids. IBM's DBDA [11] designs IMS databases. Such systems rely upon the given information, which is in the form of various data relationships, frequencies of accesses to data items or groups (in [16]), or knowledge of all user queries (as a set of production groups in [10]). The goal of these aids is to produce "optimal" schemas with the given specification of structural requirements, user constraints, and the constraints of the DBMS environment. They do not allow users to specify alternate schemas for evaluation, once the optimal solution is presented. The internal capabilities of these systems to generate quantitative estimates of the amount of change in transforming one schema to another is totally lacking. Users get no feel for equivalent schema designs that would perform adequately in the particular environment of a user.

The picture in the second context of schema restructuring is not as dismal. A number of implementations of systems to perform "static restructuring" (as defined earlier in Section 10.4.2) have been developed at the Universities of Pennsylvania [27] and Michigan [3, 18, 33] and at IBM [28, 29]. The most comprehensive of these efforts are those at Michigan (UMDTP: University of Michigan Data Translation Project) and at IBM (XPRS: A Data Extraction, Processing and Restructuring System). The UMDTP and XPRS have both addressed the problem of schema restructuring as a part of the wider problem of data translation. The terms *data translation* and *data conversion* are generally used to include a physical reorganization as well as a logical restructuring of data. They deal with translating databases from a source system to a target system with possible changes in hardware, storage organization, system software, and so on, and target databases are designed on the bases of different data models. Schema restructuring is mostly unavoidable during a changeover. Even when the source and target DBMSs are identical, users may wish to restructure a database to suit the target application environment better or for ease of use or efficiency of processing. Some of these reasons were listed in Section 10.4.2

All the above data-translation systems have followed the same three-phase approach of READ, TRANSFORM, and WRITE steps (see Figure 10.3). Furthermore, all translation systems have the common feature that a high-level data-description language is used to describe the source and target databases in their respective DBMSs. The translators also employ another language; for example, CONVERT [29] is a language used in the XPRS system [28] which is general enough to describe a large variety of restructuring situations arising in different systems. RSL [18] and APSL [32] are examples of other restructuring-specification-oriented languages. With the above specifications as input, the generalized translator performs the intended translation involving some inherent schema restructuring.

In considering how these systems have been implemented, the following characteristics are noteworthy. The University of Pennsylvania translator exemplifies the *program-generation approach*. The translator generates programs in a standard programming language (e.g., PL/1 in the Penn translator) on the basis of the input specifications. These programs are then compiled and run with the source database files as input to create the target database. A second type of translator takes the *interpretive approach*. The UMDTP translator, which exemplifies this approach, operates as follows. The stored data-definition language and translation-definition language are processed by an analyzer, which produces an object version of the source code in the form of encoded tables of data description and translation definition. These tables drive the translator, and the intended translation plus schema transformation operations are performed interpretively. The XPRS system of IBM uses a hybrid approach combining the above two. Some components of the system that are general enough are designed to handle a standardized stream of input to generate a standardized stream of output. However, the front end of the READER or the back end of the WRITER needs to be system specific. To deal with that, the XPRS translator generates specific PL/1 programs for reading from source files or writing to target files.

The UMDTP and XPRS translators have demonstrated that it is possible to process a wide variety of databases in a generalized translator and perform a variety of schema restructuring operations. The UMDTP translator performs both hierarchical and network schema transformations, whereas the XPRS system processes "forms," which are tabular descriptions of database files incorporating embedded hierarchies. Questions, however, still remain regarding the use of the generalized translation systems in a real-world environment involving high volumes of data and a multitude of users and incorporating complex structures specific to locally developed software. The usability of these systems depends upon the ability of the users and conversion analysts to understand and effectively use the high-level languages provided by these translators. Moreover, the generalized approach needs to be efficient and reliable enough in a real conversion effort; otherwise there is a tendency to write one-shot conversion programs to transfer files. The UMDTP, XPRS, and ADAPT [11] systems have been used and tested in the field. Taylor [34] has reported on the experience gained from XPRS, which is available as an IBM program product. A detailed discussion of the approaches to data conversion and implications for program conversion may be found in [9]. From the standpoint of generalized schema restructuring, there is still a long way to go beyond the generalized translators.

10.7 PROGNOSIS

This chapter has surveyed the issues and problems related to schema implementation and restructuring. Some approaches to schema restructuring have been outlined and features of existing generalized translation software which incorporates schema restructuring have been briefly discussed.

The state of the art of technology related to the above problems is not yet very advanced. With the proliferation of database management system software during the 1970s, many large organizations faced the problem of designing databases to contain all existing data in scattered files. A lack of well-understood methodologies, the inability of designers to cope with complex design problems manually, and the dearth of usable design tools has led to many ad hoc designs of databases which perform very poorly. Redesign of such databases is imminent and calls for further work in schema restructuring. Current database design aids do little to help the users in considering alternate structures for their databases, nor are they very efficient to use for large problems. There is a particular need for research in mapping global information models to commercially available DBMSs (for example, see [20]).

As far as the types of schema restructuring are concerned, transformations of hierarchical structures are much better understood than those of networks. Further research is required in development of high-level restructuring specification languages. The relational model offers a great redeeming feature in that restructuring a set of relations with preservation of all information is a much simpler and more manageable problem. If relational DBMSs become the wave of the future, users and designers will enjoy considerable relief as far as the schema implementation and restructuring problems are concerned.

REFERENCES

1. ANSI/X3/SPARC, "Study Group on Data Base Management Systems, Interim Report," *FDT*, Vol. 7, No. 2 (Feb. 1975).
2. Berelian, E., "A Methodology for Data Base Design in a Paging Environment," Ph.D. dissertation, The University of Michigan, Ann Arbor, 1977.
3. Birss, E.W., and J.P. Fry, "Generalized Software for Translating Data," *Proc. 1976 National Computer Conference*, Vol. 45, pp. 889–899. Montvale, N.J., AIFPS Press.

4. CINCOM Systems, *OS/TOTAL Application Programmer's Guide*, Publ. No. PO2-1236-00. Cincinnati: CINCOM Systems, 1976.

5. CODASYL Systems Committee, *Feature Analysis of Generalized Data Base Management Systems*, 520 pp. New York: ACM, 1971.

6. Dahl, R., and J. Bubenko, "IDBD: An Interactive Design Tool for CODASYL-DBTG Type Data Bases," *Proc. Eighth Int. Conf. on Very Large Data Bases*, Mexico City, Sept. 1982, pp. 108–121.

7. Deppe, M.E., "A Relational Interface Model for Database Restructuring," Technical Report 76 DT 3, Data Translation Project. University of Michigan, Ann Arbor, 1976.

8. Fry, J.P., "The Technology of Data Base Translation, Data Base Conversion, and Data Base Restructuring," Report #s 24-01-10 and 24-01-11, *Data Base Management Reports*, Auerbach Publishers Inc., 1978.

9. Fry, J.P., S.B. Navathe, et al., "An Assessment of the Technology for Data and Program Related Conversion," *Proc. 1978 National Computer Conference*, Vol. 47, pp. 887–907. Montvale, N.J., AFIPS Press.

10. Gerritsen, R., "A Preliminary System for the Design of DBTG Data Structures," *Comm. ACM*, Vol. 18, No. 10 (October 1975).

11. Goguen, N.H., and M.M. Kaplan, "An Approach to Generalized Data Translation: The ADAPT System," Bell Telephone Laboratories Internal Report, October 1977.

12. Hebalkar, P.G., "Application Specification for Distributed Data Base Systems," *Proc. Fourth Int. Conf. on Very Large Data Bases*, W. Berlin, Sept. 1978, pp. 442–229.

13. IBM, *Database Design Aid: General Information Manual* and *Designer's Guide*, Publication Nos. GH 20-1626-0 and GH 20-1627-0, 1975.

14. Irani, K.B., S. Purkayastha, and T.J. Teorey, "A Designer for DBMSs—Processable Logical Database Structures," *Proc. Fifth Int. Conf. on Very Large Data Bases*, Rio de Janeiro, Brazil, October 1979, pp. 219–231.

15. Lum, V.Y., et al., "1978 New Orleans Database Design Workshop Report," *Proc. Fifth Int. Conf. on Very Large Data Bases*, Rio de Janeiro, October 1979, pp. 328–339.

16. Mitoma, M.F., "Optimal Data Base Schema Design," Ph.D. dissertation, The University of Michigan, Ann Arbor, 1975.

17. Mitoma, M.F., and K.B. Irani, "Automatic Data Base Schema Design," *Proc. First Int. Conf. on Very Large Data Bases*, Framingham, Mass., October 1975, pp. 286–321.

18. Navathe, S.B., "A Methodology for Generalized Database Restructuring," Ph.D. dissertation, University of Michigan, Ann Arbor, 1976.

19. Navathe, S.B., "Schema Analysis for Database Restructuring," *ACM Trans. on Database Systems*, Vol. 5, No. 2 (June 1980), pp. 157–184.

20. Navathe, S.B., and A. Cheng, "Database Schema Mapping from an Extended Entity Relationship Model into the Hierarchical Model," *Proc. Third Entity-Relationship Conf.*, Anaheim, Calif., October 1983, North-Holland.

21. Navathe, S.B., and J.P. Fry, "Restructuring for Large Databases: Three Levels of Abstraction," *ACM Transactions on Database Systems*, Vol. 1, No. 2 (1976), pp. 138–158.

22. Navathe, S.B., and S.G. Gadgil, "A Methodology for View Integration in Logical Database Design," *Proc. Eighth Int. Conf. on Very Large Data Bases*, Mexico City, September 1982, pp. 142–165.

23. Navathe, S.B., and B. Ip, "Network Restructuring," Working Paper, New York University, 1977.

24. Navathe, S.B., and M. Schkolnick, "View Representation in Logical Database Design," *Proc. ACM-SIGMOD Int. Conf. on Management of Data, June 1978.*

25. Nijssen, G.M., "A Gross Architecture for the Next Generation Database Management Systems," *Proc. IFIP TC-2 Working Conf. on Data Base Management Systems,* Freudenstadt, W. Germany, January 1976.

26. Purkayastha, S., "Design of DBMS-Processable Logical Database Structures," Ph.D. dissertation, The University of Michigan, Ann Arbor, 1979.

27. Ramirez, J.A., "Automatic Generation of Data Conversion Programs Using a Data Description Language (DDL)," Ph.D. dissertation, University of Pennsylvania, 1973.

28. Shu, N.C., et al., "Express: A Data Extraction, Processing, and Restructuring System," *Transactions on Database Systems,* Vol. 2, No. 2 (1977).

29. Shu, N.C., B.C. Housel, and V.Y. Lum, "CONVERT: A High Level Translation Definition Language for Data Conversion," *Comm. ACM,* Vol. 18, No. 10 (1975), pp. 557–567.

30. Steel, T.B., Jr., and J.A. Jardine, "ISO Report on Concepts for Conceptual Schemas," *Proc. Sixth Int. Conf. on Very Large Databases,* Montreal, October 1980, pp. 321–325.

31. Su, S.Y.W., and D.H. Lo, "A Semantic Association Model for Conceptual Database Design," *Proc. Int. Conf. on Entity Relationship Approach to System Analysis and Design,* Los Angeles, December 1979, pp. 147–171.

32. Swartwout, D., "An Access Path Specification Language for Restructuring Network Databases," *Proc. 1977 SIGMOD Conf.,* pp. 88–101.

33. Swartwout, D.E., M.E. Deppe, and J.P. Fry, "Operational Software for Restructuring Network Databases," *Proc. 1977 National Computer Conference,* Vol. 46, pp. 499–508. Montvale, N.J., AFIPS Press.

34. Taylor, R.W., *Using Generalized Data Translation Techniques for Database Interchange,* IBM Research Report RJ 2866, July 1980.

35. Wiederhold, G., and R. El-Masri, "A Structural Model for Database Systems," *Proc. ACM-SIGMOD Conf. on Management of Data,* June 1978.

36. Zloof, M.M., and S.P. de Jong, "The System for Business Automation (SBA): Programming Language," *Communications of the ACM,* Vol. 20, No. 6 (June 1977), pp. 358–396.

Index

A

Abstract objects, 140–41
 record-based model lack of, 123–25
Access cost, *357**
 definition, 319
Access-path specifications, 352–53, 389–90
Accurately Defined System (ADS), in requirements
 process, 23
Actigram, 29
Action-means association, 132
Action-purpose association, 132
Activity analysis, in requirement process, 20
Add instance, 142
ADS (*see* Accurately Defined System)
Aggregation, 316
Algorithms:
 database design use of, 232–51, 312–16, 319–21,
 346–48
 design-assistance, schema implementation use
 of, 366
Analysis reports, in PSA use, 43
Ancestor, definition, 83
ANSI/SPARC architecture:
 data models and, 66–114, 109–12
 external schema proposal for, 73–75
 hierarchical systems in, 81–88

**Page references to figures are indicated
in italic.

relationships in, 76–81
 strengths of, 73
 user classes for, 68–69
ANSI/SPARC Report, 6
Application events, in semantic database models,
 145
Application-requirement model, 362
ARDI method, in requirements process, 23
Assign variable, 142
Associations, 257–58
Associative entity type, 225
Attribute-analysis report, 271–74
Attributes:
 definition, 6, 212
 diagrams, for entity types, 197–99
 entity relationship to, 71, *72*
 in relational data models, 100
 surrogate values in, 132
 of relationships, representation of, 80, *80*
Attribute value, definition, 212
Automation, of database design process, 321–23
AUXCO method, in requirements process, 23
Average fanout information, 345–46

B

Bachman diagram, 78
Backward-forward approach, in requirements
 process, 19–20

397

Base object classes, definition, 297
Binary relationships, 76
Bottom-up approach, in requirements process,
    18–19
Boyce-Codd normal form, 231
Bridge facility, 59

C

CADES, 38
CADIS, 37–38
Canonical logical schema, 260
Cardinality value, 297
CASCADE, 38
Cause-effect association, 132
Chaining, 316
Change anomalies, 230
Characterization association, 131
Chen, Peter P. S., "Database Design Based on
        Entity and Relationship," 174–210
Child, definition, 82
Clemons, Eric K., "Data Models and the
        ANSI/SPARC Architecture," 66–114
CODASYL network proposal, 88–89
    characterization of, 89–91
    design of, 91, 91, 92–94, 93
        many-to-many relationship removed in, 92
        recursion removed from, 92, 92
    evaluation of, 99–100
    language in, 94–98, 96, 97
    limitations and enhancements of, 98–99
    subschema facility of, 73–74, 89
Combined nodes, 339–44
Common attribute group, 310–11
Complex association, 258, 258
Complex-associations reports, 284–89
Composite entity identifier, 183
Composition association, 132
Compression, definition, 377–79
Computer-Aided Design and Evaluation System
        (CADES), 38
Computer-Aided Design of Information Systems
        (CADIS), 37–38
Computer-Aided Systems Construction and Docu-
        mentation Environment (CASCADE), 38
Computer-aided techniques:
    in hierarchical database design, 255–93
    in requirements process, 37–38
"Computer Assisted Hierarchical Database Design,"
        by George U. Hubbard, 255–93

Conceptual data model, (see Functional data model)
Conceptual schema, 69
    design of, under relationship
        restrictions, 78–79
Conditional association, 258, 258
Conditionality, definition, 7
Confluent hierarchy, 304
Connection trap, 76
Connectivity, definition, 7–9
Constituent relations, definition, 298
Content-preserving, 229
Contents Report, in PSA use, 52–53, 53
Corporate constraints, 151
Criterion, definition, 12
Currency indicator, 95

D

DAPLEX, 136
Data, view types of, 266–67
Database, 21
Database design:
    algorithms for, 232–51, 312–16, 319–21, 346–48
    automating process of, 321–23
    computer assistance in, 255–93
    constraints in, 215–17
    entity and relationship basis of, 174–210
    entity-relationship diagram in, 177–86
    evaluation of, 351–58
    hierarchical, 206–7
    interactive system for, 325–60
    logical DL/I, 260–64
    logical problems of, 175–76, 175
    logical steps in, 193–203
    network, 294–324
    normalized relations in network, 310–16
    process in, 226–32
    processing-requirement modeling in, (see
        Requirements process)
    relational, 211–54
    requirements for, 1–4
"Database Design Based on Entity and Relation-
        ship," by Peter P. S. Chen, 174–210
Database navigation, definition, 74
Database operations, 154
    order of, 169
Database systems:
    architecture of, 109–12
    CODASYL, 88–89
        characterization of, 89–91